Amateur Gemstone Faceting

Volume 1

The Essentials

T OM H ERBST

FACE
TABLE
BOOKS

Scan this code to visit
www.facetingbook.com

Book design and formatting: Tom Herbst
tom@facetingbook.com

ISBN-13: 978-3-00-047474-3

"True glory consists in doing what deserves to be written; in writing what deserves to be read; and in so living as to make the world happier and better for our living in it..."

- Pliny the Elder

Table of Contents

NOTE: Volume 1 (this book) contains Chapters 1 to 9 and the Glossary. Chapters 10 to 20 appear in Volume 2. You can search by topic in the merged index appended to each volume.

Volume 1

Volume 2

Foreword to Volumes 1 and 2

F.1 Welcome

If you are new to the hobby, welcome to the world of gemstone faceting.

I think that I know why you are here. You probably have a friend or colleague who cuts gemstones, or you somehow learned that creating these minor miracles of Nature is within the grasp of average people.

Like me, you may live and work in a world governed by logic, mathematics, and the type of activity broadly characterized as "left-brain" in pop psychology. Gemstones are an anomaly in our world. While completely explicable in terms of refraction, absorption, and so forth, the seemingly magical interaction of light and matter evident in a well-cut gemstone transcends the purely physical and becomes a unique fusion of science and art. I can write down the mathematical formulae which determine how a gemstone looks, but I cannot for the life of me explain why they captivate my imagination so totally. Hopefully, this book will help you have your own faceting epiphany, that moment when you discover that you, too, can create an object of sublime beauty.

Alternatively, you may be an artistic type, a "right-brainer" looking for another means of self-expression. Here, too, gemstones are an anomaly in the world, precisely because they bridge the artistic and scientific domains. Unlike other creative pursuits, gemstone faceting requires at least some knowledge of science and mathematics. Faceting also demands proficiency with precision equipment. These requirements should in no way deter you, since you can pick up the needed skills as you progress, and there is a wealth of material – including this book – which can guide you along the way.

If you are an experienced gem cutter, welcome to you as well. I think that you will find plenty here to expand your understanding, involvement, and enjoyment of the hobby. In particular, if you began faceting before the dawn of the digital era, you will find that the world has changed. Whether it is the wealth, both intellectual and interpersonal, of online discussion groups, or the ready availability of software to design, optimize, and even visualize gemstones before putting stone to lap, the information age has entered our workshops. This book will not only update you on the latest tools and techniques, it should also provide an easy gateway into faceting in the 21st century.

F.2 Why Facet?

Why facet? To an amateur gem cutter, this is a bit like asking, "why eat chocolate layer cake?" Faceting is fun, absorbing, challenging, fascinating, rewarding, surprising, therapeutic, and a half dozen other adjectives. And, unlike chocolate cake, you can indulge as much as you want without guilt.

Amateur gemstone faceting is simply a great hobby. I cannot speak to the issue of faceting professionally, since I have never done so, but amateur faceting is all these things and more. Indeed, the word amateur comes from the Latin *amare*, which means to love, and so I guess by definition, amateur faceters have to love their hobby. Turn to Chapter 1.4 for a longer love letter on the hobby of faceting…

F.3 Who is This Book Intended For?

This book is intended for both the eager beginner and the seasoned faceter. Clearly, that's a fairly broad target audience, but I have separated the book into two volumes to allow readers to focus on the areas and skill level appropriate to them. The first volume presents the essentials, including a detailed, visual tutorial to guide the complete beginner through his or her first gemstone. There are chapters providing guidance on selecting gem rough, faceting machines, laps, and additional equipment, as well as lengthy explanations of cutting and polishing technique. It concludes with a chapter on further reading to help you continue your faceting journey. In summary, Volume 1 targets the beginning to intermediate faceter.

Volume 2 should be of interest to all skill levels, including the beginner. It provides simple-to-follow explanations of exactly what goes on when light enters a gemstone, and equips your with the mathematical tools to maximize your enjoyment of the hobby. There are chapters on gemstone properties and treatments, as well as a useful overview of common materials that amateurs actually cut. Volume 2 continues with several chapters that should expand your faceting horizons, including discussion and tutorials on advanced pre-forming techniques, faceting on the computer, and creating your own unique gemstone designs. The final chapter provides ideas for several do-it-yourself projects, ranging from building a better drip tank to adding a digital angle indicator to your faceting machine.

Eager to dive in but not sure where? Chapter 1.6 provides a more detailed chapter-by-chapter overview of the book, and both volumes contain a complete index.

F.4 Why Rewrite the Bible?

This is by no means the first book on amateur gemstone faceting. In fact, several excellent textbooks have appeared over the past forty years or so. Names like Vargas, Wykoff, Dake, Broadfoot, and Collins have achieved legendary status within the community, and their books on amateur faceting are widely regarded as "bibles."

Why rewrite the bible? After all, to quote the real Good Book, "There is nothing new under the sun," (Ecclesiastes 1:9).

Here's why: Ecclesiastes' great wisdom may apply to Man's spiritual quest during his brief time on this planet, but in the field of amateur gemstone faceting, a great number of new things have appeared under that life-giving, yellow orb.

New techniques, new gem materials, and new tools appear every year. For example, improved manufacturing methods have pushed some cutting laps completely off the market, to be replaced by more reliable and consistent options. Legislative changes are beginning to limit access to essential chemical solvents and even incandescent light bulbs, yet viable alternatives exist. Perhaps most importantly, the advent of the affordable personal computer and the explosive growth of the Internet have fundamentally changed the way we cut stones.

Thus, this book is an attempt to update, not rewrite, the bible. I have also tried to compose it in a more modern, accessible style, with clear, effective figures. The information is organized in a linear, hopefully logical progression, with individual sections that are more or less self-contained. This, coupled with a complete index, should help you rapidly identify the relevant chapter and section and get the information that you need.

In short, this book is the book that would have helped me. I hope it helps you.

> ### While We're on the Subject...
>
> As with many modern reference books, I have also tried to intersperse the nuts and bolts detail with a few highlights, anecdotes, and (hopefully) humorous observations. They are set off from the main body of the text in shaded boxes like this. I hope that this approach makes the material more interesting and adds an additional dimension to your enjoyment. And please laugh at my occasional lame joke...I won't tell anyone.

F.5 About This Book

Note: This section isn't about faceting. It's about books. If you are not interested in the logistics and economics of producing a book on the lapidary arts, skip ahead to Chapter 1.

When I first began toying with the idea of presenting an updated view of the world of amateur gemstone faceting, I soon recognized that there was a problem with how books for hobbyists are made and marketed. The economics of modern publishing has skewed significantly to the mass-market fiction paperback, and the prospect of a publishing house taking an interest in a limited-distribution production run targeting a few thousand hobbyists around the world was very remote indeed.

Perhaps it was always so. In fact, the "bibles" listed in the previous section all came from small or self-published houses. Glenn and Martha Vargas brought *Faceting for Amateurs* to market under their own label, and had it printed and bound commercially. Broadfoot and Collins did much the same with *Cutting Gemstones* and their GemInfo imprint. Wykoff published *The Techniques of Master Faceting* with Adamas Publishers, again a homegrown affair.

The problem with small publishing houses, including author-owned imprints, is that they have a great deal of trouble establishing and maintaining inventory. Printing and warehousing a large number of volumes makes no economic sense if the books trickle out slowly over a period of years.

Clearly, the old system doesn't work for this kind of thing. Luckily we can ignore the old system, and perhaps it will go away...

Welcome to the world of computer controlled typesetting and Print-On-Demand (POD) books. In the last decade or so, several companies have begun offering efficient and economical book printing services intimately integrated with online sales and marketing. Modern printing presses can produce single copies of requested books almost instantly and at a very competitive price. Type your search term into amazon.com or other online bookseller, double-check that it is what you want, and then click "Buy." The book will be printed as a single unit within hours and should arrive on your doorstep within days. Goodbye warehouses, goodbye out-of-print notices, and goodbye $600 prices (see "Bibliophilic Blues" below). For focused, limited-audience publishing, the world has become a very nice place indeed.

After evaluating several options, I selected Createspace, a division of Amazon, to print this book. The other companies, including Lulu and Lightning Source, offered very attractive conditions, but the close integration with amazon.com sealed the deal.

Bibliophilic Blues

Not convinced of the value of POD publishing? When I first tried to buy Wykoff's book, the only copy that I could easily locate online was $630 used.

You read that right. A book which initially retailed for $24.50 in 1985 – about fifty bucks in 2010 inflation adjusted terms – was on sale "in good condition" for a typical worker's weekly salary. Wow.

I eventually located a more or less beat up copy for about a tenth of that breathtaking price, or only slightly more than what a brand spanking new book would cost after accounting for inflation.

My difficulty in tracking down Broadfoot and Collins' excellent *Cutting Gemstones* was no less eye-opening. Produced in limited runs by a commercial printer in Brisbane, Australia, a brand new copy set me back about $90, including shipping to Europe. It would have been considerably more, had I opted to have it sent by something faster than a boat. The book arrived almost two months after I placed my order...

The imprint, FaceTable Books, is my own, just as it was with Vargas, Wykoff, *et al*. The name is an obvious play on words between the adjective indicating that a piece of rough can produce a gem and the noun *facetable*. Never heard of it? Think *facepalm*, only worse. The online urban dictionary can help if you are stuck (see Chapter 15.8.13).

F.5.1 Text, Photographs, and Figures

All of the text, unless otherwise credited, is my original work. Turn to the overleaf of the title page for the customary caveats. Unless otherwise stated, I created all the figures in this book. Full credit for additional material appears at the end of each volume.

for Inge

1

Gems and Faceting

G reat!

You've made it to Chapter 1, so you are obviously seriously committed to cutting faceted gemstones and are eager to begin!

This chapter provides a general introduction to the hobby, including explanations of exactly what a gemstone is, why faceting is a wonderful hobby, and how to get started. It also contains a guide to the remainder of this book for those who like to jump around.

1.1 Gems

Let's begin with a seemingly straightforward question: What, exactly, is a gem?

That wonderful, ultimate reference book, the *Oxford English Dictionary*, defines a gem as "a precious stone of any kind, especially when cut and polished for ornament."

The reason that the OED is so wonderful and ultimate – it immodestly refers to itself as "the definitive record of the English language," after all – is that it poses more new questions with every answer. It invites you to explore.

What is a stone? What is precious? What is cutting and polishing?

Let's follow that invitation and do a little exploration…

Figure 1-1   A precious stone of any kind, especially when cut and polished for ornament…

1.1.1 Minerals, Rocks and Stones

To the everlasting disappointment of the editors at the OED, we tend to be lazy and imprecise in our language. Most people would agree that a mineral is pretty much a rock, which in turn is pretty much a stone.

Nothing could be further from the truth. In fact, these words have fairly precise meanings in the world of geology and mineralogy.

A **mineral** is a naturally occurring solid material with a specific chemical composition, regular crystal structure, and characteristic properties. Three clear requirements: **chemistry**, **structure**, and **properties**. Some experts insist that the definition should include a requirement on geological, rather than biological origin, but this remains controversial. Fans of amber and pearls can scan ahead to the definition of mineraloids for comfort. There are currently almost five thousand known minerals, with more being added each year. The website www.webmineral.com can help keep you up to date.

The **chemical** makeup of minerals ranges from pure elements to salts to extraordinarily complex molecules. Gold is an elemental mineral, while the table salt at your local diner is an ionic halide mineral. The more complex silicates constitute about 90% of the Earth's crust, and this group of minerals includes some familiar names, including garnet, zircon, topaz, and peridot. Turn to Chapter 12.2 for more on gemstone chemistry.

The regular crystal **structure** of minerals can be expressed in seven common forms: cubic, tetragonal, hexagonal, trigonal, orthorhombic, monoclinic, and triclinic. These are fancy terms for describing the arrangement of the component atoms and molecules in the larger organizational structure of the crystal, the *lattice*. Chapter 12.10 contains a great deal more information on crystal systems, including some neat 3D pictures.

Gem cutters tend to group the **properties** of a mineral into two broad categories: optical and physical. The optical properties determine the visual appearance of a gemstone and include colour, refractive index, and dispersion. The physical properties, such as hardness, density, crystal system, and cleavage, relate more to identifying and working with a particular mineral. Again, Chapter 12 provides more detail, while Chapter 14 lists the optical and physical properties of common gemstone materials.

Mineraloids are what you get when you throw out the "regular crystal structure" requirement on a mineral. Mineraloids can also display a huge variety of chemical compositions – a much greater range than is generally accepted for "proper" minerals. Prominent among the mineraloid gems are opal and moldavite (Figure 1-2), which are not true minerals because they are not crystalline: the molecules stick together in a formless, glassy, mass. Amber, pearl and jet, in addition to being of biological origin, are also mineraloid gems, due to their amorphous structure.

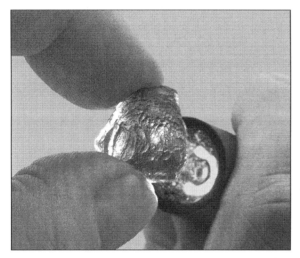

What, then, are rocks and stones?

Mineralogically speaking, a **rock** is an aggregate of one or more minerals and mineraloids. Rocks may also include organic materials. Thus, limestone is a common rock composed mostly of the mineral calcite. Granite is a rock containing varying amounts of the minerals quartz, mica, and feldspar.

Figure 1-2 Moldavite, a mineraloid gemstone, perhaps produced by the impact of a meteor in central Europe some fifteen million years ago.

The whole definition thing gets a little murky when it comes to **stones**. For many, the term is a catch-all, referring to minerals, rocks, and just about everything else, including gems. A hobbyist faceter will talk about polishing stones, but will not boast about a beautifully cut rock. Others insist that rocks and stones are the same thing and that the distinction is one of size: stones are small, whereas rocks are big. Yet another faction argues that the location is key: rocks are part of the earth's surface. As soon as they get picked up and used for something – like building a cottage – they become stones. For what it is worth, the Oxford English Dictionary comes down on the side of the size distinction. In this book, I will use the term stone in the catch-all sense. As you will see, dear reader, this is just one of the many ways that this book is not the OED…

1.1.2 Precious and Semi-Precious Gems

I saw the Hope Diamond at the Smithsonian when I was a kid. In addition to its lengthy and more than a little turbulent history, I remember being struck by the notion that something that could easily fit in my hand would have a value of many tens of millions of dollars.

The value of an object, particularly one that is unique, is a very slippery thing. For example, some sources insist that the Hope Diamond is worth a quarter of a billion dollars, while other valuations make it a relative bargain. The last time the diamond was sold at a publicly disclosed price was over a century ago. A New York Times article in October 1910 stated that the gem was for sale for $150,000, which is now about $3.5 million in inflation adjusted terms.

There is a deeper message here. Human perception enters the equation when you consider value. Nowhere is this clearer than in the often-tangled distinction between precious and semi-precious stones. Back when I was visiting the Smithsonian, I was told that there were only four precious stones: diamonds, rubies, sapphires, and emeralds. I did not realize at the time that rubies and sapphires were chemically virtually identical, effectively reducing the membership of this exclusive club to three.

Figure 1-3 Crowds flock to the Smithsonian Museum of Natural History in Washington DC to gaze at the Hope Diamond.

In principle, then, all other gemstones are semi-precious. Try to convince yourself of this the next time you go shopping for tsavorite garnet, which in decent quality can rival the price of diamonds. Paraiba tourmaline, a very rare blue-green variety originally discovered in Brazil, can put to shame all but the finest diamonds and rubies in terms of cost (see "Tulips and Tourmaline" on page 213). Until huge finds came to light in the 19th century, now-lowly amethyst was considered precious, one of the group of "cardinal gemstones," which also included diamonds, rubies, sapphires, and emeralds – all of the "precious gems" of today.

Here's the short version: In modern, practical terms, the distinction between precious and semi-precious stones is meaningless. The individual characteristics and rarity of a particular gem, in addition to its current popularity in jewelry, will determine its value.

Note that Chapter 6 expounds at great length on the value of rough gemstones and gives you tips on paying the right price.

1.1.3 Artificial Gemstones

Sharp-eyed readers may have noticed the wording "precious stone *of any kind*" coming from the definitive record of the English language. While you can fairly use "of any kind" to include your favourite organic mineraloid, there is no doubt that the OED's wise definition also allows *artificial gemstones*. This category includes *synthetics*, which mimic the real thing at a chemical level, and *simulants*, which strive to achieve only the look and feel of a natural gem.

"Aha!" you cry. "Manufactured gemstones cannot be precious – they come in bulk from a factory!"

Fair point. Wrong, but fair.

In fact, a substantial number of synthetic and simulant gemstones fetch per-gram prices that are comparable to the real thing. For example, synthetic gem-quality diamonds have only recently become economically viable, and it is still a challenge to fabricate an absolutely colourless, D-type stone. Hydrothermally grown synthetic emerald can cost up to ten times as much per carat as pale natural aquamarine, despite being chemically virtually identical. There are even some types of synthetic gemstones that have been created in the lab, but they cannot compete in the market with the same natural material. From a practical amateur faceter's viewpoint, such synthetics simply don't exist.

The history and technology of artificial gemstones is quite fascinating. Turn to Chapter 6.6 to learn more.

Perceived Value and Value Perceived

Diamonds have been the king of gemstones for your entire lifetime, and indeed the lifetime of almost everyone still walking around. You could, with carefully calibrated irony, state that diamonds are the gold standard in terms of precious gems. Part of this calibration, of course, is the fact that diamonds are far more valuable than gold, at least on a per gram basis (see "A Weighty Matter" on page 9). This is reflected in the fact that the traditional 50th wedding anniversary gift is one of gold – you have to hang on for at least sixty years to celebrate with diamonds. Curiously, traditional couples exchange rubies after only forty years of matrimonial bliss, although by any reasonable measure, rubies are the most valuable gemstones of all. In any case, diamond is currently king.

It wasn't always so.

In medieval Europe, rubies and emeralds ranked higher, and indeed by some accounts, diamonds were not even in the top ten. This is not surprising, since most diamonds rely on proper cutting and sparkle for their appeal, and proper angles were not understood until the early 20th century (see page 240 of Volume 2).

In fact, some experts decry the "king of gemstones" for its blandness: almost all gem quality diamonds are effectively colourless. Robert N. Proctor, a historian of science at Stanford University, has memorably characterized diamond as "the Velveeta cheese of the gemstone kingdom, albeit priced like Reggiano Parmesan…" Interestingly, he argues that the value of diamond stems from its uniformity, rather than its uniqueness, and points to the troubled history of Africa as one of the consequences of this value. The rise of the diamond is inextricably entwined with finance, politics, and the changing role of marriage in society. Unsurprisingly, the DeBeers company was involved. It makes for a very interesting story – Chapter 9.4 can help you learn more.

1.2 Cutting and Polishing of Gemstones

Excellent progress! There are clear answers to several of the questions posed by the one-line definition of gemstones on page 2: Gems are stones (Section 1.1.1), which are precious (Section 1.1.2), and can be of any kind (Section 1.1.3) The last bit of the OED's definition, namely the "cutting and polishing for ornament" part, is going to take up the remaining 800 pages of the two volumes of this book. Yippee!

Actually, not all gemstones are cut and polished. A fraction of ornamental jewelry uses gemstone crystals in their natural form, and of course there is a significant subculture of people who believe that altering a natural gem in any way drains it of its transcendent internal energy. That group will not appreciate the next 800 pages…

There are two broad categories of cut and polished gemstones. Opaque and translucent materials most frequently appear cut **en cabochon**, that is, as smoothed, rounded domes. You can also find transparent gemstones cut as "cabs," although this tends to be restricted to lower refractive index material, such as amber. Cabochons show certain unique optical properties to best effect. A prominent example is star sapphire, which exhibits multi-rayed stars due to internal needle-like inclusions (see Chapter 12.7.3). Tiger-eye and opalescent stones also look great as cabs.

This book isn't about cabs.

This book is about the other category: **faceted gemstones**. The technique of faceting places multiple, tiny windows on the surface of the gemstone with the goal of maximizing visual interest and light return from the environment. A faceted gemstone *sparkles*, although sometimes the emphasis is on displaying colour to greatest effect (see Chapter 16.5).

Faceted gemstones share a few defining characteristics (see Figure 1-4). Specifically, faceted gems:

- almost always have some symmetry. Even symmetry (four-fold, eight-fold, twelve-fold, etc.) is the most common type, and faceted gems are usually mounted such that the viewer looks directly down the axis of this symmetry.

- have an upper part, called the *crown*, and a lower part, called the *pavilion*. The pavilion is almost always deeper than the crown.

- usually have a crown featuring a large *table* facet perpendicular to the symmetry axis. The pavilion, on the other hand, usually comes to a point, called a *culet*, or to a long ridge, called a *keel*.

- have an "equator" separating the crown from the pavilion. This equator is known as the *girdle*, and its facets lie parallel to the symmetry axis of the stone. Serious amateur faceters tend to take great care in producing a finely polished, faceted girdle, whereas commercially cut stones often have a rough-ground girdle.

- have (usually) flat facets that intersect at a relatively small number of vertices, called *meet points*. Some facets have special names, such as the table and girdle mentioned above. Other named facet types include the *break* facets ad-

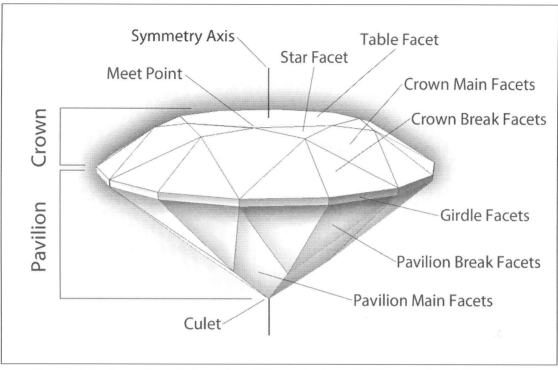

Figure 1-4 Anatomy of a typical gemstone. This standard round brilliant has eight-fold symmetry.

jacent to the girdle and the aptly named *main* facets, which are frequently the largest and most important.

• are almost always *convex solids*. This means that all the edges defining the intersection of the facets bulge out from the volume of the stone, rather than being indented. The requirement of being a convex solid arises due to the geometry of faceting machines (Chapter 2.1), and it places significant constraints on the form that gemstones can take. For example, a true heart shape is not possible using conventional faceting techniques (see Figure 1-5).

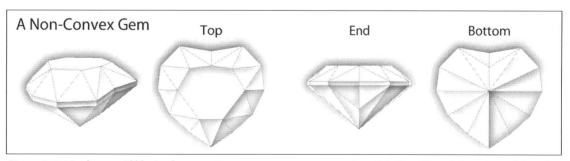

Figure 1-5 Much as we'd like to do so, cutting non-convex gems, such as this "true" heart, is not possible using conventional techniques.

1.3 Gemstone Cuts

You should not view the characteristics of a faceted gemstone listed in the previous section as limitations. Rather, they represent a framework within which artists can express their creativity. Far from being sharply confined, gemstone designs span an almost unbelievable range

Faceted Gemstones – A Collaboration between Nature and Man

Did you ever have that earnest conversation with friends about a tree falling in the forest? For me, it occurred in freshman year at college: a group of us would gather together to sample various libations and discuss the important issues, like the meaning of life and what's the point of it all.

The whole tree falling issue centers around the question of whether physical phenomena and objects have an identity outside of human perception. Usually expressed as "if a tree falls in a forest and no one is around to hear it, does it make a sound?" this philosophical musing is attributed to the Irish philosopher George Berkeley, Bishop of Cloyne, who advanced the notion that "to be is to be perceived" in the early 17th century.

Berkeley's idea was that objects do not exist without our perceiving them. In other words: No Man, no sound. While certainly an active topic of debate for the last three hundred years, particularly among freshmen, there is no doubt that gemstones (remember them? – that is why you are reading this book) do not have an independent existence. In other words, if a sapphire fell in the woods, and there was no one around to facet it, would it be a gemstone? Definitely not.

Faceted gemstones are a collaboration between Nature and Man. Nature contributes the raw material, and the wonderful mechanisms through which light interacts with matter. Man, armed with knowledge of these mechanisms and an artistic drive, manipulates the stone in a way which captures its internal beauty and mystery.

History does not record what, if any opinion Bishop Berkeley had of the craft of gemstone faceting, but I think that he would have approved. As a devoted mathematician and scientist, as well as a philosopher, he understood that Nature and Man share an intimate connection. Faceters express that connection every time they lower a gemstone to the lap.

of shapes and reflectance patterns, and the wide availability of inexpensive design software (Chapter 15.3) means that the number and breadth of gemstone cuts grow daily.

There are, however, a few standard shapes that have withstood the test of time. Indeed, these designs are actually the product of the test of time, since they were developed over decades by expert cutters with no software tools whatsoever. By far the most popular gemstone cut is the standard round brilliant, also commonly known as the SRB (Figure 1-6). The SRB produces wonderful sparkle and fire in even the most affordable gem materials.

Ironically, there is nothing "standard" about the standard round brilliant, and in fact, variants exist with all sorts of symmetry and modifications to the facet layout (see Chapter 16.2)

The emerald or step cut (Figure 1-7) is widely used to emphasize the body colour of a gem over sparkle. As with the SRB, there are many, many variants of the emerald cut. Other common gemstone cuts include, in alphabetical order, the baguette, briolette, heart, kite, marquise, oval, pear, princess, radiant, square, trapezoid and trillion. The great gem designers Robert H. Long and Norman W. Steele have attempted to categorize gemstone cuts. Their taxonomy includes almost fifty diverse forms – turn to Figure 16-3 and be amazed…

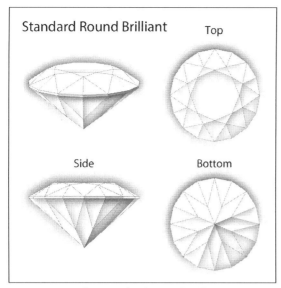

Standard Round Brilliant — Top — Side — Bottom

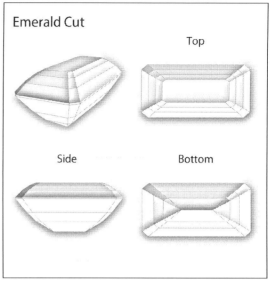

Emerald Cut — Top — Side — Bottom

Figure 1-6 . The Standard Round Brilliant empha-sizes sparkle and fire.

Figure 1-7 The emerald or step cut emphasizes gem-stone colour.

For a beginning amateur gemstone faceter, the message is both encouraging and a little daunting: the range of gemstone designs available to you can represent a lifetime of cutting. Depending on your talents and inclination, you can focus on a few classic designs while exploring different gem materials, or try many different cuts in your favourite type of stone. Or both. Or create your own design. This book should help you along, no matter which path you choose. Turn to Chapter 19 to explore some new and unique gem cuts, or learn what different gem materials can bring to your favourite design in Chapters 12 and 14, or follow the advice in Chapters 16-18 to begin blazing your own trail.

A Weighty Matter

The standard unit for weight in the coloured gemstone business is the *carat* (abbrevi-ated to ct). One carat is a fifth of a gram, or 200 milligrams. The name probably derives from the Greek word *keration*, which refers to the seed of the carob plant. These seeds were thought to be particularly uniform in size and weight (it turns out that they are not), and hence would make an excellent reference for balance scales. In his seminal book – sorry for the pun – *Gemstones of the World* (see Chapter 9.3), Walter Schumann suggests that the term "carat" may come from either the carob seed or from the term *kuara*, the seed of the African Coral Tree.

In any case, at a fifth of a gram, one carat is not very heavy in traditional terms – amus-ingly, a small pea weighs about a carat, whereas a carrot weighs considerably more. One carat can be a lot for gems, however. Premium materials, such as sapphire, blue tourmaline, and grossular garnet, can fetch more than a thousand dollars per carat in these "small" sizes. A flawless one-carat E-type diamond runs about ten to twenty thou-sand dollars at current prices. For this reason, diamonds have their own, even smaller unit of weight – the *point*. One point is 0.01 carat, or 2 milligrams. A 25-point accent gem is thus equivalent to ¼ carat.

Many people confuse gemstone carats with gold carats. The latter is a measure of the purity of gold alloy, quantized in 24ths, of all things. For example, 24-carat gold is 100%

gold, while 18-carat gold is 75% gold, 12-carat is 50%, and so on. To help minimize confusion, North American jewelers use the term *karat* (abbreviated to kt) for gold. Things are even simpler in Europe, where the *millesimal fineness scale* has replaced all this business with seeds. This scale denotes the percentage of gold as a three-digit number. For example, 18-carat gold is 75% pure and has fineness 750.

Pop quiz: Which would you rather have: a one-carat diamond mounted in a 24 carat gold ring, or a 24 carat diamond mounted in a 1 carat gold ring?

1.4 Gemstone Faceting as a Hobby – A Love Letter…

Faceting is a great hobby. It is great for a number of reasons. The first arises out of the fact that faceting transcends the traditional categories of leisure time activity: whether it is arts and crafts, science, handiwork, or just plain knock-out beauty that turns your crank, you will find a great deal of satisfaction in faceting. Faceting also has the wonderful virtue of going at the speed you want. Unlike some hobbies – golf and gourmet cooking come to mind – the clock is irrelevant. You can proceed at your own pace. Some cutters manage up to ten gems a day, while others can take ten or more hours per stone. Given your available time, this can mean producing anywhere from a few to a few hundred gemstones per year.

Faceting is also relaxing. The recommended practice of "cutting a little, looking a lot" (page 161) can be very soothing, and it is only the occasional minor polishing disaster that throws a monkey wrench into the experience. I suspect that gem cutting shares a great deal of the absorption and peace of meditation.

On the other hand, you can facet while pursuing another activity. Some faceters have a TV on in the workshop, while others limit their external stimuli to music or talk radio. I have not heard of anyone setting up a treadmill or stationary bicycle in front of his or her machine, but it is only a matter of time…

You will probably also take pleasure in the simple act of operating precision machinery and operating it well. This is probably where words like "craftsman" start creeping in, but the appeal is undeniable. Mastering a challenging art form on a beautiful piece of equipment is a thrill. If you are a do-it-yourselfer, you can even upgrade and improve your faceting hardware (see Chapter 20).

All of these benefits neglect the fact that faceting actually *produces* something. You will not soon forget the experience of seeing your first gemstone emerge. The fact that you actually turned a more or less shapeless lump of rock into *that* will floor you. Since antiquity, gemstones have had a special power over Man and a special place in society. Whether mounted in a royal scepter or in a ring of betrothal, gems have been simultaneously both transcendent and very much a part of this world. And you just made one. It's like capturing mystical fire.

Guess what? That feeling doesn't go away.

Gemstone Faceting as a Hobby: A Pep Talk

If you are anything like I was as a beginner, the whole concept of being able to create a sparkling gemstone is a little overwhelming. As a typical, shortsighted scientist (both opthalmologically and philosophically), I had a decent understanding of how light interacts with matter, as well as the ability to remove my eyeglasses and hold up a gemstone close to my eye to try and figure it out. At some point in my early twenties, I had the opportunity to examine a pale blue topaz exactly this way.

I was amazed. Our friends at the *Oxford English Dictionary* might even say gobsmacked. Although it was an inexpensive mall-outlet gem, it seemed to be covered with an infinity of flat, perfectly intersecting facets. Despite this apparent complexity, stepping back and replacing my eyeglasses made it clear that all of this tiny detail worked together harmoniously to produce a type of visual magic. Wow.

It was clear even at that initial epiphany that I wanted to learn more. I wanted to *do this*.

I didn't start right away. In fact, I was held back by my general ignorance of lapidary techniques, coupled with a lingering uncertainty about my abilities and the financial situation typical of college students. Truth be told, I am not an artistic type. In fact, when I have to provide a signature in a public place, the bank teller or cashier inevitably looks up at me to check that I really am an adult. It's that bad.

The good news is that you don't have to be an artistic genius to create magnificent gemstones. As the Foreword to this book makes clear, faceted gemstones occupy a unique place at the intersection of art, mathematics, and science, but you don't need to be a master of any of these domains to execute a seemingly perfect gemstone. There is a wealth of explanatory information out there to help you learn. This includes Web resources such as online forums, as well as more traditional media such as the one you are holding in your hands. Lapidary clubs, both real and virtual (see Chapter 15.1.3) abound, as do the number and variety of gemstone designs. Finally – and most importantly for people like me – modern faceting machines are precise and easy to use, removing much of the mechanical barrier between the non-craftsman and this craft. If only I had started earlier....

The message here? Go for it.

1.5 Getting Started with Faceting

How do you actually get started?

I apologize in advance for the pedestrian response, but your options here are pretty similar to those of any other activity in life:

- have a faceting friend help you
- take a class at a lapidary club
- acquire the equipment and have at it

Of these three options, I strongly recommend the first two over the last. While I admire the spirit of those willing to grab the bull by the horns, the financial investment involved in even a beginner's faceting setup is substantial. A few thousand dollars substantial, so you should be pretty darn certain that you want to pursue this hobby before diving in.

Unfortunately, however, our widely connected yet widely distributed world means that there may be no clear options for direct contact with other faceters. For example, I would have to travel some 500 miles from my home in southwest Germany to meet face-to-face with my closest gem cutting acquaintance. In these circumstances, an excellent fall-back is to take a concentrated course from a faceting school. These typically last a week or two and can fit readily into a scheduled vacation. Chapter 15.8.2 points you toward possible solutions.

Whichever of these three paths you follow, this book should help you along the way. The next section explains how to use *Amateur Gemstone Faceting* and provides a chapter by chapter overview of both volumes.

1.6 Using this Book

Not only is this book not the Oxford English Dictionary (see Section 1.1), it is also not a novel. This means that you don't have to read it from beginning to end, methodically ticking off the sections and chapters as you go.

You can focus in on a particular aspect of faceting, following the topic using the cross references in the text or the index. Alternatively, you can browse, opening the book randomly and finding something of interest. I have tried hard to make things work in this non-linear way. For example, whenever a certain point assumes an understanding of a different subject, you should find a helpful pointer where to follow up.

Oh…it should also work as a traditional book, so feel free to read it from front to back.

The two volumes separate roughly along the lines of The Essentials and Expanding Your Horizons. Thus, the first volume contains information on equipment and techniques, while the second focuses on aspects which should broaden and enhance your enjoyment of the hobby.

Here's a rough breakdown by volume and chapter:

Volume 1 – The Essentials

Foreword – A welcome to the wonderful world of amateur gemstone faceting, including a brief explanation of the who, what, why, and how of producing this book.

1. Gems and Faceting – This chapter. Explains the nature and types of gemstones and introduces the hobby of faceting.

3. Faceting Machines – Provides an overview of the mechanics of faceting machines, including a section on evaluating and paying the right price for your dream machine or even building your own. A final section contains a snapshot of the current faceting machine market, along with contact information for manufacturers.

3. Laps – Explains the basics of cutting and polishing laps and the relative advantages and disadvantages of each type. An overview of commercial offerings should help you make the best choice, while a final section lists typical lap sets for the beginner and advanced faceter.

4. Additional Equipment – Faceting involves a great deal more than just machines and laps. This chapter discusses the additional equipment you will need or want, ranging from dop sticks to polishing compounds to lighting.

5. GeM101: Your First Gemstone – A detailed illustrated tutorial to guide you through cutting and polishing your first gem, from selecting the rough stone to showing off your handiwork.

6. Gem Rough – Provides advice on finding gem rough, selecting the right piece, and paying the right price for it. The chapter also discusses synthetic and simulant gemstones and concludes with a section on orienting your gem rough for maximum visual impact and yield.

7. Dopping – The act of dopping – that is, gluing a piece of gem rough to a dop stick – can be a major challenge to the beginner. This chapter explains traditional dopping practice and introduces a hybrid method, which simplifies the process substantially. The chapter ends with a discussion of dop transfer technique to ensure proper alignment of the pavilion and crown.

8. Cutting and Polishing – Explains the techniques of cutting and polishing, including sections on pre-forming, lap and facet sequencing, meet point faceting, polishing theory, and charging laps with compound. Extensive troubleshooting discussions should help you avoid, or at least correct, common cutting and polishing problems.

9. Further Reading – An expanded reading list on multiple faceting related topics.

G. Glossary of Faceting Terms – A reasonably complete list of faceting terms, including brief explanations and more importantly, direct pointers to the chapter and page where you can learn more.

Volume 2 – Expanding Your Horizons

10. Gemstone Mathematics and Geometry – Introduces the essentials of trigonometry needed for faceting and provides a detailed explanation of how to do tangent ratio scaling. The chapter then discusses gemstone symmetry and transposing designs to a different index wheel. The final section addresses the question of gem size and maximizing yield from a piece of rough.

11. Gemstone Optics –Explains the wave nature of light and how its interaction with matter produces colour, refraction, and reflection. A simple analogy clarifies Snell's law of refraction and subsequent sections discuss how total internal reflection and luster give gemstones their sparkle. The last part of the chapter follows several rays of light from the environment on a 3D journey through a gemstone.

12. Gem Material Properties – Explains the optical properties of gemstones, including colour, refractive index, and dispersion. This includes a discussion of the origin of various optical phenomena in gems, such as saturation, colour change, birefringence, and pleochroism. The second half of the chapter deals with the physical material properties of gems: density, hardness, crystal structure, cleavage, and inclusions.

13. Gemstone Treatments – A short chapter addressing gemstone treatments, from heat and radiation to oiling and exotic procedures. The chapter concludes with a discussion of the ethics of gemstone treatment.

14. Common Gem Materials – Contains easy to read tables of properties for the dozen or so most common gemstone materials. The presentation focuses on information useful to an amateur faceter, such as colour, cleavage, and the best solutions for polishing. A more abbreviated table lists basic properties of less common materials.

15. Faceting on Your Computer – Explains how to harness the computer revolution to maximize your enjoyment of faceting. The chapter begins with a discussion of getting online to learn about the hobby, connect with enthusiasts, and conduct online commerce. The next sections deal with commercial and freeware gem design and optimization software. The chapter ends with a description of three-dimensional rendering – literally cutting the gem inside your computer. This includes a detailed tutorial on how you can use freely available software to get started.

16. Designing Your Own Gemstone – Provides guidance on expressing your individual artistic urges via gemstone design. Begin with simple modifications to existing cuts, and then build steadily to the point where you can create your own, new, unique, gems. Although it is impossible to "teach" artistic creativity, this chapter provides numerous real-world design principles and tips to help you on your way.

17. Establishing the Gem Outline – Describes advanced techniques for establishing the outline of a gem. This information is useful for both cutters and designers. Separate sections explain the CAM, OMNI, CLAM, and ECED pre-forming methods and give detailed examples of each.

18. Case Study: Designing the Briar Rose – A case study in gem design. This chapter chronicles the conception, development, and execution of a novel hexagonal cut. The text gives hints on channeling inspiration into actual facets, and provides a detailed explanation of how to optimize a gem design for maximum visual impact. Although technically about the design process, this case study will also improve your skills with the GemCAD and BOG computer programs.

19. New Gemstone Designs – More than twenty new and unique gemstone designs, ranging from straightforward and easy cuts for the beginner to challenging designs for the more experienced faceter. Step by step instructions with figures assist the novice for the beginner's cuts.

20. Do-It-Yourself Projects for the Frugal Faceter – A collection of do-it-yourself projects to improve your faceting hardware and increase your enjoyment of the hobby. These range from building a better drip tank, to fabricating an inexpensive dichroscope, to adding a true digital angle encoder to your faceting machine.

I know. That is a lot of material and the two volumes of this book contain a lot of pages.

It could have been worse. Covering this breadth of subject matter without unnecessary repetition is not a trivial exercise. For example, the GeM101 tutorial in Volume 1 contains a great deal of material that, by necessity, appears elsewhere. Striking the best balance between completeness and repetitiveness was a challenge. I hope that you think that I got it about right.

To ease navigation, both volumes contain a full Table of Contents and Index. Note also that updates and errata will appear on the "official" website of *Amateur Gemstone Faceting*. Point your browser to:

www.facetingbook.com

to learn more. Techies can simply aim their smartphones at the QR code on the overleaf of the title page.

Whew! Enough introductions…you were, after all, seriously committed to this hobby and eager to begin. Turn the page and enter the wonderful world of amateur gemstone faceting.

2

Faceting Machines

A faceting machine is an electro-mechanical device for precisely placing facets onto a gemstone. Exactly how it does this is an interesting topic involving all sorts of considerations of angles, symmetry, and precision. These considerations have lead to a few general principles, which have found form in two basic layouts of machine: the mast type and the platform type.

In addition to their interesting geometrical and mechanical properties, faceting machines can be distressingly expensive and will no doubt represent the largest and most important investment in your hobby (that is, until you acquire a distressingly and perhaps uncuttably large collection of gem rough – see Chapter 6).

Faceting machines also come in a wide array of configurations. Selecting the right one can be difficult and more than a little intimidating for the beginner. Mast or platform? Left or right-handed? New or used? How to select from the bewildering variety of models from dozens of manufacturers? How about building your own? In addition to explaining the mechanics of faceting machines, the overall goal of this chapter is to guide you through the process of identifying and acquiring your particular dream machine.

2.1 A Machine Tailored to the Task

Faceting machines are highly specialized devices tailored to the task of turning an often very valuable piece of rough gem material into a work of visual art. An understanding of what these machines must do will increase your appreciation of how well they work, and it will almost certainly make you a better faceter.

We can start with a pretty fundamental question: What, after all, *is* a faceted gemstone?

Chapter 1.2 provided a brief introduction, but it is worth a short review, this time looking at the nature of a gemstone from a machine's point of view. A faceted gemstone is a piece of usually transparent mineral whose volume is defined by the intersection of many flat planes, known as facets. Such gems share a number of characteristics, although there may always be exceptions. These characteristics include symmetry and the presence of a pavilion, girdle, crown, and table. Less obvious is the fact that faceted gemstones are *convex solids* – that is there are no indentations. See page 7 for more on this.

These gemstone characteristics drive the design of any well-constructed faceting machine. For example, the symmetry characteristic requires that the machine have a mechanism for placing facets at certain well-spaced locations around the symmetry axis. The existence of tables and girdles impose the need for an angle adjustment mechanism between 0° and 90° from the symmetry axis. Ideally, this mechanism would allow ±90° adjustment to cover all possible angles from culet to table, but such an arrangement would make holding the stone itself problematic. Finally, the goal of accurate meet points means that the machine should be robust and reproducible in its settings.

2.1.1 A Multi-Faceted Approach

How, then, does one go about designing a machine to facet gemstones? Clearly, there needs to be a way to define the location of the facets in some straightforward and systematic way. Facets are geometric planes. More accurately, they are areas defined by the *intersection* of multiple geometric planes, since the planes themselves are by definition infinite in extent. This is perhaps a detail for the hardcore geometry freaks, but an individual facet doesn't really have an outline until all of the intersections with its neighbours are in place.

Casting your mind back to high school geometry, you may recall that geometric planes can be defined by two quantities: the *orientation* of the plane – in other words, which way it faces – and its *distance* from a reference point. The orientation, in turn, is given by a pair of angles defining the direction perpendicular to the surface of the plane, something called the "normal vector." You therefore need a total of three numbers: a distance and two angles. At this point, the Greek letters (ρ, θ, ϕ) and the phrase "spherical coordinates" may be stirring in the dusty halls of memory. Figure 2-1 explains the situation.

Don't remember high school geometry? Don't worry. Here's an easy way to understand how to define a specific geometric plane: Imagine for a moment that you are given the task of constructing a football field somewhere. The field is essentially a small plane on the surface of the earth, a tiny facet on our big, beautiful, blue chunk of gem rough. What do you need to know before starting?

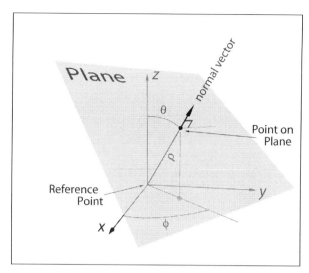

First, you will require the exact location of the field. The conventional way of defining such a location is the latitude and longitude (there are your two angles). You need one further piece of information before firing up the bulldozer, however: the altitude of the field. This can either be the distance above sea level, or more appropriately for our gemstone analogy, the number of miles from the center of the earth (there's your distance).

Figure 2-1 Spherical coordinates. Two angles, θ and φ, along with a distance ρ, define a plane.

Let's neglect whether the field runs north-south, east-west, or some other direction, since the *edges* of the plane (for example, where it intersects other features such as grandstands) determine this orientation. As described above, "cutting the neighbours" will take care of the outline of the field.

And so, whether you are an analytic geometer or just someone who really likes bulldozers, the answer is straightforward: a faceting machine must allow easy setting and control of two angles, the analogues of θ-φ or latitude-longitude, and one distance from a reference point, which conventionally is set to the center of the gem.

Let's strain the analogy even further. Figure 2-2 highlights a single facet of an impossibly large standard round brilliant. How do you locate this geometric plane? Your (extremely large) faceting machine must allow you to reproducibly adjust the "latitude," "longitude," and "altitude" of the cut.

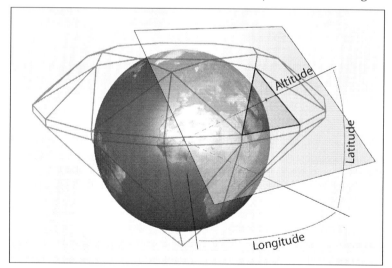

Figure 2-2 In order to cut a gem (or build a football field), the faceter (or bulldozer operator) must know the facet angle (latitude), the index (longitude), and the center distance (altitude). Yes, it is rather spooky that this particular football field is triangular and floating several thousand miles above the Great Pyramid of Giza...

There are a number of ways to do this, but essentially all faceting machines have settled on three separate mechanisms: some type of protractor to set the latitude, or *facet angle*, a toothed wheel to select various regularly-spaced intervals of longitude, or *index*, and some sort of adjustment mechanism to place the facet at the right altitude, or *height*.

2.2 History and Types of Faceting Machines

Although rotating abrasive wheels have been around for thousands of years, the earliest device in common use that we would identify as a faceting machine is the so-called "jamb-peg" faceter (Figure 2-3). This machine employs a stick-like hand-piece that can be inserted in various holes to set the cutting angle and height. The operator selects the index angle manually by rotating the stick. Some jamb-peg hand-pieces are octagonal in cross-section, forming a crude index wheel; laying each face on a stationary rest simplifies the cutting of stones with eight-fold symmetry.

Producing quality gemstones with a jamb-peg machine requires great skill on the part of the cutter. Although quite common in mass production facilities until recent years, the jamb-peg faceter is steadily being replaced by accurate commercial and custom machines. Nevertheless, a small number of manufacturers still offer what is effectively a jamb peg machine that would be recognizable and usable by our forebears of half a millennium ago. Consult Section 2.8 to indulge your historical passions, or better yet, read Glenn Klein's excellent *Faceting History* (see Chapter 9.4).

Jamb-peg devices are certainly of historical interest to the hobbyist of the 21st century, but you probably wouldn't want to use one on a daily basis. The added skill and experience required to operate such a relatively crude machine simply drain attention and effort away from the fun part of our hobby: working with and concentrating on the stone itself.

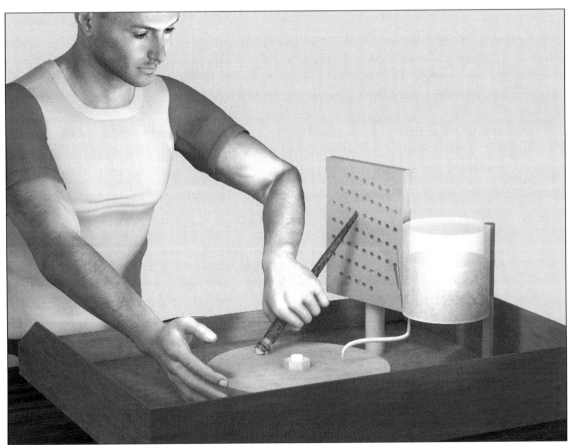

Figure 2-3 A jamb-peg faceting machine. You can learn much more about the history of gem polishing hardware in Glenn Klein's book Faceting History. See Chapter 9.4.

Fortunately, there is a wide selection of modern machines, both commercially available and custom built, that are accurate, reproducible, and easy to operate. Some may lament the loss of the truly unique manual skills that jamb-peg faceting demanded, but modern machines allow both the professional and hobbyist to achieve spectacular results without worrying about unreliable and inconsistent hardware. There is enough to think about already, such as matching the gem design to the rough or achieving a high quality polish.

Modern faceting machines fall into two general categories: the mast type and the platform type. Although different in external appearance, the two categories offer the same functionality: a simple, reproducible way to establish the facet angle, index, and height (see previous section).

2.2.1 Anatomy of a mast type faceting machine

Figure 2-4 shows a typical mast type faceting machine. It consists of two major components: a drive assembly to provide rotation and lubrication of an abrasive wheel or lap, and a mast and head assembly to bring the gemstone precisely and reproducibly into contact with the surface of the lap.

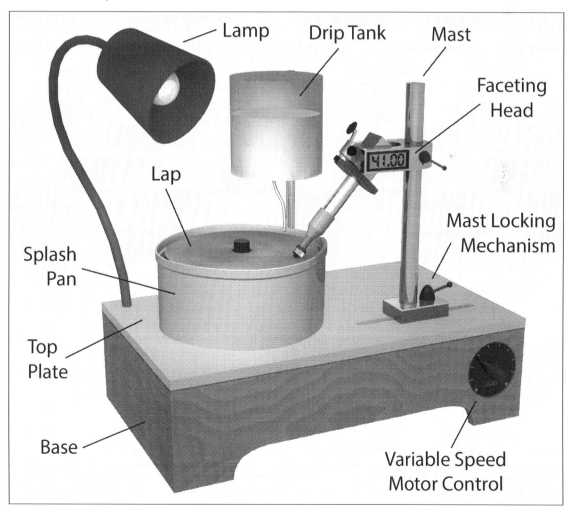

Figure 2-4 A typical mast type faceting machine.

Drive Assembly for Lap Rotation and Lubrication

The motor, arbor and platen (Figure 2-5) take care of the lap rotation part. Typical hobbyist faceting machines will have DC motors ranging up to half a horsepower (350 W) and either a direct drive or belt coupling arrangement. Most modern machines offer a variable speed motor, since different laps and gem materials prefer different cutting rates. Some also include the option of reversing the lap direction, which can help when polishing stubborn facets (see Chapter 8.17). The arbor contains the precision components, including a very straight and true drive shaft and sealed, preloaded ball bearings. All of these parts serve to convey rotation to the platen, which forms the mechanical interface to the underside of the lap. A central retaining knob or nut holds the lap in place.

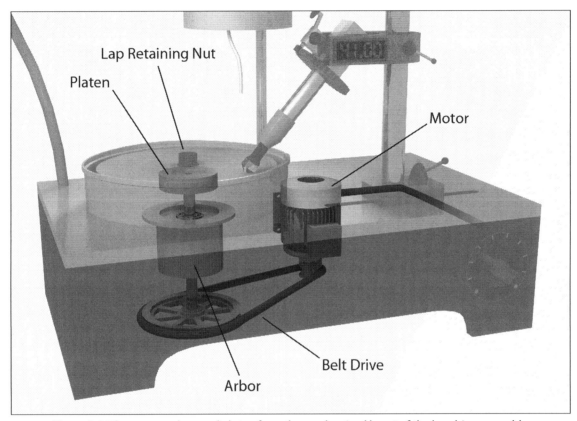

Figure 2-5 The motor, arbor, and platen form the mechanized heart of the lap drive assembly.

Accurate and consistent performance is an essential requirement on all parts of a faceting machine, but it is easy to overlook how critical a seemingly simple task such as spinning a metal disk can be. Solid steel cutting laps can weigh upward of 6 pounds (3 kg), and coarse pre-forming may call for rotation rates in the neighbourhood of 1500 revolutions per minute. That corresponds to edge speeds in excess of 50 feet per second or about forty miles per hour (60 km/hr). Needless to say, any excess wobble or play could be very destructive to valuable gem rough, to say nothing of your nerves. And you definitely don't want your arbor and platen to fail at those speeds.

At the same time, the motor, arbor, and platen must allow very slow, precise rotation for cutting fine facets or polishing. Specifically, the hardware must have sufficient torque at low lap speeds to prevent slowing and stopping when the gem makes contact. Those of us who tend to be heavy-handed know this phenomenon well.

Accurate alignment between the lap rotation axis and the remainder of the machine, for example the mast, is essential for consistent cutting results. Most commercial faceting machines offer some means of adjusting the orientation of the arbor and platen.

The remaining components of the drive assembly, the drip tank and splash pan, take care of lap lubrication, cooling, and the removal of cutting residue or swarf. The drip tank must allow a steady, controllable amount of water to fall onto the selected area of the lap, flow across the surface, and exit safely over the edge into the splash pan. Contamination is a constant concern in faceting, and small pieces of gem material removed earlier in the cutting process are one of the most insidious culprits. A well-functioning tank and splash pan will help keep these nasty fragments under control.

Note that the cutting of girdle facets requires that the dop and quill be horizontal, an arrangement that would collide with a continuous, circular splash pan. For this reason, manufacturers provide flexible splash pans or removable panels at the appropriate location (Figure 2-6).

Figure 2-6 Flexible materials (left) or removable panels (right) on the splash pan allow cutting of girdle facets.

Mast and Head Assembly for Gem Positioning

The mast and head assembly is responsible for making sure that the gem makes contact with the abrasive surface of the lap in a controlled and controllable way. Specifically, it must take care of the now-famous two angles and one distance: facet angle, index, and height (see Section 2.1.1). The mast and head assembly is also usually the most costly and complex component of a faceting machine.

Figure 2-7 shows the mast and head assembly for a typical mast type machine. The gemstone and dop stick are attached to the quill, a (usually) cylindrical metal bar that can rotate around its long axis in the trunnion to set the desired facet index. This is done in concert with the index wheel, which restricts this rotation to a series of equally spaced angles, and the index locking mechanism, which keeps the quill in place. The cheater, sometimes also known as the index splitter, allows minor adjustments to compensate for cutting errors (see "Cheat to Win…" on page 25).

The trunnion itself rotates up and down in the yoke to set the facet angle. A mechanical protractor or digital readout gives the angle, usually to a tenth of a degree. While the trunnion can freely swing upward to raise the gem from the lap, a hard or soft stop prevents the stone from moving down past the desired angle (see Section 2.4). Higher end machines may have a fine adjustment to allow precise selection of the facet angle once the stop has been engaged.

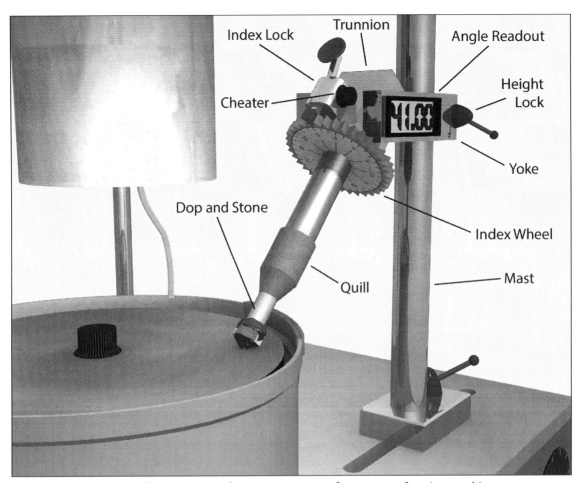

Figure 2-7 The gem manipulation components of a mast type faceting machine.

The mast serves as an accurate vertical guide to allow the head assembly to move upward and downward as necessary to set the correct height. *Absolute* height markings are not necessary, since there is no simple relationship between the measured height of the head assembly and the distance of the resulting facet from the center of the stone (draw a sketch if you don't believe this – the length of the dop stick and even the size of the gem play a role). Instead, examination of cutting progress determines the correct location. Fine-tuning of the *relative* head height is a prerequisite for accurate cutting, however, and premium faceting machines usually come with some sort of fine-adjustment mechanism.

The simple geometry of the mast type faceting machine requires two more types of motion. The first and most obvious is head rotation about the vertical axis of the mast to allow sweeping of the stone back and forth across the lap during cutting and polishing. The second required motion is a little more subtle. As the facet angle changes, the distance between the mast and the point of contact of the gemstone with the lap varies as well. For example, the star facets on a standard round brilliant (Figure 1-4) are cut with the gem much closer to the mast than when cutting the girdle. If the mast were fixed at a certain distance from the lap spindle, it would be impossible to always work at the ideal cutting location on the lap. To correct this situation, mast type faceting machines have a slide and lock mechanism to allow shifting of the mast and head assembly (Figure 2-4 and Figure 2-8).

Additional Components

A mast type faceting machine contains a few additional components beyond the drive and mast/head assemblies. The most important of these is the base, which supports the top plate on which the other assemblies are mounted. The base assembly also includes the electrical infrastructure for the drive motor and it can serve as a mounting point for the drip tank, lamps, clipboards, and just about anything else that you might want to have at hand.

Although seemingly prosaic in comparison to the precision manufacture of the other assemblies, a properly made base can spell the difference between faceting fun and frustration. Specifically, the top plate must not just hold everything together – it must do so accurately and repeatably. The previous section mentioned the importance of parallelism between the mast and the rotation axis of the lap. It also noted that the mast and head assembly must slide back and forth to accommodate different facet angles. Any yaw, pitch, or roll of the mast induced by imperfect flatness of the top plate will result in facet angles, index settings, and even height adjustments that vary with mast location. Yikes.

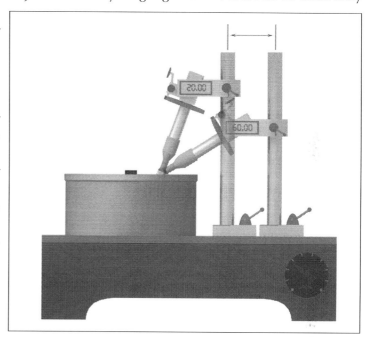

Figure 2-8 Depending on the current facet angle, the user adjusts the mast location to place the contact point at the ideal spot on the lap.

Cheat to Win...

Ahhh...the cheater.

Maligned by some, loved by many, the cheater mechanisms on our faceting machines are an endless source of discussion and controversy. Opinions span the gamut from those who believe that no skilled faceter should need such an abomination to those who view the cheater as the solution to many, if not all, of life's problems.

As with most such debates, the truth lies somewhere between the extremes. There are very legitimate reasons for splitting your indices. Machine misalignment, scalloped lap surfaces, or slight shifting of a dopped stone can all be managed by adjusting the cheater. Even more fundamentally, achieving a near-perfect dop transfer in the real world simply requires some means of adjusting the rotation reference of the index wheel (see Chapter 7.6). Getting the alignment right for the repair or re-polish of damaged gemstones is another circumstance demanding an index splitter. Finally, the mechanics of most 45° table adapters (Chapters 4.15 and 5.8) depend on the presence of a device for rotating the quill in increments much smaller than a single tooth of the index wheel.

You should not view the cheater as a cure-all, however. Yes, minor adjustments to the cutting angle and index can correct small errors, but it is a delusion to assume that you can productively and practically cheat your way through all the facets of a gemstone. In other words, it is a far better idea to understand and correct the source of your difficulty than it is to cheat your way through it.

The bottom line? Cheat to win. Don't just cheat because you can.

Variations on a Theme...

The most popular mast type commercial faceting machines include models from Ultra Tec, Facetron, and Poly-Metric (for a more complete list, see Section 2.8). While Figure 2-4 could have been extracted from the instruction manual of any of these manufacturers, there are commercially available and popular variants of the classic mast type faceting machine.

For example, one of the premium commercial machines, the GemMaster from Fac-Ette (Figure 2-9 and page 43), places the axis of the protractor at the end of the quill, not somewhere in the middle. This goes a long way toward removing the tedium of frequent height changes, since the stone rotates in "latitude" more or less about its center, not around the pivot point of the quill. The Gem-Master also claims to eliminate the need for a 45° adapter for polishing the table: because of the large protractor arrangement, the quill can be oriented vertically above the cutting surface. However, some users report skittering and jamming difficulties with this configuration and feel more comfortable with a conventional 45° tabling adapter.

The "Tradition Française" machine from l'Atelier Des Lapidaires in southwestern France represents another unique take on the concept of a mast type faceter (Figure 2-9). This device combines a relatively conventional drive assembly with a mast-mounted pegboard and handpiece guide – effectively a 21st century jamb peg machine. Everything old is new again...

Figure 2-9 The Fac-Ette GemMaster (left) quadrant design uses a unique combination of protractor and mast, while the Tradition Française faceter (right) is a hybrid of conventional mast type and jamb peg machines.

Humble Heritage

A little rumination about what a mast type machine actually does, rather than how it looks, should lead to a small epiphany: mast type faceting machines are the direct descendants of the humble jamb-peg device (Figure 2-3).

Yes, an accurate mechanical or digital protractor has replaced the series of crude holes, and yes, the simple octagonal hand-held dop now finds its role overtaken by an exchangeable index wheel, but the basic function – and arguably much of the form – of the mast type machine is essentially a jamb-peg faceter. It's hard to keep a good idea down…

In fact, the connection between the jamb-peg and the mast type faceting machine is very real and current, as a glance at the right panel of Figure 2-9 will make clear.

2.2.2 Anatomy of a platform type faceting machine

The platform type faceting machine in Figure 2-10 owes its design heritage to classical diamond cutting hardware. In fact, some users refer to this type of machine as a "tang" type, after the tool for holding diamonds. The platform faceter also shares many components with the mast type. For example, the drive assembly, including motor, platen, arbor, and splash pan, is functionally identical to that of a mast type machine. The platform faceter adopts a completely different strategy for manipulating the gem, however.

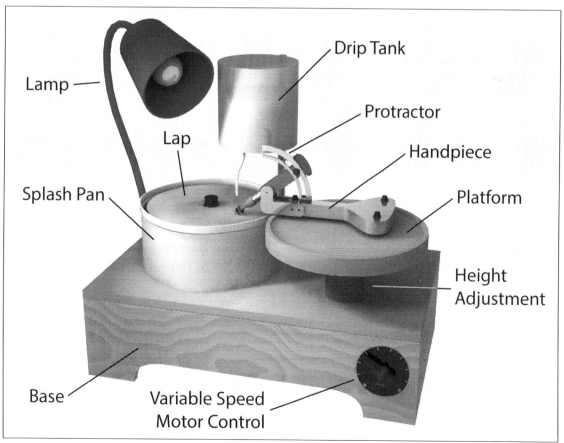

Figure 2-10 A typical platform type faceting machine.

Head Assembly

Rather than using a tall mast and head, the platform type machine incorporates all of the angle adjustments and sweeping motions into a single hand-piece that moves across a platform, hence the name (see Figure 2-11). As with the mast faceters, there is a protractor and index wheel for setting the facet angle and index, respectively, while the platform itself moves up and down to adjust the height. The hand-piece rides freely across the platform on three smooth feet, and the unit can be simply lifted off the platform to examine progress on the gem, make fine adjustments, etc. This arrangement makes it easy to work the stone on various parts of the lap, including orienting the hand-piece to reverse the cutting direction. Doing so can be helpful in polishing stubborn facets and with gem materials whose physical properties vary along different crystal directions.

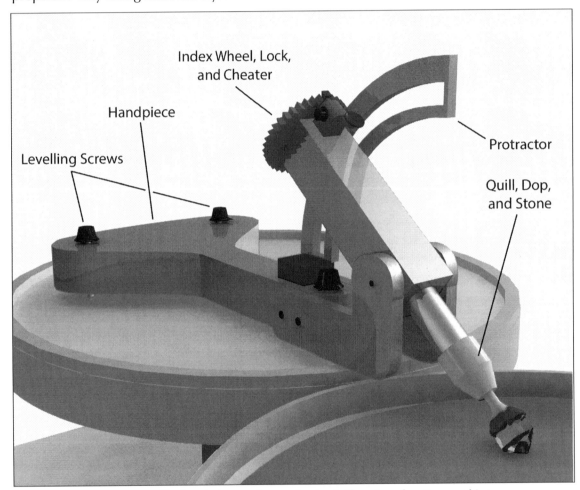

Index Wheel, Lock, and Cheater

Handpiece

Levelling Screws

Protractor

Quill, Dop, and Stone

Figure 2-11 The hand-piece and controls of a platform type faceting machine.

2.2.3 Mast or Platform: Which is Better?

As with many aspects of faceting, the choice of machine type is very much an individual decision. And, along with other issues such as dopping techniques (see Chapter 7), when faceters get together, endless discussions of the pros and cons of each machine type are the rule, rather than the exception.

Proponents of the platform type inevitably point to the ease of examining progress on the gem – simply pick up the hand-piece and look. Mast aficionados retort that wear and tear on the platform and the three feet on the hand-piece lead to inaccurate and frustrating cutting. Both sides are right and both types of machine can cut high quality gemstones. Listen to the arguments politely and make your own choice, hopefully by trying out both types.

At the end of day, the decision may not be in your hands, however. Most hobby gem cutters use commercial machines, and sadly, the platform type is becoming less and less of an option. To my knowledge, only three manufacturers – one American, one Brazilian, and one Japanese – continue to produce platform type machines, and the Raytech Shaw Faceter, which is for many the most readily available of these, has only recently returned to production after Scott Manufacturing acquired the rights from the original company (see Section 2.8). If you really want a platform style machine, your choice is limited to a small number of current commercial offerings and of course, the ever-present option of purchasing a used machine or building your own.

The Best of Both Worlds

Torn between the robustness of a mast type faceter and the ease with which a platform type machine lets you examine your work? Why not get the best of both worlds? I spotted the Lapida machine pictured in Figure 2-12 at a gem show in France. It offers all of the features of a mast type machine, combined with the removable cutting head of a platform faceter. Popping the quill out to examine the stone and then returning it to its proper position takes only a second or two.

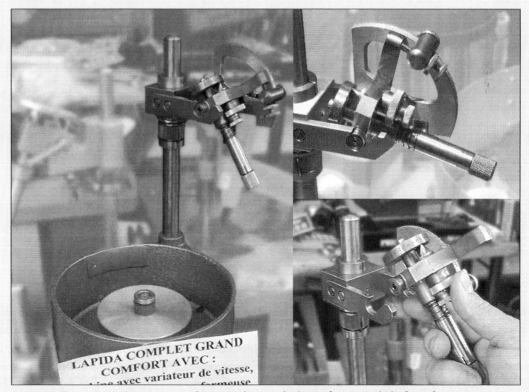

Figure 2-12 A custom machine combining the best of mast and platform faceters.

There are many good ideas out there in the world, but relatively few truly original ones. The machine pictured above was apparently inspired by an earlier-generation American / Lee "OK" faceter. In addition to standing the test of time, good ideas tend to spread as well. Although less well known to North-American cutters, it turns out that several European and Australian manufacturers of mast type machines offer removable hand-piece mechanisms (see Section 2.8).

2.3 Left Versus Right-Handed Machines

Yes, faceting machines, like people, come in left-handed and right-handed models. As we all know, handedness in people refers to the dominant side of the body as expressed by writing, throwing a ball, etc. In the world of faceting, handedness distinguishes machines with the lap on the left from those with the lap on the right. Interestingly, it is by no means clear or consistent whether a left-handed faceting machine has the lap to the left or the head to the left. Guess what? Faceting curmudgeons debate this as well.

So...you are right handed (the ten percent of lefties out there are used to this presumption, but I apologize for it nonetheless). Should you choose a machine with the lap on the right or one with the lap on the left?

At this stage, you will not be surprised to learn that the answer is "yes."

During cutting, one hand will typically grasp the stone and sweep it across the lap, while the other takes the leading role in making adjustments to the facet angle, index, and cutting height. Which hand does a better job at which task is a matter of personal opinion and practice, and again you should try both arrangements if possible before making a decision.

The good news is that most people should be able to accommodate either configuration with a little practice. I am right-handed, and I learned on a Graves machine which has the lap on the right (Figure 2-13). After trying an Ultra Tec with the opposite arrangement, I chose to assemble my own hybrid commercial/homemade machine with the lap on the left (see Figure 2-23). This decision did not reflect a real preference, however. Robustness, build quality, and cost drove my decision on the commercial parts, and it just turned out that a lap-on-left

 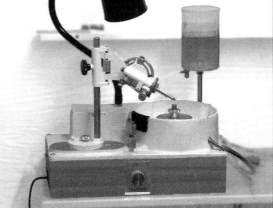

Figure 2-13 These Poly-Metric (left) and Graves (right) machines represent the two sides of the handedness debate. I have happily cut stones on both.

configuration was the standard for my chosen supplier. Note: some manufacturers offer both left and right-handed versions.

Incidentally, a few years after completing my hybrid faceter, I learned from reading Vargas' *Faceting for Amateurs* (see Chapter 9.1) that "the most satisfactory method is to be facing the machine so that the lap is to the right, and the quill to the left...The quill to left position is far simpler for the right-handed individual." Well, all I can say is "not for this right-handed individual."

The Sound of One Hand Lapping...

The faceting hobby inevitably involves a substantial investment in hardware and workspace. Or does it? For a number of years, an amateur faceter from Ohio produced what may be the ultimate in portable faceting machines. The Lap-Lap, from Jack Lahr, is essentially a hand-piece from a platform faceter and nothing more – no motor, splash pan, or drip tank. Instead of motorized, rotating laps, the user simply rubs the stone back and forth across a stationary surface covered with the appropriate abrasive or polishing material. For example, any tabletop can be converted into a faceting machine using the Lap-Lap and a copper plate charged with diamond. You can even facet on an airplane, if you can get the Lap-Lap through security.

Although it is perhaps the best-known hand powered faceting machine, the Lap-Lap is by no means the only or the first of its kind. In the 1970's and 80's enthusiastic cutters in the Pacific Northwest developed a variety of handheld machines, including offerings from Stevie's Lapidary (Mission, BC), Francis Manchester (Bellingham, WA), and Western Gems (Aldergrove, BC). More recently, Mountain Gems near Vancouver, BC produced a more refined design with an actual index gear and cheater mechanism.

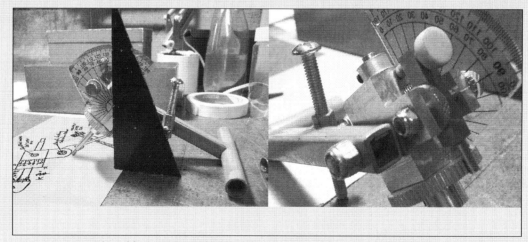

Figure 2-14 A hand faceting machine from the Pacific Northwest. Note the protractor (with set square to help read it), index wheel, and cheater mechanism. Image credit: Walt Heitland.

Due to their simplicity, the Lap-Lap and its brethren were also considerably less expensive than other faceting machines. New units cost approximately one hundred dollars, one-tenth the investment needed for a full, motorized rig.

There are of course disadvantages to these devices. By far the greatest drawback is faceting speed. The human arm simply cannot sustain the rapid motion that a motorized lap provides. Users of hand faceters estimate that completing a gemstone takes roughly ten times as long as with a motorized machine.

On the other hand, for many hobby gem cutters, the journey is the destination, and having a prolonged, intimate interaction with the emerging gemstone more than makes up for lower efficiency.

Unfortunately, Jack Lahr passed away in December 2005, throwing the availability of the Lap-Lap into limbo. The brief flowering of hand powered machines from British Columbia and Washington State has also apparently come to an end. As a result, devoted fans of hand faceting have had to resort to searches on eBay for used machines in recent years.

This sad state of affairs took a dramatic and happy turn in 2010, however, with the appearance of the Tes Faceting Machine, a direct spiritual descendant of the Lap-Lap. A couple of unique features of this machine set it apart from previous takes on the hand faceter theme: first, the kit includes a *digital* cutting angle gauge – I kid you not – and the index wheel cleverly incorporates 32, 64, and 96 index dials within a single disk. See Section 2.8 below for further details.

2.4 Hard Versus Soft Stop

Sooner or later, you will discover that it can be alarmingly easy to over cut a facet. Lost in a Zen-like state of grinding bliss, you fail to notice that things have gone too far, and you cut beyond the desired protractor angle. An over-cut facet will almost certainly require remedial action, ranging from re-cutting an entire tier to starting over from the beginning, with the grim prospect of producing a considerably smaller and less valuable gem.

For this reason, essentially all commercial faceting machines come equipped with a *hard* or *soft stop* to restrict and/or monitor the cutting angle. The exact type and configuration of stop varies considerably from manufacturer to manufacturer, but a few general distinctions can be drawn between the two types. A hard stop provides a physical barrier to further cutting. One common configuration is an adjustable screw, which just makes contact with the quill of a mast type machine at the desired protractor angle, thereby physically blocking further vertical motion toward the lap.

Soft stops don't actually stop the cutting. Rather, they provide a visual or auditory signal that the target angle has been reached. The soft stop often takes the form of an adjustable dial indicator, whose needle makes steady progress during cutting until the desired pre-set depth has been attained.

As with so many other aspects of our hobby, opinions diverge wildly on the relative merits of hard versus soft stops. The hard stop has the clear advantage of not allowing over cutting, even if your transcendent state is particularly deep. On the other hand, soft stop proponents argue that their preferred scheme offers greater control. It also discourages the mild over cutting that can arise due to mast flexure against a hard stop.

Which type of stop should you select? The best advice is to seek out a local lapidary club and give them both a try. Gaining some cutting experience with each variety will help you enormously in your decision. Sadly, this may not be a simple option given geographical constraints – faceting clubs are few and far between. Another alternative is to select a machine that offers both hard and soft stops. For example, I use a Poly-Metric Scintillator faceting head, which sports a dial indicator soft stop, as well as an adjustable screw hard stop.

2.5 Machines for Polishing Diamonds

All beginning faceters will at one point ask themselves whether it is possible to facet a diamond with their machine. The answer is probably not.

The first difficulty is that diamond is very, very hard. Although only one unit higher on the Mohs' scale than corundum – 10 versus 9 – diamond is in actuality approximately 140 times harder (see Chapter 12.9). It is really, really hard. In fact, the only thing that can cut and polish a diamond is another diamond, and the process can be excruciatingly difficult and slow.

Figure 2-15 Cutting a diamond requires special equipment and procedures.

Professional diamond workers typically use large diameter (20″-30″ or 50-75 cm) cast iron disks charged with diamond bort and rotating at a breathtaking 3000 RPM. Working the rough against this disk can produce an ear-splitting shriek, and disintegration of the lap and consequent serious injury to the operator, while rare, is not unknown.

Diamond also has the frustrating property of having radically different hardness and cutting speed in different directions. Successful faceting therefore requires considerable planning, patience, and experience.

Oh yes…and the gem rough can be a bit expensive and hard to find.

Amateur faceters are nothing if not stubborn, however, and many have successfully cut diamonds on machines completely unsuited to the task. There is even one commercial faceting machine – the Diamonte from Imperial Gem Instruments – that offers diamond-cutting capability out of the box. Fac-Ette, the manufacturer of the GemMaster machine, is also apparently developing a diamond cutter (but see the note on page 43). The best advice would be to contact others who have tried and learn from their experience. Wykoff's book, *Techniques of Master Faceting* (see Chapter 9.1), has a chapter on cutting diamonds, and you should be able to track down further tips on the Web.

2.6 Your Perfect Machine

So how do you find the perfect machine?

You must begin by realizing that there is no overall perfect machine, but there may be an (almost) perfect machine for you. Different people facet in different ways, and the relative importance of some strengths or features versus others will vary from individual to individual. These preferences will also almost certainly evolve as you gain experience and skill.

The best approach is a "try before you buy" strategy. This basically means finding a club or get-together where you can take a number of different machines for a spin. Unfortunately, as mentioned above, hobbyist faceters are pretty well dispersed throughout the world, and the nearest club may be a substantial distance away. Another alternative is to take a faceting course. This is an excellent idea for the beginning faceter anyway. Check with the teacher or school on the availability of different types of faceting machines. Planning an extended trip to take advantage of a club or faceting course is also an excellent means of focusing your energies and thoughts on exactly what you want.

The larger gem shows will attract dealers in all types of hardware, including faceting machines (Figure 2-16). Although you won't be allowed to actually sit down and cut a stone, these get-togethers provide a unique opportunity for side-by-side comparison of features, build quality, and price.

The web-based discussion groups (Chapter 15.1.3) are also a useful source of information on faceting machines, but be warned: this is yet another area in which opinions are strong.

Figure 2-16 Large gem and mineral shows provide an excellent opportunity for comparing machines from different manufacturers (see Chapter 6.2.2).

Given the potential financial investment, and even more importantly, the potential disappointment with a less than ideal machine, you should take your time, do plenty of reading, and if at all possible, try several different types before you commit to a purchase.

Inevitably, you will find annoying quirks and shortcomings with any hardware. Note: others may view these as "features." If you find that you have simply made the wrong choice, all is not lost. Faceting machines, as with other precision devices, tend to lose resale value very slowly when properly maintained. If you end up with a machine that you simply do not want, selling it onward is a very real and reasonable option.

2.6.1 Things to Look For in a Faceting Machine

This chapter began by emphasizing that gemstone faceting means control over two angles and one distance – effectively the cutting angle, index wheel setting, and the height. It should come as no surprise, then, that the most important thing to look for in a faceting machine is the ability to control these quantities and to control them well.

This basically boils down to precision, accuracy and ease of use. Incidentally, precision and accuracy are not the same thing. Precision refers to how repeatable an operation is, while accuracy measures how close to the desired target it comes. Turn to page 392 of Volume

2 for more on accuracy versus precision and a neat drawing of an archery target to demonstrate the difference.

Cutting a gemstone requires **precision** – that is, repeatability – because the standard workflow involves at least three distinct visits to each facet, one for rough cutting, one for fine cutting, and one for polishing. A machine lacking precision will require adjustment at each of these visits for each of the dozens of facets on a gem – hardly a prescription for enjoyment of a hobby.

Faceting also requires **accuracy**. Many modern gemstone designs use the intersections of existing facets for the placement of subsequent cuts – the so-called "meet point" technique (see Chapter 8.7). Inaccuracy in cutting leads to incorrect meet points, which in turn leads to incorrect facet placement, which in turn leads to another generation of incorrect meets, and so on. The words "and so on" at the end of the previous sentence are really just a polite way of saying disaster and frustration. Incidentally, traditional non meet point cuts often require the same or even greater accuracy.

The final piece of the puzzle is **ease of use**. Don't forget that faceting is a hobby, and your enjoyment will be directly influenced by how pleasant or unpleasant it is to interact with your machine. Do the math. Amateur cutters typically produce tens or even hundreds of gemstones per year. At perhaps five hours per stone, you will probably spend more time with your faceting machine than with any other device in your life, with the possible exception of the TV remote control, if you could only find it. An easy to use machine is truly a joy and makes faceting a relaxing, occasionally transcendent experience. An uncomfortable, balky, machine, on the other hand, can make faceting a chore, even worse than having to walk over to the television to switch channels…

So.

How can you evaluate the precision, accuracy, and ease of use of a faceting machine?

The best way is clearly to cut a few gemstones with it, but this may not be a viable option, particularly if you don't have access to a large lapidary club or a group of very accommodating faceting friends. There are a number of less direct ways to evaluate a particular machine, however. The following paragraphs list some critical questions you can ask yourself in assessing a candidate faceting machine for precision, accuracy, and ease of use.

How good is the **construction quality** of the machine? The old adage warns you not to judge a book by its cover, but for mechanical devices, external professionalism is often an indicator of internal quality. The "fit and finish" of a faceting machine will reflect how well it was put together by the manufacturer, and if you are considering a used machine, how well it was maintained by the previous owner.

Is the machine **mechanically "tight"**? With everything locked down, there should be no play in critical components such as the quill angle, rotation, and height. The lap, platen and arbor should also be free of play when stopped and free of rumble when at maximum speed. A corollary to this question is whether all critical mechanical components are properly sealed. The most precise bearings in the world will be of no help if they are subjected to a constant barrage of water and abrasives. Look carefully at all joints and flexures – if you can see the bearings, your cutting swarf can probably find them.

Are the components **solid without being overly heavy**? Spindly parts will flex under hand pressure, reducing both accuracy and precision. On the other hand, massive components may reflect a shortcut in engineering and will add weight without improving either accuracy or precision. Cast versus machined parts may point to such shortcuts, although there are very prominent exceptions.

Are the **critical angle settings** – facet angle and index wheel – clear, easy to use, repeatable and tight? Nothing can ruin your day faster and more effectively than a missed angle or index. Large, legible, and unambiguous indicators are a must. Examine the cutting angle display, for example. Can you readily interpret the exact angle? If it is a mechanical device, is the scale cramped or hard to read? How easy would it be to make an error of 1 degree? How about 5 degrees or even 10 degrees? Digital displays are not perfect either. Try dialing in a particular cutting angle. Raise and lower the quill a few times. Go away for a coffee and come back. Is the angle reading the same? Try setting a particular index a few times while seated in front of the machine. Was it easy? Did you make a mistake?

How repeatable and easy is the **height setting**? Some machines offer a calibrated absolute height scale while others have limited visual feedback. You don't need an absolute reference, but the height control must be precise and allow fine adjustment (see also page 24). If circumstances permit, try lowering a piece of scrap stone until it just touches a rotating lap. Raise the cutting head and try again. You should be able to return to the correct position using the visual indicators alone. Does the mast height adjustment allow rapid changes, or will you have to crank and crank going from the main facets to the girdle?

Almost the exact same questions apply to **the cheater** or index splitter. Actually, you should begin by asking a more fundamental question: does the machine even have a cheater? Some older faceting machines do not, reflecting the perverse and happily outmoded attitude that any mistakes are clearly operator error. Presuming an index splitter exists, can you reliably return to a particular cheater setting time after time? A real world test using a piece of scrap can help here as well. Cut a flat into the stone and mark it with indelible ink. Adjust the cheater back and forth, then return it to its original setting and do another light cut (Figure 2-17). Was the ink mark removed uniformly?

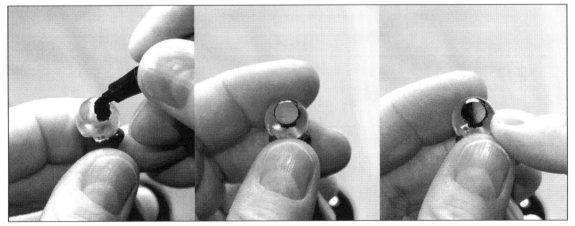

Figure 2-17 An inked flat cut into a piece of scrap, for example a marble, can test the repeatability of the cheater. The middle frame shows that the ink disappeared simultaneously across the facet, indicating a consistent cheater setting. The right hand image points to a problem.

What about the **angle stop**? Opinions vary on the value of hard versus soft stops (Section 2.4), but no one disputes the importance of repeatability in this area. Does the angle stop mechanism appear robust and easy to use? If you have the opportunity, you can test the precision of the stop by lowering a piece of scrap until you just hear the "tick-tick" of contact between the stone and a rotating lap. Set the stop as recommended and then repeat the procedure. Do you always end up at the same reading on the cutting angle display? Do you always hear that satisfying "tick-tick"?

Mast type faceting machines will have an additional, less obvious mechanism – the **mast slide** which places the stone at the desired working point on the lap for different cutting angles (see Figure 2-8). Examine the mast slide mechanism. Is the mating surface smooth, hard, and of machine quality? If you are considering a used machine, is there evidence of wear and / or other problems with the slide? Try unlocking the mast and moving it back and forth. Was it easy and straightforward? Can you imagine doing it dozens of times for every stone you cut?

How does the **motor** look? Does it appear undersized or oversized for the job? Are the electrical connections solid and professional looking? Would you be comfortable using these high power electrical components with water spraying everywhere? Older faceting machines on the resale market may not be equipped with a variable speed motor – a serious disadvantage, since optimal cutting and polishing can demand radically different rotation speeds. In fact, different individual facets on a single stone and lap type may react better with different spin rates. Most modern faceting machines offer reversible motors. This can be a real life-saver on certain gemstones, particularly those with cleavage plane problems. Note that you can achieve the same effect by operating on the opposite side of the lap (see Figure 8-32). Any machine without a reversible motor should at least allow the quill to reach both sides.

How about **low speed torque**? Some polishing situations call for very low rotation speeds: one revolution per second or even slower. There can be significant friction between the lap and stone, and uncontrolled variations in speed lead to uncontrolled results. Try mounting a lap on the machine and setting the motor to its slowest setting. Can you easily stop the lap with your finger? At the other end of the speed spectrum, you may find yourself confronted with a large chunk of low priced rough. Hogging out the rough gem shape will require a coarse lap and high speed, unless you have the luxury of a lapidary saw or grinding wheel (see Chapter 8.3.1). Try cranking the motor to maximum revs. Does the machine rumble, vibrate, or otherwise display suicidal tendencies?

New vs. Used

My first car was a new car.

I was young. I was stupid.

Since that time, my annual income has gone up by perhaps a factor of ten, yet my current set of wheels cost me less than that long-forgotten, long-ago-scrapped dream machine. You may disagree with my automotive philosophy, insisting that buying a used car is just buying somebody else's problems. You may disagree with me, but you would be wrong.

The "newer is better" philosophy does apply to faceting machines, however, at least in general terms. Used faceting machines carry the very real risk of having suffered years of neglect and abuse by their previous owners. This translates into difficulties with alignment, mechanical precision, and general wear and tear. And unlike with a car, cranking up the tunes doesn't make the problem go away.

Faceting machine manufacturers are constantly adding new features. As a result, older machines will likely be more difficult to use. Recall from earlier in this chapter that the (essential) cheater mechanism was one such feature. Compared to other industries, the faceting machine manufacturers are surprisingly well "connected" with their owner base, and will likely offer upgrades to older machines, in order to bring them in line with the features of the current product line. Such upgrades will not be free or cheap, however, and any such costs should enter into your "new vs. used" calculations.

On the other hand, a used faceting machine can be up to a factor of two less expensive than the factory-new model. Although this depreciation rate is considerably slower than with automobiles, the potential savings may mean the difference between being able to afford a faceting machine and not being able to do so. Needless to say, you will need to pay greater attention to the condition of a pre-owned machine. Note also that a number of manufacturers offer a lifetime service warranty, but only to the original purchaser. Although it is extremely unlikely that they would refuse service to a second or subsequent owner, it is equally unlikely that such service would be free.

The short version? Caveat emptor…and drive safely.

2.6.2 Other Factors

A precise, accurate, and easy to use faceting machine will almost always satisfy, but there are a few additional factors that you may want to examine before committing to a particular machine. The following paragraphs address these factors, in no particular order.

Index Wheels   The overwhelming majority of modern gemstone designs assume a 96-tooth index wheel. This choice has become popular, since it allows two, three, four, six, eight, twelve, and sixteen-fold symmetry. Prominently missing from this impressive list of symmetries is five-fold, which usually calls for an 80-tooth wheel. It also excludes the seven, nine, and tenfold symmetry provided by 77, 72, and 80/120-tooth wheels, respectively. Turn to Chapter 10.7 for more on gemstone symmetry and how it relates to index wheels.

The conclusion? The ability to switch index gears is definitely a desirable feature in a faceting machine, but it is not absolutely essential. Here's a concrete example: I own 80, 96, and 120-tooth index wheels, but over 95% of the gems I have cut have been on the 96 gear. You can cut a lifetime of gemstones with just this one index wheel. Note that many older faceting machines are equipped with fixed, 32 or 64-tooth wheels. My advice on these machines? Stay away, unless you are content with cutting a limited range of classic designs.

Eight-inch versus six-inch laps   Although the majority of modern faceting machines use eight-inch diameter laps, a few manufacturers offer six-inch versions. Although they are generally more compact and perhaps less expensive, there are at least a couple of good reasons to avoid the smaller machines. First, six-inch laps do not represent an overall economic saving: the smaller cutting area does not usually come at a proportionately smaller price. Also, the popularity of eight-inch laps means that they are more readily available in a greater variety of types. See "False Economies" on page 59 for additional reasons why you should look for an eight-inch machine.

Keyed Dops A number of critical stages in gem cutting depend on establishing and maintaining the same relative rotation of the stone with respect to the index wheel. These stages include the dop transfer, where the primary goal is to ensure alignment of the pavilion and crown facets (see Chapters 5.6 and 7.3.2). Touching up the crown star facets after completing the table in a 45° adapter is another circumstance requiring precise control over rotation.

Many faceting machines support a rotational keying system – a fancy way of saying dop sticks with a built in reference point (see Figure 4-5). In principle, such a system allows you to remove the dop and stone from the quill and replace them without losing rotational reference on the index gear. I say "in principle" because in my experience, rotational keying systems don't work that well – at least not well enough for my admittedly over-inflated standards. The short version? Keyed dops are a plus, but they are definitely not a necessity. Chapter 4.4 contains more punditry on this issue.

Portability Do you belong to a lapidary club? If so, you may want to experience the shared enjoyment of faceting in a group setting. Not only can you pick up great tips on polishing, but also such circumstances provide almost limitless opportunity for discussing the relative merits of wax versus epoxy, scoring laps versus not scoring, and so on. Of course, participating in this type of activity requires a portable faceting machine. If this is important to you, ask yourself whether you can imagine lugging your potential purchase around and setting it up in various locations. Even if you are a lone cutter, the workspace available may force a portable solution. For example, your spouse may not agree that your fine piece of machinery makes an excellent permanent guest at the dinner table.

Accessories and Add-Ons It is all too easy to neglect the range and quality of accessories when purchasing a faceting machine. This is particularly true if you are considering used hardware. Essentially all new machines come with a water drip system, a selection of dops, a transfer fixture, and a 45° table adapter, but this is by no means guaranteed with something pre-owned. Here's an educational exercise: point your web browser to the site of a commercial faceting machine manufacturer and spend fifteen minutes scanning their accessories section. You will find that it is alarmingly easy to drop several hundred dollars on items that ship with a new machine. That bargain doesn't sound so great anymore, does it?

Of course, even a brand new set of accessories is of no help if they are of poor quality. The accuracy and precision (those words again!) of your cutting depend on these accessories just as much as they do on the machine itself. Bent dops, a crappy transfer fixture, or an awkward tabling adapter can wreck your gem just as quickly as a bad angle indicator. Check that the water system is sensible and easy to use. Note: the water system includes the drain!

Manufacturers and especially previous owners of faceting machines display great imagination in creating add-ons to improve the cutting experience. These include pre-forming tools, girdle rests, motorized quills, depth of cut indicators, concave faceting tools, and on and on and on. Such doodads are definitely a mixed blessing. On the one hand, they can genuinely make your hobby more enjoyable. On the other hand, many such devices are not really necessary, and they offer additional opportunity for things to go wrong. Be particularly wary of home-brew modifications. Commercial machines represent the wisdom of manufacturers and users accumulated over decades. Somebody's "great idea" cooked up in the middle of the night and executed with a hand drill and glue may not be so great after all. Besides, acquiring an unmodified machine allows you to try out your own ideas, which are of course truly great. Chapter 20 will help you get started.

2.7 Making the Purchase

Faceting machines are expensive. In fact, beyond vehicles, housing, and sending the kids to college, a faceting machine and its accessories can easily represent the single largest investment you make in an adult lifetime. Luckily, unlike essentially all vehicles (see page 37), some housing, and too many college educations, faceting machines depreciate relatively slowly, and with proper maintenance, can give a lifetime of service.

As a result, you should not undertake such a purchase decision lightly. When it comes to buying lapidary equipment, there are pitfalls out there beyond the purely technical. Even the finest faceting machine in the world can arrive on your doorstep amid a disappointing fog of dealer mistrust, suspicion of overpayment, or miscommunication of features and included accessories. Ask yourself the following question: is the stereotype of the dishonest car salesman associated with any particular brand of automobile? No. It is associated with the *process* of buying a car. And, as with your next automobile purchase, care and preparation in advance will ensure that your faceting machine buying experience will be as smooth and enjoyable as possible.

This section lists some of the non-mechanical things you should watch for in purchasing a faceting machine. As before, they are presented in no particular order, but you should feel comfortable about all of these items before signing the cheque.

The **cost** is the most obvious – and often startling – aspect of buying a faceting machine, but surprisingly, it can be one of the least important. The reason for this is that the faceting machine market is relatively small: there are simply not a large number of amateur cutters out there. As a result, neither economies of large scale manufacture nor strong competitive forces can have a strong influence on price. We are inevitably in the situation of paying premium prices for premium products.

Don't misinterpret this situation. There can be qualitative differences in price between the various dealers and models, and you should certainly try to negotiate both price and included accessories in your chosen faceting package. The online resources listed in Chapter 15.8 can help in identifying suitable sellers and machines. Just don't expect a free lunch.

The positive corollary to the maxim of higher price is the fact that you can and should expect excellent **dealer support**. Whether you buy directly from the manufacturer or from an authorized distributor, you will find that an unusually strong and positive relationship exists between the producers and consumers of faceting machines. This arises from an additional corollary to the law of higher cost: the manufacturers are not getting terribly rich building faceting machines. I can only interpret their continued production as genuine loyalty to their customers and a love of faceting. Cynics may label this behaviour as self-serving insincerity, but name another industry which routinely gives lifetime warranties to the purchasers of mechanical equipment. Call me a blue-eyed optimist and fool if you want, but when I correspond with the owner of the company which built my machine components, I use his first name and he uses mine. My conversations with fellow hobbyists tell me that this situation is by no means unusual.

The short version of this is that you cannot go wrong by working either directly with the manufacturer of your chosen machine or with one of their authorized representatives. Of course, doing so can be more difficult if you purchase used hardware. In that instance, you should very seriously consider shipping the machine to the original manufacturer for a check-up (see the comments on return policy below). If all goes well, this can serve as the initial exchange of a satisfying, long-term relationship.

You should not overlook **company reputation**. All manufacturers have confronted design flaws and unhappy users, but not all have worked equally hard to make things right. Community experience and guidance can be a big help here, but don't neglect the natural human tendency to emphasize shortcomings and gloss over satisfaction. The newspapers, after all, are not full of stories about all the airplanes that managed to stay aloft yesterday…

Company longevity is another important, but not critical factor. Manufacturers regularly go out of business or, more likely these days, are "acquired" by larger concerns with less interest in hobbyist faceters. Should this happen with your machine, you may find yourself without a supplier of spare parts, repair services, and so forth. A number of leading manufacturers have been producing commercial machines for decades. While in principle, this gives some assurance of their continued interest and existence, the small scale nature of faceting machine manufacture means that the long term prospects of a particular company may be tied to a single (mortal) individual. None of these concerns should be a showstopper, however. Provided that you select a reasonably well-known brand, there should be a substantial established user base for spare parts and support.

All sellers of new or used faceting machines should provide a generous and reasonable **return policy**. Specifically, you should be able to return an unused machine and receive a full refund. Given their size and weight, you may reasonably be expected to pay shipping charges. Negotiate with the seller of a used faceting machine. You should be permitted to cut a stone or two on it before committing to the final payment. You should also be allowed to ship the unit to the original manufacturer (at your expense) for a thorough check-up and evaluation of repair cost. At a bare minimum, you should check the serial number of a used machine with the manufacturer to get a history of repair and upgrades. Be reasonable in your expectations and dealings with sellers of both new and used machines. Nothing will be perfect in all respects, but you will be surprised at how willing lapidary people can be to give satisfaction on all sides.

Finally, in the case of a used machine, you should at least understand the **reason for sale**. A casual reading of the online discussion groups and a few visits to ebay.com scattered over several months will tell you that top faceting machine brands do not often appear on the re-sale market. There is a very good reason for this: satisfied owners. In dealing with private individuals, it is entirely appropriate to ask why the machine is for sale. Usually, the reasons relate to financial difficulties, loss of interest, or health issues with the previous owner. Just make sure that there are no underlying problems or frustrations with the machine.

Faceting for Eternity

I tried to avoid making this discussion morbid.

I honestly tried, but there is no real way to avoid the fact that one of the best sources of well-maintained, top quality faceting machines is other faceters, who for reasons of poor health (or worse) have been forced to abandon their hobby.

Look around you at your next lapidary club meeting. There are probably more people who remember the Eisenhower administration than those who can climb ten flights of stairs unassisted – this is a comment on both age and health, by the way.

The simple, perhaps awful fact is that no one lives forever, and the end can come suddenly or with a steady loss of vision, manual dexterity, and so on. Often, information about the availability of used machines will come through contacts with club members or estate sales. Keep your eyes and ears open, but of course, exercise all due restraint and respect. The last thing you want is a perception that you are a vulture.

On later reflection, I honestly don't think that all this talk about faceting for eternity has been morbid after all. When it is my turn to go to the great rough pile in the sky, I would rather have my beloved faceting machine giving joy to a devoted hobbyist than moldering away in a box in some nephew's garage. I suspect that it can be of some comfort to surviving relatives that a little part of their loved one lives on in the happy production of yet more objects of beauty and mystery.

Whew.

There is clearly plenty to think about and plenty of things to look for when you go hunting for that ideal new or used faceting machine. To provide additional guidance, the following sections attempt to capture a snapshot of the current landscape of commercial offerings. This is followed by a short excursion into the world of homebuilt hardware and add-ons. Whether you have the mechanical skills to build an entire faceting machine from scratch, or the partial skills to combine the best of commercial hardware with do-it-yourself components, building or enhancing a machine that is perfect for you can be a very attractive option.

2.8 Commercial Faceting Machines

This section provides an overview of commercial faceting machines. Although by no means exhaustive, the list includes both current models and those which are commonly available on the resale market. Of course, manufacturers come and go, as do their individual product lines. This compendium reflects availability in 2013. The online resources listed in Chapter 15.8 can provide more up-to-date information.

Note also that a detailed review and opinion of individual faceting machines is well beyond the scope of this book. Not only do machines evolve, but also the pros and cons of a certain brand are very much a matter of personal taste. And, as noted above, some initially annoying aspects of a machine may become a valued feature with time.

A final caveat: few individuals, myself included, have the time and resources to evaluate all the faceting hardware on the market. And, although I have twiddled the knobs on many of the machines listed below – the faceting equivalent of kicking the tires – I have only really cut gemstones on two different types of faceter. Nevertheless, this section should provide you with enough background information to get you started in making intelligent choices among commercial faceting machines.

2.8.1 Manufacturers and Models of Common Faceting Machines

This section lists make and model information for commonly available faceting machines. Note: I admit to and apologize for a North American bias in deciding which models are more or less common.

Fac-Ette (GemMaster II, GemMaster Jr., GemMaster Diamond)
Leland, NC, USA
www.fac-ette.com
$3,000 - $5,000 depending on included features
See Figure 2-9

Many consider the Fac-Ette GemMaster series to be the Rolls Royce of faceting machines. Although it is more expensive than competing brands, the GemMaster has unquestioned high build quality and a vocal, devoted user base. Distinguishing features of the Fac-Ette machines include a strain-gauge based depth of cut indicator and a novel protractor arrangement which can eliminate the need for tabling adapters. Fac-Ette has announced the development of the eponymous GemMaster Diamond, which will, unsurprisingly, be capable of faceting diamonds. *Note: As this book entered final production, the faceting world received news that Fac-Ette had ceased production. At this time, the future of the GemMaster line is unclear.*

The Graves Company (Mark I, Mark IV, Mark 5XL)
Pompano Beach, FL, USA
www.gravescompany.com
$1200 (Mark IV) – $1700 (Mark 5XL)
See Figure 2-13

If Fac-Ette is the Rolls Royce of faceting machines, then Graves is the Volkswagen. Affordable and in very wide use, the various generations of Graves machines are a fixture in the world of amateur gemstone polishing. Although now rarely seen, the venerable Mark I model is the direct ancestor of the ubiquitous Mark IV. Most recently, Graves has acquired the rights to manufacture the Gearloose XS3 digital faceting head as the Mark 5XL. The 5XL can serve as a retrofit to the Mark I or Mark IV platform, or it can replace the original mast assembly on a number of models from other manufacturers, such as the Facetron.

Jarvi Tool Co. (Facetron)
Anaheim, CA, USA
www.facetron.com
$2700

The Facetron from Jarvi Tool Co. is perhaps the most popular faceting machine among amateurs, and it represents an excellent choice for beginners and experienced cutters alike. Unique features of the Facetron include the micrometer-based fine height adjustment at the top of the mast and the dial-type mechanical protractor, which allows precise angle settings to a tenth of a degree (see Figure 20-20).

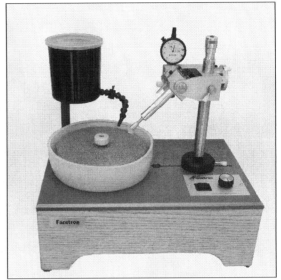

Figure 2-18 The popular Facetron machine.

Jersey Instruments (Patriot, Tom Thumb, OMNI)
Huntsville, AL, USA
www.jerseyinstruments.com
Patriot $2200 (for 6" laps) – $2400 (for 8" laps); Tom Thumb $1800

Jersey Instruments is a relative newcomer to the field of commercial faceting machines, although the original OMNI drew inspiration from the classic Australian Hall Xtra machine. The latest version, incorporating new technologies and customer suggestions, is called the Patriot. The Patriot has a couple of distinguishing characteristics: the machine is very compact (particularly the 6" lap model), and all recent Jersey Instruments faceting heads ship with true

digital encoders, a definite plus. See Chapter 20.8.3 for more on this issue. Recently, the firm introduced the Tom Thumb Faceting Machine, a smaller footprint, analog-only cousin of the Patriot. My favourite aspect of the Jersey machines is the statement on their website declaring that "Our list of products include aircraft mufflers, digital chronometers, pedestrian crossing timers, aircraft test instrumentation, experimental aircraft and others." I guess that faceting machines are among the "others."

Figure 2-19 The Patriot faceting machine from Jersey Instruments.

Poly-Metric Instruments Inc. (Xristal-Tek '99', Scintillator 88, O.M.F, Xristal-Tek 87)
Clayton, WA, USA
www.polymetricinc.com
$2200 – $4000 depending on model and features
See Figure 2-13

Founded in 1990, Poly-Metric Instruments is also a relative youngster among faceting machine manufacturers, although the owner and his father were involved in the lapidary business for over thirty years before that date. Poly-Metric is perhaps best known for innovating the OMF or "optically magnified facet" machine, the first widely available concave faceter.

Ultra Tec (V5, V2, Concave, and Fantasy)
Santa Ana, CA, USA
www.ultratec-facet.com
$4000 (V2 analog) - $5000 (V5 digital)

Ultra Tec has been manufacturing premium faceting machines for over 45 years, and they have a large, devoted following in the hobbyist community. The V5 and V2 models operate on 110 or 220V and can be ordered with a fully digital encoder offering true, 0.01° precision. Ultra Tecs use a belt-free direct drive, and the overall build quality, the "fit and finish," of these machines is without peer in the business.

Figure 2-20   The Ultra Tec V5 faceting machine with a Digital Angle Display.

2.8.2 Less Common Models

This section lists the manufacturers and models of less common faceting machines currently on the market. Some of these are true rarities, while others appear here due to my admitted bias toward North American hardware. Nevertheless, you should be able to track down further information via the websites listed.

Addexton Company (Jamb-Peg)
Woodland, CA
www.thelapidarycompany.com

Addexton sells a jamb-peg faceter. Really. A genuine jamb peg faceter. Actually, it is just the pegboard. You have to supply the spinning lap and quill. The device can be used with your current machine to regain an appreciation of true manual craftsmanship.

Anand Engineering Works (FPK, FPID, FPIT machines)
Trichy, India
www.anand-gems.com

The Anand lapidary machines seem geared to larger scale production. The FPK and FPID machines have dual arbors and a single mast, allowing you to cut and then polish the same facet without changing settings. The FPIT has two arbors and four faceting heads.

Astro-Tel – (Hall – various models)
Cairns, Australia
www.turbofast.com.au/astrotel/faceting.html

Astro-Tel makes multiple models (2000, Mark V, Heavy Duty Deluxe, Xtra), and created the design for the American-made OMNI (see previous section). The Hall faceters are conventional mast type machines with analog protractors.

l'Atelier Des Lapidaires – (Tradition Française model)
Thédirac, France
http://www.taille-pierre-precieuse.com/materiel_tarif.html
See Figure 2-9

The "Tradition Française" faceting machine is a hybrid, combining a jamb peg unit with an otherwise traditional mast type configuration. The company offers training to help new users master this unique machine.

Atelier La Trouvaille – (various models)
Remoulins, France
http://www.atelierlatrouvaille.com

This company offers various combinations of faceting heads, bases, and accessories. These include the LTFAC removable quill model, as well as a "Vernier" jamb-peg unit for use on a conventional mast (similar to the Tradition Française). They also carry HAMAG hardware (see below).

Otto Eigner e. K. (FM series)
Idar Oberstein, Germany
www.ottoeigner.de/html/maschinen/seite3_z_fm1.html

Manufactured at the epicenter of the European coloured gem industry, the FM series of faceters from Otto Eigner are very compact but otherwise conventional mast type machines.

Gemmarum Lapidator – (GL 501, BSF1, BSF2)
Cavalese, Italy
www.gemmarum.it

Although most of the world has gone to mast type machines, there are still manufacturers out there who understand you. One of these is Gemmarum Lapidator, who fabricate several models of platform type faceting machines.

HAMAG Maschinenbau (various drive assemblies and facet heads)
Buchloe, Germany
www.hamag-maschinenbau.de

In the distant shadow of the Bavarian Alps lies the town of Buchloe, home to HAMAG machine works. This company produces a huge variety of lapidary equipment, including the "XV Nova" and "Präzisions" faceting heads, which mate to a variety of bases and lap assemblies from HAMAG and other manufacturers.

Homberg and Brusius
Kirschweiler, Germany (near Idar-Oberstein).
http://www.homberg-und-brusius.de/index.html

Homberg and Brusius produce the "Facettier", a compact mast type machine with an analog protractor and a removable hand-piece (see Figure 2-12 for another example of this concept).

Igon Faceting Machines - Gemcut MK1
Tootgarook Australia
No web site.

The Gemcut MK1 is a relatively conventional mast type machine with a traditional analog protractor.

Imahashi (FAC-8)
Tokyo, Japan
http://www.imahashi.net/english/imac_001.htm

Imahashi produces the FAC-8, a compact platform type faceter that is widely used in Asia.

Imperial Gem Instruments (Alpha Taurus, Diamonte, Imperial)
Santa Monica, CA
http://iginstruments.com/IGInstruments/Welcome.html

The Alpha Taurus is a relatively conventional mast type faceting machine (although I really like the red anodized trim). Imperial Gem Instruments also manufactures the Diamonte model, which is suitable for faceting diamonds. The Imperial Faceting Machine was discontinued in 1988 but may appear on the resale market.

Jack Schmidling Productions, Inc. (EasyGem)
Marengo, IL, USA
http://schmidling.com/eg.htm

The EasyGem is an inexpensive mast type faceting machine incorporating fine angle adjustment and a dial indicator for depth of cut. The website is worth a visit, if for no other reason than perusing the range of Mr. Schmidling's products and interests listed on his home page.

KLM Technology (Jang 1D, Jang 12D)
New Brunswick, NJ / Incheon, Korea
www.klmtechnology.com

KLM Technology produces robotic faceting machines (1 stone or 12 stone). These are high tech wonders, with liquid crystal touch panel controls and full automation. The 1D model has dual arbors, allowing sequential cutting and polishing without changing laps. Definitely cool, but probably misses the point for hobbyists.

Lapidart (Lapidador)
Belo Horizonte, Brazil
http://www.lapidart.com.br

Lapidart produces a series of professional grade faceting machines featuring stainless steel construction, Fac-Ette type arc protractors, and recirculating filtered cooling systems. They have also developed a fully robotic faceting machine which can cut and polish fifteen stones an hour.

LWD Engineering (Drabsch)
Weston, ACT, Australia.
No web site - telephone (+61) 2-6288-7752

The Drabsch machine is a compact unit with a Fac-Ette type quadrant protractor.

Rajasthan Tools and Spares (3D and industrial production machines)
Jaipur, India
www.rajtools.com

Like Anand Engineering (see above), the faceting machines from Rajasthan are oriented toward commercial customers. The 3D unit is a double arbor machine for sequential cutting and polishing, and the company offers a triple-arbor, six-head faceter for larger production.

Sapphire Engineering (VJ Faceting Machine)
Rockhampton, Australia
No web site - telephone (+61) 79-28-2119

The VJ model from Sapphire Engineering has a unique lap platform which moves up and down, along with a Fac-Ette type arc protractor.

Scott Manufacturing (Raytech Shaw Faceter)
Littleton, CO, USA
http://raytechshaw.com

Fans of platform type faceting machines, rejoice! Raytech Industries ceased production of the Raytech Shaw Faceter a few years ago, but now the machine is back on the market thanks to Scott Manufacturing.

Shell-Lap Supplies (GEMMASTA GF4, GF5)
Mile End (Adelaide), Australia
www.shell-lap.com.au

The Gemmasta GF series are relatively conventional mast type faceting machines that are very popular down under. The more expensive GF5 model ships with a larger motor and a "meet point indicator" (precise soft stop). The removable chuck allows inspection of the stone without disturbing the alignment.

Stone Tes Faceting (Tes Faceting Machine)
Mansfield, OH, USA
http://www.stonetes.com

The Tes Faceting Machine is a (non-motorized) hand faceter, a so-called "human powered faceting instrument" which draws its inspiration from the Lap-Lap device (see "The Sound of One Hand Lapping..." on page 31). The basic kit includes the hand-piece, copper lap "cards," a transfer fixture, and polishing compound – in other words, everything you need except muscle power.

TheGemConnection.com (CJP Faceting Machine)
Port Charlotte, FL, USA
http://www.thegemconnection.com

Gerald Wykoff, master gemcutter, author, championship middleweight boxer, and all-round Renaissance man is also in the business of fabricating affordable faceting hardware. The Calibrated Jamb Peg (CJP) Faceting Machine is a kit for building your own stand and peg board for cutting gemstones the way that 600 years of wisdom have instructed. You will have to supply your own motorized base and lap drive, but the website offers numerous instructional books and CDs to get you going.

2.8.3 Models Out of Production

This final section lists information on manufacturers which are no longer actively producing faceting machines but whose products may appear on the resale market. Note that some of this information was hard to track down, and the commercial environment changes continuously. The entries below should help you sniff out further details, but they may not be accurate or complete in all instances.

Abrasive Technology Inc. (Crystalite Faceting Machine)
Lewis Center, OH, USA

American Facetor (AmFac Faceting Machine)
Cornwell Hts, PA, USA

A unique design that shipped with special index wheels for various gem shapes (pear, oval, etc.) and had special faceting head mount locations for working on the girdle and table.

Arrow Profile Company (Sapphire Faceting Machine)
Hazel Park, MI, USA

Mast type faceter with analog protractor. Not to be confused with Sapphire Engineering in Australia – see above.

B&I Manufacturing Co. (Gem Maker)
Burlington WI, USA
See Figure 2-21.

Figure 2-21 An advertisement for the Gem Maker faceting machine from the July 1946 issue of Popular Science. A bargain at less than thirty dollars.

Covington Engineering (Covington Faceting Machine)
Redlands, CA, USA
www.covington-engineering.com

This company used to make a faceting machine but now focuses exclusively on other types of lapidary equipment.

Daniel Lopacki Co. (Lopacki Faceting Machine)
Cliff, NM, USA (current location)

A version of the original Lee machine manufactured in China.

Franz Eisele Engineering (Exacta Faceting Machine)
Oceanside, CA, USA

Conventional mast type.

Gearloose (XS3 Faceting Head)
North Easton, MA, USA

This digital faceting head became the Graves 5XL. More details at www.gearloose.com/xs3.html

Glen Engineering (Topaz Tec Faceting Machines)
Everton Park, QLD, Australia

Sturdy, mast type faceting machine.

Gus Meister (The Facet-Meister – formerly Alta Faceter)
Altadena, CA, USA

Highland Park Faceting Machine
Manufacturing location uncertain

A re-branded version of the Prismatic (?)

Irv's LLC (Irv's Faceting Machine)
Spokane WA, USA

See www.irvsshop.com

J. F. W. Engineering (Agatemaster)
Brisbane, Australia

Mast type analog faceter with a large, stable foot on the mast slide assembly.

Jack Lahr (Lap-Lap Hand Faceter)
Mt. Vernon, OH, USA

See "The Sound of One Hand Lapping…" on page 31.

Lee Lapidaries Inc. (The Lee Faceting Machine)
Cleveland OH, USA

Removable hand-piece. Spawned many imitators.

Maja Manufacturing (Maja Faceting Machine)
Woodland Hills, CA, USA

Removable quill mast type. One of the many Lee imitators.

Francis Manchester (Hand Faceting Tool)
Bellingham, WA, USA

Hand faceting machine, originally available for $55. See page 31.

Charlie Mandelkow (Mandelkow Faceting Machine)
Stanthorpe, Queensland, Australia

Hybrid handpiece faceter based on the O'Brien machine (see below).

MDR Manufacturing (Master, Model 300-C, Others)
Kingwood TX, USA

Conventional mast type faceting machines. Ceased production ca. 2003, although rumours of renewed manufacturing and support persist.

Mountain Gems (Hand Faceter)
Burnaby, BC, Canada

Hand faceting machine with index gear and cheater. See page 31.

Norris and Mollin (The Taylor Faceting Machine)
Location uncertain

Conventional mast type machine with analog protractor.

Dan O'Brien (O'Brien Faceting Machine)
Burlington, WI, USA

Hybrid design using a free-floating quill with a polygonal index plate, which rides on a mast-based platform.

Pos-A-Pin
Manufacturer, location uncertain

More or less conventional mast type with fixed, "pinned" angle settings.

Prismatic Instruments (Prismatic H Series, Accura-Flex, Viking models)
Spokane WA, USA

Information on these mast type faceting machines is available at the Poly-Metric site: www.polymetricinc.com

Glenn and Martha Vargas (Fac-A-Gem Faceting Machine)
Thermal, CA, USA

Platform type machine manufactured by Glenn and Martha Vargas, the authors of *Faceting for Amateurs* and other books (see Chapter 9).

Stanley Lapidary Company (Stanley Ultra Tec)
Santa Ana, CA, USA

The original Ultra Tec, manufactured by Howard Stanley until 1970, when he sold the company to Joe Rubin, the current owner.

Stevie's Lapidary (The Canadian Facetor)
Mission, BC, Canada

Relatively conventional mast type faceting machine with brass fittings (see http://www.the-gemdoctor.com/facetor.html). The company also produced a hand faceter in the 1970's.

Western Gems
Aldergrove, BC, Canada

Hand faceting machine with protractor. See page 31.

2.9 Alternatives: Building your own machine

The previous sections emphasized the importance of "try before you buy." For the more mechanically skilled (or perhaps just the more adventurous) hobbyist, there is an alternative: building your own.

Homebuilt faceting machines can take almost any form, provided that they supply the basics of control over facet angle, index, and height (Section 2.1.1). The current commercial "conventional wisdom" is by no means the final word on the design of the ultimate faceting machine. Just imagine it and you can probably build it.

Having said that, manufacturing your own faceting machine is by no means trivial. Accurate, reproducible results require precision mechanics, and these are not easy to fabricate on equipment available to most amateurs. For example, the "run-out" or variation in lap height with rotation for commercial faceting machines is often quoted in tens of micrometers (a few thousandths of an inch). Working with and aligning high-speed precision bearings is also a challenge, and don't forget that all this fancy equipment must work in a daily bath of water and abrasives. You may also face challenges in producing reliable and safe electrical connections, given the amount of spray and drips that can occur.

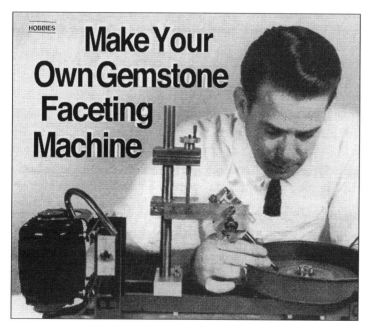

Well, enough of me *emptor*-ing my *caveats* – after all, "buyer beware" only really applies to someone who is going to *buy* something. You want to get your fingernails dirty, right? If you feel that you have the chops, go for it.

Figure 2-22 An article in the February 1971 issue of Popular Mechanics explains how to build your own faceting machine. Although more than four decades old, the text and technical drawings are an excellent starting point. Image courtesy of Popular Mechanics. Originally published in the February 1971 issue.

A Hybrid Commercial-Homebuilt Faceting Machine

As mentioned in Section 2.3, I learned to facet on a commercial Graves machine at a local lapidary club. I also had the opportunity to try hardware from Ultra Tec and Face-tron. Each of these machines had their strengths and weaknesses. None was a perfect match.

I have some training as a machinist, and I know a couple of masters of the lathe and mill. I am also blessed with the three character traits essential to any do-it-yourselfer: I am persnickety, stubborn, and, most importantly, cheap. This fortuitous combination of circumstance and character prompted me to explore the possibility of building my own faceting machine.

Unfortunately, my ambition to build the ultimate gem cutter soon slammed into the harsh reality outlined in Section 2.9. Given my set of experience and skills, it was simply out of the question for me to produce a machine that would meet my own standards. Reluctantly, I went back to the catalogs of the commercial manufacturers.

While glumly flipping through the various offerings (particularly glumly with the price lists), I was struck by an idea – why not build what I could build and buy what I could not? A number of companies offer individual components and assemblies, in addition to complete machines. Yes! I would reluctantly fork over the cash for a precision arbor mechanism, but who the heck wants to spend forty bucks for a drip tank?

Thus was born the hybrid commercial-homebuilt faceting machine shown in Figure 2-23. The hard to build stuff, including the mast, head, and arbor, are from Poly-Metric, but everything else is home-built or otherwise acquired by unconventional means.

Here are some specifics: The splash pan is literally an empty potato salad tub from my office cafeteria. In order to accommodate the spindle, I cut out the bottom of the tub and replaced it with a PVC toilet flange and some scrap rubber sheeting (Figure 2-24). The drain pipe is a length of clear plastic tubing. Total cost: less than $5, mostly in silicone bathtub sealant…I used a lot of that.

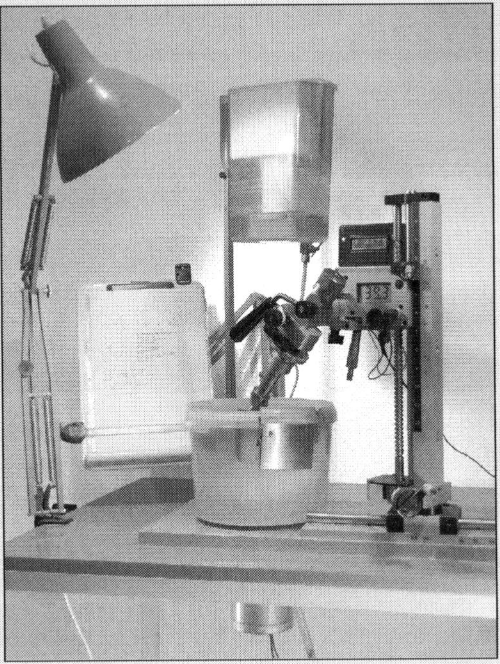

Figure 2-23 My hybrid commercial / homebuilt faceting machine. Readers familiar with Poly-Metric hardware may notice a few add-ons to the faceting head. Chapter 20 provides details.

The drip tank is a modified water filter jug. Having read horror stories about sand and other grit in tap water making its way onto the lap surface, I decided early on to always use filtered water when I cut. At home, we had a commercial filter jug system from Brita in the kitchen. Staring at it one day, I realized that Brita-on-a-Stick would kill two birds with one stone – the perfect drip tank. After investing in a small brass water tap, a bit of plastic tubing stiffened with wire, an aluminum rod from the scrap heap, and another embarrassingly large amount of silicone bathtub sealant, I was in business. Total cost: $5 and an explanation to the wife about the fate of our water jug. Turn to Chapter 20.5 for an explanation of how you, too, can build your own filtering drip tank

The base assembly consists of three parts. The table was recovered from a junk heap. I simply hacked out a hole large enough to allow the motor to pass through (more on this later). The drive motor itself also comes from the junk pile. Based on the vague recollections of its prior owner, the motor spent its earlier life in some sort of ventilation system. After a few tests with a power supply ($60 new), I realized that a direct drive, flex-coupler configuration would work – no need for complicated belts and pulleys.

Figure 2-24 An empty potato salad container and a PVC toilet flange find new life as a home-brewed splash pan. This viewpoint cleverly obscures the embarrassingly large amount of silicone bathtub sealant necessary to make the whole thing work.

The top plate was a different story altogether. As emphasized in Section 2.2.1, accurate co-alignment of the drive spindle and mast are a prerequisite to problem-free cutting. How could I produce a large machined plate with sufficient precision? I turned to my friend, the master machinist, who was interested enough to do the job for the cost of raw materials. Raw materials in this instance included the aluminum for the top plate of the faceting machine and beer for the machinist. Yes, I was careful to ensure that the deadly mix of alcohol and serious metalworking equipment did not occur.

Total cost of the base assembly: less than $100, including the power supply for the motor but not including the deposit on the beer bottles.

Putting it all together took less time and was a lot easier than I expected. Of course, it was a great help to start with new, high quality commercial components and the best custom machined hardware that beer can buy. With a couple of borrowed tools, including a steady base and dial indicator, I had the machine aligned and up and running in a couple of evenings. There are several excellent articles on faceting machine alignment out there on the web, and these proved invaluable (see Chapter 15.8.13).

The Bottom Line

In the end, I estimate that I saved over a thousand dollars by scrounging and building the low-tech parts of my hybrid faceting machine – at least that is the price difference between the components that I purchased and assembled versus the full-up machine from the same manufacturer. Those thousand dollars were more than enough to buy a full suite of laps, accessories, and gem rough.

In addition to the financial savings, rolling your own will give you greater insight into how faceting machines work and how they can be made better. For example, you will be forced to learn how to align things properly. In all likelihood, you will also be more

Figure 2-25 The base assembly of my hybrid faceter. (left) The black anodized flange and the platen and spindle above it are commercial parts; everything below is homemade. Note the machined surface of the aluminum plate below both the arbor and the mast slide to the right. These were produced during one machining operation on a mill, ensuring coplanarity. A few slivers of shim stock below the black flange (see right side above) remove any residual tilt. Note that the motor attaches directly to the spindle on the underside of the table via a simple flex coupler, like the one shown at right. You can see the motor peeking out from under the workbench in Figure 2-23.

willing to try modifications and add-ons which could improve your faceting experience. Chapter 20 relates more of my do-it-yourself adventures.

The less tangible reward for building your own faceting machine lies in the personal satisfaction that comes from working with hardware of your own creation. Every cutter remembers the look of wonder on friends' faces when they ask, "did you really create that gemstone?" The same satisfaction comes when people ask, "did you really build that machine?" Of course, you may also have to deal with the brother-in-law, who will inevitably ask, "is that really a toilet flange?"

3

Laps

The "lap wheel," or more conventionally just the "lap," is what actually does all the work of cutting and polishing your gems. Whether they are constructed of steel, plastic, ceramic, or some high tech composite, all laps serve the basic function of containing or supporting the abrasive material which cuts or polishes the stone. To do so well, they must be flat and run true without wobble or shake

This chapter explains the basics of both cutting and polishing laps, and presents a brief overview of the current (2013) selection of commercial products. Note that other parts of this book, specifically Chapters 5.5 and 8, give explicit instructions for preparing, charging, and using your laps.

3.1 Laps for Faceting

Have you ever visited a large astronomical telescope? The experience is well worth it, particularly if you have a soft spot in your heart for large pieces of polished SiO_2. Although dwarfed by the newer generation of giant facilities, the 200" Palomar Telescope will always be the granddaddy of them all. On your tour, the guide may remark to you that the hundreds of tons of steel and glass serve no other purpose than to maintain accurately the shape of a few grams of aluminum – the actual reflecting surface of the giant mirror. In the same way, you could argue that all of the complex mechanisms of a faceting machine act only to hold and turn a few microscopic diamonds against the raw gemstone.

In fact, both points of view oversimplify the situation, in the sense that, for both the faceting machine and the telescope, all of the additional hardware works together harmoniously to ensure that the abrasive action – and the reflecting of light – takes place in exactly the right way.

Figure 3-1 A large precision mechanical device for supporting 10 grams of aluminum. Note the human at bottom center for scale.

3.1.1 Keeping it Smooth and Steady

The lap is the last link in this chain for a faceting machine. To ensure top performance and user satisfaction, the lap wheel should be free of irregularities, ripples, and scalloping on the surface. It must also run true. Shortcomings in any of these areas will lead to irregular cutting and polishing, leading in turn to considerable frustration and headache. In severe cases, a poorly spinning lap may cause irreparable damage to shock-sensitive gem materials.

Short version: Take care of your laps. Don't drop them, for instance. Not only can this cause damage and dislodgement of the abrasive, but also it can bend the darn things. Oh, and at up to 7 lb (3 kg) apiece, laps can do serious damage to your flooring, footwear, toes, etc.

3.1.2 A Lap for All Seasons…

Faceting laps come in many forms and even a few sizes. For hobbyists interested primarily in coloured gemstones, there are two basic types: laps designed for cutting and those tailored to polishing. Of course, such categorization neglects the continuum of lap types and their application. For example, pre-polishing is an important stage of gemstone production, and it can be carried out using a variety of fine-grit cutting *or* polishing laps.

Most commercial and home built faceting machines can accommodate both 8" (20 cm) and 6" (15 cm) diameter laps. There are a variety of standards for the size of the central hole, so double-check your machine's user manual before placing your order.

False Economies

The ready availability and lower cost of 6" diameter laps has prompted some frugal faceters to opt for the smaller size, even though their machine was designed for 8" laps.

Opinions vary on the wisdom of this strategy. The "smaller is better" proponents point to the lower unit cost and the comfort of the additional finger-room between the lap and splash pan when switching grits.

A little math and some bitter experience may convince you otherwise. A 6" lap has a surface area of approximately 26 square inches (170 cm²). Its larger cousin sports an expansive 48 square inches (310 cm²), almost twice as much. Increased area translates directly to more abrasive and more cutting power and lifetime. Does an 8-inch lap cost twice as much as the 6-inch version? No. Case closed.

There are a couple of additional reasons why you may want to use the larger lap. That wonderful extra finger space around the rim is also a yawning chasm waiting to swallow up your innocent, unsuspecting gem rough. Having a half-completed stone grind its way over the brink is an experience you don't want to have, or having had it, don't want to repeat (see "Cutter Beware" on page 299). Working with an eight-inch lap, you will find that the contact of your thumb against the edge of the splash pan is an excellent tactile warning of the lurking dangers.

Larger laps also provide the luxury of more real estate and a greater range of instantaneous cutting speeds. The edge of a spinning lap moves, and hence cuts, much faster than the region near the hub. In fact, some users report difficulty in cutting long thin facets, for example those in step cuts, due to variations in lap speed across a single facet! I must admit to some skepticism about this claim, but the effect of increasing lap speed with radius is very real.

Lap wear also has a profound influence on cutting speed. Over its working lifetime, the lap will experience different wear at different locations on its surface. These areas will have different cutting efficiency, with the more worn regions providing slow, smooth cutting action, and the fresher zones acting more aggressively. An experienced faceter will take advantage of these variations, working at different spots on the lap as the need arises (see "Your Lap's Sweet Spot" on page 72). A larger lap permits greater flexibility in exploiting these effects.

Finally, depending on the geometry and configuration of your faceting machine, you may experience difficulty in cutting girdles with an undersized lap. Typically, the machine will be scaled to allow you to work at 90° on the outer portion of the lap. In designing the various adjustment mechanisms, the manufacturer may have presumed that the rim of the lap is just inside the splash pan, not an inch or two further away.

The thickness of cutting and polishing laps varies between a fraction of a millimeter for the flexible Mylar Ultralaps to half an inch (12 mm) or more for solid steel cutting laps. To help maintain that all-important flatness, laps thinner than ¼ inch (6 mm) should always be used in conjunction with a thicker reference lap, called a *master lap*.

Cutting and polishing laps have been fabricated from a bewildering variety of materials, ranging from leather to solid steel. Softer metals, such as tin, zinc, and various alloys, dominate the field of polishing laps, although composite disks made of resins and plastics are growing in popularity. Even quite exotic materials, such as glass, wood, wax, and fabric, can be found spinning around on faceting machines. In fact, if a substance can be formed approximately into a disk, some gem cutter somewhere has probably tried to make a lap out of it.

The following sections describe the types of cutting and polishing laps available to the amateur. Note that, due to their similar construction and use, pre-polish laps are grouped with the cutting laps. The chapter concludes with suggestions for a beginner's set of laps. Please refer to Chapters 5 and 8 to learn how to use your laps effectively.

3.2 Cutting Laps

Cutting laps are the workhorses of the faceting world, charged with the task of bringing an irregular lump of rough close to its final gemstone form. At that point, the polishing lap – the more delicate, thoroughbred species – can take over.

Most commercially available cutting laps are of metal, most commonly steel or copper. Laps constructed of other metals, such as nickel, brass, tin, or lead, are also available. The latter two, tin and lead, are very soft and hence are particularly suited to cutting shock-sensitive gem materials.

The modern era has seen an explosion in the importance of plastics, ceramics, and other composite materials in a wide variety of applications. This technological tsunami has also swept through the faceting community, with most amateur's owning and using at least one resin composite or plastic cutting lap.

Despite the wide variation in construction materials, essentially all modern cutting laps use a single type of abrasive: diamonds. Their hardness, cutting efficiency, long life, and availability simply have no peer (see "Origins: Pliny the Elder on Faceting" on page 124 of Volume 2)

3.2.1 Grit sizes

The cutting and polishing processes employ different-sized diamond particles for different purposes, with the larger particles used for cutting and the smaller ones for polishing. The coarseness or fineness of abrasive grit is usually enumerated by the *mesh* number. Manufacturers sort abrasives either by liquid flotation, in which the larger, heavier particles sink first, or by sieving the material through a series of finer and finer woven meshes.

The mesh number refers to the number of strands per inch of the weave which sorts out a particular batch of abrasive. Table 3-1 lists common lapidary diamond grits used by faceters and their respective particle sizes. Sharp-eyed readers will notice that the typical particle

Table 3-1 Common diamond grit sizes used in faceting.

Mesh	Particle Size (μm)	Application
100	150	Very coarse grinding
260	90	Coarse cutting (large stones only)
600	30	Coarse cutting
1200	15	Fine cutting / pre-polish (NuBond)
3000	6	Very fine cutting / pre-polish
8000	3	Pre-polish
14,000	1	Fine pre-polish / coarse polish
50,000	0.5	General polish
100,000	0.25	Fine polish
200,000	0.12	Very fine polish

sizes are smaller than the value expected by the mesh number. For example, a 1200 mesh weave has strands separated by 1/1200 of an inch, or about 21 microns. The actual particles of 1200-mesh diamond are only 15 microns across, however. The reason? We have yet to invent usable strands of mesh material with zero thickness: although the strands are 21 microns apart, the holes between them are 15 microns wide.

Note that very coarse laps – say, those with 260 mesh and larger – can chip the facet edges of some types of gemstone material. Quartz and topaz are particularly vulnerable. If you plan to use such a coarse lap for pre-forming, make sure you stop well before the final size of the gem.

Will It Go Round in Circles...

How fast do your laps rotate? Chapter 2.2.1 touched on this briefly in the context of understanding the need for high precision bearings in the drive assembly of a faceting machine.

Don't cheat – keep your eyes away from the user's manual and guess how fast your laps spin.

If you've cut and polished a variety of gem materials, you know the answer: it depends on how fast they are turning. This is not a frivolous joke. Different types of gem rough and different stages in the gem cutting process demand different rotation rates. Because of this, essentially all modern faceting machines offer a variable speed motor, and many will allow you to reverse lap direction (see Chapter 2.6.1). Consult your user's manual (it's Ok now) to understand the relationship between the speed knob setting and the revolutions per minute. Absent such information, you could try calibrating your motor control. See "Spin Doctoring" on page 65.

So, to kick this investigational can further down the road, how fast *should* your laps rotate? The answer, you will have no doubt guessed, is that they should spin as fast as they need to in order to get the job done.

In practical terms, this means from dead slow – less than one revolution per second – up to about 1500 RPM, or 25 revolutions per second. Many perfectly fine machines peak out at 1000 RPM, or about 15 turns per second. Note also that some laps may have a speed limit above which they can potentially disintegrate in a very nasty way. Check with the manufacturer before cranking a new lap up to top speed.

These rotation rates are considerably lower than the 3000 plus RPM of diamond cutting machinery (see Section 2.5). Nevertheless, having a 7 lb lap zipping around at 1500 RPM is a striking multi-sensory experience: the sight, sound, and feel of a rapidly spinning cutting lap makes a strong impression. Note that if smell is one of these sensations, it's time to turn things off and check the bearings…

Each individual stone and your growing experience will dictate the optimal lap speed for each stage of cutting and polishing. Nevertheless, there is conventional wisdom in this area. Table 3-2 lists typical rotation speeds for various circumstances. Use these values as a jumping off point, but feel free to experiment with the speed knob.

Table 3-2 Typical lap speeds. Approximate conversion: Slow 0-200 RPM; Medium 200-400 RPM; Fast 400-1500 RPM. When two speeds appear, you should adjust the first value somewhat toward the second. In other words, Medium - Slow is somewhat slower than medium, whereas Slow - Medium is somewhat faster than slow.

Activity	Speed
Pre-forming with diamond bonded or sintered laps	Fast
General cutting with diamond bonded or sintered laps	All Speeds
Fine cutting with diamond bonded or sintered laps	Medium - Slow
Pre-polish with NuBond laps	Medium - Slow
Polish with Ultralaps	Slow - Medium
Polish with composite laps (Last Lap, Pol-A-Gem, etc.)	Slow - Medium
Polish with oxides on metal laps	Slow - Medium
Polish with diamonds on metal laps	All Speeds
Polish with diamonds on ceramic laps	Very Slow

3.2.2 Hand Charged Cutting Laps

Cutting laps fall into two broad categories: those that must be charged manually with loose grit and those that are permanently charged. The hand charged type was the only option in the good old days. Hand charging and even fabrication of cutting laps was part of the ritual and tradition of faceting, back when men were men and amateur cutters were part inventor, part machinist, and 100% handyman.

Thankfully, those days – and particularly all that "man" stuff – are largely a thing of the past. Hand charged cutting laps have become less popular in recent decades, due to the advent of high quality and affordable permanently charged laps. Nevertheless, hand charging remains a viable option, particularly for those who enjoy cutting very large stones, or "doorknobs." Hogging out a single 1000-carat gem corresponds roughly to 100 one-carat stones (it goes by surface area). This corresponds to a significant fraction of the working lifetime of a commercial permanently charged lap.

Essentially all modern hand charged cutting laps use diamond grit. Silicon carbide enjoyed some popularity in the past, but has since disappeared from the amateur's shop (see "True Grit," below). By far the most common hand charged cutting laps are of copper, or an alloy of copper and bronze. Copper is harder (Mohs 3) than other common lap metals, and it has the excellent property of hardening with use. This means that it is relatively easy to embed the diamond in the surface of the lap, while the work hardening ensures a solid grip on the particles. Copper is also (relatively) affordable. See "Making Your Own Copper Lap" on page 64

True Grit

In the past, loose silicon carbide grit was a popular option among amateur faceters. Charging a cutting lap meant mixing the grit with a carrying fluid such as kerosene and spreading the resulting slurry across the surface of a metal disk. The cutting process inevitably involved the flinging about of large amounts of loose silicon carbide grains, all in a stinking cloud of kerosene vapour.

Needless to say, cleanliness was a constant concern and cross-contamination of laps a regular occurrence. In addition to the dangers posed to valuable gem rough, kerosene may be a carcinogen in large doses, exposing the valiant faceter to additional dangers beyond disappearing in a ball of flame.

Those were the days of true grit among cutters. Fondly remembered but happily long gone.

Charging a Copper Lap with Diamond

The procedure for charging and using copper cutting laps is relatively straightforward, and the classic references, Vargas, Wykoff, and Broadfoot & Collins, provide detailed guidance (see Chapter 9.1). This section gives the Reader's Digest version, and in the interest of full disclosure, I admit that I have not explored this particular route to cutting happiness: I am a fan of permanently charged laps – see Section 3.2.4 below.

To begin, distribute the diamond bort across the surface of the lap, either in powder form or pre-mixed with mineral or olive oil to a thick slurry. Use approximately 1.5 carats of diamond for a first charge on a new lap. Recharging should require roughly half that amount.

If you choose to use dry diamond powder, a light pre-oiling of the lap surface will help keep the grains in place. The down side of oil is that it has a great surface affinity for diamond. In fact, diamond miners use oiled bands to extract rough crystals from the surrounding ore. Some claim that this affinity can cause balling-up of the abrasive, producing effectively larger particles, which leads to scratching. If you encounter this difficulty, consider using a synthetic carrier such as Teflon grease.

With the diamond well distributed, use a piece of agate, synthetic sapphire, or an embedding tool to force the diamond into the copper (see also Figure 8-26). Coarse grit, say 200 and below, will require considerable effort to embed properly, while fingertip pressure should suffice for the finer grades (above 1000). Some users insist that the lap should be scored before applying coarser grit diamond bort. See "To Score or Not to Score" on page 328 for more information and opinion on scoring laps. If you choose to score your copper disk, make sure to smooth out the bumps and ridges using a piece of agate or synthetic corundum before subjecting your precious gemstones to the lap.

A few minutes of work should lead to a well-charged lap. Give the surface a final wipe with a paper towel, and you are ready to go. Use a light water drip to keep things cool and to remove cutting residue.

You will notice that your freshly charged lap will cut very aggressively, but things will settle down as the diamond particles become dull, sink into the copper, or abrade away. Cutting on a worn-out charge is a very bad idea. Not only will it take forever, but also the pressure of the stone can cause deformation and ridging of the copper – it should be riding on diamonds, not metal. Note that the difficulty resulting from exposed copper is another reason for ensuring even distribution of the diamond when charging. It is certainly time for more abrasive if you see any telltale traces of copper on your gem.

Making Your Own Copper Lap

Want to roll your own? A solid copper lap 8 inches in diameter weighs about 6 lb (2.8 kg). At current prices, that represents an investment of less than $50 for the raw material. Copper is relatively easy to machine, although it requires sharp tools and relatively high speeds. Even a moderately skilled machinist using a mediocre lathe should be able to produce a disk whose flatness and parallelism match the quality of any commercial lap.

Another option is to fabricate a "topper," a thin copper disk which can be bonded to a master lap. Standard printed circuit board material consists of a 0.0014-inch (35 micrometer) thick layer of copper, laminated to epoxy filled fiberglass. A glance at Table 3-1 tells you that this is enough copper for 1200 mesh or finer diamonds. You should be able to track down circuit board material with a heavier copper coating. For example, so-called "two-ounce" and "three-ounce" boards have a copper layer two and three times thicker, respectively.

Cut the circuit board material to shape and glue it to a master lap. Some argue that this approach of using a thin layer of copper on a rigid backing avoids the difficulty of grooving and deformation inherent to solid copper laps. The raw materials can (arguably) be considerably cheaper, no heavy-duty machining is required, and resurfacing is straightforward: peel off the old topper and glue on a new one.

Spin Doctoring

My faceting machine is a hybrid of commercially available parts and homebrew kludges, some of which work fine, and others which depend on an embarrassing amount of silicone bathtub sealant (see Figure 2-24). One of the better kludges was the lap drive motor and controller, but due to their mixed heritage, it was impossible for me to consult the manual to understand which knob setting corresponded to which RPM value.

How could I measure how fast my laps spin?

Needless to say, knowing the true RPM of machinery is a fairly important issue, and there is a great deal of instrumentation available for making extremely accurate measurements. Perhaps the most common of these instruments is the *variable stroboscope*, also known as a *photo-tachometer*. These devices are essentially electronic flashes with precisely controllable repeat rate. By adjusting this rate, the operator can arrange for exactly one complete revolution of the motor between flashes. A reference mark on the shaft then appears to be "frozen," even though the motor is turning.

Such photo tachometer / stroboscopes are fine pieces of equipment and undoubtedly cool, but they can cost hundreds of dollars. Faced with the prospect of investing far more on such a measurement tool than on the actual motor drive hardware, I was forced to rephrase the question:

How could I measure how fast my laps spin without spending any money?

Several ideas flitted through my mind. I could install a small light source on the lap and use a photocell coupled to an oscilloscope to measure the speed. Of course, this would require some soldering and an oscilloscope, which costs at least as much as a photo tachometer. Also, the prospect of a battery plus light source taped to a lap spinning at 1500 RPM struck me as more than a little unsafe.

I also thought of cannibalizing the speedometer from my bike. Here's the idea: simply attach a small magnet to the lap and hold the remote sensor at the edge. Of course, the eight-inch lap is considerably smaller than my 26-inch bicycle wheel, but correcting the reading is simply a matter of multiplication.

Two factors argued against this scheme. First, at that point, my bicycle was locked in the garden shed under a heap of snow, and second, bicycle speedometers don't measure the type of rotation rates we're talking about here. My speedometer can in principle measure up to 99 km/hr (62 mph). This is based on counting the number of digits in the display and thankfully not due to actual personal experience. An eight-inch lap turning at 1500 RPM corresponds to my bike traveling at about 190 km/hr (118 mph).

I finally settled on a completely different scheme which requires no potentially lethal objects taped down on the lap and no specialized equipment. The idea is based on the fact that fast-moving objects appear blurred in photographs. I own a fairly old but fairly decent digital camera with full control over the shutter speed. By taking an image of the spinning lap with a known exposure time, I should be able to measure the amount of blurring and extract the rotation rate. Simple!

Figure 3-2 shows the sum total of additional equipment I prepared: a black line on a white piece of paper placed on a master lap. When spun up, the line blurs to a wedge, which is readily measurable using a protractor.

A little doodling leads directly to the relationship between the angle of blur θ and the number of revolutions per minute of the lap: RPM = θ / 360° / ExpTime * 60. For example, the right hand panel of Figure 3-2 shows an exposure of 1/50th of a second. The measured wedge angle is 32°. This means that the lap rotation rate was 266 RPM.

Figure 3-2 (left) A black line on a piece of white paper serves as the target for the RPM measurement. Note the three desk lamps to provide plenty of light – as you can imagine, this technique doesn't work with your on-camera flash. (right) With the lap turning, rotation blurs the line out to a wedge with angle θ. Note: I have adjusted the image brightness and contrast to make the measurement easier.

Figure 3-3 plots the results of my experiment. Each point in the figure represents half a dozen different measurements and the bars indicate the scatter in each group.

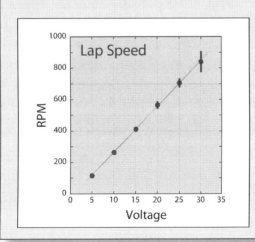

What have I learned? First, the motor peaks out at about 1000 RPM for the maximum voltage on my power supply. This is more than enough for even the most aggressive of preformers. Second, the system is very linear: each volt on the power supply corresponds to about 30 RPM. Finally, measurements at high rotation rates are more difficult and uncertain. This is because the higher speeds demand shorter exposure times, resulting in grainier images for

Figure 3-3 The lap rotation rate as a function of motor supply voltage. See text for further information.

a given amount of illumination. Also, interesting effects due to the exact way that the camera shutter operates begin to show up.

You may find yourself in a similar situation, either without accurate manufacturer's information about motor speed or with a retrofit that changes the calibration.

Do I recommend this exercise?

Not really. On the one hand, knowing the exact RPM of your faceting machine is interesting, and it certainly makes sense to verify the numbers in the manual. On the other hand, the number of revolutions per minute doesn't really matter. As explained in "Will It Go Round in Circles..." on page 61, it is very important to be able to tailor the rotation rate to the current lap and gemstone material, but the exact RPM value is irrelevant. You should be guided by the maxim, "if it works, do it."

Next project: calibrating the thickness of silicone bathtub sealant...

3.2.3 Permanently Charged Cutting Laps

As their name suggests, permanently charged cutting laps come with diamonds pre-embedded in some matrix bonded to the lap surface, and they never need re-charging. The matrix can be metal, resin, or plastic, depending on grit size, manufacturer, and application.

Metal Bonded Laps

The metal bonded, permanently charged cutting laps are widely used for all phases of cutting, ranging from hogging out a coarse pre-form to executing a fine pre-polish. There are a number of varieties of metal bonded cutting lap, but all of them share a common feature: the diamond particles are bonded and held to the lap by a hard metal, such as nickel (see "My Name is Bond..." on page 70). The major difference between the various manufacturers' offerings lies in price and usable lifetime. You guessed it...longer life means higher price.

The so-called "toppers" lie at the inexpensive end of the price-lifetime spectrum. These are thin metal disks with a bonded diamond surface and an adhesive backing. Because they are so thin – typically 1/16" or 1.5 mm – they must be glued or placed on a reference lap, such as a master lap. Of course, gluing a topper down to one side of your master lap will take that surface out of circulation for other purposes. Users who just use the lap nut to hold the topper in place have complained about unevenness and wobble during use. For roughing out a gem early in the cutting process, toppers represent a reasonable, economic choice. Expect to pay in the neighbourhood of $40 apiece for these laps.

Thicker bonded metal laps represent the next step up from toppers. These laps are ¼ inch to ½ inch thick and do not require additional support and stabilization. The less expensive variety is made of aluminum, with the nickel diamond matrix bonded to its upper surface. A slightly more expensive and durable option is the solid steel bonded lap, which, as its name suggests, is made of solid steel. Yes, at 3 kg (7 lb) apiece, this is the toe crusher. To prevent corrosion, the steel may be encased in a thin copper coating.

Solid metal bonded laps, both the aluminum and solid steel variety, have front and back surfaces that have been machined accurately parallel, and, at $100-$200 per lap, depending on grit size, they represent an excellent investment for the amateur faceter. As the lap wears down, it will start to cut less aggressively and perform like a finer grit. Metal bonded laps that are clogged with stone debris can be cleaned with a dressing stick, although this will shorten the lifetime of the lap (see Chapter 4.9.1).

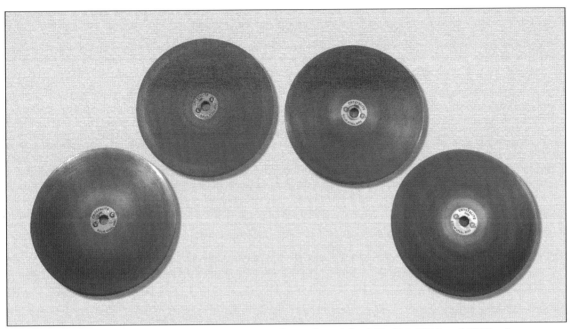

Figure 3-4 Bonded cutting laps from Crystalite. Left to right: 260, 600, 1200 and 3000 grit.

Sintered Laps

Sintered laps are the top of the line in terms of cutting laps. Instead of a thin layer of nickel-bonded diamonds, the sintered laps have a thick cutting layer of diamond matrix that provides extremely long life and uniform cutting performance. Here, the metal is usually bronze. Although equally susceptible to differential wear and dishing as the bonded variety, sintered laps can be cleaned and refreshed many times with a dressing stick with little effect on lifetime (see Chapter 4.9.1) .

Premium performance and lifetime come at a premium price, however. Sintered metal laps list for roughly $500 apiece, which means that even a beginner's set of cutting laps could cost more than the faceting machine itself. On the other hand, for high volume and commercial cutters, sintered laps are the way to go. See "My Name is Bond..." on page 70 for more on the economics of bonded versus sintered laps.

Lapidary Pavé

Wandering into my workshop one day, my young son was surprised and impressed with the sparkle on the surface of a new Crystalite bonded cutting lap. His surprise turned to wide-eyed wonder when I explained that the sparkle was diamonds.

"Real DIAMONDS!?"

In many ways, a modern, permanently charged cutting lap is like lapidary *pavé*, the art of "paving" a piece of jewelry with many small diamonds. Of course, the "gems" on the lap are considerably smaller and less well-formed, and they are not set in place meticulously by hand, but a cutting lap is in many ways like that fancy Rolex in the magazine.

At least that was what I tried to tell my son.

With his wonder trending rapidly toward skepticism, I enthusiastically explained that the diamonds on the lap were synthetic, since natural diamond dust is more irregular, needle-like, and hard to work with.

At this point, my son's attention was drifting over to the computer at the end of the room, and the possible video games therein.

"But see how it sparkles! It's diamonds…Real DIAMONDS!" I declared.

"Cool," was his response, and his response was certainly cool.

The moral of this story? In conversation as with gem cutting, the key is knowing when to stop.

Non-Metal Cutting Laps

When you mention cutting laps, most faceters think metal – both the permanently charged type (bonded and sintered) and those used with loose abrasive. However, there are at least a couple of workhorse cutting laps out there which take a radically different approach to supporting and spinning that thin layer of cutting diamonds.

NuBond Cutting and Pre-Polish Laps

Perhaps the most ubiquitous of these non-metal cutting laps is the NuBond from Raytech Industries (see Chapter 15.8.9 for contact information for the manufacturers of this and other laps). The NuBond laps use a layer of resin-bonded diamonds on a relatively thin aluminum back plate. According to the manufacturer, this technology allows "a higher concentration of friable, self-sharpening diamond" to be brought to bear against the gem rough. Sounds good to me. All I know is that my NuBond lap cuts reliably and well.

My Name is Bond...

It is easy to confuse metal bonded laps with sintered laps, at least until you get to the cash register. They look very similar, and they both have a cutting matrix consisting of diamond particles embedded in metal. This metal prevents tumbling and aggregation of the abrasive, and as it slowly wears, the matrix exposes more of the diamond particles.

Metal bonded laps have a thin layer of diamond, usually electroplated in place with nickel. With use, this thin layer breaks down and starts cutting like a finer grit. Sintered laps, on the other hand, have a very thick (3-6 mm) cutting matrix. To paraphrase the chelonian* cosmological ruminations of such luminaries as Bertrand Russell, Stephen Hawking, and Antonin Scalia, "it's diamonds all the way down." This contributes to a much longer life and steady, aggressive cutting performance.

Although no firm statistics exist on the long-term economics of metal bonded versus sintered laps, you can probably count on at least a factor of ten more cutting from the more expensive lap. In fact, a sintered lap can easily provide a lifetime of steady, reliable performance. At a cost only 3-4 times higher than the bonded variety, this can make a great deal of sense. On the other hand, for beginning faceters who are unsure about making a lifelong commitment to the hobby, such savings may never be realized.

*look it up. I had to.

RayTech produces the NuBond in three grits: 325 (coloured gray), 600 (brown), and 1200 (blue). Note, however, that these laps cut considerably less aggressively than their grit numbers suggest. In fact, you will get best results by considering the NuBonds to be one or more steps finer: the 325 cuts like 600-800, the 600 like 1200-2000, and the 1200 like 3000-4000. This softening of the cutting action is particularly noticeable once the surface of the lap has been broken in and takes on a glazed appearance. The original performance can be restored by RayTech's recommended procedures, but many hobbyists prefer the ultra-fine cut and pre-polish possible with a broken-in NuBond.

The 1200 grit NuBond lap is by far the most popular of the three, precisely because of the wonderful pre-polish that it can place on quartz and beryl. Every beginner's lap set should include that lovable blue disk (see Section 3.4 below). Expect to pay $100-150 for your NuBond lap, and expect to use it a lot.

A couple of cautionary notes deserve mention before you place your order. First, these laps are relatively thin and

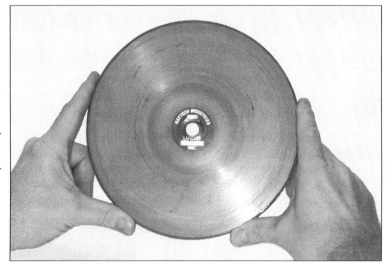

Figure 3-5 The NuBond cutting laps have a composite resin matrix surface layer embedded with diamond.

flexible. Use them with a master lap to ensure consistent cutting results. Second, and more insidiously, the NuBond laps can produce pitting problems with gemstone materials harder than 7 on the Mohs scale (see Chapter 12.9). This phenomenon is normally called the "orange peel" effect in the online discussion groups, or the "@%#^$% orange peel effect" when it happens to you. Polishing out orange peel can be particularly wasteful of time and gem rough. You have been warned. You will be warned again on page 341.

Ultralaps for Cutting and Pre-Polish

The other common type of non-metal cutting lap is the Ultralap from Moyco Precision Abrasives Inc. Yes, the Ultralap. Not the standard beginner's cerium oxide polishing disk, but rather its diamond impregnated big brother. Ultralaps are available in a variety of abrasive types and grit sizes (see Section 3.3.2). Among these combinations are 1200 and 3000 mesh diamond – arguably pre-polish laps, but certainly capable of moving facet meets around.

The diamond impregnated Ultralaps are more expensive than those containing oxide polish, but at $10-20 each, you won't need to mortgage your home to give them a try. Installing and using these thin Mylar sheets is straightforward. See page 170 for pointers.

Although there are only two common non-metal cutting laps currently on the market, the field of composite materials evolves rapidly. Keep your eyes and ears open: there will inevitably be newer and better technologies available as these developments filter down to the amateur faceting world.

3.2.4 Why Use Permanently Charged Cutting Laps?

Beyond their obvious ease of use, permanently charged cutting laps offer a number of distinct advantages to the hobby faceter. First, and perhaps most importantly, the abrasive is uniform in both particle size and distribution over the surface of the lap. Hand charged metal laps can suffer from balling up of abrasive, to say nothing of the phenomenon of some diamond particles sinking deep into the metal, while others protrude above the surface. The result is uneven cutting and in the worst instances, bad scratches.

The second major advantage of permanently charged laps is that they have virtually eliminated the problem of cross contamination in the cutting process. Yes, you will hear stories of how a diamond grain or two broke loose from this or that manufacturer's lap and ended up causing problems at a later, finer cutting phase. Think about that complaint for a moment and hearken back to the days of loose abrasive grit cutting (see "True Grit" on page 63). We are in a different world.

The moniker "permanently charged" may be a bit of an exaggeration – these laps do wear out, after all – but they can, in fact, last a very long time. Exact lifetimes are difficult to judge, since different gem materials can have a radically different effect on your laps. Corundum, for example, exhibits a cutting resistance almost ten times higher than that of quartz (see Chapter 12.9.1), yet quartz has a well-deserved reputation for gumming up laps. Gem size also plays a role: a 10 mm gem has twice the surface area – and hence incurs twice the damage to your lap – as does a 7 mm stone of the same material and design.

Your Lap's Sweet Spot

Do cutting laps, like baseball bats, have a "sweet spot," that is, a location where everything goes right and nothing goes wrong? The spot you always try to hit?

The answer is yes and no. Yes in the sense that a certain radius out from the lap nut will seem to produce smooth, problem-free cutting. No in the sense that you shouldn't use this sweet spot all the time.

The trouble is that laps wear down with use. The primary symptom of wear is reduced cutting efficiency, but there is a more insidious side effect of sticking to the sweet spot. Always cutting at the same location on the lap will result in excess, localized wear and tear. This can produce "dishing" or curvature of the lap, which in turn can lead to minor cutting errors.

Actually, experienced faceters take advantage of differential lap wear without letting it get too far. For example, some radii on a workhorse lap will cut very gently, while other areas – typically near the center and edge – will remove gem material as aggressively as a new lap. Understanding and tracking the surface characteristics of your cutting laps will lead to greater efficiency and fewer nasty surprises. See "False Economies" on page 59 for more on this issue

The second message here is that the specified cutting grit of a lap refers to its performance out of the box, not after months and years of use. In fact, it is not uncommon for a cutter to seemingly break the rules while cutting a stone, for example using a well-worn 600 after a brand new 1200. Grind truth is ground truth.

Hand charged laps require regular refreshing of the cutting abrasive, a process which can be messy and time consuming. Between charges, the lap will display cutting behaviour that evolves rapidly with time. Initially, the lap will have plenty of "bite," removing gem material at an aggressive rate. As the protruding diamond particles sink, abrade, or are chipped away, the cutting action will slow considerably and soon it will be time to recharge. Although some look positively on the fact that this requires attention to and awareness of current lap conditions, I prefer more deterministic cutting when I sit down at the machine. See Section 3.2.2 for more on hand charging of laps.

There are additional distinct advantages of permanently charged laps, due to the mere fact that the abrasive is bonded to the surface. Held in place by metal or composite material, the diamond grit is not free to tumble across the surface and aggregate into larger particles, which can scratch. Finally, keeping the diamonds in place eliminates the need to clean them up off the splash pan, faceting head, operator's fingers etc. Less cleaning time means more cutting time.

As a result of these great strengths, the permanently bonded cutting laps have essentially taken over the amateur faceting field. They are not without their shortcomings, however. Despite their long life and steady performance, permanently bonded cutting laps are not indestructible. Like people, they will generally wear down with age and cut slower and slower. This can be turned to your advantage, however – see "Your Lap's Sweet Spot" above and "Aging Gracefully" on page 316.

Permanently charged laps, particularly the bonded solid steel variety, are also not cheap. Coarser grit wheels will be more expensive, but you should count on spending at least $100 for a good hobbyist-grade solid steel lap. Is this expensive? Initially, yes, but a careful look at the economics of faceting laps may tell a somewhat different story (see "My Name is Bond…" on page 70).

Oh…one more thing. Don't let your permanently charged lap run dry. Damage to the lap and stone are a distinct possibility. A steady stream of water for cooling, lubrication, and swarf removal will make sure that both you and your lap remain happy cutters.

Partisans will argue the strengths, economics, and even the "traditional faceter values" of the hand charged cutting lap. Feel free to give them a try. In addition to the classic books, there are additional resources on the web which explain the care and feeding of loose abrasive cutting laps. For example, the online discussion groups include several active users of hand charged laps who contribute their advocacy and wisdom. See Chapter 15.8.1 for links.

Cleaning and Storing your Lap

Attention to cleanliness is the key to a long and happy relationship with your collection of laps. Contamination by coarser grits or even gemstone fragments can lead to scratching, while the build up of cutting swarf, dopping adhesive, and even (oops!) dop metal will reduce the predictability and efficiency of cutting action.

Luckily, there are a few easy ways to strengthen your lap relationship. Storing your laps in a sealed container between uses will reduce the chance of contamination (see Chapter 4.9.2), as will the ritual of performing a general cleanup of your machine, work area, and hands when you switch to a finer grit size (see "Keep Things Clean" on page 158). To inhibit rust, I usually give my steel laps a quick spray with an aerosol oil such as WD-40 before putting them away.

There are various options out there to help you clean and maintain your cutting laps. For example, a simple nonmetallic scrubbing pad and running water can do wonders for a lap that has seemed to slow down before its time. Girdle cutting can cause wax build up near the edge of the lap. A quick squirt of alcohol, followed by a few minutes soak and a careful wipe with a paper towel can clear things up. Finally, there are specialized tools for cleaning and "sharpening" cutting laps. See Chapter 4.9.1

3.3 Polishing Laps

Ahhh…polishing.

Loved by some, hated by many (particularly beginners), polishing is what truly sets faceting firmly in the category of art, not science. The challenges posed by different gem materials, and even different samples of a single material, have led to the development of an astonishing variety of polishing laps. And, while commercial gem production houses are satisfied by a finish that looks acceptable to the untrained eye, many amateurs strive for that elusive perfect polish. Sections 10 through 17 of Chapter 8 provide an introduction to the mystical realm of successful polishing. Here, we examine the variety of polishing laps that amateurs use to put that otherworldly shine on their gems.

As with cutting laps, there are a few broad categories of polishing lap. And, as before, the most significant distinguishing characteristic is whether the lap requires hand charging or not. Table 3-3 summarizes the properties of the various types of common polishing lap, and the subsequent sections provide additional information on each category. Innovation in polishing technology leads to a constantly changing landscape of commercial products, so the online resources listed in Chapter 15.8 are the best place to look for the latest and greatest.

Table 3-3 Overview of polishing laps.

Lap	Type	Manufacturer / Application / Comment
Zinc / Tin alloys	Metal, hand charged	Available from a variety of manufacturers. Used with both oxides and diamond
BATT / BA5T	Metal alloy, hand charged	Available from www.gearloose.com and other suppliers. Excellent all-round lap suitable for both oxides and diamond. See page 76
Lucite	Plastic, hand charged	Various manufacturers. Used with powdered cerium oxide or alumina. Can also serve as a master for Ultralaps (see below)
Last Lap, Fast Lap, Darkside Lighting Lap	Resin composite, hand charged	The Last Lap from Crystalite and the Fast Lap by Raytech Industries use pelletized metal embedded in resin to hold diamond polishing compound. The Darkside from gearloose.com is a polymer composite used with both oxides and diamond. Marsh Howard produces the Lightning Lap, a plastic composite disk available with or without pre-charged compound.
Ceramic	Ceramic composite, hand charged	Multiple manufacturers. The hardest lap, used with diamond, resulting in the flattest facets and sharpest edges. Can be difficult to use.
Home-brew	Miscellaneous, hand charged	Various suppliers, including home-made. Hand charged. Includes wax laps for very soft stones, Corian laps, etc.
Ultralap	Plastic, permanently charged	A product of Moyco Precision Abrasives. Impregnated Mylar sheets for use with a master lap. Excellent for beginners.
Pol-A-Gem, Dyna Disk, Greenway Creamway	Composite, permanently charged	Excellent for quartz. The rigid structure produces flatter facets than do Ultralaps. The Pol-A-Gem can be ordered with either alumina or cerium oxide coating, while the Dyna Disk is CeO_2 only. The Greenway has a chrome oxide composite surface. The Creamway uses zirconium oxide.

3.3.1 Hand Charged Polishing Laps

Hand charged polishing laps must, as their name suggests, be manually loaded with polishing compound by the user. Depending on the gem material, lap type, and personal preference, this polishing compound can be either finely graded diamond or one of the metal oxides (usually that of cerium or aluminum – see Chapter 4.12).

Experienced faceters generally prefer the hand charged type of polishing lap, since they are more economical in the long run. A single lap can also be used with multiple types and grades of polishing compound (within limits, of course – see below). Finally, by varying the amount and type of compound, you can fine-tune the intensity of polishing action.

Hand Charged Metal Polishing Laps

Hand charged metal laps are the traditional tool of the gemstone polisher, and a wide variety of metal types and alloys have been employed to address the equally wide variety of challenges encountered during the polishing phase. Decades ago, pure elemental metal laps, such as those made of copper, lead, and tin, dominated the scene, although they suffered from significant drawbacks. For example, copper has a great affinity for diamond abrasive, but it can produce mixed results and scratching as the particles are embedded, exposed, and released. Tin, like copper, is an element which has excellent physical properties, but it is relatively expensive and deforms easily under pressure. Lead is soft and ductile, which can lead to ridges and bumps on the lap with extended use. It also oxidizes readily and requires a rubdown with Vaseline after every use. And, as almost daily headlines about imported products remind us, lead can cause serious health problems if ingested through the nose, mouth, eyes, or breaks in the skin. Such ingestion is not impossible, given how we use our laps.

All of these difficulties have motivated innovation in the manufacture of polishing laps. The most obvious improvement in recent decades has been the replacement of pure tin and copper laps with the bonded variety, in which the metal is layered on the surface of a rigid reference lap. Other elemental metals have also been tried. Zinc, for example, is slightly harder than tin and has enjoyed some popularity, but zinc laps can be difficult to find. Cast iron, especially the proprietary Meehanite variety, is the universal lap material in the diamond industry, and it can be used to good effect on harder stones such as corundum. Of course, iron laps rust all too readily, and they do not work well with oxide polishes or on softer stones. Despite all this experimentation with the Periodic Table, the true solution to the problems of pure metal laps lay elsewhere…

Alloys – mixtures of elemental metals. Simplicity and genius…take the best properties of individual metals and make the resulting mixture better than any of its constituents. Bronze is a prominent and historically important example. This alloy is a mixture of copper and tin, yet it is harder and more durable than either pure metal. Oh. And it also got us out of the Stone Age.

Although bronze is not a typical lapidary alloy, other mixtures have become essential to our craft. Typemetal, a combination of tin, lead, antimony, and other trace elements, enjoyed great popularity due to its excellent mechanical properties, low cost, and ready availability. In fact, in the mid-20th century, it was not unusual for amateur faceters to cast their own typemetal laps, although this practice has now essentially disappeared along with other "rough and ready" techniques (see "True Grit" on page 63).

The modern hobby faceter will likely encounter and use only two types of hand charged metal lap: the tin lap, which is actually a tin-lead alloy bonded to a master lap, and the BATT, a high-tech mixture of tin and other metals produced by Jon Rolfe (see "Holy Polish BATTman!" on page 76). Depending on the age and curmudgeon coefficient of the membership at your local lapidary club, you may still occasionally encounter the copper polishing lap.

Note that some metal laps are initially quite soft and can leave metal residue on facets as you polish. Not to worry - in general, these laps will work harden, leading to somewhat different polishing properties with use. The flecks of metal should also go away.

Purchasing and Using Metal Polishing Laps

Acquiring and using metal polishing laps has never been easier. Lapidary suppliers offer a wide selection, and you can take advantage of the online resources listed in Chapter 15.8 for cost comparisons, additional opinion, etc. Metal lap prices vary considerably, depending largely on current bulk material costs. Expect to pay from below $100 for a basic metal lap to several hundred dollars for premium products. Chapter 8.14 provides detailed instructions for hand charging metal laps with oxide or diamond. Note that many metal laps can be re-surfaced on a standard metalworking lathe if they become damaged or deformed. The manufacturer may offer this service, but if you use an independent machinist, warn him or her if the lap contains embedded diamonds.

Holy Polish BATTman!

Starting in 1997, an intrepid inventor and amateur faceter named Jon "Gearloose" Rolfe began producing a series of polishing laps tailored to the needs and finances of amateur cutters. Extolling the virtue of "10 dollars per inch of diameter," Gearloose has invented and successfully marketed several affordable and effective polishing laps over the years:

BATT – The original. A "High Fractal Dimension Microstructural" alloy that works wonders with both oxide and diamond. Used for quartz, beryl, tourmaline, topaz, cubic zirconia, corundum, and just about anything else you can throw at it. The original BATT is the only metal polishing lap that I regularly use – actually I have two (Figure 3-6).

BA5T – A somewhat harder, smoother big brother of the BATT. More expensive and targeted at very serious amateurs and commercial polishers.

Darkside – A polymer composite material bonded to a rigid aluminum reference lap. The Darkside works with both oxides and diamond on most gem materials.

Greenway – The Greenway permanently charged composite lap has apparently solved the staining problem of working with chrome oxide polishing compound (see Chapter 4.12.1). This lap works well on pretty much all but the hardest of gemstone materials.

Figure 3-6 My pair of BATT laps, charged with 50,000 diamond (left) and 8000 mesh for pre-polish (right). Yes, I thought about cross-contamination in deciding which lap should be above the other for the photo. And yes, I washed my hands and put the 50k away first.

The Matrix – A ceramic composite lap with a porous microstructure to hold the polishing compound in place. One of several collaborative efforts with Adamas Instrument.

The Dominatrix Dual Lap – The best of BATT and Matrix, with an outer BATT band for pre-polish and an inner MATRIX band for polishing. Centrifugal force keeps contamination problems to a minimum.

Creamway – Another joint venture with Adamas, the Creamway lap features a permanently charged zirconium oxide ceramic polymer layer on a rigid backing. The **Skyway** lap is a premium version on a full-thickness aluminum base.

Lightside – A smooth and durable specialty lap for polishing soft and delicate materials, the Lightside replaces the classic wax lap.

BATTSTIK Charging Sticks – These crayon-like applicators were designed to eliminate the mess and waste of traditional oxide slurries. Gearloose sells cerium, alumina A, chrome, and zirconium oxide versions. Also available with diamond (DIASTIK).

In addition to the Dominatrix, Gearloose has experimented with other combinations of pre-polishing and polishing surfaces on a single disk. These hybrid laps typically take the name "wing." For example, the "Redwing" combined an inner disk of BATT material with an outer pre-polish annulus of copper. Although it still has a strong user base, high copper prices killed the Redwing ($10 per inch was simply not possible). Other "wing" laps include the BATTWing and GreenWing. No doubt, more interesting laps and fanciful names will appear.

I recognize that the foregoing sounds more like an advertisement than unbiased information, but I do love my BATT laps. Early on, I had more or less given up trying to polish with anything other than Ultralaps (see Section 3.3.2), but the BATT changed everything. Also, a quick survey of online discussion forums (see Chapter 15.1.3) will show you that Gearloose is uncommonly helpful and forthcoming with information, customer support, and general good neighbourliness. If that doesn't deserve a free ad, nothing does.

Hand Charged Composite Polishing Laps

In the 1967 classic movie "The Graduate," Dustin Hoffman plays a young man at loose ends after finishing college. A family friend assures him that the future can be summarized in just one word: plastics. Although he was certainly not referring to the lapidary industry, Hoffman's putative mentor did, in fact, capture the sense that materials science would change the world in the second half of the twentieth century. We can argue endlessly about the reality and consequences of such a view, but there is no doubt that polishing laps fabricated from plastics – and more generally high-tech composite materials – have revolutionized the way we cut gemstones.

The first and most widely used hand charged plastic polishing lap was the Lucite or Plexiglas lap. Available from a variety of manufacturers, these plastic laps are inexpensive and reliable performers, effectively polishing the softer materials such as quartz and beryl when used with alumina or cerium oxide. This simplicity and low cost comes with a significant drawback, however. Lucite and Plexiglas laps tend to generate considerable frictional heat, which can be a problem with sensitive gem materials. This heat can also cause dop wax to soften, leading to the nightmare of a slightly shifted stone.

More recently, composite polishing laps have appeared. These laps can be used with either oxide polishes or diamond. They consist of a layer of resin or polymer composite bonded to a stiff master lap. In the case of the Fast Lap produced by Raytech and the Last Lap manufactured by Crystalite, metal particles are mixed into the resin layer. This combination can improve the diamond-holding properties of the matrix without introducing the problem of grooving and gouging inherent to all-metal laps. In 2008, Jon Rolfe introduced the Darkside, a polymer composite on aluminum polishing lap that has received very positive reviews (see page 76). The Lightning Lap, developed by Marsh Howard, is a plastic composite lap that bridges the gap between the hand charged and permanently charged types. Although usable in its raw form with both oxides and diamond, the Lightning Lap is available with one side pre-charged with cerium oxide.

Corian polishing laps have become popular in recent years. Corian is a thermosetting acrylic polymer developed by Dupont Corporation. By far its most widespread use is in kitchen and bathroom counter tops. In fact, the first homebrew Corian laps came from the salvaged cutouts for household sinks. Used with diamond, Corian polishes a wide variety of gem materials, ranging from beryl to topaz.

Purchasing and Using Hand Charged Composite Polishing Laps

Hand charged composite laps represent a similar financial investment to the lower-end, all metal laps – prices typically hover around $100. Corian can be surprisingly expensive, as a quick visit to your local home improvement center will demonstrate. Finished Corian laps cost $30-$60, but if you are at all adventurous and know someone with a recently installed sink, you might want to try producing your own. Lucite laps involve considerably simpler manufacturing procedures and lower raw material costs. Expect to pay $10-$30 for a Lucite lap. Charging plastic and composite laps is straightforward. See the individual manufacturer's instructions and Chapter 8.14 for further information. Online message forums can also be a great source of wisdom on the idiosyncrasies of individual lap types (see Chapter 15.8.1).

Hand Charged Ceramic Laps

Compared to the metal or plastic composite types, ceramic laps represent a qualitatively different approach to polishing, in that the substrate of the ceramic lap is as hard as, or harder than, the gemstone material itself. Ceramic laps are used exclusively with diamond, and the physical nature of the polishing action is quite different, since the diamond is free to tumble around on the surface, producing *three-body abrasion* (see page 286)

Ceramic laps are essentially corundum – Al_2O_3, the stuff of rubies and sapphire. This material is extraordinarily hard (Mohs 9). Other lap materials have a Mohs hardness ranging from around 1.5 for the softest met-

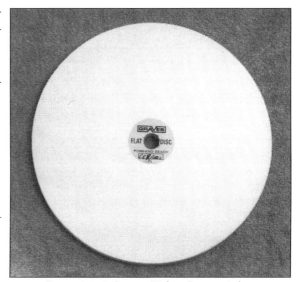

Figure 3-7 A Graves "Falcon" ceramic lap.

als to about 3.0 for harder metals and composites. Clearly, the embedded diamond particles, with hardness 10, are doing all the work on these softer laps (and clearly cerium oxide, which has Mohs hardness 6 yet can readily polish tourmaline with hardness 7.5, remains a mystery – see Chapter 8.11).

Due to its hardness, the ceramic surface exhibits no flexure under the pressure of a passing gemstone. The result is exceptionally flat facets and essentially zero edge rounding. If you want to win competitions, you want to use a ceramic polishing lap.

Purchasing and Using Ceramic Polishing Laps

Of course, perfect facets come at a cost. In addition to the initial investment – expect to pay upward of $200 – ceramic laps require skill and patience. Especially patience. Some ceramic laps need to be broken in, a process which can take hours. Slow spindle speeds work best, and the lap may need re-frosting if it becomes glazed with use. Charging ceramic laps is also a challenge, since almost everyone makes the mistake of using too much diamond (oxides are never used with this lap). In fact, charging a ceramic is essentially an exercise in removing diamonds, not adding them. Chapter 8.14 contains a discussion of the trials and rewards of using ceramic laps. Note that the new Matrix ceramic composite lap from Gearloose seems to have addressed some of these difficulties (see page 76).

Hand Charged Custom Laps

Ever wonder where that old Glenn Miller album went? Does your faceting friend like to try weird, soft, gem materials? Do his unique gemstones exhibit curious, slightly curved grooves, like those on a vinyl record?

The quest for ever more exotic gem materials, as well as the inventive spirit of amateur faceters, has led to a bewildering variety of custom polishing laps. Wax, wood, felt, pitch, and, yes, vinyl, among many others, have all been tried. These materials find particular application in the polishing of softer gem materials, where mechanical shock can lead to disaster. Unfortunately, such soft laps also usually lead to rounded facet edges.

The art of fabricating, charging, and using these exotic laps is beyond the scope of this book. The classic references listed in Chapter 9.1 contain some information, and as always, the Web represents a surprisingly rich yet occasionally risky resource. As mentioned at the beginning of this chapter, whatever you may think of trying, someone out there has probably given it a go and is willing to talk about it.

3.3.2 Permanently Charged Polishing Laps

Permanently charged polishing laps come pre-loaded with polishing compound. Again, both diamond and metal oxide versions are available, with the compound locked in a carrier matrix. These laps are an excellent choice for beginners, since they are relatively inexpensive and easy to use. On the down side, most types of permanently charged polishing laps produce some rounding of facet edges, a definite turn-off for persnickety expert cutters. Also, permanently charged polishing laps are far from permanent, although they can be "freshened up" by manually charging with oxide or diamond.

Ultralaps

The Ultralap is far and away the most popular permanently charged polishing lap among amateurs (as in Chapter 2.8, I apologize in advance for a North-American-centric viewpoint). Ultralaps are very forgiving in terms of technique, and are therefore an excellent choice for beginners. I polished my first few stones (mostly quartz and beryl – see Table 5-1) with an Ultralap and had little idea of the polishing horrors to come with more difficult materials and laps.

The high purity "Spectra" cerium oxide Ultralap is the workhorse of the group, and almost every amateur faceter will have a few of these ubiquitous thin blue plastic disks at hand. Other popular options include aluminum oxide and diamond. Table 3-4 lists the various types of Ultralap available and their particular application.

Table 3-4 Ultralap types and colour coding.

Polishing Compound	Colour	Application / Comment
Cerium Oxide (Spectra type)	light blue	Excellent all-round choice for quartz, beryl, tourmaline
Aluminum Oxide	white	beryl, garnet, topaz, peridot, tourmaline
Chrome Oxide	green	tourmaline, peridot
Tin Oxide	cream	tourmaline, garnet, soft stones
Diamond	blue, white, cream, etc.	Available in 1200, 3000, 8000, 14k, 50k, and 100k mesh. Coarser grits are used for pre-polish on most materials. The finer mesh is suitable for polishing harder stones such as corundum

Purchasing and Using Ultralaps

Most lapidary supply houses carry Ultralaps, and you should expect to pay about $2 apiece in packages of five. Depending on the gem material, stone size, and your hand pressure, you should manage to complete several gems before the lap becomes significantly worn. At a couple of bucks a throw, Ultralaps are truly disposable, but the frugal faceter can always re-charge a worn lap using the appropriate oxide or diamond.

Needless to say, you will need a master lap or other reference surface to support the Ultralap. Surface tension adhesion using water droplets can keep the lap in place. Chapter 5 explains how to mount an Ultralap on a master lap in this way (see page 170).

Note that the "give" of the thin water film between the Ultralap and the master can lead to facet rounding. If this is a concern, you can purchase Ultralaps with an adhesive backing. Of course, this strategy will prevent you from using at least one surface of your master lap for other purposes, and peeling off a worn adhesive lap can be tedious. Finally, at least some of the facet rounding comes from the compressibility of the plastic film of the Ultralap itself. Less hand pressure and more patience may be a better solution than going the self-adhesive route.

As you gain experience, you will become less and less satisfied with the rounded, occasion-ally "ripply" appearance of facets polished on an Ultralap. At that point, it will definitely be time to move on to a harder polishing lap, either metal or ceramic. Nevertheless, I have found on countless occasions that one or two facets on a gem will stubbornly refuse to polish out with my metal lap and diamond. When all else fails, I return to the Ultralap, and it usually solves the problem.

Permanently Charged, Rigid Composite Polishing Laps

Complaints about facet rounding with Ultralaps have led to the popularity of rigid, permanently charged polishing laps. The most well known of these, at least to North Americans, are the Pol-A-Gem, the Dyna Disk, and the Greenway. These laps are an excellent choice for polishing quartz, beryl and other materials.

Glenn Vargas, one of the founding fathers of modern faceting, originally pioneered the Pol-A-Gem, and it is available in both cerium oxide and alumina impregnated models. The Dyna Disk (also spelled Dyna Disc) cerium oxide laps are a product of Fac-Ette Manufacturing Inc., who also produce the top-end GemMaster faceting machine (see Chapter 2.8). Jon "Gearloose" Rolfe introduced the Greenway permanently charged polishing lap in 2010. The Greenway has apparently solved the long-standing problems and mess associated with chrome oxide polish. The Creamway zirconium oxide lap followed in 2012 (see page 76).

Purchasing and Using Permanently Charged Rigid Composite Polishing Laps

The Pol-A-Gem, Dyna Disk, and Gearloose laps are all available by online order from their respective manufacturers. Consult Chapter 15.8.9 for contact details. You can expect to pay $60-$100 per lap. A couple of additional notes about availability: The Pol-A-Gem is manufactured in seasonal, limited-production runs. Contact the manufacturer directly about current stock. The Dyna Disks have been difficult to find in recent years, although production of the new "System 2" laps appears to be ramping up (but see the note about Fac-Ette on page 43).

Using these rigid laps is straightforward: start a steady water drip and use moderate lap rotation speeds. Note that, although they are theoretically permanently charged, these rigid composite laps will wear out. To address this, the manufacturers provide instructions for "refreshing" the laps with polishing compound.

Figure 3-8 The Pol-A-Gem permanently charged polishing lap.

> ## One More Lap...
>
> My wife once asked me why I had to purchase yet another expensive polishing lap. After all, she reasoned, I only have one coarse cutting lap – why four different polishing laps?
>
> The previous sections have explained that certain gemstone types behave better with specific laps and polishing agents. And although most hobbyists have a favourite "go-to" polishing lap, they also cut a wide variety of different gem materials. Working with multiple materials means multiple laps and multiple jars of polishing agent (see Table 8-1 and Chapter 14).
>
> Faultless logic...of course, it doesn't explain all those *unused* polishing laps in my collection...

3.4 A Starter Set of Laps

So. Lots of laps.

How to choose, particularly if you are a beginner?

There is surprising consensus on the best selection of beginner's laps – surprising not only given the diversity of options out there, but also given the diversity of opinion on almost every aspect of our hobby.

Table 3-5 lists a typical starter set of laps, while Table 3-6 shows a reasonable way of expanding your collection as you gain experience and commitment to faceting. Careful planning of your lap purchases makes a great deal of sense, since the array of laps in these tables could easily cost as much as the faceting machine itself.

The final table in this chapter shows the ultimate lap collection. Needless to say, I have yet to assemble such a collection, but a guy can dream, can't he?

Table 3-5 A starter set of laps

Type	Purpose
260 bonded steel cutting	pre-forming large stones
1200 bonded steel cutting	fine cutting to final shape
1200 NuBond	pre-polish
CeO_2 Ultralaps	spectra type for polishing
Master lap	to support Ultralap

Table 3-6 An expanded set of laps

Type	Purpose
260 bonded steel cutting	pre-forming large stones
600 bonded steel cutting	pre-forming / rough cutting smaller stones
1200 bonded steel cutting	fine cutting to final shape
1200 NuBond	pre-polish
CeO_2 Ultralaps	spectra type for polishing
BATT lap	for 50k diamond
Lucite lap	for CeO_2, Alumina
Master lap	to support Ultralaps, BATT lap

Table 3-7 A dream set of laps

Type	Purpose
260 sintered steel cutting	pre-forming large stones
600 sintered steel cutting	pre-forming / rough cutting smaller stones
1200 sintered steel cutting	fine cutting to final shape
3000 sintered steel cutting	very fine cutting
600 NuBond	fine cutting
1200 NuBond	pre-polish
CeO_2 Ultralaps	spectra type for polishing
Pol-a-Gem, Dyna Disk or Greenway lap	CeO_2 or chrome oxide for quartz
Darkside	CeO_2 for quartz
Lucite lap	for CeO_2, alumina
Last Lap, Fast Lap, or Darkside	for 50k diamond
BA5T lap 1	for 8k diamond (corundum pre-polish)
BA5T lap 2	for 50k diamond
BA5T lap 3	for 100k diamond
Ceramic lap 1	for 50k diamond
Ceramic lap 2	for 100k or 200k diamond
Master lap	to support Ultralaps, Pol-a-Gem, etc.

4

Additional Equipment

W^hew!

You've successfully acquired the major hardware – a faceting machine and laps – and your bank manager is still willing to look you in the eye. Don't stop now! There are a few additional pieces of equipment you will need before putting stone to lap.

This chapter discusses these additional items in (approximately) alphabetical order. Much of this stuff is essential, although you can postpone some acquisitions, such as a trim saw and precision scales, until your budget (and banker) can stand it.

4.1 Adhesives

The time has come," the Walrus said, "To talk of many things:
Of shoes—and ships—and sealing-wax— Of cabbages—and kings—

- Lewis Carrol, Through the Looking Glass

Good old C. -L. Dodgson had it right. In a desperate attempt to keep their gemstones in place, amateur cutters have talked of (and tried) many things. Although there are no recorded successes with cabbage, the previous item in the list, sealing wax – or its lapidary equivalent, called dop wax – has been the traditional faceting adhesive for centuries. More recently, alternative adhesives, in particular cyanoacrylate glue and epoxy resin, have enjoyed increasing popularity

4.1.1 Dop Wax

Modern faceters can choose from a variety of dop wax types. These are typically distinguished by colour, each indicating a particular melting temperature (see Table 4-1 and Chapter 7.2.1). Note that modern dop wax is actually a mixture of wax, shellac, and neutral fillers. Generally speaking, more shellac means a higher melting temperature but a more brittle bond. Dop wax typically costs a few dollars a stick, enough for dozens of stones.

Table 4-1 Dop wax types and melting temperatures

Dop Wax Type and Colour		Softening / Melting Temperature	
		°F	°C
Cabbing Wax	Green or Red	160	70
Standard Dop Wax	Black	170	77
Diamond Setter's Wax	Brown	180	82

Excess heat on the lap, particularly during polishing, can soften dop wax and cause shifting of the gem. This, in turn, will force you to do a great deal of cheating to get things right. This, in turn, will cause you to pull your hair out. I use and strongly recommend the high temperature brown diamond setter's wax. Of course, heat sensitive stones may force you to a lower temperature mix or a cold dopping technique.

4.1.2 Cyanoacrylate Glue and Epoxy Resin

The other important adhesives used in faceting are cyanoacrylate (CA) glue and epoxy resin. CA is often known by the trade name "Krazy Glue," although there are multiple manufacturers throughout the world. Your local hardware store will charge about five dollars for a small tube of cyanoacrylate. Although seemingly costly, a little bit of CA goes a very long way, and my experience is that the tube dries out or gets hopelessly gummed up long before you actually run out of glue.

There is a huge selection of epoxy resins on the market, ranging from "instant" epoxy, which takes approximately a minute to set, to slower resins, which can remain workable for hours.

Bug Juice

When I was a kid, my school cafeteria used to serve a beverage universally known as "bug juice," a grayish-orange mixture of unidentifiable fruit concentrates and water. This drink was the traditional accompaniment to their other signature dish: "mystery meat."

I did not like bug juice nor bugs generally, and thus it came as a bit of a surprise to me to learn that "real" bug juice plays a central role in the hobby we all love. It turns out that dop wax contains shellac, and shellac comes from bugs.

More specifically, shellac is a refined product made from *lac*, a resinous secretion of the lac bug, known formally to the scientific world as *Laccifera lacca*. These industrious insects swarm on several types of tree native to India and Thailand, ingesting the sap and secreting lac resin in the form of tubes. Workers harvest these cocoon-like structures and process them to remove residual tree bark and insect parts. What remains is dried flakes of shellac, which can range from pale yellow to deep brown, depending on the type of tree and season. Dissolving these flakes in denatured alcohol produces liquid shellac, unquestionably the most important wood sealant and finish over the last five hundred years. Incidentally, I do not recall whether my school cafeteria had "resinous secretion" on its menu, but it would not surprise me.

Shellac has had some other, rather surprising uses beyond the furniture industry. As a natural polymer, shellac can be mixed with other agricultural products to form a solid mass that is for all intents and purposes a plastic. In fact, phonograph records were made exclusively from shellac compounds until the advent of vinyl in the 1950's.

Despite – or perhaps because of – its insect origin, shellac is edible, and in fact, it is still used regularly as a protective coating on pharmaceutical capsules and pills, as well as (gasp!) for candy. Have you used confectioner's glaze in any of your culinary experimentation? Yup. Bug juice.

The list of uses for shellac could go on forever. Perhaps my favourite – beyond dop wax, of course – is as a fuel and colourant for fireworks. Although now largely supplanted by other materials due to cost, shellac was an essential ingredient for coloured flame fireworks. Apparently, this versatile substance produces unusually pure blue and green flame, an effect difficult to achieve with other fuels.

So the next time you hold that stick of dop wax over an alcohol lamp, give a moment's thought and a healthy dose of respect to good old bug juice, a substance that has been enriching our lives for millennia. Oh. And give the mystery meat a pass…

Typically, the longer the setting time, the more durable the ultimate bond. On the other hand, even the fastest setting, weakest epoxies are much stronger than you will ever need. I tend to use the five-minute type.

Note that epoxy resin has a finite shelf life, and may need to be refrigerated after opening. As a result, the larger, "economy" tubs of resin may not be a real value, unless you are some sort of otherworldly faceting speed-demon. The smaller, toothpaste-sized tubes cost a few dollars and represent a better choice. Although somewhat more expensive, the dual "injector" type packaging automatically dispenses the resin and hardener compounds in the correct ratio for mixing (Figure 4-1).

4.1.3 The Best Adhesive?

Which is the best adhesive for dopping stones?

It depends whom you ask and the exact circumstances. On the one hand, dop wax is the traditional adhesive, and partisans argue that it is the only way to go. On the other hand, the more modern glues also have their adherents in the faceting community, particularly among careless users of cyanoacrylate...Sorry, I could not resist the joke.

Chapter 7 contains a detailed discussion of the pros and cons of each type of adhesive and how to use them. It also tries to convince you that the whole of

Figure 4-1 Still life with glue...Common faceting adhesives include (clockwise from left) dop wax, epoxy resin (in both tube and injector packaging), and cyanoacrylate glue.

the faceting adhesive world may be greater than the sum of its individual parts: I almost always use a hybrid wax and epoxy bond with my gemstones. As a beginner, your best strategy is to buy a little of each type and try them separately or in combination. Compared to the value of your gem rough, to say nothing of your time and sanity, the financial investment is trivial.

4.2 Alcohol lamps and Torches

A stick of dop wax is just an unattractive paperweight without heat. Managing this heat, that is, bringing the right amount of warming to the right location, is at the heart of successful dopping. Lapidary wax softens and melts at a temperature of 160-180°F (70-82°C – see previous section). Raising, and more importantly, controlling the temperature of dop wax can be difficult, particularly with a gemstone in one hand and a dop stick in the other.

Enter the adjustable alcohol lamp (Figure 4-2). This humble device, used for hundreds of years for purposes as varied as glass blowing and sterilization of medical implements, is an essential tool for every faceter. When turned down to minimum flame, the alcohol lamp enables you to apply small amounts of heat to dop wax. This can be particularly valuable for fine adjustment of the gemstone position, a situation in which you need softened, not molten, wax. Increasing the flame means more heat and more heat means liquid wax. With practice, this wax can be carefully controlled and directed onto a dop-stone joint.

Figure 4-2 Alcohol lamps (center) and small butane torches, both hand-held (left) and free-standing (right). Note the knob on the left of the alcohol lamp to control flame size. A heat and drip-proof working surface is an excellent idea when using these tools.

In recent years, the miniature gas torch has grown in popularity among gem cutters. These refillable burners use butane or butane-propane gas, the kind intended for cigarette lighters. Gas torches produce very localized, intense heating (see "The Heat is On…" on page 91). The smaller units require continuous thumb pressure to maintain gas flow, and can only be used hand-held. Their larger "blazer" type cousins boast a stable plastic base and an easily adjustable gas valve, allowing their use hands-free.

4.2.1 A Hot Debate…

Which is better – an alcohol lamp or a gas torch?

Surprise surprise! It depends. Surprise surprise! Faceters argue about this.

The alcohol lamp allows gentle warming over a fairly large area, while the torch provides intense, localized heat. The lamp is less likely to overheat your dop wax, or even set it on fire, but it can be difficult to warm only a small area of the wax joint. Of course, every alcohol lamp sits stably on your worktable and operates hands-free. The gas torch is unquestionably extremely hot, which can be both good and bad. Unlike the lamp, it can be used in any orientation, and it is often easier to bring heat to the work piece, rather than the other way around.

I use both alcohol lamps and gas torches of various sizes and configurations. In fact, Figure 4-2 shows only a fraction of my collection of burners. Yes, there are several more, and no, I am not a firebug. The investment is tiny in comparison to other aspects of our hobby. A decent alcohol lamp costs $5-7, and while a fancy butane torch could set you back ten times that amount, perfectly usable economy models range from $3-20. Short version: get and use both.

A word of caution: both the alcohol lamp and gas torch will produce drips of burning hot wax if you are not careful. In principle, the lamp is safer in this regard, because the work – and hence at least one of your hands – is always above where the drips will fall. In fact, my alcohol lamp seems particularly skilled at catching these drips (Figure 4-2). On the other hand, the more localized heat of the gas torch is less likely to lead to widespread melting and dripping catastrophes.

Note that both alcohol lamps and gas torches provide a very useful source of secondary heat: warming a scalpel blade in the flame will let you cut through dop wax with ease. A well-heated blade can even make short work of epoxy resin, although take care not to inhale the fumes.

Candle Candle Burning Bright…

Your first inclination may be to use a candle to heat dop wax.

Bad idea.

Candles inevitably leave soot everywhere. And while I know of no study examining the influence of soot particles on the strength of dop wax, getting everything black is a headache that is very easy to avoid.

Incidentally, soot consists of impure carbon particles resulting from less than complete combustion of hydrocarbons, such as the wax found in modern candles. The soot situation could be worse, or at least more disgusting: in the old days, the main ingredient of candles was the rendered fat of slaughtered animals.

Here's another bit of faceting-related candle trivia: you have certainly noticed that an alcohol lamp burns with a pale blue, almost invisible flame, yet a candle produces a bright, warm, yellowish light. The reason? Our old friend (and enemy): soot. The candle flame heats the tiny soot particles until they are yellow hot, producing that romantic, golden, glow. The atavistic charm of candlelight may be a purely modern phenomenon: to my knowledge, history does not record whether the glowing residue of slaughtered animals was considered romantic. In any case, a sootless candle, although arguably better for us lapidary folk, would sort of miss the point.

4.3 Chemicals

As a hobby faceter, you will always have two common solvents, alcohol and acetone, near to hand. Both should be available at your local hardware store or pharmacy, although concern about the use of these liquids in the manufacture of methamphetamine has made procuring them somewhat more complicated. For example, some governments will require identification to purchase alcohol or acetone, and trying to buy both chemicals at the same time may set off automatic warning bells.

Alcohol is used for both cleaning and burning. It has the admirable property of safely and easily dissolving dop wax, as well as removing grease, oil, and other contaminants. Every hobby faceter will also have an alcohol lamp for dopping (see Section 4.2). Alcohol is available in a variety of forms, including mixtures with scent agents and other additives. Your best bet is probably denatured alcohol, sometimes known as methylated spirits (see "Better Living Through Chemistry" on page 92).

Acetone is the other big gun in your solvent holster. It, too, dissolves dop wax, although its harsher odour and greater volatility will make alcohol a better choice for this purpose. Ac-

> ## The Heat is On...
>
> The manufacturers boast that their blazer-type torches can produce temperatures of 2500°F or 1370°C.
>
> How hot is 2500°F? We know that lapidary dop wax melts at 160-180°F (see Section 4.1.1). Gem quality amber melts at 400-700°F. Your aluminum and brass dops will melt at 1200-1600°F, and even the steel of your faceting machine may soften and begin to flow at 2500° F.
>
> How hot is 2500°F? Hot enough. Be careful.

etone really comes into its own when you use alternative adhesives, specifically epoxy resin (see Section 4.1). Most epoxies will soften and break apart after a good soak in acetone.

Note that acetone will also attack a variety of other materials, including plastics, flooring, etc. Acetone fumes sink in air and can flow across surfaces and ignite in the presence of open flame or sparks. It is also nastier to the skin than alcohol. In other words, use acetone only when you need it.

There are a few other chemicals you may encounter while faceting, for example machine oil or synthetic lubricants. I spray down my steel laps with WD-40 after use to inhibit rusting, and regularly clean and lubricate the mechanical parts of my faceting machine with synthetic silicone lubricant. Some cutters insist that drip tank additives such as vinegar (acetic acid) or liquid soap will improve polishing performance. The jury is definitely still out on the advisability of this practice, particularly since vinegar will slowly corrode your machine (see "Lube Job" on page 298 for more on this).

Although more aggressive options exist (see "Serious Solvents" on page 93), these three or four chemicals are all you really need for faceting. Make sure that you use re-sealable small containers for alcohol and acetone, since these volatile liquids won't be there in the morning if you leave them exposed to air. For acetone, you should also check that the bottle itself won't dissolve.

4.3.1 Shellac – Alcohol Mixture

Alcohol has one additional essential function, beyond being a great solvent and fuel for your lamp (and perhaps parties). When dop wax dissolves in alcohol, it produces a shellac-alcohol mixture that is great for preparing your dop sticks and gemstones. Chapters 5.4.1 and 7.3.1 explain how to use shellac-alcohol mixture to improve adhesion. Here, we discuss how to make the stuff.

Fill a small jar half full with denatured alcohol and add a few chunks of dop wax (1/3 of a stick or less). Overnight, the dop wax will dissolve, producing a brownish liquid containing alcohol, shellac, and wax. You will also likely find solid residue on the bottom of the jar. This is filler material that has settled out as the dop wax dissolved. You can either just leave the filler in place, or pour off the clean liquid into another jar. Voilà! Shellac-alcohol mix!

Better Living Through Chemistry

Alcohol has many uses beyond being an excellent solvent. You may now give thanks to your favourite deity.

Perhaps as early as the Stone Age some 10,000 years ago, ancient man recognized the intoxicating effects of fermented sugars, and there is no question that alcohol has played a significant role in many cultures in the intervening millennia.

Beer, wine, and spirits contain pure ethanol. Most modern countries impose strict controls and taxes on this type of alcohol, and these levies can be substantial: pure ethanol can cost $50 per liter or more. Short version: don't use the good stuff for faceting.

Gem cutters are more likely to use *denatured* alcohol, which is typically 90% ethanol combined with additives that make the mix unpalatable, poisonous, or both. These additives frequently include *methanol*, which causes blindness and death, *denatonium*, the most bitter chemical compound known to man, and *ipecac*, which is an emetic (it induces vomiting). Some denatured alcohols even contain 10% aviation gasoline. Short version: don't use the denatured stuff for cocktails.

Actually, some claim that the additives in denatured alcohol can leave a residue on your gemstones. The best advice is to try a couple of different brands and see which works best. Isopropyl alcohol (rubbing alcohol) is a great alternative, although check the label for additional ingredients. If you can afford it (and find it), a small bottle of pure ethanol does a great job of producing that final clean shine on a stone.

Over time, the level of shellac-alcohol in your jar will drop lower and lower. You can freshen the mix with fresh solvent and wax. Transferring or completing a gemstone always yields bits of used dop wax. Don't throw them out – add them to the jar.

Furniture aficionados will point out that shellac has a very finite shelf life after mixing with alcohol. Within a year, a process known as *esterification* converts the resins in the shellac into a sticky, gummy substance that doesn't dry properly. I have noticed this effect on my dops – older shellac-alcohol mixture can remain somewhat sticky. Dop sticks are not furniture, however, and I have not noticed a reduction in adhesion using older solution. If you encounter a problem, consider mixing up a fresh batch.

Figure 4-3 Adding dop wax to a jar of alcohol will produce shellac-alcohol mix for dopping.

Serious Solvents

Losing patience with just acetone and alcohol? Does that epoxy bond simply refuse to give up? You may be tempted to call in the solvent cavalry.

For example, there are a number of methylene chloride based products on the market which are specifically formulated to dissolve epoxy resin. Although more aggressive and effective with epoxy, these solvents are dangerously volatile, inflammable, and toxic. In fact, the European Union recently banned many methylene chloride based solvents due to health concerns. Acetone, like denatured alcohol, is poisonous if consumed, but it is in the minor leagues of dangerous substances in comparison to methylene chloride. Rather than the instant gratification of methylene chloride, I suggest a leisurely soak in acetone for all epoxy bonds. Take a walk. Get some fresh air. The bond will eventually give up.

4.4 Dops

A *dop stick* or *dop* is a short, straight rod, usually of brass or aluminum, which holds the gemstone in place for cutting and polishing. As such, dops form the critical interface between the raw gem rough and the precision mechanics of the faceting machine. Dops come in a variety of configurations and sizes tailored to specific purposes or gem shapes (see Figure 4-4). And, although quite simple in principle, the humble dop stick can be a source of unending frustration if it is bent or otherwise damaged.

By the way, don't confuse the noun *dop* with the verb *to dop*. The dop is the metal stick, while dopping is the action of gluing the gemstone to the dop stick.

By design, or perhaps more accurately, by necessity, faceting machines can cut and polish only one half of a gem at a time. Chapter 2.1 explains why. To complete a stone, you will need to perform two separate dopping operations. The standard practice is to begin by dopping to the table area and cutting the pavilion, followed by a transfer to a second dop and cutting of the crown (but see "The Great Debate" on page 304).

As Chapter 5.7 makes clear, the orientation of the stone with respect to the faceting machine must be maintained during these two phases. If the stone rotates or shifts arbitrarily during transfer, the facets of the crown and pavilion will not line up properly. A *transfer jig* can help ensure consistent dop-to-dop orientation (see Section 4.16 below and Chapters 5.6 and 7.6).

Figure 4-4 Dop sticks come in a variety of forms and materials.

4.4.1 Purchasing Dops

New faceting machines typically ship with a minimal set of dop sticks to get you started. You will want to acquire more. Trust me. Not only will dop sticks wear out with use and abuse, but also, inevitably, the one particular dop you need will already have a half-finished stone attached to it or be otherwise indisposed.

Compared to other faceting hardware, dops are cheap, so you can treat yourself to a decent collection without breaking the bank. Note that dops are also very easy to make. If you have any machining skill whatsoever, you should be able to fabricate your own from brass or aluminum rod stock. For example, Figure 4-31 shows a few homemade dops and spare rod stock lurking in my toolbox, and my skills are only half a notch above whatsoever...

Keying Systems

In order to help maintain rotational alignment during transfer, most commercial manufacturers use a mechanical reference point or *key* on the dop, faceting machine, and transfer jig. This key may be a groove or hole in the dop stick, mated to a reference pin in the quill and jig (Figure 4-5). Alternatively, the back (*i.e.* non-gem) end of the dop may be cut at an angle or with a flat to fit a corresponding part in the faceting head and transfer jig.

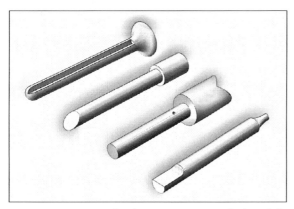

Figure 4-5 Various dop keying systems, including (left to right) grooves, angled tips, pinholes, and flats.

Do you need to use keyed dops?

Definitely not. The keying system can help with proper alignment of the gem, but it is no substitute for knowing and understanding how to orient the dop stick in the faceting machine and transfer jig. The shape of the gem rough, not the location of the reference key, should determine the optimal initial orientation of the stone, while the completed pavilion or girdle facets give the rotational position after transfer. Even the highest quality mechanical keying system will have some slop, and it is a simple geometric fact that if there is some offset in angle between the keying system and the index wheel, the error will double after transfer (you might have to make a sketch to convince yourself of this). Like me, you will probably realize that cutting a test row of facets is the best way to guarantee an accurate transfer. Chapters 5.7.1 and 7.6 focus on these alignment issues. Turn to page 251 for more on keying systems and to Chapter 7.7 to learn about cutting test tiers.

Which Dops, How Many?

Which dops should you get?

Dops are machine-specific, due to differing shaft diameters and keying systems between manufacturers. Many faceters, including me, choose to not use the mechanical reference key, relying on other techniques to ensure proper orientation after transfer. In this instance, you can use dop sticks from other machine types, provided they have a compatible diameter. I use Poly-Metric, Graves, and homemade dops with my machine (Figure 4-4).

How many dops do you need?

That is a bit like the classic rhetorical question: "how long is a piece of rope?" Some faceters prepare multiple pieces of gem rough at once, and have many stones simultaneously "on the dop." This strategy clearly demands a larger collection. At a minimum, you should acquire dops covering the range of sizes of gemstone that you anticipate cutting. For each size, you will need a flat dop and a cone dop for round (or nearly round) gem designs, as well as a vee dop for keeled stones. Table 4-2 shows a good starter set.

You will certainly acquire more dops as you gain experience and develop your own cutting style. And as mentioned above, dops are inexpensive, typically a few dollars each. Having a broad selection to match any potential gemstone is a very affordable luxury.

Table 4-2 A starter set of dops.

Diameter		Types
in	*mm*	
1/8	3	flat, cone, vee
3/16	4	flat, cone, vee
1/4	6	flat, cone, vee
1/3	8	flat, cone, vee
1/2	12	flat, cone, vee

4.4.2 Dop Types

Flat Dops

As their name suggests, flat dops have a flat mating surface suitable for bonding to a similar area on the gem rough (Figure 4-6). In conventional pavilion-first faceting, the initial bond is between a flat dop and what will eventually become the table. Rough pre-grinding on a wheel or a coarse lap can produce a bonding area on the stone, if no suitable surface exists (see Chapter 5.4).

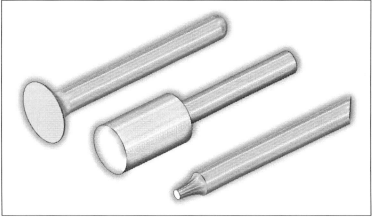

Figure 4-6 Flat dops come in a number of different shapes from different manufacturers.

Cone Dops

Cone dops resemble the flat type, but with a conical cup machined into the end which holds the gem (Figure 4-7). This cup accepts the pavilion of a partially cut stone. Cone dops are clearly tailored to round gems, but with a suitable buffer of dop wax or adhesive, they can also be used for almost any design with a more-or-less conical pavilion.

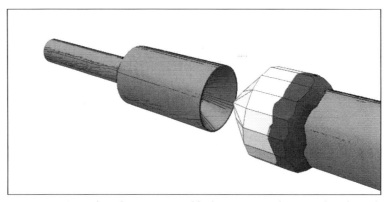

Figure 4-7 Cone dops have a conical hole to receive the completed pavilion of a gemstone that is approximately round.

The closed cup shape of cone dops can complicate the release of the completed gemstone when used with epoxy resin or cyanoacrylate glue. See Chapters 7.3.2 and 7.3.3 for tips on using cone dops.

Vee Dops

Vee dops provide a V-shaped surface for bonding to the pavilion of gemstones with a long, ridge-like pavilion or keel (Figure 4-8). The emerald and step cuts belong in this category. As with the cone dop, sufficient buffering by either wax or adhesive ensures a good fit and can adapt the dop to a range of elongated gem designs.

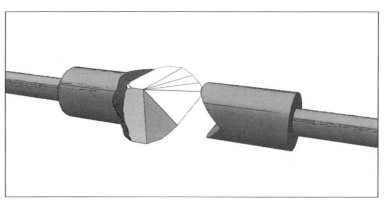

Figure 4-8 Vee dops are suited to long designs with a keel.

Specialty Dops

In addition to the standard flat, cone, and vee dops, you may encounter specialty dops tailored to more exotic gemstone forms. In particular, manufacturers provide specialty dops for trillion, briolette, and very long keeled designs.

Opinions vary on the necessity of specialty dops. Even for very unusual shapes, I have had no problems using standard dops and careful buffering by wax. In other words, you can probably get by without specialty dops. The only exception would be a T-shaped dop for very long designs – for example, very long rectangles cut from crystals of beryl or tourmaline.

4.4.3 Brass versus Aluminum Dops

Brass or aluminum. Which is better? As with many aspects of faceting, your individual style and preferences should drive the choice between brass and aluminum dops. Both materials work well, and the differences between the two metals are considerably less important than their similarities. Also, manufacturers usually provide only one or the other; choosing whether or not to use the keying system can make the decision between brass and aluminum for you.

The essential differences between the two types are:

Heat Retention. Brass retains heat considerably longer than aluminum. This can simplify or, for some, complicate the task of wax dopping. It can also lead to burnt fingertips for the unwary. You will just have to try both to see if the additional heat capacity of brass is a help or a hindrance.

Weight. Brass is also denser than aluminum. This means that, even for large gems, the metal will dominate the weight and heft of the dopped stone. This can lead to less "gem-centric" handling and hence accidents such as dropping or impacts.

Corrosion. Brass corrodes readily, leading to discolouring and in extreme cases, surface changes that may make accurate clamping and centering difficult. Brass dops left soaking for long periods in alcohol may emerge looking worse than before the cleanup. Aluminum, on the other hand, oxidizes even more readily than brass, but aluminum "rust" is corundum, which is hard, transparent, and durable, like sapphire. In fact, exactly like sapphire. Note that etching problems may occur with both materials and harsh solvents.

Adhesion Properties. Some experienced faceters suggest that dop wax doesn't stick as well to aluminum as it does to brass. Nevertheless, you should always pre-coat the dop with a layer of shellac-alcohol mixture before applying the wax. I have never noticed a difference in adhesion with proper preparation. Note that brass may interfere with the chemistry of some fast-setting epoxies. Hybrid wax-epoxy dopping techniques avoid this issue entirely (see Chapter 7.4).

4.4.4 Damaged Dops

With all the handling, heating, soaking in solvents, and rough grinding on the faceting machine, dops inevitably get damaged. There is a simple solution when you notice a damaged dop: throw it away. Bent dops can cause endless headaches in terms of misaligned facets, spiral cuts, and so forth. Dops cost a couple of dollars each and are always cheaper than either gem rough or blood pressure medicine.

There is a simple test to determine whether a dop is bent or not. Place the suspect dop in the quill and tighten as usual. Then, setting the cutting angle to 90° (*i.e.* for the girdle), lower the faceting head until there is a tiny gap between the dop and a reference lap. A master lap works well, as do any of the thicker, solid steel cutting laps.

Come Get Some…I've Got Dops of Steel!

If dops need to be resistant to damage, why not make them out of some serious material, like steel?

Good question. Steel undoubtedly has excellent structural properties, and it is without question the material on which the industrial revolution was built. Steel dops would be strong dops, indeed.

On the other hand, steel has some distinct disadvantages. It rusts readily in a wet environment, for instance, and your dops are definitely going to get wet. Stainless steel does not rust, but it can be particularly expensive and difficult to machine.

Also, bounds of reason should apply to the strength requirement on dops. Most manufacturers supply dop sticks that are 1/4 - 3/8 inch (6-10 mm) in diameter. If you are regularly bending brass or aluminum dop sticks, you should seriously re-examine your faceting style or cut down on the coffee. Your friendly neighbourhood machinist will also warn you about using tools that are as hard as, or harder than, your machinery. Steel dops could potentially damage or deform your quill: when you clamp down on the collet mechanism, something has to give.

The final argument against macho dops, whether they be of steel, titanium, or kryptonite, is that your dops will sooner or later make contact with your laps. In such an encounter, you definitely want the laps to win. Damaged, dented, and delaminated cutting laps are no laughing matter from both the financial and hobby-enjoyment points of view. Figure 4-10 shows what should happen.

Release the index wheel mechanism so that the quill can rotate freely, and place your eye close to the plane defined by the reference lap. You should see a small, perfectly straight gap between the dop and lap (Figure 4-9). If not, adjust the cutting angle until the gap is parallel. At this point, you might be able to spot any bending directly. Now rotate the quill. The gap should not vary in thickness or shape. Note, however, that if you see variations, this could indicate other problems with your machine, particularly the quill and collet, so double-check with a known, good dop stick.

Fair warning: this test may be difficult, depending on the type and diameter of dop. For example, some larger diameter dops look like golf tees (Figure 4-6) and don't have a long reference edge that can be brought close to the lap surface. In this instance, a small,

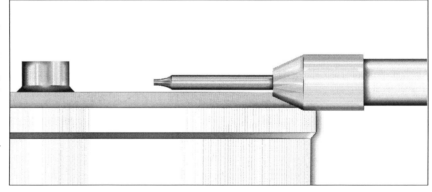

Figure 4-9 Place the suspect dop in the quill at 90°, and rotate the quill. Variations in the gap between the dop and lap could indicate a problem.

accurately square block of wood or metal placed on the lap may help. You can also try rolling the suspect dop stick across a piece of flat glass. There should be no bowing or irregularity as the dop rotates. The test described in "The Jig is Up" on page 121 may help as well. Whichever test you employ, the simple message is: "when in doubt, toss it out..."

While you should immediately discard bent dops, other types of damage are completely harmless. For example, many beginners choose an oversized dop to ensure a solid bond, and then end up cutting into the dop itself when forming the girdle of the gemstone. There is again a simple solution to this difficulty: keep on cutting! Unless you are right at the beginning of the process or a very large amount of

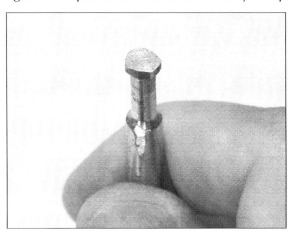

the dop will be cut away, there is little harm in continuing. Both brass and aluminum are softer than most gemstones, and will not gum up cutting laps in small amounts. Note however, that a severely "modified" dop stick (Figure 4-10) may make initial alignment of subsequent pieces of gem rough more difficult.

Figure 4-10 An oversized dop will be cut away during the faceting process. While this is mostly harmless, the resulting modified dop stick may be a more difficult target for accurate centering of gem rough.

4.5 Immersion Fluids

Sooner or later, you will have the awful experience of discovering a previously unseen, seemingly fatal inclusion in a half-completed gemstone. Why couldn't you have spotted that earlier?

It turns out that evaluating the internal condition of gem rough can be extraordinarily difficult, particularly for the higher refractive index materials. Sadly, these are usually the more expensive types.

Beyond the presence of obvious surface gunk, there are two physical processes which limit your ability to see inside a stone. The first effect is so-called *Fresnel loss*. What Augustin-Jean Fresnel demonstrated (see Chapter 11.8) is that even a perfectly smooth surface will reflect some light if it represents the interface between two materials of different index of refraction, for example, gemstone material and air. The amount of reflection, and hence the amount of distracting light confusing your view of the inside of a stone, depends directly on the difference in refractive index. For garnet (n~1.76) in air (n=1.0), things can be difficult indeed.

The second challenge arises due to microscopic surface roughness, which scatters light in all directions. This is the same effect which prevents you from seeing the filament of a frosted light bulb, despite the fact that the glass clearly can transmit light.

Enter the immersion fluid.

Long ago, our forebears noticed that placing gem rough in water allowed a clearer view of internal flaws. The reason is simple. Water has a refractive index of 1.33, considerably higher than that of air and closer to that of the stone. This reduces Fresnel losses and hence distracting reflections. Presto! You can see inside.

Immersion Etiquette

Despite the obvious advantages of such a strategy, you will probably not be permitted to go from table to table at a gem show, dropping pieces of rough into your jar of Refractol. Although it is considerably more benign than other immersion fluids (see opposite page), Refractol leaves a bit of a smelly mess, and of course, the dealer may actually have something to hide inside those stones.

All reputable gem dealers should allow you to use some water, a flashlight, and a loupe to examine their wares. In fact, many will allow a proper, leisurely examination, including Refractol. This is particularly true for repeat or larger-lot customers. Gem show etiquette demands that you ask for this privilege in advance. Refusal on the part of the dealer, particularly if the circumstances are not overly hectic, should tell you more than you need to know about his or her ethical business practices. Turn to Chapter 6.2.2 for more tips on getting the most out of gem shows.

Water helps a lot with surface scattering effects as well, since the liquid wets and "fills in" the microscopic roughness. Snell's law (Chapter 11.4) tells us that the amount of refraction or bending of light at a tilted interface also increases with the difference in refractive index. Less difference means less bending and hence less scattering at the rough, convoluted surface of the stone. Equipped with the information in Chapter 11, you should be able to make a sketch of the situation and convince yourself. Of course, you could always just rub some spit into that frosty piece of quartz to show this. To heck with equations…

What's good with water should be even better with a liquid of higher refractive index. In fact, Fresnel and Snell tell us that for a perfect index match, the surface of the stone should disappear completely, allowing a clear view of internal colour and other effects, such as inclusions. Commercial immersion fluids take exactly this approach. Refractol, produced by the endearingly named Bob-A-Lou Rock company, is far and away the most popular immersion fluid among amateur gemcutters (Figure 4-11). It has an index of 1.567, comfortably located between quartz and beryl. It is also relatively inexpensive and non-toxic (see "High Index Immersion Fluids" below). As such, it is the ideal immersion liquid for gem materials ranging from opal (n~1.43) through tourmaline (n~1.63). Glycerol, with a refractive index of 1.47, is an excellent and more readily available alternative.

Figure 4-11 Refractol is a commercial immersion fluid suitable for many gem materials.

Expect to pay five to ten dollars for a small jar of Refractol. Note that you could very easily recover this investment by avoiding a disaster on your first purchase of gem rough. With proper care and cleanup, one jar should last for many years. Chapter 5.3.1 contains more information on using immersion liquids.

High Index Immersion Fluids

How about these for uplifting words?…

"…skin irritation…eye irritation…vomiting, diarrhea, burning sensation in mouth, chest, stomach, and rectal area, abdominal cramps, dizziness, double vision… mutagenic…over-exposure can result in death…"

No, these are not stage directions for the latest Wes Craven splatterfest. Rather, they are an extract from the Material Safety Data Sheet (MSDS) of a high index gemological immersion fluid.

Yikes!

Scanning further down the supplier's web page, you note that these charming substances can range from $100 upwards for a small jar of liquid.

Why on earth would you want to play with this stuff?

Well, the reasons are clear, or more precisely, clarity. The adjacent text explains why an index-matching liquid can really help in identifying internal flaws in gemstone rough, and higher index gem material is usually more costly gem material. As a consequence, a number of suppliers offer immersion fluids with higher refractive indices, ranging up to approximately that of corundum.

Table 4-3 lists the most common immersion fluids. I cannot in good conscience recommend any of these nasty liquids, beyond water, glycerol and Refractol. For what it's worth, the most commonly used immersion fluids after these three are benzyl benzoate and methylene iodide. Please be careful…

Table 4-3 Common immersion fluids.

Liquid	Refractive Index	Liquid	Refractive Index
water	1.33	bromoform	1.59
ethanol (pure)	1.36	cinnamon oil	1.59
kerosene	1.45	carbon disulfide	1.63
glycerol	1.47	1-bromonapthalene	1.66
benzyl benzoate	1.54	methylene iodide	1.74
Refractol	1.567	methylene iodide saturated with sulfur	1.78

4.6 Index Gears

As explained in Chapter 2.1 , the index gear carries the responsibility of controlling the rotation of the gemstone as you cut and polish. For those who have not yet had enough of the metaphorical excesses of that chapter and section, we are talking "longitude" here.

Because they offer discrete settings, index wheels bear a direct relation to the symmetry of the gemstone. Stated briefly, the number of teeth on the index wheel determines which type of gem you can cut. Chapter 10.7 provides a full discussion of gemstone symmetry and index wheels.

In all likelihood, your machine arrived with a 96-tooth index wheel and the option to exchange it. While a very large fraction of modern gemstone designs can be executed with such a gear, you will sooner or later want to branch out to alternate symmetries. Index wheels are machine specific, so consult your manufacturer's catalog for available types. The most common ones have 32, 48, 64, 72, 77, 80, 96, or 120 teeth. Math mavens, or those who have peeked ahead at Chapter 10.7, will recognize that this group of gears allows symmetries from two-fold through twelve-fold and a couple of higher ones to boot. Plenty of opportunity for exploration...

If you already have a 96-index wheel, what is the best choice for the next one? The answer depends entirely on what you want to cut. My personal preference would be an 80-index gear, since it opens the door to the many excellent, five-fold symmetric designs. On the other hand, older faceting diagrams – the "legacy cuts" – are much more likely to be matched to a 64 or 72 index wheel. Consult Chapter 10.7 for further wisdom.

Expect to pay $20-120 each for add-on index wheels. Incidentally, you should be able to spot one of my spare gears in Figure 4-31, and it's not the 80-tooth. That one was on my faceting machine when I took the picture...

4.7 Loupes and Magnifiers

Sight is by far the most important of the five senses in both creating and appreciating a fine gemstone. Although a sensitive touch and the ability to hear what is going on are both helpful, you simply cannot make your meet points without looking, and looking carefully.

Some sort of magnification or viewing aid is absolutely essential. Given the diversity of personal cutting styles, it is fortunate indeed that loupes and magnifiers come in a wide variety of sizes and configurations (Figure 4-12). For faceting, you will want a comfortable magnifier in the range 10-15X that lets you quickly move back and forth between cutting and inspecting.

Hand Loupes

Hand loupes are essential to a wide variety of hobbies and disciplines, ranging from stamp collecting to linen inspection. Available magnifications range from 3-15X, and are often adjustable by swinging an additional lens in or out. Although many faceters swear by them, I do

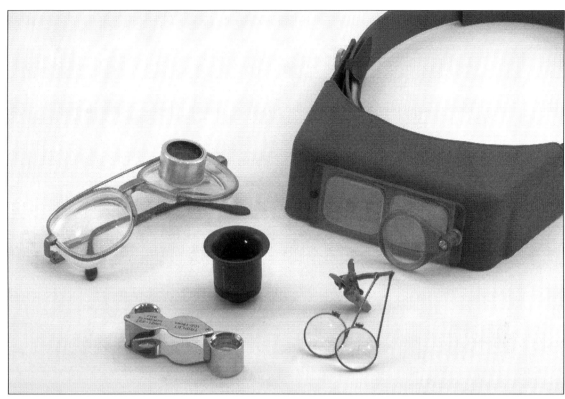

Figure 4-12 Gem cutters can choose from a variety of magnifiers. The dark plastic cylindrical object at center left is an eye loupe. Clockwise around it starting in the upper right are a head visor with auxiliary magnifier, a dual-lens, clip-on loupe, a conventional hand loupe, and a custom 22X magnifier built into a pair of eyeglasses.

not use a hand loupe because, as the name implies, you need a free hand to use one. With one hand on the gemstone and the other on the various machine controls, I simply don't have an extra hand to spare when cutting. When I am inspecting my work, I use those hands to hold the gem and adjust the lamp, respectively. Again, I simply run out of hands.

Nevertheless, you may already have a hand loupe, so give it a try. The fold-out type is particularly convenient, since you can hold it by looping your finger through the cover and letting it just hang from your finger when not in use.

Eye Loupes

Eye loupes are what most people imagine when they think of how a watchmaker or jeweler works. These magnifiers are held against the eye, monocle-style, freeing both hands once in place. The range of available magnification is similar to that of hand loupes. I own and occasionally use an eye loupe, but a number of disadvantages limit its practicality. First of all, you have to "plug" the loupe in to your eye before inspecting the gem. In addition to being an additional, albeit small, time waster, some may find wearing an eye loupe uncomfortable. And of course for those of us who wear glasses, eye loupes carry the double disadvantage of requiring an extra step – removing your spectacles – and worsening whatever vision you had with the other eye. Yes, there are eye loupes with small clips to fit over glasses, but in my experience they do not work reliably. Finally, eye loupes fall out – for example when you go wide-eyed upon seeing a horribly over-cut facet. Things that fall get broken, and they tend to break other things while they're doing it.

Head Visors

The head-mounted visor is a common sight in precision workshops, and it can be particularly helpful for fine work as one ages and loses near point vision. I use a visor during dopping, cleaning, and other operations (but I am not getting old, darn it!). Although very practical for these activities, head-mounted visors are simply not available with the required magnification for inspecting meet points and polish. Yes, add-on lenses can bump up the typical 3-4X by a small factor, but you will find that this is not enough to achieve the results you want. I also tend to bonk the visor part against things, like the faceting machine, lamps, etc.

Clip-On Loupes

Clip-on loupes attach to the arm of a pair of glasses and place one or more lenses in front of the eye. Typically, these lenses can be swung away to permit unobscured vision, or inserted singly or in pairs to vary the magnification. With magnifications in the range 8-15X, clip-on loupes enjoy many of the advantages of the other types with few of the drawbacks. For example, they are truly hands-free in operation, and even when in place, a clip-on loupe permits peripheral vision. The only real down side is that, if you don't wear eyeglasses, there is not much for the loupe to clip on to. Nevertheless, they are otherwise so comfortable and practical that I know faceters who have bought cheap reading or sunglasses and knocked out the lenses, just to be able to use a clip-on loupe.

Custom Magnifiers

This is a catchall category that includes a variety of approaches. For example, I really like high magnification to ensure near perfect meets, and my 11X clip-on loupe doesn't quite do it for me. As a result, I made a custom 22X magnifier by gluing a modified telescope eyepiece into a hole drilled in the (plastic) lens of an old pair of eyeglasses (see Figure 4-12). This provides a wonderfully magnified, wide field of view for really fine work.

Buying Loupes and Magnifiers

Loupes and magnifiers vary significantly in price. You should expect to pay $15-30 for a simple eye or hand loupe. Head visors are also moderately priced ($20-30), but you will probably also want the add-on lenses for increased magnification ($10-20). Clip-on loupes are the most expensive commercial option, running about $30-60, depending on the manufacturer and number of lenses.

4.8 Lighting

Proper lighting plays a very important role in amateur faceting, improving both the final product and your experience at the machine. You are, after all, a craftsman enjoying a wonderful leisure time activity. Poorly polished facets and eyestrain are not the goal here.

Although some faceting machines come equipped with a small lamp, you should seriously consider adding at least one additional source of lighting. Adjustability is the key, since the best illumination conditions can vary from one stage of cutting and polishing to the next, and from one gem material to another. Consider, for example, the geometry of a mast type faceting machine while working on girdle facets versus crown stars. Swinging the quill up to examine the stone places the gem and your eyes at radically different locations. Fixed lighting simply cannot cope with this, particularly in those final polishing phases which call for careful control over illumination. A large, articulated office desk lamp is an excellent choice, since it can be moved through a substantial three-dimensional volume, and can even be swung completely out of the way when not needed (Figure 4-13).

Figure 4-13 Articulated office lamps provide flexible illumination. Where'd the ball go?

Opinions vary among faceters on the merits of bare filament bulbs versus frosted. In my experience, the frosted bulb makes facet meets easier to see, while a bare bulb viewed just off direct reflection can really pick out microscopic scratches (see Figure 5-51). Higher power bulbs (75-100W) produce more photons, but can be uncomfortably warm for close work. In my rig (Figure 2-23) I have a frosted 75W bulb on the left and a bare 100W filament on the right. Your mileage may vary – try different combinations until you hit on a winner, but be careful not to exceed the lamp manufacturer's power limit. Also note that many jurisdictions are phasing out high-powered incandescent bulbs on ecological grounds. You might want to stock up, but even if they are no longer available in your region you can, like me, find such bulbs on the Internet.

A Clean, Well-Lighted Place

Although critically important, localized lighting represents only one visual aspect of your workspace. Ambient conditions, including room lighting, wall coverings, etc. also play a role. You see much more than just the light bulb when examining facets. For this reason, I find that an unfrosted bulb in an otherwise darkened room produces best results for hunting down those final, faint scratches.

To improve visibility, I always keep a small piece of white paper towel close to hand. Not only does this allow a quick swipe of the facet prior to inspection, but also moving the paper around brings different reflection conditions into play for maximum visibility of meet points and remaining scratches (see page 125 for more about paper towels).

You may also want to think about the decor around your workbench. I initially had a bright, multi-colour flag hanging on the wall above my faceting machine, but it soon became apparent that the presence of a changing coloured background was negatively affecting my ability to assess facets. The current interior decoration in my clean, well-lighted place?

Nada.

4.9 Lap Accessories

4.9.1 Dressing Sticks

A clean lap is a sharp lap, and a sharp lap produces steady, satisfying results. Perhaps as early as your first few stones, however, you will notice a change in performance of your cutting laps. Two things are happening. First, the sharpest exposed diamonds on a new lap will have worn or abraded away. This is a good thing, part of the "breaking in" process. The second effect is a general slowing of the cutting action due to build up of stone residue, dop wax, and generalized glop on the surface of the lap. This is a bad thing, but there are plenty of ways to deal with it.

Perhaps the most important of lap accessories is good old H_2O. You can avoid much of the problem of swarf buildup with a proper flow of water from your drip tank. A quick going-over in the sink with a non-metallic scrubbing pad can also be a great help. Occasionally, you may be forced to cut away a fair amount of dop wax while forming the girdle of your gem. This leaves a brownish (or blackish or greenish – see Section 4.1.1) ring of dop wax on the periphery of your lap. Soaking the affected areas for several minutes in a puddle of alcohol, followed by a wipe with a clean paper towel, should eliminate the problem.

If these modest efforts at lap maintenance do not give satisfaction, it may be time for more aggressive measures. Lapidary supply houses offer sintered boron carbide dressing sticks to rejuvenate diamond cutting laps.

Boron carbide is such an amazing material that it deserves a very brief side bar for the material science fans out there. Lightweight and tough, boron carbide is an essential ingredient in the manufacture of tank armor, padlocks, nuclear reactors, and bulletproof vests. It also scores an impressive 9.3 on the Mohs hardness scale, leaving just about everything outside of diamond in the dust (literally).

Available under the brand name Norbide among others, boron carbide dressing sticks re-sharpen your lap by scrubbing away some of the metal matrix and diamond, exposing a fresh layer below. This rejuvenation comes at a price, however. Most metal bonded laps can only stand a few such treatments before the entire surface layer is worn away. Sintered laps are an entirely different matter: their thicker layer of diamond and metal allows regular sharpening with a dressing stick. See Chapter 3.2.3 for a discussion of metal bonded versus sintered laps.

Figure 4-14 A commercial dressing stick for re-sharpening laps.

Note that you can also use a boron carbide dressing stick to prepare and charge ceramic laps. Coupled with the diamond abrasive, the hard substrate of the stick knocks down all the ridges and machining marks of a new ceramic lap, speeding the "breaking-in" process considerably. The edge of a Norbide stick also makes an excellent tool for distributing bort across the lap, effectively taking the role of the razor blade in the description of charging ceramic laps in Chapter 8.14.

Dressing sticks aren't cheap – typically $50 or more – but investing in one will be worthwhile if it can rescue each of your $150 cutting laps a few times over. On the other hand, you may choose to just let your cutting laps get duller and duller. The gentle cutting action of a gracefully aged cutting lap can be a major boon (see page 316).

4.9.2 Lap Containers

This type of lap accessory is the most important (along with water, of course). Laps spend only a tiny fraction of their lives spinning around on your faceting machine. The remainder of the time, they sit around accumulating dust, grit, and abrasive particles from their fellow laps. As my grandmother used to say, it's the idle time that can lead to problems.

At a bare minimum, you should store your laps separately, in other words, not touching, and vertically, for example in a dish rack. This is the bare minimum, and given the stakes involved, arguably a reckless minimum. Custom lap containers cost a few dollars each (Figure 4-15). Suitable zip lock bags cost a few pennies each. Use them.

Figure 4-15 Custom lap containers provide convenient, safe storage for your valuable laps. Note how labeling both halves of the container can help reduce the possibility of confusion and contamination.

4.9.3 Scoring and Embedding Tools

Two other types of lap accessory, namely scoring and embedding tools, may find their way onto your workbench. The scoring tool produces regular ridges and gullies in a metal polishing lap, the theory being that such surface features can better hold the polishing compound and provide a safe place for cutting residue to hide. Many faceters point an accusing finger at balled-up stone fragments and excess polishing compound when unwelcome scratches appear. It should be noted, however, that such accusations and even the practice of scoring are not without controversy. Turn to page 328 for more on this.

The embedding tool does exactly what its name implies – it embeds. Specifically, an embedding tool is a hardened metal roller used to push diamond particles into the surface of a metal polishing lap. It can also be used to flatten out any extremes of topography left by the scoring process. Happily, the practice of embedding is completely uncontroversial.

Both types of tool – scoring and embedding – are available as commercial products, but both functions can be accomplished with bits and pieces you probably already have in your workshop. A section of hacksaw blade is an excellent scoring tool, and a standard ball bearing or chunk of synthetic corundum does a great job of embedding diamond (see Chapters 3.2.2 and 8.14).

4.10 Logbook

You should own and use a logbook to keep track of exactly what is going on while you facet. This includes noting down the angle, height, and cheater settings, particularly if you have to adjust things slightly at the pre-polish phase. It is no fun hunting around again for the correct cheater adjustment once you get to the final polish. You should also record unusual circumstances – inclusions, slight cutting errors, etc. – for later reference.

The laboratory type notebooks are an excellent choice. Chapter 8.8 shows one way of keeping track.

Old School

Chapter 15 attempts to convey a sense of the impact of personal computers on society in general and on the gem-cutting hobby in particular. However, to fully appreciate how profoundly the world has changed, I encourage you to visit a local university or community college and sit through a lecture.

Gone are the days of students hunched over their papers, desperately scratching away in an effort to capture the professor's fleeting ideas presented using only voice and chalk. In all likelihood, you will see a computerized graphical presentation and a room full of students tapping away on laptop computers or tablets.

Despite my admiration – and use – of such technologies, I believe that the faceter's workshop emphatically remains the exclusive domain of the (paper) notebook and pencil. Independent of the wisdom of having your laptop bathed in a spray of water and cutting residue, it is simply not yet practical, for example, to execute a quick sketch on the computer showing the location of an internal veil.

4.11 Machine Add-Ons and Accessories

In their well-intentioned effort to improve the experience of cutting and polishing gemstones, the faceting machine manufacturers have developed and marketed a remarkable array of add-ons and accessories. Some of these add important functionality, while others are a mere convenience. The following paragraphs briefly describe some of these doo-dads, but your specific machine manufacturer, combined with opinion from online discussion groups, will be a better source of information.

4.11.1 Dial Indicators

Most faceting machines support either a hard stop or soft stop angle mechanism to prevent over cutting. While opinions vary on the benefits of each type, with an add-on dial indicator, you can bring soft stop goodness to your hard stop machine. The exact way to accomplish this will vary from machine to machine. See Chapter 2.4 to learn more about angle stops.

4.11.2 Pre-Forming Tools

This category of accessory encompasses a variety of mechanisms to assist in pre-forming gem rough into non-round shapes. These devices range from simple offset dops for grinding oval and marquise outlines to complex hinged cams with templates for standard sizes and shapes.

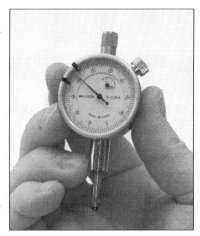

Figure 4-16 An add-on dial indicator can add soft-stop capability to a hard-stop machine.

I have never needed or used a pre-forming tool. I tend to cut more valuable gem materials, which, given my limited financial resources, translates directly to smaller and more carefully selected (i.e. well-formed) pieces of rough. The advent of meet point techniques for establishing gem outlines has also largely eliminated the need for pre-forming tools. Chapter 17 describes these methods in detail. Like me, you may find that a 360, 600 or 1200 bonded lap may be the only pre-form tool you ever use. See page 291 for more.

4.11.3 Quill Sweepers and Rotators

Also known as an *oscillator*, the quill sweeper automatically swings the dop and gem back and forth across the rotating lap. In other words, once things are set up, you can just sit back and watch. The rotator performs the same function for quill rotation, turning the process of free-wheel pre-forming into yet another spectator sport. Chapter 8.3.2 explains free-wheel pre-forming.

While they may be suitable for commercial production, I believe that these accessories miss the mark somewhat in terms of faceting as a hobby. I *like* to hold and sweep my gemstones. That is kind of the whole point. You will also miss the tactile feedback that warns of impending problems with such devices.

4.11.4 Girdle Rests

The girdle rest provides a rigid and stable support for the quill while cutting at 90°. This reduces machine flexure and leads to more accurate gemstones. Such stability and accuracy are particularly important for designs which depend on an initial girdle cut to establish the proper outline (see Chapter 17.2). However, most modern cutting prescriptions build on an initial center point and rely on meet points for an accurate girdle. GeM101 in Chapter 5 is an example, and Chapter 17 discusses this issue further. Nevertheless, if you have difficulty cutting consistent girdles on your machine, a girdle rest mechanism may be the ticket. Look for high quality construction and an easy and repeatable means of adjusting the height of the rest.

4.11.5 Depth of Cut Indicators

In addition to the hard or soft stop, some faceting machines offer the option of a depth of cut indicator. In its basic form, this is a simple electric circuit which closes and sends a signal – either light or sound – when the quill makes contact with an electrode on the stop mechanism. Minor height variations in every lap will cause momentary on and off contact just as the quill reaches the final cutting angle. A simple mechanical damper, such as the needle of an analog meter, smooths out the flickering current and provides a reliable and repeatable indicator of depth of cut. Alternatively, a matched resistor-capacitor circuit can provide electrical damping (see Chapter 20.7.2). More sophisticated indicators use strain gauges to monitor both the cutting angle and hand pressure.

Although they are commercially available, constructing your own home-brew device is relatively straightforward and fun. I soldered together my first depth of cut indicator in about ten minutes from an inexpensive voltmeter module, some wire, a battery, alligator clips, and about five cents worth of additional electrical components. Chapter 20.7 shows how you can do the same. My current indicator is a hardware and software add-on to the digital optical angle encoder described in Chapter 20.8.

4.11.6 Digital Angle Indicators

Modern gemstone designs, particularly those that depend on the meet point technique, usually call for cutting angle accuracy of 0.1° or better. The need for greater accuracy, say 0.01°, is a matter of debate (see "Sufficient Accuracy" opposite), but there is no question that you will experience heartache and pain if you can't hit your target angles to within a tenth or two of a degree.

For an analog protractor with a radius of 2 inches (50 mm), a tenth of a degree corresponds to markings at the periphery that are 3 one-thousandths of an inch (88 microns) apart. That is about the width of a typical human hair. Yes, vernier systems exist that can in principle manage this accuracy, but they can be uncomfortable and difficult to use.

The solution? A *digital angle indicator*. Available as standard equipment on a number of premium faceting machines, a digital angle indicator greatly simplifies the setting of cutting angles. It also eliminates the frustrating syndrome of dialing in an angle precisely one, five, or ten degrees different from that called for in the design (this is a "can't see the forest for the trees" situation: focusing on getting the fine vernier markings to line up, you fail to realize that you are not on the correct whole angle setting...).

Almost all commercially available digital angle indicators use precision *potentiometers*, a fancy word for variable resistors, coupled to an accurate metering system. These indicators work well, but they can be sensitive to thermal and electrical drifts that limit both their accuracy and precision to less than the advertised amount (see page 392 of Volume 2 for a complete discussion of accuracy versus precision).

For the ultimate in performance, look for a "true" digital angle indicator based on an optical encoder. These devices use light sensors and imprinted disks with alternating black and transparent zones. Measuring an angle is then simply a matter of counting the zones as the disks rotate past the sensor. As you can imagine, this process is immune to thermal and electrical changes. At least two faceting machine manufacturers offer true digital encoder-based angle indicators, and the response of users has been very positive (see Chapter 2.8).

Unfortunately, commercial encoder-based indicators can cost almost as much as an entire low-end faceting machine, putting them well outside the budget of many hobbyists, including me. As a result, I designed and built my own optical-encoder-based angle indicator that achieves absolute rock-steady accuracy and precision better than 0.05°. The cost of parts was about a tenth of the asking price of commercial units. Want to give it a try yourself? Chapter 20.8 contains complete instructions.

4.11.7 Saw blade adapters

Every hobby gem cutter has experienced the anguish of grinding away a great deal of valuable gem rough at the pre-forming phase. It literally almost hurts to see all that beautiful, expensive material disappearing down the drain of your splash pan, and this agony is not decreased by the knowledge that the additional wear and tear is shortening the life of your expensive cutting lap.

You begin to develop an unnatural longing for a proper trim saw (page 128). With such a machine, you could save and use the chopped-off bits of gem rough and reduce lap wear as well. But trim saws are expensive, and it can be difficult to make precision cuts with the stone hand-held or glued to a piece of wooden dowel.

A saw blade adapter can help eliminate this pain and longing. Again, the exact configuration will vary from manufacturer to manufacturer, but all saw blade adapters share the function of attaching a standard 4-6 inch (10-15 cm) diamond saw blade to the platen of your faceting machine. You can then use the precise angle, height, and index controls to achieve the perfect cut.

Commercial adapters exist, but it is by no means necessary to spend money on anything more than the saw blade. I use a couple of old CD-ROMS and large washers to hold my saw blade in place (see "Sawing Rough on Your Faceting Machine" on page 294).

Sufficient Accuracy

How good is good enough?

Essentially all modern faceting diagrams quote cutting angles to a tenth or even a hundredth of a degree. Is this accuracy necessary or even possible?

The answers to these questions are a qualified yes and a definite yes, respectively.

Let's deal with the second question first. As Chapter 20.8.3 makes clear, commercial and homebuilt encoders can easily achieve 0.1° accuracy or better. Case closed, as long as you are ready to make the financial or time investment.

Is it worth it? Achieving 0.1° accuracy is unquestionably necessary for some gem designs, particularly those with adjacent facets at close angle and index settings. Figure 16-33 shows a concrete example for which cutting errors of order 0.1° produce unacceptable results. For most designs, however, 0.1° accuracy is more than enough, and almost all gem cuts are amenable to tweaking at the polishing stage.

Of course, in all of these discussions, you must keep clear the distinction between accuracy and precision, a topic which Chapter 20.8 discusses in detail. The short version is that accuracy measures how close to the *correct* answer you get, while precision relates to how consistently you end up with the *same* answer. In the case of the closely spaced facets from the previous paragraph, precision counts more than accuracy. In other words, as long as you get the relative angle between adjacent facets close to the correct value, you will be in good shape.

If a tenth of a degree accuracy is sufficient, why do all those diagrams quote angles to a hundredth?

Great question. The masterful gem designer, Jeff Graham, had a great answer. Three, actually. First, some machines are more accurate than others, and the design should not penalize those who can do a better job of dialing in angles. Second, commercial faceting machines are unquestionably improving with time. The emerging availability of absolute encoders is a vivid demonstration of this. The prescription should therefore foresee better hardware. Finally, it is always a good idea to carry around a few more digits than you actually need, since a number of processes reduce the delivered accuracy. Round-off errors are an obvious example. Dialing in 42.05° on an otherwise perfect machine with 0.1° markings will result in some error. Tangent ratio scaling is another instance in which manipulating the numbers – this time mathematically – can lose accuracy through round-off.

4.12 Polishing Compounds

Here's where the rubber meets the road, or perhaps more appropriately, the stone meets the lap. Or even more appropriately, where the stone meets the polishing agent. Hand-charged laps, and even worn-out permanently charged laps, need polishing compound for the magic to happen.

Chapter 8.11 explains how polishing actually works, or at least our best current understanding of the microphysics involved. Polishing on a faceting machine involves dispersing some compound, either by hand or in the manufacturing phase, over the surface of the lap prior to use. The actual compound used depends on the gemstone material, the type of polishing lap, and perhaps most importantly of all, the experience, taste, and prejudices of the faceter.

This section provides an overview of the two main polishing compounds in use by amateur faceters: the metal oxides and diamond bort. Note that Chapter 8.14 explains how to charge a lap with these agents.

> ## Invisibly Small
>
> All polishing compounds, whether they be metal oxides or diamond grit, consist of small abrasive particles, whose size range from about 1 micron (14,000 mesh – see Table 3-1) down to 0.1 micron (200,000 mesh). It is no coincidence that these dimensions correspond roughly to the wavelength of visible light (0.5 micron for green light). In classical polishing theory, an abrasive particle will produce micro-scratches and other surface features of a size comparable to that of the grit itself, and it is a consequence of the wave nature of light that photons cannot "see" structures that are smaller than a wavelength ("Ultimate Accuracy" on page 306 explores this phenomenon as well). In other words, tiny grit particles will produce invisibly small scratches.
>
> Yes, things are actually a bit more complicated. Chapter 8.11 provides further gory detail.

4.12.1 Metal Oxides

With the exception of diamond, which is pure carbon, all of the common polishing compounds happen to be oxides of metal. This does not mean that they are all similar: for example, cerium oxide has Mohs hardness 6, while aluminum oxide has hardness 9.

Many metal oxide compounds have been tried over the years. Among the more interesting varieties is *jeweler's rouge*, which is iron oxide – Fe_2O_3 to chemists, plain old rust to you and me. Rouge was the most important lapidary agent in the past, and it also played a crucial role in the fabrication of optics. Amateur telescope builders inevitably have fond memories of the terrible mess and red-stained hands that resulted from polishing with rouge. Chrome oxide was a festive alternative, producing a green stain that was almost impossible to remove from skin and clothing alike. Another oddball compound was *tripoli*, also endearingly known as *rotten stone*. Tripoli is pure silica (SiO_2), often in the form of fossilized ancient algae. Tin oxide was popular in the past, but nowadays, its use is largely restricted to cabochon cutters. This development has helped those of us who readily get confused. No longer is there a choice between tin oxide on an aluminum lap and aluminum oxide on a tin lap…

Despite this great (and occasionally alarming) variety, only two compounds, cerium oxide and alumina, dominate the current field of metal oxide polishes. Chrome oxide and zirconium oxide find occasional use for particular gemstone species, and there are new approaches to minimizing the classic problems of staining and mess – see page 76.

Cerium Oxide (CeO_2)

Cerium oxide is a pale yellow-white or pink powder that has largely replaced rouge as the primary polishing agent in the optics industry. CeO_2 is widely available from lapidary supply houses. Note, however, that there are two grades of cerium oxide in common use, the so-called "optical cerium," a reddish-pink powder which is 90% pure, and the top grade type, which is almost white and 99.9% pure. Users have complained of scratching with the 90% cerium. The higher purity version produces much better results at only marginally increased cost, so go for the top grade here.

Cerium is the polish of choice for quartz, beryl, tourmaline, opal, and many soft stones. You can use CeO_2 with all types of polishing lap except ceramic.

Alumina (Al_2O_3)

Alumina polishing agent is the powdered form of that ubiquitous and seemingly miraculous material, Al_2O_3. Not only is aluminum oxide among the most treasured of gemstone materials, namely ruby and sapphire, but also it has proved amazingly useful in a variety of high tech applications ranging from hip replacement components to superconducting quantum devices. It also happens to be a great abrasive.

Alumina polishing compound is a whitish powder consisting of finely graded Al_2O_3 particles. Check the manufacturer's specification for the actual grit size. "Alumina A" should contain 0.3 micron (100,000 mesh) particles, while "Alumina B" is roughly 5-10 times finer. The "B" material produces a better polish according to some, but its considerably slower action has limited its use to softer and specialty stones. Beware of unmarked, and particularly non-white batches of alumina. These are often cabochon grade abrasives, which will produce unacceptable scratching on your gems.

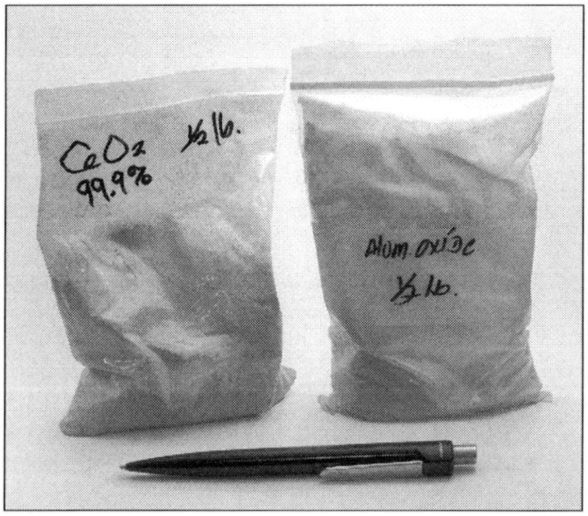

Figure 4-17 Cerium oxide (left) and alumina A polishing compound. In both cases, insist on the highest quality, faceting-grade material.

Lapidary alumina is often referred to by the trade name of Linde, a leading manufacturer. Thus, Linde A and Linde B have become synonymous with Alumina A and Alumina B. Alumina is used primarily on garnet, tourmaline, topaz, peridot, spinel and beryl. Like cerium oxide, alumina works well with both metal and plastic/composite laps.

The metal oxide polishing compounds are a very good value, given the investment needed in other aspects of our hobby. Expect to pay roughly $20 per pound ($44 / kg) for top-of-the-line cerium oxide, and roughly 2-3 times that amount for Alumina A. Such quantities will last for many years, even for the most ambitious of amateurs.

4.12.2 Diamond Bort

As the hardest of all natural substances, diamond is the one polishing agent to turn to when lesser materials break down and fail. Diamond powder, known as *bort* (or occasionally *boart*) may be either natural or synthetic. Surprisingly, the synthetic form of diamond powder is usually more expensive than its natural cousin, but the added cost can easily pay for itself. First, natural diamonds come in a huge variety of sizes and shapes, and you are depending on the manufacturer to not miss a single outsized crystal in his shipment of bort. Size and shape control is considerably easier with synthetics. Second, the synthetic powders include so-called *friable* diamond. This material is designed to maintain its sharpness even as the diamond particles break apart with use. Natural octagonal diamond crystals tend to get rounded but not break. Note, however, that only the hardest polishing laps – ceramic and composite – can take full advantage of the friable property of top grade synthetic diamond. The smaller, albeit still sharp, broken pieces of friable diamond will embed themselves and disappear into the surface of a softer metal lap or be washed away.

Most amateurs will use 3,000 or 8,000 grit diamond for pre-polishing and a 50,000 mesh for final polish. For that competition-grade finish, try 100,000 or even 200,000. Note however, that unlike with the oxides, it is a very, very bad idea to mix different diamond compounds on the same lap. Use separate mesh sizes on each (clearly identified) side of your metal lap, or better still, use separate laps for different grades of diamond.

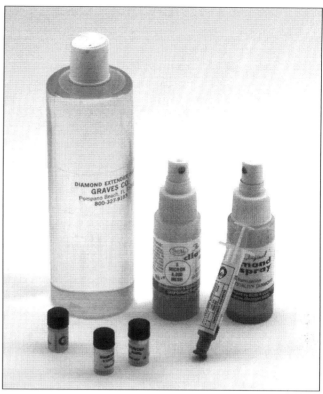

Figure 4-18 Diamond bort in powder form (small jars), slurry (spray bottles), and paste form (syringe). The large container on the left holds extender fluid, used for lubricating the abrasive.

Diamond can polish almost any gemstone, although it is most widely used (and necessary) for the harder materials, such as corundum, chrysoberyl, and cubic zirconia. All of the metal laps, as well as ceramic and the harder composite laps, can be used with diamond.

Lapidary diamond bort is available as a powder sold in small jars, or as a slurry or paste pre-mixed with an appropriate carrier (Figure 4-18). See Chapter 8.14 for detailed instructions on using each type. Most manufacturers have adopted a standard colour code for pre-mixed slurry – see Table 4-4.

Unlike the metal oxide polishing agents, which are sold by the pound, diamond polish comes in small 1-5 carat (0.2 – 1 gram) portions. They are diamonds, after all. Expect to pay $2-3 per carat for top quality bort. A single, 5-carat container should last for dozens of stones.

Table 4-4 Standardized colour coding for diamond bort in slurry form. Note that the entries below include mesh sizes for both cutting and polishing.

Mesh Size	Particle Size (µm)	Colour Code	Mesh Size	Particle Size (µm)	Colour Code
325	40-60	brown	14,000	0-2	cream
600	22-36	red	50,000	0-1	gray
1,200	10-20	blue	100,000	0-0.5	
3,000	4-8	orange	200,000	0-0.25	
8,000	2-4	yellow			

Not a "Real" Polish

Believe it or not, hobby faceters engage in friendly arguments about polishing compounds as well.

In fact, the divide between the oxide users and the diamond users is almost as deep and impenetrable as that between the wax doppers and the glue doppers (see Chapter 7.2). Yes, everyone agrees that diamonds are the way to go with sapphire, and cerium oxide will work better with quartz, but ask which is better for tourmaline or garnet and then watch the fur fly.

The standard complaint against diamond is that it produces a "greasy" finish, perhaps due to the many ultra-fine scratches that it leaves. In fact, in *Faceting for Amateurs*, referred to elsewhere in this book as "The Bible," Glenn and Martha Vargas memorably opine that "anything produced by diamond must be viewed as not a true polish." Oxides, on the other hand, may lead to non-flat facets, largely because they don't work well on the hardest laps, such as ceramic. Oxides can also produce a terrific mess in your work area, even if they no longer leave you with red or green fingers (see page 113).

How should the beginner deal with these conflicting opinions? It's easy…try both types of polishing agent and use what works best for you. In fact, there is a significant and growing constituency in the faceting community which argues that using both diamond and oxide on a single gem produces better results than either alone. Several of the masters suggest that the way to perfect polish involves starting with diamond to produce an ultra-flat facet with sharp edges, followed by a "kiss" of oxide to pop in the ultimate surface finish.

4.13 Protective Gear

Is faceting safe?

Compared to other hobbies and activities, the answer is unquestionably yes, but cutting and polishing gemstones is not without hazard. We are, after all, using some high-speed machinery to grind away rock. We also tend to play around with very flammable solvents and open flame, as well as high current motors and water spray.

It goes without saying that you should follow conventional safety procedures when faceting. The following table lists some potential risks and their countermeasures.

The last item is a sensitive and serious topic. For example, every few months, someone in the online discussion groups raises the issue of faceting uranium glass (also known as Vaseline glass), which is a lovely yellowish green. Unfortunately, it is also radioactive. Most uranium glass is harmless if used normally. Here, "used normally" means looking at a bunch of flowers in a glass vase, not grinding the stuff up into dust and breathing it (see also page 149 of Volume 2). If in any doubt about the safety of your gem rough, read the Material Safety Data Sheet (MSDS), consult reliable online sources, and wear a mask. Better yet, find something else to cut.

Independent of the gem material, you should always use plenty of water to keep the dust down.

Table 4-5 *Faceting hazards and their countermeasures.*

Hazard	Countermeasure
Injury while grinding or using a rock saw	Protective hand and eye gear, dopping to a wooden dowel.
Injury while cutting and polishing	Exercise care, particularly when reversing lap direction. Don't reach into the gap between the lap and splash pan. Avoid loose clothing and jewelry while working.
Injury while dopping	Take extra care with razor blades. Always cut in a direction away from body parts. Try to keep your hands above molten or dripping wax.
Inhalation of fumes from solvents, epoxy resins, etc.	Work in a well-ventilated area.
Skin irritation due to solvents, burns, etc.	Rubber gloves or other suitable protection. Moisturizer.
Fire (dop wax, solvents,…)	Work on a fireproof surface. Remove nearby flammable items (curtains, etc.). Obtain (and maintain!) a suitable fire extinguisher.
Electrocution	Inspect motor wiring regularly. Use low voltage DC motors only. Don't allow water spray near electrical equipment.
Eyestrain, repetitive motion injury	Take frequent breaks. Use adjustable seating and lighting.
Inhalation of rock dust	Suitable mask over nose and mouth. Use plenty of water.

4.14 Scales

Your eyes should not be the only judge of your progress as a faceter. As you gain experience, you will undoubtedly begin trying more expensive gem materials. At ten or more dollars per carat, *yield* suddenly becomes at least as important as looks. A set of precision scales will let you monitor how much weight retention you are achieving, as well as set a fair price for any gems you choose to sell. They will also let you verify the honesty of your rough dealers, at least after the fact (see page 200)

Having made the decision to spring for a set of precision scales, you are immediately confronted with the next question: how precise? You should also be asking how accurate? (see page 392 of Volume 2).

Manufacturers of commercial scales offer a huge range of products spanning the gamut from pocketable devices the size of a hand calculator up to laboratory grade instruments capable of measuring to a tenth of a microgram. They also span the price range corresponding to two movie tickets plus popcorn all the way up to a pretty decent luxury automobile. How to choose?

The short answer is that you should purchase as much accuracy as you can afford, within reason. And the good news is that, as with calipers (see below), technological advances and market forces have driven down the price of precision scales in recent years. For almost all purposes, a specified measurement accuracy of 0.05 carat (0.01 g) will be more than enough. Such a device should set you back less than the cost of three carats of good tourmaline rough, about $30-40. For approximately double that amount, you could move up to a set of scales with 0.01 carat (0.002 g) accuracy.

When you go shopping, you will notice a relatively standardized way of specifying performance in terms of maximum capacity and accuracy. For example, a manufacturer may offer a set of scales for $30 with the specification "50x0.01 g". This means that the device can measure objects up to 50 g with 0.01 g accuracy. Although at the bottom end of commercial scales in terms of maximum weight capacity, fifty grams is a lot of gem rough, and the 0.01 g accuracy should be fine.

In addition to capacity and accuracy, there are a couple of other features you should look for in a set of precision scales. Portability can be an important factor if you want to take your measurements on the road (but see page 200). Also, the ability to switch between grams, carats, and other units (ounces, pennyweight, etc.) is a definite plus. The device should have a "Tare" button, allowing you to zero the scales. This lets you compensate for small drifts and offsets,

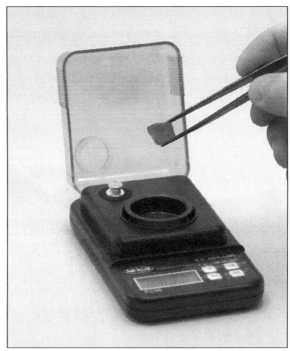

Figure 4-19 My precision scales can measure up to 50 carats (10 g) of gem rough with an accuracy of 0.01 carat (0.002 g). Note the calibration weight stored next to the measuring tray.

and occasionally, you may want to measure something *differentially* – for example, weighing an empty container and then weighing it again with something in it. Finally, premium scales may ship with a calibration weight on board (see Figure 4-19). This lets you quickly verify proper performance.

Incidentally, you can use your precision scales to do more than just weigh things. Chapter 20.2 explains how to build a simple gizmo that, combined with your scales, lets you evaluate the density of gem rough.

4.15 Tabling Adapter

It's a simple mechanical fact. Faceting machines do not like to cut at very low angles, that is, when the quill is almost vertical.

There are very good physical reasons for this, which Chapter 5.8 explains in detail. It all has to do with force vectors and machine flexure and so forth, and things unquestionably get worse closer to vertical. The upshot of the situation is that most machine manufacturers provide an adapter to help you cut and polish the table at 0°.

These adapters take many forms (Figure 4-20), but they all share a common, simple function. By introducing an additional 45° bend, the tabling adapter lets you work at a much more comfortable 45° cutting angle.

Note that the strategy for fine-tuning the gem orientation is subtly different with the tabling adapter in place. Typically, you will leave the index wheel alone and adjust the cutting angle and cheater settings to ensure that things are coming in correctly. Again, turn to Chapter 5.8 for more detail.

As with all your equipment, you should look for high quality in a tabling adapter. Pay particular attention to ease of use and alignment. For example, some adapters have a flat surface that you can match with the surface of a lap to ensure that everything is square (Figure 5-76). Note, however, that it is not terribly important that the adapter be machined to exactly 45°, since the normal alignment and angle adjustment procedures that you execute while working on the table will account for any minor offsets.

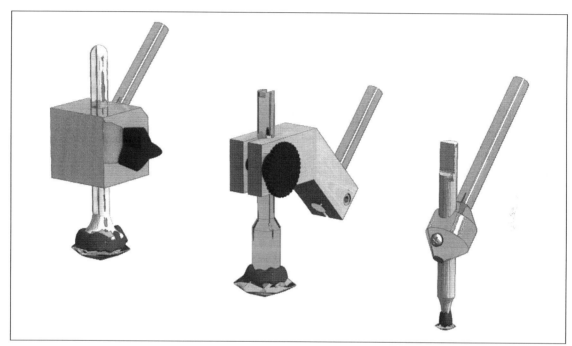

Figure 4-20 Tabling adapters let you cut and polish the table near 45°.

4.16 Transfer Jig

Establishing and maintaining alignment of the stone with respect to the faceting machine is at the heart of gem cutting success. Chapters 5.6 and 7.3.2 explain why. Given a decent machine and a carefully maintained logbook (see Chapter 8.8), you should be able to navigate the dangerous waters of gemstone alignment, as long as the dop and stone stay in place.

There is one critical phase of faceting when the gem must leave the aligned and secure confines of the machine, however. This dangerous time is the *dop transfer*.

Fear not! There is an essential tool, called the *transfer jig*, which can help you in this time of peril. The transfer jig is a precision device for holding two dop sticks exactly concentric, while allowing at least one dop to slide along its length to bring the stone and second dop into contact.

Here's how the transfer jig assists in the handover from one side of the gem to the other. With the first half of the stone – conventionally the pavilion – complete, remove the dop from the faceting machine and lock it in one side of the transfer jig. Prepare and install the second dop stick on the other side. When you are ready, that is when your favourite adhesive has been prepared, bring the stone and target dop together to complete the transfer. Chapters 5.6 and 7.3.2 provide all the gruesome details.

Like the tabling adapters, transfer jigs take many forms, but share a simple function, as outlined in the previous paragraph. Figure 4-21 illustrates two variations on the basic design, while Figure 4-22 shows a third configuration and labels its essential components. As with the faceting machine itself, build quality and precision are

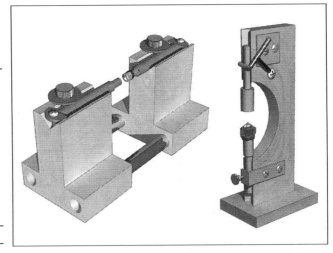

Figure 4-21 Two common configurations of transfer jig.

the most important qualities in a transfer jig. Additional features you should look for include a compatible dop keying system (see Section 4.4) and heat proof components. The latter is essential for dopping with wax, since many of your open-flame activities will take place with the transfer jig front and center.

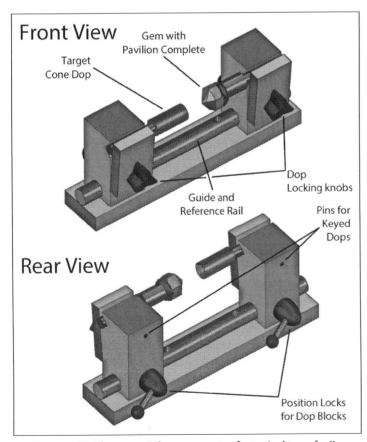

Front View
Gem with Pavilion Complete
Target Cone Dop
Dop Locking knobs
Guide and Reference Rail
Pins for Keyed Dops
Rear View
Position Locks for Dop Blocks

Figure 4-22 The essential components of a typical transfer jig.

A final, less obvious feature of some transfer jigs is the ability to work with the dops arranged either horizontally or vertically (Figure 4-23). This can be an enormous help in both applying the adhesive and in aligning the rough for maximum yield. In fact, I end up using my jig for all kinds of things beyond its designed purpose of dop transfer.

Unlike other accessories, you will more than likely receive a transfer jig with your faceting machine. This does not mean that you shouldn't consider an upgrade. Sadly, the transfer jigs supplied by some manufacturers are, frankly, crap. A precision jig based on accurate steel rails and slides will run about $100-$250. Given the endless headaches induced by a poor transfer, this is a good investment.

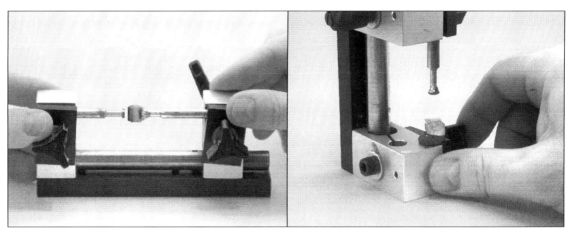

Figure 4-23 This transfer jig from Poly-Metric works well either horizontally or vertically.

The Jig is Up (or Down or Left or Right)

It should be clear to you by now that a faulty or misaligned transfer jig will lead to disaster. If you find that you need an inordinate amount of cheating to bring in the facets on the second half of your gemstones, you may have a problem.

There is a relatively simple test to check the quality and alignment of your transfer jig. Take two dop sticks of the same diameter, for example a matched flat and cone dop. Install them as usual in the transfer jig and bring their ends together.

There should be no detectable misalignment at the contact point between the two dops. Run your fingernail up and down the sides of the dops. Are there any abrupt systematic jumps? If so, your jig may need to be checked. Rotate one of the dops with respect to the other and repeat the test.

Of course, bent dops can also produce misalignment, so double check any non-uniformity with a second (or third) pair of dops. And yes, this is an excellent way of checking for bent dops as well (see Section 4.4.4).

4.17 Miscellaneous

You will need and acquire a number of additional accessories and tools as you progress as a faceter. This section deals with these miscellaneous items, again alphabetically, and gives an idea of their cost and importance. Turn to Section 4.18 for some ideas on organizing all your stuff.

Brushes – Essential for Oxide Polishes

Mixing and spreading oxide polish can make a mess. Correction. Mixing and spreading oxide polish *will* make a mess. Small artists brushes can help. Having a brush at hand simplifies the process of adding polishing compound to the lap and keeps your fingers (and everything else) clean. Given the minor investment, you should have a separate brush for each type of compound (cerium oxide, alumina,…), and don't forget to store them separately. Zip lock bags are a good choice. For more, see Chapter 8.14.2.

Calipers – Essential

Gemstone size is often at least as important as weight. For example, if you are producing a replacement gem for an existing setting or cutting for competition, you will need to know very precisely how big your stone is. Also, some gem designs require a pre-form with a fixed length-to-width ratio. Fritz15 in Chapter 19 is an example. Cutting an accurate gem means measuring small distances, say 1 to 20 mm, very reliably.

Standard mechanical calipers can help you make such measurements. Two types exist: analog and digital. The more traditional analog type includes those with classic vernier scales, as well as mechanical dial displays. Digital calipers are a relatively new innovation and are at least as precise as their analog brethren. Prices for electronic calipers have dropped in recent years, and there is now little difference in cost between the analog and digital models.

Traditional calipers are made of hardened steel to ensure a long lifetime of accurate measurement. This type of steel is harder than many gemstones, so scratching or chipping is a serious concern. You should consider purchasing non-metallic calipers. These tools are fabricated from plastics, composites, or fiberglass, and they are much more gentle on your valuable gemstones. Beyond deformation due to abuse, non-metallic calipers can be just as accurate as the hardened steel variety.

Despite recent price reductions, you can always spend a great deal of money on precision measuring equipment, and calipers are no exception. Increased accuracy translates directly to increased cost, so how accurate is accurate enough?

For essentially all gem-cutting purposes, caliper accuracy need not exceed 0.1 mm. An error of this magnitude corresponds to a roughly 0.05 ct. difference in a 7 mm gem. Calipers providing this performance are not costly. A quick survey of online shops should reveal a variety of options for under $30.

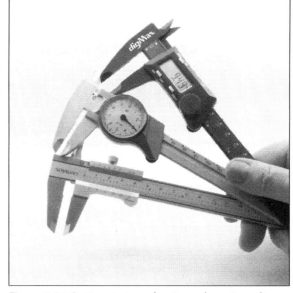

Figure 4-24 Bottom to top: classic steel vernier calipers, composite dial calipers, and composite digital calipers.

Dental Tools – Desirable

Gem work is close work, and you will frequently find yourself peering through a loupe or head-mounted magnifier, picking away at dop wax, stone chips, and various other debris. Your friendly neighbourhood dentist goes through a similar exercise each day, although hopefully dop wax and stone chips are a rare find in his or her daily oral explorations.

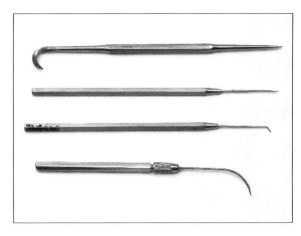

Dental implements, ranging from small blades and picks to clamps and hemostats, are a great addition to your lapidary toolbox. Expect to pay $2-$20 apiece, depending on the type of tool and where you buy it. My collection has grown slowly but steadily over the years (see Section 4.18). Now that I've mastered the ceramic lap…root canals!

Figure 4-25 Small dental tools for probing and picking at dop wax, surface dirt on gem rough, etc.

Display Boxes – Desirable

While subsequent paragraphs on setting tools and stone holders cast indirect aspersions on display boxes, nothing beats a portable case for transporting and showing off your gemstones. After all, it seems a shame to spend hours and hours transforming a lump of rock into a beautiful, sparkly gemstone, and then to wrap said gem in a piece of paper and file it in a drawer. Yes, I know that this is what the pro cutters do.

Display boxes are the solution. They allow an easy and fingerprint-free way of showing off. You can pass them around individually or in fitted cases (Figure 5-82).

I prefer the glass topped variety of gem box, simply because I find that the plastic ones scratch extraordinarily easily. Viewing a gem through scratched plastic is almost as disappointing as looking at it through fingerprints…

One other tip: I find that the boxes with white backing are unquestionably superior to those with black backing. Not only does a white background give a better sense of the true colour of the stone, but also some light will inevitably enter the gem through the pavilion and exit through the crown. Why deny your precious gemstones this added bump in brightness?

You should be able to pick up a case containing a dozen or so gem boxes for $10-20, an excellent investment. See Chapter 5.9 for more.

Dop Alignment Aids – Optional

Aligning your gemstone rough for maximum yield can be a real challenge, and it is a distressing fact of faceting life that the loss due to alignment errors grows rapidly for smaller, in other words, more expensive, gems (see Chapter 7.8) For this reason, a number of manufacturers offer dop alignment aids.

These devices use a variety of mechanisms, ranging from adjustable screws to magnets to silicone putty, all of which assist in holding the piece of gem rough at an exact location while the adhesive solidifies (see "Stone Alignment Gadgets" on page 244).

Dop alignment aids can be a real boon to your dopping technique, but be warned that they can also be surprisingly expensive. If you have difficulty getting the initial dopping step right, give them a try. High quality gem rough is also costly, and one of these alignment tools could easily pay for itself.

On the other hand, a small blob of household putty can achieve pretty much the same results (see Chapters 5.4 and 7.3.1). Most putty is not terribly heat resistant, however, so try different types until you find something that works.

There is one additional type of alignment aid known as a *target dop* or *centering dop*. These are large diameter, flat dops featuring a series of concentric circles engraved or printed on the mating surface. These markings can assist you in centering rough, particular if you need to re-attach a symmetric stone. You shouldn't use a target dop for cutting. Instead, use the guide markings for proper centering when attaching a stone to a dop held on the other side of your transfer fixture. This technique is popular among fans of the "open transfer" method (see page 256).

Dust Cover – Essential

Throughout this book, you will encounter exhortations about cleanliness and the danger of cross contamination by wayward grit particles. I'm going to do some more exhorting here.

Common household dust is surprisingly nasty for gemstones. As discussed in Chapter 12.9, quartz makes up a significant proportion of the general debris flying around our homes, and quartz is harder than many of the gem materials we polish. Nasty, harder bits will inevitably be part of the mix, particularly if your machine is in a basement workshop environment. The possibility of engendering "mystery" scratches is very real.

The simple message? Keep things clean (there's the exhorting). The easiest way to do this is to simply cover your machine when it is not in use.

Look for a well fitting cover that protects the cutting head and lap area, particularly from above. Note that you do not want a perfect seal, since humidity can build up, leading to rusting. The commercial machine manufacturers offer custom fitted covers, but you can also rig something together from cloth, shopping bags, or sheet plastic. My "custom" dust cover is a plastic bag from the University of Arizona bookstore.

Microfiber Cloths – Highly Desirable

On the mountain slopes of eastern Europe, particularly Romania, the Balkans, and the Caucasus, there wanders a species of small antelope that is breathing a bit easier these days. These charming animals, known as *Rupicapra Rupicapra* to scientists and *chamois* to you and me, used to be highly prized – and highly hunted – for the soft, absorbent leather produced from their skins.

Chamois leather is an excellent material for cleaning and polishing, as any teenager with a fancy automobile paint job can tell you. This material works wonders on gemstones as well, and a number of the classic faceting references recommend it strongly for wiping things clean during polishing.

Luckily for the Rupicapra, microfiber cloth, a development of the Japanese textile industry in the 1960's and 1970's, has largely supplanted their skins in the cleaning and polishing world. Today, you can purchase a package of microfiber cloths for a fraction of the cost of chamois leather.

I keep a microfiber cloth beside my faceting machine during polishing, particularly when using diamond. This makes it easy and quick to give the gem a swipe prior to examination under the loupe.

Note that if you use different grades of abrasive or polish, you should use and store separate cloths for each. If you are really paranoid (like me), you can even wash them separately.

Paper Towels – Essential

In addition to microfiber cloths, I always keep a roll of paper towels near my work area. This allows me to wipe down a gem during the cutting phase to examine progress. Paper towels are also ideal for doing general cleanup around the machine when changing grit sizes.

This raises a number of questions. For example, why use both paper towels *and* microfiber cloths? The answer is basically cost and disposability. Although considerably less expensive than a decade ago, good microfiber cloths are not cheap, and it pains me somewhat to clog them up with rough cutting residue. Paper towels are very inexpensive, and it causes almost no emotional stress to throw them out, particularly if you live in an area with active recycling. You can readily rip up a paper towel into pieces of the exact right size, and if, like me, you want to be really green, you can hang them up to dry and use them again (see "Go with the Flow…" on page 159). As noted below, paper towels will produce lint, which is fine at the cutting phase, but which can complicate the search for faint scratches during polishing. As a result of all this, I tend to use paper towels exclusively for cutting and microfiber cloths exclusively for polishing.

A couple of additional notes on paper towels deserve mention. First, I always use the pure white type, without a printed design. This lets me use a small corner of paper towel to both wipe the stone and to serve as a mobile source of reflected light when examining the gem with a loupe. You will be surprised at how much you can improve the visibility of scratches and meet points by moving white paper around behind the gem (see "A Clean, Well-Lighted Place" on page 105).

The second note is a cautionary one. Some experienced gem cutters warn sternly against the use of paper towels due to lint and the possible aggregation of this lint with grit and cutting residue. The idea is that such tiny balls of abrasive nastiness can ruin both your gemstones and your faceting machine. In their classic book, Broadfoot and Collins suggest in the strongest possible terms that paper towels do not belong in a faceter's workshop. I have not encountered any problems, however, and since I use bonded cutting laps exclusively, there shouldn't be much loose abrasive flying around. Nevertheless, if you encounter unexpected scratching problems, consider eliminating paper towels from your workflow.

Razor Blades / Scalpels – Essential

You will end up doing a lot of cutting while cutting, so to speak. Whether it is trimming wax after transfer, cutting dop bonds, or using a blade to apply diamond bort to a ceramic lap, the razor blade or scalpel is an essential faceter's tool.

These tools come in a variety of shapes and sizes, ranging from straight razors for removing facial hair to surgical scalpels made of titanium, ceramic, or even diamond (Figure 4-26).

Look for a comfortable, easy to use scalpel with a replaceable blade. The classic cylindrical "X-ACTO" hobby knives are another excellent option. A curved blade may make working with wax somewhat easier, but you will definitely want a straight blade as well. My toolbox contains both types.

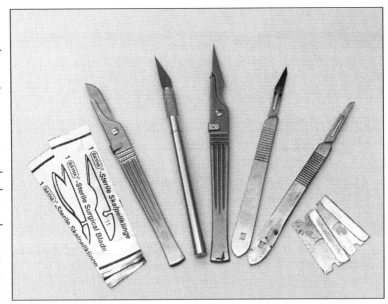

Figure 4-26 Scalpels and blades. Yes, some of these implements have been in a flame.

Note that you may find yourself heating up your razor blade or scalpel in order to cut through dop bonds, etc. This will result in extra soot and other residue on the blade. You may want to acquire a separate scalpel with spare blades for such hot work.

Setting Tools – Optional

Ask a hobby faceter friend how many stones he or she has cut, and you will likely get an answer in the hundreds. When you follow up by asking where they all ended up, there is a very good chance that the response will be something like "errr, well, I have a few display boxes on the shelf in my workshop..."

I am as guilty of this as any amateur cutter, but it doesn't have to be this way. Yes, glass-topped display boxes are a fine way of showing your handiwork to friends and family (see the remarks on display cases above, as well as Chapter 5.9), but it somehow defeats the purpose of the whole exercise to work for hours producing a tiny piece of art that magically manipulates the light in its environment, only to lock the thing away in a dark drawer.

You can get your gemstones out into the world by mounting them in jewelry. Most larger towns will have a professional jewelry shop that can do custom work, including mounting gemstones. Their services can range from adjusting pre-existing settings all the way to designing and fabricating original jewelry to hold your gems.

While I have used professional jewellers on several occasions, their efforts do not come cheap, and it is very easy to spend considerably more on the setting than on the gem rough itself.

There is an interesting alternative: mounting your own gems. A number of companies market pre-fabricated settings, also known as *findings*, and most lapidary supply houses will carry the necessary tools. Chapter 15.8.11 lists a number of online resources to help you get started.

It is well beyond the scope of this book to explain the process of mounting gemstones in jewelry, let alone the process of fabricating settings. Working with the pre-made findings is relatively straightforward, however. It is basically a process of adjusting and bending prongs (Figure 4-27). After conquering this challenge, many faceters move on to more ambitious pursuits, including soldering or casting their own custom settings.

There are multiple advantages to setting your own gemstones, beyond the obvious cost savings. First and foremost, you have done it yourself, and somehow, your having mounted the gem personally puts the icing on the creative cake of your efforts. Second, you have complete control over the process and can actively manage things to accommodate thicker girdles, non-standard sizes, odd shapes, and so forth. Finally, you will be in a position to make repairs or remount the gemstone should anything go wrong.

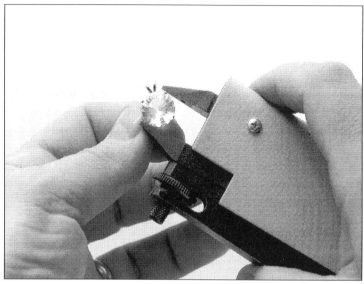

Figure 4-27 Setting tools let you easily mount your gemstones in pre-fabricated commercial findings.

Gem setting is not without its challenges, however. For example, it is quite easy to scratch the soft metal while bending the prongs, and you may not have the appropriate buffing equipment to cover your tracks. More seriously, gem-setting pliers exert a great deal of force, more than enough to literally crush most gemstones. Take extra care while setting delicate gem materials, such as those with cleavage planes.

Small Jars and Squeeze / Spray Bottles – Essential

Back in the day, they actually served meals on airline flights. Hard to believe, I know, but they did. One of the highlights for me on overnight flights was breakfast, because they handed out jam and marmalade in small, glass jars.

Why get so worked up about jam? Well, the jars that it came in were perfect for my faceting workshop, and I ended up using them a lot. You should accumulate your own supply. Whether to clean stones, store oxide polishes, or mix up alcohol-shellac (Section 4.3.1), you will covet and hoard small glass jars.

Spray bottles are equally useful, particularly if you use oxide polishes or diamond bort on a ceramic lap. I have yet to find an airline which hands them out with breakfast, however. Check your local hardware store or pharmacy.

Stone holders (3-4 prong) – Desirable

To heck with their uniqueness and swirling, individual beauty, I hate fingerprints. Nothing ruins the appearance of a finely polished gemstone like skin oil, so if you want to show off your handiwork outside of a display case, you will need stone holders.

These devices are available in a variety of shapes and sizes, and I have seen them in three, four, and (occasionally) five prong models (Figure 4-28). This diversity is important: because stone holders grip the gem very firmly, it can be qualitatively more difficult to pick up a stone if the prongs don't match its symmetry. For example, you will go crazy trying to grab and display a trilliant gemstone with a four-prong holder.

Note that almost all gem holders are constructed of steel and / or other hard metals. Exercise appropriate caution with softer gem materials.

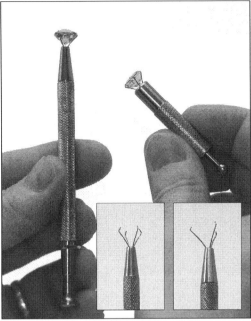

Figure 4-28 Stone holders are available in different sizes and with prongs tailored to various gem symmetries.

Trim Saw – Optional

A trim saw can be a very worthwhile investment, particularly if you like to cut larger rough, since it can spell the difference between saving usable scraps of stone and sending valuable gem material down the drain. Small lapidary trim saws range from $100-300, however, so you may want to defer this purchase until you are certain of your commitment to the hobby. On the other hand, trim saws are useful for all kinds of lapidary work. In fact, even if you choose not to purchase your own, your local lapidary club will almost certainly have one that you can use.

The main thing to watch for in a trim saw is the thickness of the blade. Thinner is almost always better, since thinner blades produce thinner cuts (or *kerfs*) and hence save gem material. A saw blade suitable for faceting rough will be 0.01" (0.25 mm) or thinner.

Figure 4-29 A small hobbyist's trim saw.

Note that you can mount and use trim saw blades on your faceting machine. See Section 4.11.7 above and page 294 for additional information.

A final word of caution: Thin saw blades can be extraordinarily dangerous to your fingertips. Be very careful (see also Chapter 8.3.1).

Tweezers – Essential

Stone holders are a fine way of picking up and displaying your completed gems, but you will need tweezers to handle things earlier on. I have accumulated a rich diversity of tweezers over the years. Figure 4-30 shows a fraction of my collection, and I use almost all of them... or at least most of them...and besides, they're not that expensive...

Even if you are not an obsessive collector of small tools, you will want to have one or two different types of tweezers. The locking variety (second from left in Figure 4-30) is particularly useful, since you can grasp them anywhere, once the stone is locked in place. Note also the plastic-tipped tweezers in the middle. Known as "pearl sorting tweezers" in the trade, they are ideal for softer stones, although exercise caution in plunging any plastic tools into harsher solvents, such as acetone.

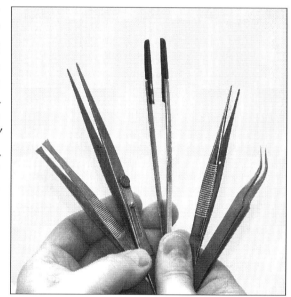

Figure 4-30 Different tasks demand different tweezers.

4.18 A Faceter's Toolbox

As you acquire experience in faceting, you will no doubt also acquire a growing collection of tools, extra dops, and various accessories. Organizing such a collection can be a nightmare, particularly if you have to share your workspace with other household activities. A faceter's toolbox can be a lifesaver in such a situation.

What is a faceter's toolbox? It is basically a container to store and organize your day-to-day tools. The toolbox can in fact be a shelf or drawer, depending on how and where you work. I personally prefer the multiple-compartment plastic toolboxes available at the corner hardware store (scratch that...when is the last time you actually *saw* a corner hardware store?). These boxes can have covers, or not, but they should have a multitude and variety of individual compartments: dop wax is generally smaller than vernier calipers, but they should both be within easy reach.

Perhaps the best way to explain a faceter's toolbox is to show one. Figure 4-31 on the next page shows how I organize my faceting tools and accessories.

Figure 4-31 My toolbox, containing a variety of dops, small tools, stone holders, measuring equipment, dop wax, spare parts, etc. etc.

5

GeM101: Your First Gemstone

This chapter leads you through all the steps needed to produce your first gemstone, from selecting the design and rough material, through cutting and polishing, to enjoying the final product.

These instructions are by no means exhaustive. As you progress as a faceter, you will recognize that there are alternative ways to accomplish the various steps that transform a shapeless lump of rock into a beautiful gemstone. The path presented here is tailored to the beginner, hopefully motivating you with how easy it can be to achieve fabulous results, while encouraging you to try different techniques with more challenging gem designs and materials. In short, these instructions are the ones that I wish I had when I started.

Note that this chapter assumes that you have access to a faceting machine and all the essential accessories. It also presumes a basic knowledge of faceting terminology and the components of your machine. Put another way, you should know your quill from your cheater before you start. Chapters 1 to 4 and the Glossary can help you with the appropriate equipment and terminology.

5.1 Which Design Should I Cut?

Everyone's first stone should be a Standard Round Brilliant, right?

Wrong.

The Standard Round Brilliant, or SRB, performs well optically, but it is far from easy to cut. First of all, it has a fairly hefty number of facets: 73 in the usual 8-fold symmetric version. In addition, the SRB is a *meet-point* design which is fairly unforgiving (see Chapter 8.7 for a complete explanation of meet-point faceting). People are also used to seeing diamonds and other high refractive index stones cut to this shape, and even a good first effort in quartz or beryl will not be in fair competition (turn to Chapter 12.5 for more on the importance of refractive index). Finally, a standard round brilliant is, well, standard. Every jewelry shop in every shopping mall in the world has hundreds or thousands of them on display. Faceting represents an opportunity to express your individuality and creativity. Why direct those energies at reproducing an everyday design?

The ideal first gem cut should therefore:

- have a low facet count
- have few or no meet points
- work well in low refractive index material
- be tolerant of cutting errors
- be different

Of course, your first gem should also be "real" in the sense of producing a very satisfying and inspiring result, all the while introducing important techniques that represent your first steps along the road to becoming an expert faceter.

5.1.1 GeM101 – The Design

Figure 5-1 shows a drawing and photograph of a beginner's gemstone design called GeM101. With only 31 facets and very few meet points, it is easy to cut. GeM101 also produces surprising sparkle, even in low index materials. In addition, it is not a "standard" round design, so don't go looking for its twin at the local jewelry store. In other words, GeM101 satisfies all the criteria in the previous section, and above all, it is fun to cut.

While Figure 5-1 shows you what GeM101 will look like (and hopefully encourages you to give the design a try), it hardly explains *how* to cut the gem.

The Faceting Diagram

Over the years, faceters have developed a common recipe format to explain to each other the steps in producing a gemstone. This recipe, or *faceting diagram*, consists of one or more drawings of the gem and a series of cutting angle and index wheel settings presented in the proper order (if you don't understand the concept of cutting angle and index wheel settings, see Chapter 2.1).

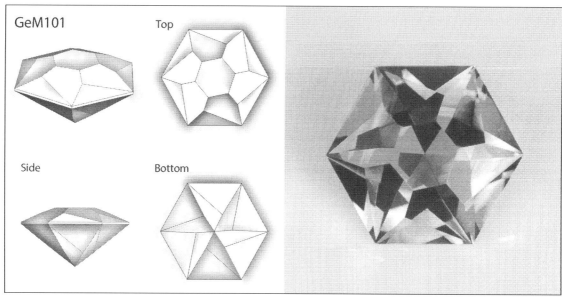

Figure 5-1   Sketch of the GeM101 design (left), and a 9.5 mm, 2.7 carat GeM101 cut in citrine (right).

Before the age of affordable home computers, faceting diagrams varied considerably from designer to designer, and some contained vague or inaccurate information. Everything changed with the appearance of GemCAD, a low-priced computer program that produces accurate, cuttable designs (see Chapter 15.3.1). GemCAD also uses a single file format and generates standardized faceting diagrams, drastically simplifying the task of publishing and sharing gem cuts. As a result, essentially all modern faceting diagrams look the same and can be readily understood and executed.

Why the Name *GeM101* ?

Readers who attended college in North America know that the naming of classroom courses in all major disciplines start with the number 101 – French 101, Geology 101, Astronomy 101, etc. Why not GeM101?

Eagle-eyed readers – those that didn't spend too many nights in a poorly-lit library at college – will have also noticed the capital M in GeM101. The other inspiration for the naming of this gem design is the famous galaxy M101 – the one-hundred-and-first entry in Charles Messier's famous catalog of diffuse nebulae (You didn't take Astronomy 101? "Diffuse nebulae" means fuzzy spots on the sky). M101 is familiarly known as the Pinwheel Galaxy.

A glance at the faceting diagram of GeM101 (Figure 5-2) makes the association obvious. Both the crown and pavilion of GeM101 resemble a pinwheel. This, coupled with the desire that your first stone sparkle like a billion stars, makes the name "GeM101" a natural…

Top, Side, End and Bottom Views

Figure 5-2 shows the faceting diagram for GeM101. The four drawings show the finished gemstone from various perspectives. The top-left figure shows the "top view" of the gem, in other words, looking down on the crown (refer to Figure 1-4 if you don't understand the terms crown, pavilion, girdle, and table). The numbers encircling the crown view correspond to the indices at which the various facets are cut. The maximum number is 96, indicating that this design is intended for a 96 toothed index wheel (see Chapter 2.6.2). You should also note the various labels – C1, C2, T, and so forth. These identify the various facets and correspond to information given in the remainder of the prescription.

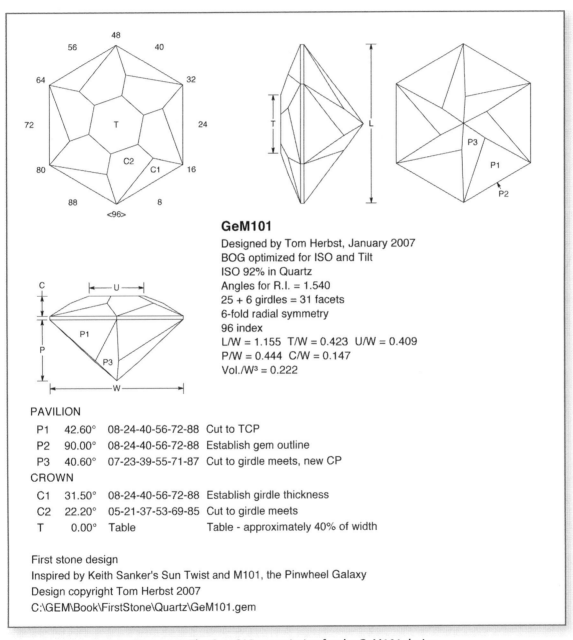

GeM101

Designed by Tom Herbst, January 2007
BOG optimized for ISO and Tilt
ISO 92% in Quartz
Angles for R.I. = 1.540
25 + 6 girdles = 31 facets
6-fold radial symmetry
96 index
L/W = 1.155 T/W = 0.423 U/W = 0.409
P/W = 0.444 C/W = 0.147
Vol./W³ = 0.222

PAVILION

P1	42.60°	08-24-40-56-72-88	Cut to TCP
P2	90.00°	08-24-40-56-72-88	Establish gem outline
P3	40.60°	07-23-39-55-71-87	Cut to girdle meets, new CP

CROWN

C1	31.50°	08-24-40-56-72-88	Establish girdle thickness
C2	22.20°	05-21-37-53-69-85	Cut to girdle meets
T	0.00°	Table	Table - approximately 40% of width

First stone design
Inspired by Keith Sanker's Sun Twist and M101, the Pinwheel Galaxy
Design copyright Tom Herbst 2007
C:\GEM\Book\FirstStone\Quartz\GeM101.gem

Figure 5-2 The GemCAD prescription for the GeM101 design.

The easiest way to understand the other three drawings is to imagine the stone sitting in the bottom of a bowl (see Figure 5-3). Moving the gem to the right slides it up the side of the bowl so that you are seeing things from the right side. This corresponds to the drawing (the "side view") to the right of the top view in Figure 5-2. Similarly, the drawing below the top view shows what the gem looks like when it slides up the bottom edge of the bowl, that is, from the side near the number "<96>." This is conventionally called the "end view." The final diagram to the upper right corresponds to moving the gem so far up the side of the bowl that it turns over. This is the pavilion or "bottom view."

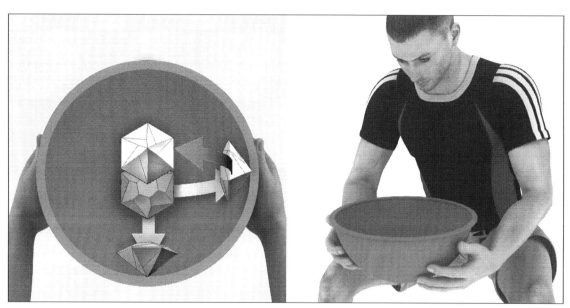

Figure 5-3 Imagine the gemstone in a bowl to understand the top, side, end, and bottom views.

Information Block

The remainder of the faceting diagram is textual and consists of two blocks of data. The upper block gives general information about the gem design, while the lower block contains the cutting recipe itself. Some diagrams, including this one, will include additional details, such as copyright information and the GemCAD filename, at the bottom of the page.

The upper information block (Figure 5-4) gives the name of the gem, followed by three lines of text supplied by the designer. These lines will vary in content from gem to gem and designer to designer, although it is customary to give information about the creator, as well as some indication of the optical performance of the gem. In the case of GeM101, the diagram indicates that the design was optimized for ISO reflectivity and tilt performance

Figure 5-4 The information block.

> ## GeM101
> Designed by Tom Herbst, January 2007
> BOG optimized for ISO and Tilt
> ISO 92% in Quartz
> Angles for R.I. = 1.540
> 25 + 6 girdles = 31 facets
> 6-fold radial symmetry
> 96 index
> L/W = 1.155 T/W = 0.423 U/W = 0.409
> P/W = 0.444 C/W = 0.147
> Vol./W³ = 0.222

(see Chapter 18.5), and that, when cut in quartz, the gem will return approximately 92% of the incoming light. The term "ISO" refers to a particular set of lighting conditions – see page 196 of Volume 2.

The remaining seven lines of the information block provide details about the target gem material and the geometry of the design. All published GemCAD output will include this information. The first two items are self-explanatory. For example, GeM101 is intended for quartz (refractive index, or R.I.=1.540) and the stone has a total of 31 facets.

You needn't worry about the meaning of "6-fold radial symmetry" at this stage. This simply refers to the degree of similarity of the stone in various directions. Chapter 10.7 provides a complete explanation of gemstone symmetry

The next line is very important, however. It refers to the type of index wheel needed to execute the gem. Most machines come standard with a "96 index" wheel, although this is by no means universal. Make sure that you have the appropriate index wheel before proceeding. The markings on it should run from 1 to 96 or 0 to 95 (index 96 is identical to index 0). See Chapters 2.2.1 and 2.6.2 for more information on index wheels.

The last three lines of the information block summarize the geometry of the completed gem. For example, the term "L/W" gives the length-to-width ratio of the design. The gem drawings at the top of the diagram identify L and W, along with the other geometric quantities listed in the various ratios. Needless to say, this information is extremely useful in evaluating whether a certain piece of gem rough can accommodate the design. As you progress as a faceter, you will be doing a lot of measurements of stones and comparisons with these numbers. Chapter 10.8 explains how.

The final line of the information block gives the ratio of the final gem volume to the cube of the width "W." As you shall see later, this information, combined with knowledge of the density of the gem material, can give you an accurate idea of the weight (and hence value) of the finished stone long before it is complete.

Recipe Block

The actual faceting instructions appear in the recipe block as a sequence of angle and index wheel settings presented in the correct cutting order (Figure 5-5). GeM101, as with most gem designs, begins with the pavilion.

```
PAVILION
  P1    42.60°   08-24-40-56-72-88   Cut to TCP
  P2    90.00°   08-24-40-56-72-88   Establish gem outline
  P3    40.60°   07-23-39-55-71-87   Cut to girdle meets, new CP
CROWN
  C1    31.50°   08-24-40-56-72-88   Establish girdle thickness
  C2    22.20°   05-21-37-53-69-85   Cut to girdle meets
  T      0.00°   Table               Table - approximately 40% of width
```

Figure 5-5 The recipe block.

Each line in the recipe block corresponds to an individual row or *tier* of facets, described by four separate fields of information. The first field is the facet identifier as labeled in the four gem drawings at the top of the diagram. Most cutting instructions designate the pavilion and crown facets as P1, P2, P3,… and C1, C2, C3,…, respectively. The table facet usually appears as "T," although it is sometimes labeled as the last (highest numbered) crown tier. Similarly, the girdle facets often get labeled with the pavilion, as they do here.

The second field gives the cutting angle for the tier of facets. The cutting angle ranges from 0° for the table to 90° for the girdle. The third field indicates the series of index settings at which to place the facets for that tier. All facets of a particular tier have the same angle and cutting depth. Chapter 2.1 contains an in-depth discussion of the importance and interplay of cutting angles, index wheel settings, and cutting depth.

The final field provides additional detail or cutting instructions for the tier of facets. This extra information typically indicates:

- the cutting target e.g. "cut to P1-P3 intersection"
- important steps e.g. "establishes size of gem"
- dangerous situations e.g. "warning – cuts very quickly"

The P1 facets of GeM101 provide an example. Here, the diagram instructs you to set the cutting angle to 42.60° and to cut six facets to the same depth at indices 8, 24, 40, 56, 72, and 88. These six facets intersect at a temporary center point ("TCP"), which establishes the symmetry axis of the stone (see Step 1 on page 158).

The remaining pavilion, crown, and table facets follow the same conventions. The format will become very familiar as you cut GeM101 following the instructions later in this chapter.

5.2 Which Gem Material Should I Choose?

As a beginning faceter, you immediately face the problem of selecting a suitable material for your first gem. The standard solution is clear quartz, since it is relatively easy to cut and very inexpensive.

Despite its rich heritage, the choice of clear quartz for a first stone is a poor one, in my opinion (and experience – my first stone was indeed clear quartz).

First of all, quartz may be easy to cut, but it is definitely not easy to polish. Even experienced faceters, with hundreds of stones under their belts, frequently have difficulty achieving a fine polish on "simple, easy" quartz. Horse-hair type scratches are a particular headache.

Figure 5-6 My first gemstone, a "Simple Jack" cut in clear quartz. This design is available online. See Chapter 15.8.4.

Also, don't neglect the fact that quartz has a low index of refraction (1.54) and dispersion (0.013) compared to the bulk of gemstone materials (see Chapter 12 if you don't understand these terms). Lower refractive index and dispersion inevitably mean a stone that has less sparkle and fire, and lower index material is more sensitive to errors in cutting angle.

The argument of low cost is also weak. Anyone contemplating faceting as a hobby is looking at a significant investment in both time and money. Yes, you will almost certainly cut away more of the stone than you should on the first try, but the difference between a few dollars versus a few cents for your first piece of gem rough is insignificant in the larger scheme of things. Selecting a material that is easier to work with and performs better optically will more than pay for itself.

So, which material should you cut for your first gemstone?

At a bare minimum, select a coloured version of quartz, either amethyst or citrine (see Chapter 14.1). The body colour of these materials can more than make up for any lack of sparkle and fire.

Also, amethyst and citrine are "real" gemstones, in the sense that they have real market value and can be compared directly with products available at the local jewelry store. Even a mistake-ridden first gem will outshine most commercially cut stones, providing you with further encouragement. Faceted clear quartz is not as widely mass-marketed.

The desire to produce a "real" gemstone with real value eliminates most man-made materials from contention. Also, despite their excellent optical properties – vibrant colours, good dispersion, and zero inclusions – synthetics can be challenging to cut.

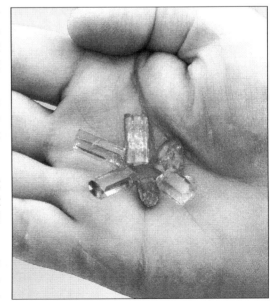

In my opinion, the best material for a first gemstone is beryl (Figure 5-7). Pale aquamarine is very inexpensive – less than $1 per carat – yet it produces fabulous gems, due to its appealing colour and somewhat higher refractive index. Beryl is also the easiest of all the common gem materials to cut and polish. Chapter 6.2 provides hints on where you can track down that perfect beginner's chunk of beryl.

For what it's worth, Table 5-1 shows what I cut for my first six stones and why these were not necessarily the best choices. I wish that I had discovered beryl earlier.

Figure 5-7 Beryl in its various forms. Clockwise from top center: Aquamarine (2 pieces), Morganite, Emerald, Heliodor (2 pieces).

Table 5-1 My first six gemstones. Note the overall poor choice of material and design.

Stone	Material	Design	Comment
1	Clear Quartz	Simple Jack	Hard to polish, low intrinsic value, difficult 16-fold symmetry
2	Blue Topaz	SRB	Difficult design, difficult material due to cleavage planes
3	Green Glass	Brilliant Jack	Simple Jack with SRB pavilion, zero intrinsic value
4	Clear Quartz	Lazy Oval	Challenging design, difficult to polish, low value
5	Clear Quartz	Sun Twist	Good beginner design (available online), difficult to polish, low value
6	Pink Tourmaline	Sun Twist	Good design, easy to polish, valuable gem material, finally sensible!

5.3 Selecting the Piece of Gem Rough

The GeM101 design has fairly conventional proportions, so you will want to select a "chunky" piece of gem rough, that is, a stone which has roughly equivalent length, width, and depth. Elongated or plate-like rough will force you to cut away too much material, resulting in poor yield. Don't agonize about this, however. You are using relatively inexpensive material.

The size of the gem rough is a more important consideration. Beginning faceters inevitably over cut a facet here or there, and this has much more severe consequences for a small stone. It is also harder to discern detail on a tiny gem. On the other hand, achieving a good polish is perhaps the most challenging aspect of learning to facet, and larger stones can be considerably trickier to polish. Unsurprisingly, the rough is also more expensive.

The best compromise between small and large seems to be a finished gem with a size in the neighbourhood of one centimeter. This of course requires a somewhat larger piece of rough – say 12-15 mm in diameter, depending on how close the shape is to the final gem. For quartz or beryl, this corresponds to approximately 3 grams or 15 carats.

Figure 5-8 Measuring the piece of gem rough with calipers.

5.3.1 Look Before You Lap…

Sad, but true…not everything in life is perfect. This can be particularly true – and consequently sad – when it comes to faceting rough. Natural materials, such as the quartz or beryl you have selected for your first gem, often contain internal flaws, or *inclusions*, which can mar the appearance and decrease the value of the finished stone. Interestingly, there are gem materials for which the presence of characteristic inclusions is a sure sign that the sample is natural and genuine, and hence more valuable (see Chapters 6.4.1 and 12.12). Quartz and beryl are not in this category, however, and you will want to start with as clean a piece of gem rough as possible.

But how can you tell if your stone is clean?

Obviously, visual examination of the rough for internal flaws is the best approach, but this can be difficult. As noted in Chapter 4.5, two effects are at play. First, gem materials have a refractive index considerably different from that of air. This means that there will be distracting partial reflections at the air-stone interface, i.e. at the surface of the rough. Refer to Chapter 11.8 for a complete discussion of this phenomenon.

These surface reflections are worse for materials with higher refractive index. Quartz and beryl have relatively modest R. I. (1.54 and 1.58, respectively) and hence surface reflections should not present too much of a challenge.

The second, more problematic effect is surface roughness. Scratches and small fractures can produce a "crazed" surface that is almost impossible to penetrate. To underline the analogy from Section 4.5, think about trying to examine a typical frosted light bulb for internal flaws, such as a burned-out filament, just by looking at it.

There are two ways to search for inclusions. The first relies on the fact that internal flaws scatter light, like snowflakes in an automobile's headlamps. Hold a small bright flashlight against the side of the stone at 90° to your line of sight (Figure 5-9). Any inclusions should show up as bright flecks. Dim room lighting and a dark background can help. Tip the rough and examine it from various angles to determine where and how deep the inclusions lie. Place the flashlight against a different side of the stone and repeat this procedure until you are convinced that you have identified any and all problems. See page 201 for more hints.

Figure 5-9 Hold a flashlight against the side of the gem rough to help reveal internal flaws.

The second technique for identifying inclusions involves an *immersion fluid*, a liquid which matches the refractive index of the stone and fills in surface roughness and flaws (see Chapter 4.5).

The most common fluid is water. Try dropping your piece of gem rough into a glass of good old H_2O. While water improves the situation, it has a considerably lower refractive index (1.33) than either quartz or beryl. It manages to fill in surface defects, but the index mismatch means that each little surface flaw produces partial reflections, and the cumulative effect can still prevent you from seeing into the stone.

Help! My Gem Rough Looks Awful!

Don't panic if you see nasty things inside your stone. As mentioned before, flaws are part of Nature. Imperfections near the surface will probably be cut out, if you orient things right (see below). Also, you will be surprised at how easily internal flaws are overwhelmed by the sparkle of a well-cut gem.

You have a few options if there are significant inclusions. Imagine where the final gem lies within the piece of rough (see Section 5.3.2). Is it possible to choose a different orientation that avoids the problem? Remember that the pavilion is essentially a cone with an approximately 90° apex angle. For most rough, this means cutting away a significant amount. Try to find an orientation that sends all the uglies down the drain of your faceting machine's splash pan. Alternatively, you can try cutting a slightly smaller stone. The most extreme option is to discard the piece of gem rough and try another.

The solution is an immersion fluid with higher refractive index. Your local pharmacist should carry glycerol, which has an index of 1.47. Commercial immersion fluids are also available. For example, Refractol (see Figure 5-10) is readily available through rock shops and, with a refractive index of 1.567, it works very well for low R. I. materials such as quartz and beryl. Professional gemologists use a range of immersion fluids with even higher refractive indices than glycerol and Refractol. These are not recommended for amateur faceters, however, since they are expensive and can be quite toxic. See Chapter 4.5 for more information.

Use locking tweezers (page 129) to hold the stone in the liquid. Why locking tweezers? Three good reasons: 1. it is always best to minimize skin contact with chemicals; 2. Refractol smells bad – you don't want it on your fingers; and 3. the locking mechanism lets you grasp the rough without fatigue and prevents annoying fumbling and dropping of the stone.

Figure 5-10 Immerse the stone in Refractol using locking tweezers. For lower refractive-index stones such as quartz and beryl, the surface will seem to disappear (right), and you can see any internal inclusions. This stone is flawless but does exhibit colour zoning.

Examine the gem rough against a light background, rotating the tweezers as necessary to see all sides of the stone. You should be able to readily identify any internal flaws. Make a sketch of the rough, indicating the location and depth of the problem areas. When you are done, remove the stone and clean it thoroughly with soap and water. Mark the location of significant inclusions with a waterproof pen directly on the gem rough – your sketch may be great, but it really helps to have the enemy in view.

5.3.2 Orienting the Gem Rough

Compare your marked-up gem rough with the faceting diagram. You should be able to identify the orientation of the rough which maximizes the size of the final gem and minimizes (or eliminates) internal flaws. For relatively clean, chunky stones, there might not be a single obvious choice.

You will learn that other factors beyond yield can drive the selection of orientation for some gem materials. For example, tourmaline can exhibit different colours in different directions, a phenomenon known as pleochroism (see Chapter 12.4). Isolating the desired hue may dictate the orientation. Other materials, such as topaz, have crystal *cleavage planes* (see Chapter 12.11.1) which drive this decision. Quartz and beryl exhibit only modest pleochroism, and they present no cleavage problems. You should therefore aim for the biggest, cleanest stone possible. Turn to Chapter 6.7 for more tips on orienting gem rough.

The outcome of this exercise should be a fairly clear understanding of exactly where your future gem lies within that irregular pebble in your hand. More specifically, you should locate where the table will be (Figure 5-11), since that is where the action takes place during the next step – dopping the stone.

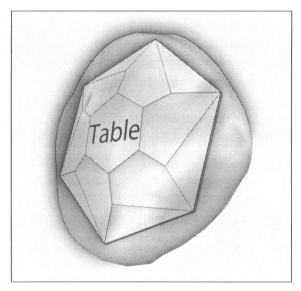

Figure 5-11 Try to visualize where the eventual gemstone and its table lie within the rough.

5.4 Dopping the stone

Dopping is the process of securely attaching a piece of gem rough to a cylindrical metal stick, or *dop*. In addition to producing a reliable bond, your underlying goal in dopping will be to position the stone for maximum weight retention or *yield*.

The first step is to select an appropriate dop stick. As with most modern gem designs, GeM101 calls for a pavilion-first cutting order. Cutting the pavilion means holding the gem on the other side, *i.e.* the table. This, in turn, means selecting a flat-ended dop (Section 4.4.2). Dops come in a variety of sizes, but here, you will want to choose one with a diameter about two-thirds that of the anticipated final gem size. In other words, if you think you can cut a 9 mm stone from your rough, pick a 5-6 mm dop.

Don't worry if the exact diameter is not at hand – choose the nearest available size. Note that a very common error among beginning faceters is selecting too large a dop stick, forcing them to either start over or to cut away part of the dop during the pre-forming process.

You will use wax (Chapter 4.1) to attach the gem rough to the dop. There are a number of alternatives, including super-glues, epoxies, and hybrid wax-adhesive methods. Chapter 7 compares these various approaches and presents my favourite technique. Nevertheless, wax dopping is a basic and essential skill for any faceter, and it works very well for larger, non heat-sensitive stones.

Why start with the pavilion?

A gemstone consists of three major parts: the pavilion, girdle, and crown (see Chapter 1.2). Because you have to hold the stone firmly while cutting, you are forced to facet the gem in (at least) two steps, holding one side while working on the other and then reversing the process to complete the gem. Here, you will use the standard modern cutting sequence: pavilion plus girdle then crown. The "pavilion first" versus "crown first" debate is one of many friendly controversies within the faceting community. Unlike with other issues, however, the decision to begin with the pavilion is very obvious and compelling. Refer to "The Great Debate: Pavilion-First or Crown-First?" on page 304 if you need convincing.

5.4.1 Dopping Pictorial

The best way to understand how to dop is to *see* it, and the best way to learn how to dop is to *do* it. This section presents a pictorial essay on dopping your first gemstone. Follow it carefully, and you should have minimal problems. Dopping can be a real challenge for the beginner, however. Don't get discouraged, and if you have difficulty, don't hesitate to clean things up and try again. You will improve with practice.

Here is what you will need for the initial dopping procedure (see Figure 5-12):

- gem rough and appropriate flat dop
- dop wax – see below
- alcohol lamp and / or small butane torch
- shellac-alcohol mixture (see Chapter 4.3.1)
- transfer jig (helpful now but essential later)
- small blob of putty
- miscellaneous – tweezers, paper towels, alcohol solvent
- a clean work area with a heat-resistant surface – see below

Dop wax is available in a variety of colours which correspond to their melting temperature. Green and black dop wax melt at a lower temperature, whereas brown wax requires more heat. In order to prevent undesired warming and shifting of the stone, I recommend the brown "diamond-setters" wax. Chapters 4.1 and 7.2.1 discuss the merits of the various types of dop wax and compare this traditional material to other adhesives.

The last item in the list is particularly important. You will inevitably drip hot wax here and there. Make sure that it doesn't do damage to either you or that fancy dining room table.

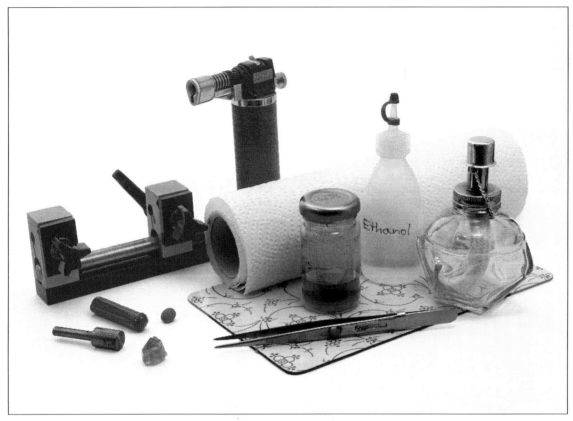

Figure 5-12 What you will need for dopping with wax. See the accompanying list for details.

Grinding a Flat for the Initial Dopping

Note: This section explains how to prepare your gem rough for dopping by grinding a flat area near the location of the future table. If your rough already has a suitable bonding area for cutting the pavilion, you can skip to the next section.

Dop wax has the admirable property of filling gaps and creating a sturdy, stable bond. This means that you do not need to have a particularly flat or smooth surface at the attachment point on the stone.

Nevertheless, it can be a great help to grind a flat area at the location of the future table. Perhaps the rough is too bumpy or irregular, requiring much too much dop wax to fill the gap. Alternatively, internal flaws may have forced you to identify a table location that is relatively deep within the stone. You will have to remove the unwanted material sooner or later, so it might as well be now.

You can grind a flat area by temporarily attaching a dop to the rough and using your faceting machine. Experienced cutters make a flat by hand-holding the stone, but I don't recommend it. Why not? First of all, it is distressingly easy to jam your fingers or hold the rough at the wrong angle, thereby removing valuable material from either your fingertips or the gem. Second, this step offers you the chance to try dopping in a situation where accuracy is not so important.

Begin by identifying a suitable temporary attachment point on the rough. This location should allow you to easily place the stone table-down on the lap at a comfortable cutting angle, say between 30° and 60°. A side of the rough that will eventually become part of the pavilion works well (Figure 5-13).

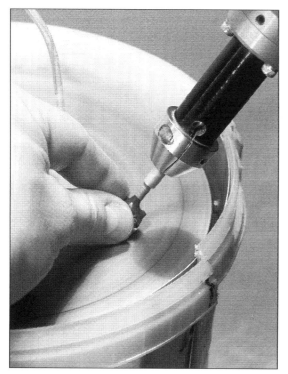

Dop the stone as explained starting at the top of the next page. Jump ahead and review that material. I'll wait here...

With the stone securely attached, place the dop in your faceting machine and adjust the cutting angle and index so that the future table area is parallel to the lap and a few millimeters above it. You are now ready to begin grinding the flat.

A coarse lap, say 600 grit, works well for two reasons. First, it efficiently removes unwanted material, and second, it produces a roughened flat area with more surface area for bonding with the wax. If you have a lot of material to remove, consider using a 260 lap.

Figure 5-13 The stone and machine adjusted to grind the flat. Dopping to the future pavilion lets you execute this step at a comfortable cutting angle.

Start a generous (3-4 drops per second) water drip and turn on the lap motor to low speed. Lower the faceting head until the stone contacts the spinning lap. Begin cutting, increasing the lap speed and lowering the gem as you understand where and how quickly the flat area develops. This surface will serve as a reference plane for cutting the pavilion, so it should be reasonably parallel to the eventual table you imagined within the stone. Adjust the cutting angle and quill rotation if necessary as you proceed (use the cheater, not the index setting, to change the quill rotation). Grind away enough material to allow a good surface for bonding with the dop, but don't go too far, since the coarse lap causes subsurface damage that can complicate things later. Aim for a flat area at least 2/3 of the dop diameter in size.

Figure 5-14 shows the resulting rough-ground surface. When you are happy, remove the dop from the machine and warm it gently over the alcohol lamp to release the stone. Apply heat to the middle of the dop, not directly on the wax or gem material. Hold the dop at the non-gem end. The wax should soften before the tip of the dop gets uncomfortably hot (see also page 193). Pull the two apart and soak both the stone and dop in alcohol to dissolve any excess wax.

Dopping the Rough for Cutting the Pavilion

With an obvious target – the future table location – in view, you are now ready to begin the actual dopping process itself. Clean the stone with alcohol, paint the table area with shellac-alcohol mixture, and let it dry (Figure 5-15).

Figure 5-14 Coarse-ground flat at the location of the future table facet.

While the stone is drying, clean the flat dop with alcohol and examine it for any damage. Dip the tip of the dop into the shellac-alcohol mix, and then place it in the transfer fixture to dry (Figure 5-16).

After a few minutes, the shellac should have dried sufficiently to ensure a good bond. Note that even when dry, the shellac may remain somewhat sticky, particularly if your mixture is somewhat old (see page 92). You can test this by touching your fingertip to the side of the dop. Don't touch the bonding surface itself, since finger oils can reduce adhesion.

Fire up your alcohol lamp and begin warming a stick of dop wax over – not in! – the flame (Figure 5-17). Don't rush things here. Watch the wax carefully and learn how the wax behaves as it slumps then flows. Too much heat can cause excessive melting, and in extreme cases, boiling and even burning of the wax. Boiling is bad since it can weaken the bond, and fire is bad because, well, fire is just bad.

After a moment or two, a droplet will flow and form on the underside of the wax stick. Make sure that it doesn't drip on anything sensitive, such as you.

Figure 5-15 Paint the future table area with the shellac-alcohol mixture. A cotton swab makes a convenient, disposable brush.

Keep the transfer jig and dop nearby. As the droplet grows and begins to drip off the wax stick, bring the dop up to the wax and capture a blob on the tip of the dop (Figure 5-17 inset).

Extinguish the alcohol lamp and set the transfer jig down on your heat-proof surface. Don't forget that the wax is still hot and sticky! When things have cooled down, remove the dop from the jig.

Center the gem rough, table side up, on one side of the transfer fixture. A small piece of putty will help you find and maintain the correct position (Figure 5-18). Install the flat dop on the other side of the jig, with its brand new wax blob facing the stone (it was obviously pointing the wrong way in Figure 5-16).

Slide the dop against the stone to check that the rough is well aligned. You can also use a larger dop stick, *i.e.* one that has a diameter similar to the final gem, in order to ensure proper centering (Figure 5-18).

Figure 5-16 Shellac drying on the stone and dop. Note the heat-proof work surface.

Note that your transfer jig may look quite different to the one pictured here. Nevertheless, you should be able to adapt this technique to your equipment. If not, you might consider acquiring a more flexible transfer fixture. As you will learn, a good jig is useful for all kinds of tasks beyond transferring gemstones (see Chapter 4.16).

Take your time getting the rough accurately centered. Look from all sides to ensure that both the location and orientation of the stone are correct. Centering is particularly important for good yield with smaller (< 5 mm) gems – see Section 7.8.

Some faceting machines use keyed dops, which either favour or require a certain orientation when inserted in the quill and transfer jig. If you use this feature, you must orient the stone to the correct rotation before dopping (see page 243 and Section 5.5.1 for more). For what it's worth, I don't use or recommend keyed dops, and they are certainly not a prerequisite to excellent results. Chapter 4.4.1 addresses the pros and cons of dop keying systems.

With everything in place, you can now begin gently heating the dop and wax. The alcohol lamp works well, but I prefer the pinpoint heat and greater control of a small butane torch (Figure 5-19).

As before, you will see the blob of wax slump and begin to flow. When it is quite liquid, but not yet dripping off, remove the heat and bring the dop and stone together. Don't push too far, or you may knock the gem out of alignment. The wax should squeeze out from between the dop and stone, form-

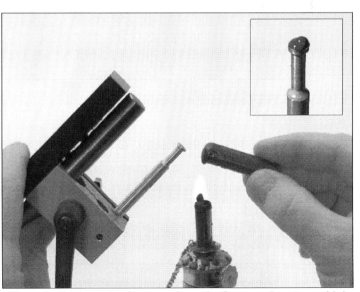

Figure 5-17 Warm the dop wax above the flame and capture a blob of wax on the tip of the flat dop (inset).

ing a convex bead (Figure 5-20). If it doesn't, you either used insufficient heat or not enough wax (or both). In this instance, you should raise the dop and try again.

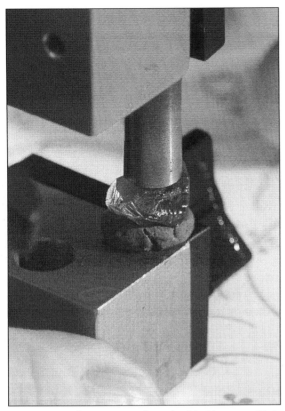

Figure 5-18 The gem rough embedded in putty. Note the large diameter dop to check centering.

You can now begin the final stage of dopping by gently heating the area of the wax joint with the alcohol lamp (Figure 5-22). Again, take things slowly here and observe the wax. Rotate the transfer jig to ensure uniform heating on all sides.

The convex shape of the wax is a sure sign of a "cold joint." This indicates that either the wax or stone was not hot enough to ensure smooth flow and strong adhesion. This is perfectly normal at this stage – you will be fixing things in a moment or two.

The joint requires additional wax to ensure a durable bond. With the dop and stone locked in place, begin warming more wax over the alcohol lamp. As the wax slumps and flows, transfer it to the area of the existing joint. This will very likely be a bit messy – don't worry about it.

The result will be an irregular mass of wax in the general area of the dop-stone bond and probably more than a couple of unwanted drips on your work surface (Figure 5-21).

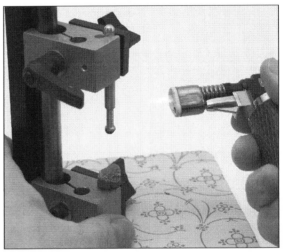

Figure 5-19 Heat the dop to melt the wax.

As the joint warms up, the wax will begin to flow across the surface of the stone and dop, making a smooth, non-convex bond. This may happen on one side of the stone before the other (Figure 5-23). Keep working your way around with gentle heat to ensure a proper bond.

It helps to keep the heat concentrated on the dop, and to a lesser extent, the wax. Try to avoid direct flame on the stone. While quartz and beryl are insensitive to heat, at least if they are free of internal flaws, other gem ma-

Figure 5-20 Note how the wax has squeezed out from between the dop and stone.

terials can fracture if you are not careful. Also, excess heat at the base of the stone may soften the putty, causing the rough to shift and ruining your careful centering.

Eventually, you should achieve a smooth, uniform bond (Figure 5-24). Note that you may have to add extra wax. When you are done, extinguish the alcohol lamp and let everything cool completely. You may have to rotate the transfer jig slowly for a minute or two before setting it down, in order to prevent slumping or dripping of the wax. Congratulations! You have completed your first dopping!

Figure 5-21 Irregular wax blob built up at the interface between the dop and gem rough.

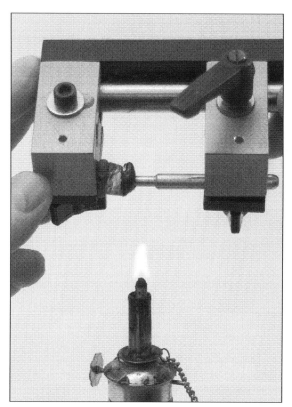

Figure 5-22 Heating the additional wax over the alcohol lamp.

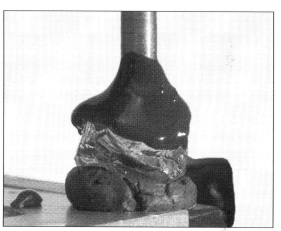

Figure 5-23 The wax has begun to flow across the surface of the stone. Note the still-cold joint on the left side.

Figure 5-24 Initial dopping complete. Note the smooth fillet between the stone and dop.

5.5 Cutting and Polishing the Pavilion

With the critical first dopping procedure now complete, you are ready to begin the true business of cutting your first gemstone. One important orientation task remains, however. As you have no doubt realized, many gem designs and essentially all pieces of natural rough are irregular in outline. Proper centering during the initial dopping procedure was the first requirement in maximizing the size of the completed gem. The second step is to optimize the rotation of the stone in the quill according to the shape of the rough and the cutting prescription. Note that if you use a dop keying system, you must take care of the rotation orientation during dopping. See page 243 for more.

5.5.1 Mounting the Dop in the Faceting Machine

GeM101 is hexagonal in outline. For this geometry, the difference in width from edge to edge versus point to point is about 15% (see the L/W ratio in Figure 5-2). Depending on the shape of your rough, getting the rotation right can make a real difference (Figure 5-25).

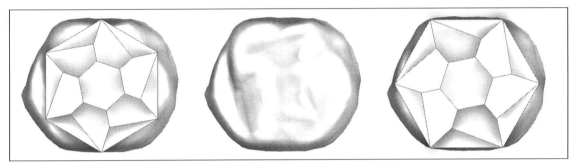

Figure 5-25 Selecting the correct dop rotation. For this piece of gem rough (center), a good selection (right) produces a gem with almost 1.5 times more carat yield than a poor selection (left). Chapter 6.7 contains more information on optimizing gemstone orientation.

Look carefully at your dopped rough and once again, imagine your completed gemstone inside it. Where would you place the girdle outline to maximize yield? Mark the stone at the location of what will become a girdle facet. This side must contact the lap when the index wheel is at one of the girdle settings: 8,24,40,56,72,88.

Begin by resetting and noting down the starting cheater value. I always set mine back to zero, near the middle of its operational range. Nothing is worse than getting to the end of polishing a gem and realizing that you don't have enough range left on your cheater to get the darn thing done (by the way, don't worry if all this discussion of cheating is unfamiliar to you. All will become clear presently).

Set the cutting angle to 90° on the faceting machine. Next, rotate the index wheel to one of the girdle settings (8, for example), and then slide the dop into the quill without clamping it. Rotate the stone until your mark is pointing exactly downward and lock the dop in place. While you are at it, perform a quick check of the other girdle indices to make sure that you have the best orientation. You are now (almost!) ready to start cutting.

5.5.2 Final Pre-Flight Check

Your rough is dopped, your machine is ready, and you are rarin' to go. Before setting stone to lap, there are a couple of last minute checks that can improve your faceting experience and chances of success.

First, make sure that your machine is in good working order. Do a visual inspection for dirt, loose parts, etc. Mechanically exercise all moving components to ensure smooth operation. Are all the locking parts tightened down? A loose mast or hard stop can ruin your entire day.

Also, make sure that your working environment is comfortable and well-lit. You will probably spend five to ten hours in that chair completing your first gemstone. Don't let it become a chiropractic nightmare.

Ok. The pre-flight check is done…You are ready to become a faceter.

Errr… you did fill the drip tank, didn't you?

Pre-Flight Checklist

- reset and note initial cheater value
- insert dopped stone with marked girdle location downward
- check all mechanical parts for smooth operation
- are all locking parts snug? (mast, angle setting, etc.)
- work environment – clean, comfortable, well-lit?
- fill the drip tank!

5.5.3 Pre-Forming the Pavilion

Unless you have been extremely lucky, your piece of rough doesn't have anything like the final shape of your gem. The process of *pre-forming* allows you to rapidly and effectively remove the bulk of excess gem material before fine cutting and polishing begins.

The goal of pre-forming is to produce the approximate outline of the final gem, but without any of the finer facets. Refer to the diagram for GeM101 (Figure 5-2). Clearly, cutting the P1 and P2 (girdle) facets will get you close to the final shape of the pavilion (Figure 5-26).

Note that some faceters will do an initial shaping of the rough on a grindstone or with a facet machine "free-wheeling," that is, with the index gear unlocked (see Chapter 8.3.2). For your first gem, I recommend executing the P1 and P2 pavilion facets just as though you were doing the "final" cut. This reduces risk of an error and gives you more opportunity to practice while the stakes are relatively low.

For efficiency, use a fairly coarse lap, for example, a 260 or 600 grit. Note, however, that although it removes material rapidly, such a lap can cause subsurface damage that will only appear later in the cutting and polishing process. To avoid difficulty, you should always stop the pre-forming process well short of the final size of the gem. For example, if your are planning a one centimeter wide stone, you should leave about a millimeter of extra material on all sides at this stage - in other words, aim for a 12 mm pre-form.

Mount the lap on the faceting machine and set the cutting angle to 42.6° for the P1 facets. In principle, you can start with any of the six index settings, namely 8,24,40,56,72, or 88. In order to not lose track, you would normally start with the first (8) and work your way through to the last (88). At the pre-forming stage, however, the rough is still quite irregular, and you don't want to cut away any more material than necessary.

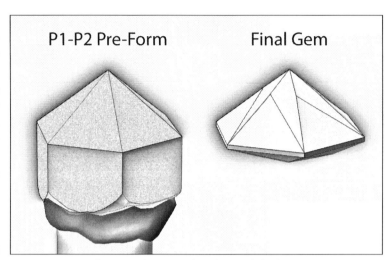

P1-P2 Pre-Form   **Final Gem**

Figure 5-26   Pre-forming the P1 and P2 facets (left) gets you very close to the final shape of the pavilion (right).

To prevent errors and minimize loss, you want to start at the index setting which requires the least amount of cutting to bring the facet into shape. Try all of the P1 index settings one by one, adjusting the height until the stone just touches the lap. The index with the lowest faceting head height is the one you are after. No other P1 facet should be cut deeper than this, so it serves as an excellent reference point for the others.

Begin with this reference facet. Start the water drip. Pre-forming is quite aggressive, so you should not skimp on the water. Aim for 3-4 drops per second. You should begin with a slow to moderate rotation speed, only increasing it as you understand how rapidly the lap removes material.

Why P1 and not P3?

GeM101 has two sets of pavilion tiers: P1 at 42.6° and P3 at 40.6°. Clearly, you should rough in the girdle facets (P2) to get the correct outline, but why choose P1 over P3 for the pre-form?

The answer should be obvious if you give it a little thought. You can always cut a lower angle (i.e. smaller number of degrees) at a certain location, but you cannot cut a higher angle. In other words, if you have already placed a facet at a certain location with an angle of 45°, you can subsequently lower that angle to 40°, but you cannot increase it to 50°: the material has already been cut away.

For this reason, you should always pre-form using the largest angle. This will ensure that you don't remove any gem material that you may eventually need.

Check that your angle stop mechanism is set, and when you are satisfied, lower the cutting head until the reference facet just touches the lap. At that point, immediately raise the quill.

Angle First, Height Second

Excellent words to live and cut by. You should always set the cutting angle before the height. It can be difficult to judge how far above the lap the stone will be for a given cutting angle. Here is the best strategy: move the faceting head to well above the final height, adjust the angle, and then lower the head carefully to bring the stone to the level of the lap. See page 297 for more.

The fun begins. Carefully lower the faceting head a little further, swing the quill downward, and begin cutting. Sweep the stone back and forth and check your progress regularly. Cut a little and look a lot (you will hear this again and again – see page 161). If you have a hard stop machine, continue removing material until you reach the stop. For a soft stop machine, cut until the index needle moves to the reference mark (refer to Chapter 2.4 for more information on hard and soft stops).

Move on to the next higher P1 index setting and cut it to the same depth. Continue through the list until you have cut all six P1 facets.

Errr…How do I actually cut the stone?

You have the faceting machine set up, the lap rotating, and the water dripping…but how do you actually cut the stone? Should you grasp the gem rough? How about the dop? Or the quill handle, if your machine has one? Should you push the stone hard against the lap or use less force? Should you use your left hand or your right?

The answer to all but two of these questions is "yes." Let's deal with the last questions first. Each faceter develops his or her own technique based on personal comfort and efficiency. There are lefties and righties among people, just as there are left and right-handed machines (see Chapter 2.3). Some cutters are hard-core heavy-handers, while others insist that only the lightest of touches is effective. Of course, you should never apply so much force that it bends or flexes the machine, rendering your accurate angle settings pointless.

The one sure thing is that you should always hold the stone, not the dop or handle. This gives you a better feel for how things are progressing, and it prevents you from applying too much force and popping the stone off the dop (not a good thing – you can read one tale of woe starting on page 259).

It is also important to sweep the stone back and forth across the lap as you cut and polish. This has two benefits. First, every lap has surface bumps and irregularities. Sweeping back and forth tends to average these out, rather than having them immortalized, mirror-imaged, on your gem. The second benefit arises from the sad fact that expensive laps wear out. Sweeping the stone spreads the wear and tear on the lap and can substantially increase its lifetime.

An interesting corollary to the last point is that the inner part of the lap – nearest the nut – gets the least workout. Experienced faceters exploit this fact, working on the inside of the lap if they temporarily need a bit more aggressive cutting (see "Your Lap's Sweet Spot" on page 72).

As you sweep the stone back and forth, take care not to hit the central nut (I once knocked a gem off the dop this way) nor fall off the edge of the lap, which can causes serious damage to the stone, fingers, and self-esteem. See "Cutter Beware" on page 299 for more dire warnings about this.

You should check your work regularly to avoid over cutting. I always have a roll of paper towels near the machine, and half a paper towel in my hand. This allows a quick swipe across the stone to remove excess water and swarf for a better view.

Finally, do what comes naturally. Although your initial cutting efforts may seem awkward and imprecise, you will soon develop a personal style that works well for you.

In all likelihood, you will have a stone which resembles a six-sided truncated pyramid with no peak (left panel of Figure 5-27). Alternatively, you might have a temporary center point, but the P1 facets do not reach to the edge of the stone (middle panel). A final possibility is that you have reached both the TCP and the edge, but a divot in the stone persists (right panel).

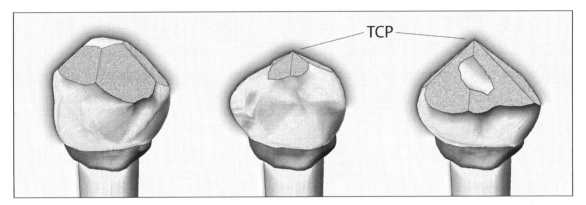

Figure 5-27 Incomplete pre-forming of the P1 facets. In all three cases, you should continue until you have six clean facets out to the edge of the stone.

All of these symptoms indicate that you have not cut deep enough to pre-form the P1 facets. Lower the faceting head slightly and cut each of the indices again.

Continue this process until the pre-formed facets are the proper size. You should aim for something like Figure 5-28. Note that you will be cutting all of these facets again with a finer lap, so you should stop short of the final depth. For example, if your TCP is the last to come in, as will happen in the left panel of Figure 5-27, stop before the final point forms.

With the P1 facets roughed in, you can move on to pre-forming the outline of the gem. Set the cutting angle to 90° and make any additional adjustments to your faceting machine required for girdle work. For example, most machines will require repositioning of the mast and / or reconfiguring of the splash pan. Also, working on the girdle generally means operating near the outer edge of the lap. You may need to adjust the location of the water drip to ensure prompt removal of cutting residue (see Figure 5-29).

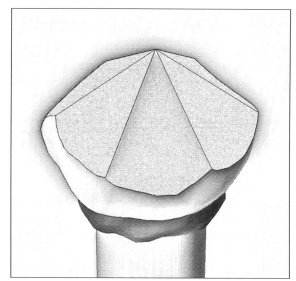

Figure 5-28 The P1 facets properly pre-formed to the edge of the gem rough.

As with the P1 facets, you can start with any of the girdle indices (8,24,40,56,72, or 88), but there will probably be an obvious best choice. All of the P2 facets lie at the same distance from the center of the stone, so setting the cutting height of the girdle ultimately establishes the gem size and yield. As before, you don't want to cut away any more material than you must. Test all of the P2 indices and begin with the one with the lowest required cutting height (see Figure 5-30).

Cut the first P2 pre-form facet until it forms a complete edge with the corresponding P1 facet (Figure 5-31). As before, you should recognize that you will be re-cutting these facets with a finer lap, so you should stop as

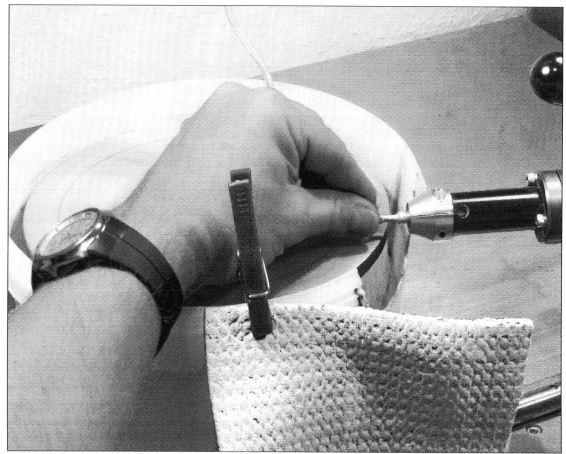

Figure 5-29 Cutting girdle facets. Most gems are considerably smaller than the quill. To prevent damage, you must work near the edge of the lap. Note the removal of a portion of the splash pan and the improvised sponge cloth to catch spray.

soon as the complete triangle appears. The intersection of this first girdle facet with the P1 tier will give you two targets for placing the next girdle facets (Figure 5-31).

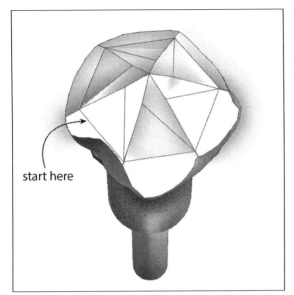

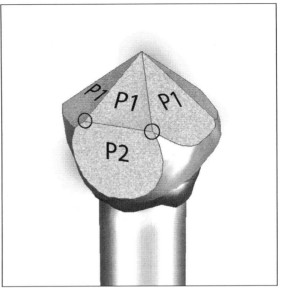

Figure 5-30   Imagine the largest possible final gem outline within the rough, and start pre-forming with the P2 girdle facet closest to this outline.

Figure 5-31 Grind the first P2 facet until P1 becomes a well defined triangle. The subsequent P2 facets should meet the lower corners of this triangle (circled).

Continue around the stone, using these two meet points to rough in the P2 facets, until you get back to where you started. Don't overdo things here. Remember that the goal is to remove the bulk of unwanted gem rough quickly, not to achieve high precision. And of course, going too far is worse than doing nothing at all. Sadly, gem material is much easier to cut away than to put back.

When you are done, you should have a reasonable approximation of the final pavilion (Figure 5-32). Congratulations, your first pre-form is complete!

5.5.4 Pre-Forming the Crown?

The process of pre-forming the pavilion has established the (approximate) proper outline of the stone. Depending on the size of the remaining gem rough, you may have considered pre-forming the crown as well. Doing so at this stage would require a dop-to-dop transfer (see Section 5.6 on page 176), so you should postpone this operation until you have completed the pavilion. Also, see page 185.

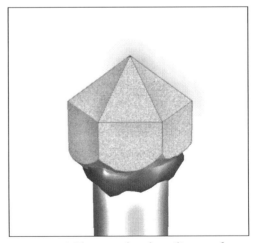

Figure 5-32 The completed pavilion pre-form.

5.5.5 Cutting and Polishing the Pavilion Facets

With a good pre-form, much of the hard, at least physically hard, work is done. Doing the actual cutting and polishing of the pavilion represents a relatively small, but much more accurately removed, amount of stone.

> ## HELP! I am cutting into the wax!
>
> It doesn't matter.
>
> A little bit of dop wax will not harm your lap, and a good bond will not be significantly weakened by this process. If a lot of wax builds up along the edge of the lap, you can remove it with a soak in alcohol followed by a wipe with tissue (see page 106).

The first step in cutting the pavilion is to select a finer lap, and unless the gem is unusually large or small, this finer lap will almost certainly be a 1200 grit stainless steel or bonded lap (see Chapter 3.2.3). The 1200 turns out to be the workhorse lap for cutting, and I use it on essentially every stone I facet.

Before installing the 1200 lap on your machine, do a general clean up, giving a quick wipe to the gem and dop, the splash pan, and the various controls. You should also wash your hands (see "Keep Things Clean" on page 158).

Finally! After all the design decisions, rough selection, dopping, and pre-forming, it is finally time to begin cutting your gemstone. You will begin again with the P1 facets. Yes, you've already been there and done that in the pre-form process, but as you will learn, the business of faceting is basically about refining previous steps with finer and finer tools.

The coarse pre-form lap not only removes surface material quickly, but also, unfortunately, causes *subsurface damage*. This means that the rough grinding of the stone has propagated inward, causing microscopic cracks and flaws below the visible surface. Every cutting lap does this to a greater or lesser extent, but the coarser laps undoubtedly do the deepest

> ## HELP! I am cutting into the dop stick!
>
> It doesn't matter. Much.
>
> Sooner or later, every faceter will mess up and select an oversized dop. Lucky you. It happened sooner.
>
> Actually, even experienced cutters are often faced with a changed situation requiring a smaller dop. For example, a previously undetected inclusion or cutting error may force a downsizing of the final gem.
>
> You have several possible choices of strategy. First, you can simply detach the stone, bond it to a smaller dop, and start over. A better option is to use your transfer jig to do a "double transfer," that is, transferring to an intermediate cone dop and then back to a smaller flat one. Refer to Section 5.6 below and Chapter 7.3.2 for more information on dop transfer. This should preserve the stone centering and orientation, saving your efforts so far. Finally, and simplest of all, you can just plow ahead and continue faceting your dop along with the stone. Most dop sticks are either brass or aluminum and are harmless to most gem materials and the lap in small amounts. See Chapter 4.4.4 for more information on dealing with damaged dops.

Keep Things Clean

I routinely do a quick clean-up of the faceting machine after finishing one cutting or polishing stage, wiping the stone, lap nut, and general work area with a (subsequently discarded) paper towel. I then get up from the machine and go scrub my hands under running water. In addition to minimizing contamination, this ritual forces a regular stretching of legs and refocusing of the eyes and mind.

Note that these precautions are particularly important when switching from coarser to finer cutting, or from cutting to polishing. Needless to say, the impact of any cross contamination is essentially zero, if you temporarily go back to a coarser grit lap for some reason.

A friend once asked me why I was so careful about keeping things clean, since I had never had a single problem with cross-contamination. My response was a wordless stare. Some questions just answer themselves.

Figure 5-33 After a good clean-up, install the 1200 grit lap to begin the real business of faceting the pavilion.

damage. Part of the reason for switching to a finer grit lap at this stage is to cut away these flaws, while doing a smaller amount of damage, which is, in turn, removed by subsequent laps.

Incidentally, it is a common error among beginners to pay insufficient attention to these intermediate grit laps. The eternal hope is to pass directly from a coarse grind to a fine polish. Such an approach inevitably leaves subsurface fracturing and damage uncorrected, a situation which becomes painfully obvious on the polishing lap. Don't try to save time by skipping the intermediate laps: at the polishing stage, you will end up wasting considerable time and several valuable bouts of profanity (you only get so many before people stop listening).

Step 1: The P1 Facets and the Temporary Center Point

Refer to the faceting diagram on page 134. The P1 facets should be cut to a TCP, or *temporary center point*. A TCP is a point on the stone defined by the intersection of a number of facets which are in this case cut at the same angle and height. Some cutting prescriptions produce a TCP from a mixture of facet types. See Chapter 17 for more.

Go with the Flow...

Every faceter will develop his or her own techniques, but there are a few general guidelines about the water drip that will help ensure consistent and successful results. First, make sure that there is a small but steady flow to wash away cutting residue. Too little water will allow build-up of swarf on the lap, produce scratches, and potentially overheat the stone. Too much water causes hydroplaning, just like on the highway, and water doesn't cut nearly as well as the diamonds embedded in your lap.

Centrifugal force will carry the water and residue to the edge of the lap and over into the splash pan. Make sure that all of the usable area of the lap is getting wet: sweeping inward onto a dry area can produce nasty scratching (Figure 5-34).

You should also regularly examine your progress. I find that having a few strips of paper towel at hand allows a quick "clean and dry" before putting the stone under the loupe.

Figure 5-34 Locate the water drip inward of the minimum radius of lap you plan to use, and ensure a steady flow of water to wash away cutting residue and prevent scratching. Wiping a clean finger from inside to outside can help distribute the water.

The paper towel strips will soon get wet. You can throw them out or be green and hang them up to dry and re-use. Needless to say, you should discard the paper towel strips when they wear out or when you switch to a finer grit lap.

Because the P1 facets are arranged symmetrically around the gem, their intersection automatically defines a point that is on the centerline or rotation axis of the quill. Think of a Native American tipi or the free-wheel pre-form described in Chapter 8.3.2 if you don't understand why such facets define a center point. By the way, you will see why this center point is called temporary soon enough.

Begin by cutting three of the P1 facets to the same depth with the finer lap. Three such facets, when distributed evenly around the stone, are enough to define the TCP. You will then have to cut the remaining P1 facets to this meet point.

GeM101 has six-fold symmetry, so selecting three symmetric facets is easy. The obvious choice is at indices 8, 40, and 72. Set the facet angle to 42.6°, fire up the machine, and start cutting at index 8. Because you have made a pre-form, this process should go relatively quickly. Stop when all evidence of the rough scratches from the coarse pre-form lap has disappeared. With experience, you will know exactly how far to go, but this is a first, learning gem, and it is better at this stage to cut away too much rather than too little (within reason, of course).

Switch to the 40 index and cut to the same depth. Your faceting machine may have a hard stop to help you here, or you may have a soft-stop needle or depth of cut indicator. In any case, try to achieve the same depth while ensuring that all of the pre-form scratches have been eliminated. Move on to the 72 index and repeat. Your stone should look like Figure 5-35.

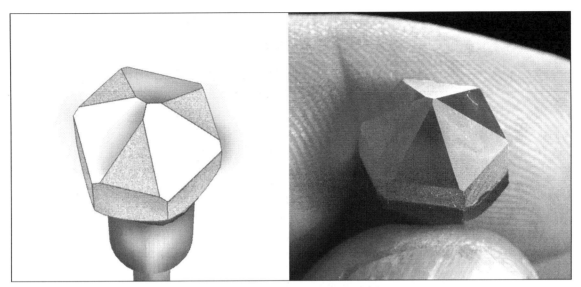

Figure 5-35 Three of the six P1 facets cut to a temporary center point.

Before proceeding with the remaining P1 facets, it is a very good idea to check the accuracy of this temporary center point. The easiest and best way to do this can vary from machine to machine. For example, a depth-of-cut indicator (see Chapter 20.7) can be very helpful, but the general procedure described here should work on almost any machine.

The basic principle involves raising the height of the faceting head and then lowering it (with the lap turning slowly) until the stone barely touches the lap. Just as the gem makes contact, imperfections and warping of the cutting surface will result in an intermittent "tick-tick" sound as the stone touches the highest points on the lap. You may have heard the expression "cutting by ear" thrown around in conversation with other faceters. Congratulations, you are now also an ear-cutter.

When you have found the right spot at index 8, move on to 40 and listen. Almost certainly, the stone will be making more or less contact with the lap, hence producing a different sound. Try again with the 72 index. The facet with the least contact has already been cut the deepest, so you should re-adjust the height and cut a little more on the other two. When all three match, you have achieved a very accurate center point. Note that the high points on the lap will almost certainly vary with radius. I mark a circle on the lap with a permanent marker and test the TCP at a constant distance from the nut (Figure 5-36).

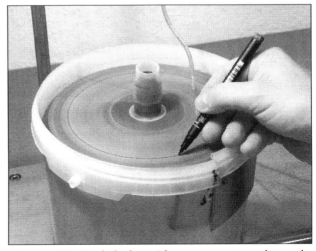

Figure 5-36 Mark the lap with a permanent marker and always test for depth of cut at the same radius.

Finally, don't rush things here. Time spent in achieving an accurate TCP is time well spent, and it will more than pay for itself later in the process. For complex gem designs or valuable rough, I will take up to half an hour or more to ensure that things are exact as possible.

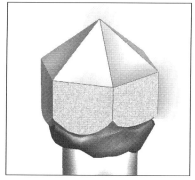

Figure 5-37 The completed P1 tier.

Completing the P1 tier should go relatively quickly and easily once you have established an accurate center point. Simply proceed through the 24, 56, and 88 index facets, cutting a little and looking a lot, until each of the facets meets the TCP (Figure 5-37).

Step 2: The P2 Girdle Facets and the Gem Outline

As discussed in section 5.5.3 above, the P2 or girdle facets define the size, and hence, the ultimate value, of the final gem. The P2 facets also form the interface between the pavilion and crown, and, again, accuracy at this stage is important to a successful stone.

Set the cutting angle to 90° and begin with the first girdle facet at index 8. As before, you want to cut away enough material to eliminate the subsurface damage from the pre-form stage. You will also be establishing and following meet points as you go along, much like you did while pre-forming (Figure 5-31). Yes, you have already cut through the meet points between the P1 and P2 pre-form facets established earlier. Not to worry – you will re-establish these reference locations soon enough. Also, if your pre-form meets were that accurate, you probably spent too much time on them.

Exercise a little extra care when you sweep the stone back and forth. Cutting the girdle means cutting near the edge of the lap, increasing the risk of having the stone fall over the edge. Take my word for it. This can produce some spectacularly nasty gouges.

Cut a Little and Look a Lot

This should be your mantra.

Not only will this prevent errors (and their consequence, which is cutting a lot and looking a lot and ending up with a smaller stone), but also you will acquire a sense of how pressure and lap time translate to removal of gem material. In other words, if you cut a little and look a lot now, you will be able to cut more and look less in the future.

Keep cutting until you are happy with the first girdle facet. Note that you have now established a new pair of meet points where the 8-index P2 facet intersects the 8-index P1 facet (Figure 5-38). One of these new points will be the target for placing the next girdle facet.

Adjust the index wheel setting to 24 and then lower the stone onto the lap to begin cutting the second P2 facet. Proceed carefully at this stage, since over cutting the meet points will force you to go back and repeat the entire tier. Completing the 24-index facet will, in turn, create the next meet point for the next girdle cut (Figure 5-39).

That was easier than the first one, wasn't it? This process of placing and meeting target meet points is at the heart of modern faceting technique, and you will rapidly gain a sense of how a complicated three-dimensional geometric form can be assembled from a few accurate angles and intersections. You will also begin to appreciate the accuracy of the meet points on gemstones cut by amateurs, including yourself, particularly in comparison to the generally execrable quality of commercially cut gems.

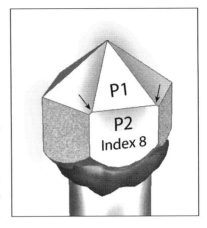

Figure 5-38 The first girdle facet with the 1200 grit lap. The previous P1-P2 facet intersections of the pre-form have been cut away and new meet points have been established (arrows).

With two meets met, you should continue around the stone, completing the P2 facet tier. Note that the last facet, at index 88, has to hit two meet points: the one created by the previous cut at index 72 and the second of the two meet points created by the first girdle facet way back at index 8. If you have been careful up to this stage and there are no major alignment problems with your machine, this last facet should float smoothly into place (Figure 5-40).

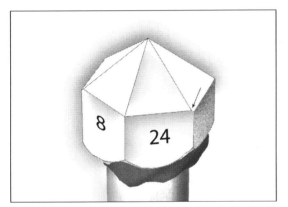

Figure 5-39 Cut the second P2 facet at index 24 to the meet point create in the previous step. This produces a new target for the next girdle facet (arrow).

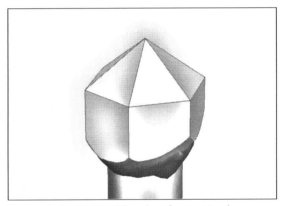

Figure 5-40 The completed P2 facets. You have now effectively refined the original pre-form and established the overall size of the gem.

Help! I can only get one of the two meet points to work!

First of all, don't panic. A small mismatch at the last facet junction is not necessarily a serious problem. Go back and check each of the other P1-P2 facet meet points for over or under cutting. If you find a problem, go back to the offending girdle facet (in the case of an under-cut) or back to its neighbours (in the case of an over-cut) and then touch up all the other facets around the gem. This should usually solve the problem.

If it persists, your temporary center point established by the P1 facets might not be accurate. Examine the TCP for problem facets, and take the necessary corrective action. This usually means going back to the appropriate P1 facet (which may be the first one), correcting things, and then working your way forward through all the subsequent steps. Yes, this can be frustrating, but many faceters find this to be excellent therapy.

Finally, keep an eye out for cumulative error. Each of the target meet points depends on the accuracy of the previous facet, which in turn depends on the accuracy of its previous facet, and so on. Significant problems can build up if you consistently under cut or over cut by a small amount. For example, you may share my obsession with perfection: even if a facet is a tiny bit short of its perfect location, I will continue to cut. This consistently leads to slight over cutting of individual facets, and hence, the entire tier.

The result of single or cumulative error can produce what looks like a spiral on the girdle (Figure 5-41).

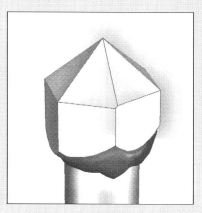

Some authors suggest that you can correct such an apparent "spiral" cut by adjusting the cheater. This is not geometrically correct nor strategically sound. In my experience, an accurate TCP, coupled with accurately-placed girdle facets, simply will not produce an over or under-cut spiral. Skirting the problem using the cheater at this stage will lead to greater headaches later on in the cutting process.

Figure 5-41 A mismatch of the final P2 facet may indicate an earlier cutting error.

Looking into the Future: A Mathematical Intermission

With the preliminary cutting of the P1 and P2 facets complete, you already know a surprising amount about your future gemstone. For example, you may have spotted a previously unseen internal flaw that will affect either your cutting strategy or the ultimate value of the gem or both (turn to page 166 for some ideas on possible ways out of serious difficulty you may encounter).

The previous section emphasized that the P2 girdle facets determine the gem outline, and therefore its size. With some information from the faceting diagram and other sources, you can also estimate the final weight and, hence, the value of your gem.

The weight of an object is the product of its volume and density (see Chapter 12.8), and you will need to know both for this calculation. The density is easy: just look it up, for example on the web or in Chapter 14. If you are working in clear quartz, amethyst, or citrine, the density is 2.65 grams per cubic centimeter. For aquamarine or other types of beryl, use the value 2.70, which is in the middle of the published range.

The mathematical part of this intermission involves deriving the weight of the gem from its linear size. Examine the information block on the faceting diagram (page 134). In addition to various length relationships, the diagram states that the ratio of the volume of the gemstone to the cube of its width is 0.222. For the GeM101 design, the width W is the distance between opposite girdle facets in the hexagonal outline (see the lower left figure in the faceting diagram, reproduced in Figure 5-42).

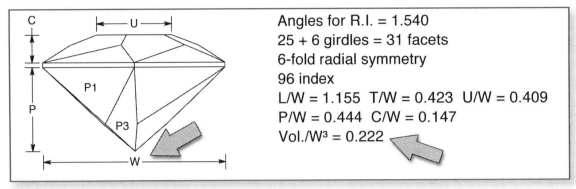

Figure 5-42 The quantity Vol / W³ *gives the ratio of the volume of the GeM101 design to its width, and the faceting diagram indicates exactly which dimension of the gem corresponds to W.*

Time to dust off your high school algebra skills. The density is the ratio of weight to volume, and the diagram gives the ratio of volume to width:

$$\mathrm{Density} = \mathrm{Weight/Volume}$$

$$\mathrm{Volume}/\mathrm{W}^3 = 0.222$$

A little mathematical manipulation leads to:

$$\mathrm{Weight} = 0.222 \cdot \mathrm{Density} \cdot \mathrm{W}^3$$

For the citrine shown here, the width W is 9.5 mm or 0.95 cm (the width has to be in the same units as the density, *i.e.* centimeters, for the equation to work). We therefore expect a final gem weight of 0.50 grams or about 2.5 carats. Market values for gemstones fluctuate considerably (see Chapter 6.5), but a well-cut, clean, citrine, amethyst, or beryl of this size in a unique design can fetch more than $50.

There are a number of reasons to view your calculation as an estimate only. First of all, you have not even begun the fine cutting or polishing, so more material will be removed, reducing W. In addition, there is significant variation in the density of some gemstone types, and the nominal Vol / W³ value is based on the girdle thickness shown in the drawing.

Finally and most importantly, this calculation presumes that you don't make a mistake or discover an internal flaw, two nasty situations that can force you to cut away a lot of additional gem rough before you are done. Like Aesop's milkmaid, you should not count your chickens before they hatch. All the more reason to use this mathematical intermission as a pause to refresh and refocus before diving back in.

Oh…and if you can't wait to find out the answer, the caption to Figure 5-1 at the beginning of this chapter shows how much the completed citrine actually weighed. The secret to this success? I used some clever girdle engineering to help. For more mathematical diversion on the subject of rough yield and girdle thickness, turn to Chapter 10.8.3.

Step 3: The P3 Facets Complete the Pavilion

A final tier of facets lies between you and completion of the initial pavilion cut. The P3 facets are different from the previous tiers in being quite close to existing facets in angle and index.

This means that relatively little material must be removed, and as a result, you should proceed with appropriate care to prevent over cutting.

The P3 facets are also somewhat challenging because they have to meet exactly at the girdle intersections and at a new center point. Note that this center point will no longer be temporary. A clean, symmetric culet adds qualitatively to the aesthetics of a gem, so you need to get this one right.

A final word of caution before you proceed. Placing the first P3 facet will cut through the original TCP, which was the fundamental reference meet point for the entire stone. For example, the P2 girdle facets, and hence the gem outline and connection to the crown, depended on this reference point. It is very worthwhile to have a final look and convince yourself that everything is Ok before cutting through the TCP with the P3 facets. From this stage forward, the girdle will serve as your reference.

Set the cutting angle to 40.6° and the index wheel to 7. With the lap turning slowly, gently lower the faceting head. As soon as you feel the slightest cutting action, stop and examine what has happened. You will probably be surprised at how quickly the cut proceeds compared to your earlier efforts. Again, this is due to the similarity in angle and index with the P1 facets.

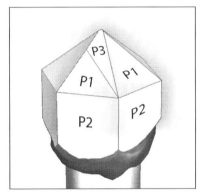

Figure 5-43 Cut the first P3 facet at index 7 until it just touches the girdle intersection.

Continue cutting a little and looking a lot until the facet just reaches the girdle meet point (Figure 5-43). You can then proceed to index 23 and do the same. The third P3 facet at index 39 will establish the new center point and define the culet. Continue around the stone, checking for good girdle and culet meets until the entire P3 tier is complete. Pay particular attention to applying constant and even cutting pressure. Mast flexure induced by a too-heavy hand will almost certainly mess things up.

If everything worked well, there should be a clean center point at the top of the gem (Figure 5-44). Don't worry about slight mismatches at this stage. They can be removed in fine cutting or polishing.

You have now completed the preliminary pavilion cut. Congratulations!

Figure 5-44 The completed initial pavilion cut

Help! It doesn't line up!

Minor P3 facet mismatches are not terribly problematic at this stage. More serious missed meet points, for example more than a millimeter or so at the girdle, may indicate an error in indexing or angle or both. Recovering from such errors is straightforward, albeit time-consuming: merely re-cut the P1 and then the P3 facets using the girdle facets as a reference. This assumes, of course, that the girdle facets are not the cause of the problem. If they are, you may have to start over from the beginning (see also "Help! I can only get one of the two meet points to work!" on page 162).

Recutting the P1 facets only makes sense if you have sufficient gem rough to shift the design downward slightly. Convincing yourself of this involves the various length ratios listed in the information block.

For example, the stone shown here has a width W of 9.5 mm. The pavilion to width (P/W) and crown to width (C/W) ratios give the total height of the gem from table to culet:

$$\text{Height} = P/W \times W + C/W \times W + \text{girdle}.$$

You should add a little extra to the required height to allow a downward shift. For W=9.5 mm and a typical girdle width of 0.3 mm (see page 46 of Volume 2), the total height of the citrine gem would be about 5.9 mm. Measuring the actual dimension of the rough gives at least 6.5 mm of stone, *i.e.* it should be Ok. If there is too little material left, you may be forced to reduce W and ultimately the size and weight of the final gem. Lowering the crown angles is another option, but I don't necessarily recommend it (see Chapter 10.5.1).

Note that this type of calculation applies to all sorts of situations beyond cutting errors. For example, the first application of a fine lap often reveals internal flaws in the stone that were previously invisible. Given the location and size of the problem, and the amount of gem material available, you may choose to shift the entire pavilion downward within the rough. The tabulated length ratios let you do this with confidence that you won't run out of stone. Chapter 10.8 deals with this type of calculation in detail.

Step 4: Fine Cutting and Pre-Polish of the Pavilion

Fine cutting and pre-polish are the next order of business. As discussed earlier, the primary goal here is to remove the scratches and subsurface damage created by the coarser laps. This is also the final, real cutting stage: all of the facets should be in excellent shape before you proceed to the actual polish.

There are a number of options in terms of lap selection for this step, but as with the earlier cut, there seems to be one workhorse lap that does the job well for almost all gem materials. I use a RayTech NuBond 1200 resin bonded lap for the final cut and pre-polish and I highly recommend it for the beginner. Finer-grit bonded laps, such as a steel 3000, are another option, although they can be a bit aggressive when new.

Remove the 1200 grit steel or bonded lap you have been using and don't forget that all-important clean up. The NuBond lap is relatively thin and therefore flexible, so it is a good idea to place it on a master lap (Figure 5-45).

Fine cutting / pre-polishing proceeds exactly as did the cut with the 1200 lap. Begin with the P1 facets, working through them in order and checking that all traces of scratching from the coarser grit have disappeared.

Is this fine cutting or pre-polishing?

Is the final preparatory stage before polishing a *fine cut* or a *pre-polish*?

Here is my answer: Is my least favourite vegetable a *turnip* or a *rutabaga*? Same thing, different names.

The coarser lap was very effective at removing bulk material and the polishing lap will do a beautiful job of producing a fine finish. The 1200 NuBond represents the perfect transition. You will still be able to influence the placement of facets and establish good meet-points. At the same time, this versatile lap should remove all the uglies from the first cut and give you a preview of what a fine polish will do for your gem.

Too wishy-washy an answer? Chapter 8.1 contains a complete discussion of the differences between cutting and polishing.

As you proceed, you may notice that the pre-polish doesn't appear uniformly across the facet. Rather, it starts on one edge and works its way across. Typically, this will be from top to bottom or bottom to top, although all directions are possible (Figure 5-46). This indicates a somewhat different cutting angle or relative quill rotation than was used with the previous lap. Double check the machine settings, but be aware that slight differences in the warping and dishing of the two cutting surfaces can produce this effect.

If the problem is slight, you can just ignore it and continue cutting. If, on the other hand, one side of the facet is completely pre-polished before the other side is touched, you should adjust the cutting angle or cheater as shown. This will ensure that all parts of the facet receive the same level of pre-polish. Whichever option you choose, make a note of any changes, so that you won't be surprised later on in the polishing phase.

If, on the other hand, you see that the cutting action is significantly different – produc-

Figure 5-45 Use a master lap as a rigid support for the NuBond.

ing a kink in the facet as it proceeds, for example – you probably have an incorrect angle or index setting and should stop to sort things out.

When you are happy with the P1 facets, proceed on to P2 *i.e.* the girdle. As before, you should target the P1-P2 intersections as the meet point for each facet as you go (see Figure 5-39 if this is not clear).

You may find that the pre-polish goes pretty slowly on the girdle, since you are cutting away at a substantial amount of stone, dop wax, and perhaps (horrors!) the dop itself. Experienced faceters recognize that there is nothing really magical about 90.00° – the girdle will be fine, as long as the angle is

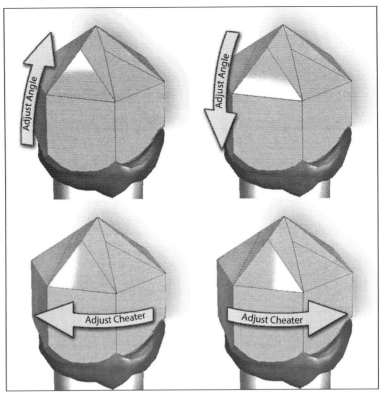

Figure 5-46 Adjust the cutting angle or cheater setting to ensure that the pre-polish advances uniformly across the facet. For example, the upper left figure shows that the pre-polish has developed at the top of the facet first. Increasing the cutting angle counteracts this.

close to 90° and, more importantly, consistent around the gem. Try setting a cutting angle of 89.9° to focus only on the area of stone that will eventually become the girdle, and aim for at least 1 mm of pre-polish (Figure 5-47).

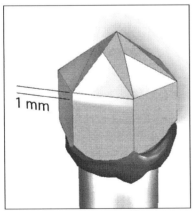

Figure 5-47 If you adjust the cutting angle to focus the pre-polish, aim for about 1 mm of girdle.

Work your way around the girdle, trying to achieve a consistent amount of pre-polish. As you go, you will notice that the tips of the P3 facets have been shifted upward away from the girdle by the pre-polish on P1. Your goal in the final stage of pavilion pre-polish on the P3 facets will be to bring these tips back to the girdle meet-points, while establishing a clean and symmetrical center point at the culet.

When you are done with the girdle, set the cutting angle to 40.6° and begin pre-polishing the P3 facet at index 7. As with the P1 tier, check to make sure that the pre-polish is coming in correctly. Even the relatively fine NuBond lap can move the meet points around fairly quickly, due to the similar angle and index to P1. As a result, the "cut a little, look a lot" mantra is definitely still in effect.

After three P3 facets, you will have again established the final culet meet point. Subsequent facets should come in fine, with one point just touching the girdle as the other reaches the culet meet. Of course, the world is an imperfect place, and one of the two meets will inevitably come in first. You should stop when you reach the first meet point to prevent over cutting. A small angle adjustment will help touch things up and match the meets in this case (see Figure 5-48). Yes, this is exactly the same type of minor adjustment you encountered while pre-polishing the P1 facets (Figure 5-46).

Before making any changes, however, you should evaluate the situation critically. Is the missed meet severe, say more than half a millimeter or so for the left-hand case in Figure 5-48? If not, you can probably manage any tweaking at the polishing stage. If you do choose to make a correction on a particular facet with the NuBond, consider completing the remainder of the P3 tier first to ensure a consistent angle setting. Also, note down any problems and adjustments you make. Later, in the polishing stage, you will need to know if there is a slight angle or index difference for a particular facet.

Finishing the P3 facets leaves only one more step for the pavilion: polishing. Oh…and don't forget to do a quick clean up before moving on…

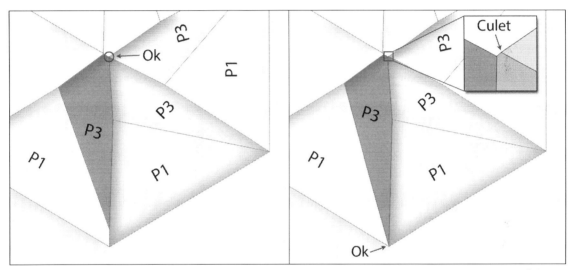

Figure 5-48 The P3 facets must hit two meet points simultaneously, the culet and the intersection of the P1 and P2 facets at the girdle. The left frame shows how the fourth P3 facet (shaded gray) has reached the culet (circled) before the girdle meet point, necessitating a slight increase in cutting angle. The right frame shows the opposite situation, which a decrease in cutting angle will correct. Note that the angular errors in the two cases above are approximately equal, but the similarity in angle and index between P1 and P3 magnifies the effect in the left frame.

5.5.6 Putting the Polish on the Pavilion

Polishing gemstones will be your greatest source of both satisfaction and frustration as a faceter. On the one hand, seeing a mirror-like finish come in and reveal the true glory of your gemstone is enormously rewarding. Even a casual examination of the quality of the polish will set your work in a category far above the commercial gems available in shopping mall jewelry stores. In short, a fine polish is truly the icing on the cake.

All too frequently, however, a stone will be obstinately, infuriatingly, seemingly psychotically resistant to your best-intended efforts. Scratches will appear from nowhere for no reason, and some facets will simply refuse to polish, no matter what you try. I would like to say that experience inoculates you against these frustrations, but it is not entirely true. There are a number of strategies that will keep polishing woes to a manageable minimum (see Chapter 8.17), but even the most experienced gem cutter will occasionally encounter a nightmare stone that refuses to cooperate.

Luckily, your first gem will not be one of these stones, since quartz and especially beryl are relatively forgiving materials and you have done a careful job of pre-polishing (right?). In fact, the majority of headaches encountered by beginning faceters during the polishing phase are actually cutting or pre-polishing problems that come to light when all the distracting haze and minor scratches disappear.

Coming to order...

Unlike during the cutting stage, there is not necessarily a fixed polishing order for the various facet tiers. All of the cutting should be complete at this point, and hence there is less worry about meet points.

Less, but not none. Experienced cutters frequently modify the polishing sequence to minimize the number of mast height and angle changes. On the other hand, you may have to make some minor adjustments, and there is nothing wrong with following the order from the faceting diagram. You have enough to think about on your first gem...

The Final Lap

The variation in polishing properties of different gem materials has led to a proliferation of polishing laps, and while some manufacturers make claims of being "universal," you will almost certainly acquire and use at least two or three different types of polishing lap as you progress. Chapter 3.3 explains the characteristics, advantages, and disadvantages of each, but for a beginner working on quartz or beryl, there is a clear recommendation: the cerium oxide Ultralap.

The Ultralaps are thin, Mylar sheets impregnated with cerium oxide and sold in lots of 5 or 10 to a package. When properly installed on a master lap, the Ultralap allows easy polishing of gem materials that can be challenging with other types of lap. Ultralaps offer other advantages. They are inexpensive, easy to use, and can be discarded when worn out, or even be recharged with powdered cerium oxide. Contamination is simply not an issue: if you notice a problem, just throw the lap away. On the down side, Ultralaps are fairly soft and hence deform slightly under the pressure of the stone. This can lead to rounded facet edges – not a problem for most people, but a definite no-no in the rarefied world of competition faceting.

Installing an Ultralap is easy, but you must follow a few guidelines. The plastic sheet adheres to the master lap via a thin film of water and surface tension. Begin by placing a clean master lap on your machine. Then, using your drip tank or a separate bottle, evenly distribute a number of water drops around the surface of the lap (see Figure 5-49). Too little water will prevent good adhesion, while too much will create a thick film of liquid, further "softening" the lap and producing more rounded facets.

With the water well-distributed, place the Ultralap on the spindle, pressing it down against the lap and squeezing out excess water. Work from the inside to the outside, eliminating air bubbles and forcing the extra water over the side and into the splash pan. When you are done, the Ultralap should be firmly fixed to the master, with no hills or valleys due to air, wrinkles, or excess water. Tighten the lap nut to complete the installation.

Ultralaps like slow speeds and a small but steady water drip. Aim for one to two revolutions per second and one to two drops per second. As a general rule, dry laps will scratch your gem, and Ultralaps are no exception. Before beginning to polish, sweep your finger from lap nut to edge, spreading a film of water over the entire lap.

Figure 5-49 Scatter water droplets on the master lap, and then press the Ultralap into place.

Finally...Polishing

All the preparations are complete, the lap is in place and turning, and you are ready to start polishing your very first facet. Set the angle to 42.6°, dial in index 8, and set the height so that the facet barely touches the lap. Once again, use your fingertip to ensure an even film of water, and then lower the quill to begin polishing. After a few back-and-forth sweeps, raise the stone, dry it off, and examine what has happened. Hopefully, you will observe that the fine scratches and haze left on the facet by the pre-polish phase have begun to disappear, and that the gem has started to take a fine, high polish. Congratulations! See? Polishing is not that difficult.

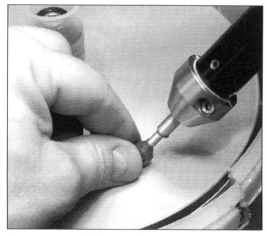

Figure 5-50 Polishing with the Ultralap. As always, you should grasp the stone, not the dop, quill, or handle.

Actually, in all likelihood, you will notice that the polish is not progressing uniformly across the facet. Rather, there may be more polish on one side. This indicates a slight problem with the angle of the faceting head, or the rotation of the quill, or both. As during the cutting stage, a small adjustment of the cutting angle or cheater should set things straight (see Figure 5-46).

After adjusting the facet angle or cheater, try a few more sweeps across the lap and see if things have improved. You may overshoot the correction, but with time, you will gain a sense of how much angle and cheater adjustment produces how much tweak. Yes, this is a variant of your mantra "cut a little, look a lot."

After a couple of adjustments, it may be difficult to ascertain whether you have improved things or not, since polish has appeared all over the facet. Any angle or index difficulties should be uniform across the entire tier of facets, so you can move on to index 24 and a fresh "canvas" for your experiments.

Once you are satisfied with the angle and cheater settings, you can begin polishing in earnest. Continue to sweep the stone across the lap, examining your progress regularly, until all traces of scratches, haze, and pits have disappeared.

When you are happy with the polish, advance to the next facet and repeat your success. Complete the P1 tier and do a final inspection before moving on to the girdle.

Help! A couple of tiny scratches and pits will simply not go away!

Congratulations!

I am not being sarcastic. Having now experienced some of the pain of polishing, you are truly becoming a faceter. Let's see how to turn that pain into pleasure…

First of all, make sure that you are actually making contact with the entire facet. Scratches that don't touch the polishing lap won't go away. One way to check that the gem is sitting flat on the lap is to ink the facet using a waterproof marker.

Try to find a marker that produces a thin, uniform layer of ink without blobs and ridges. Then, touch the facet down on the lap for a moment and examine what has happened. If the ink has disappeared on one side of the facet but not the other, you almost certainly have a slight tilt that will require an angle or cheater adjustment.

Our old friend, Figure 5-46, shows the remedy. Adjust the angles accordingly until a fresh layer of ink disappears uniformly. Record what you did and consult your notes from before: was this a problem facet that you adjusted during pre-polish? There is no sense in having an error on one facet propagate to all the others.

If you are confident that you are making good lap contact, the problem is likely subsurface damage. Among beginners, stubborn scratches are almost always the result of insufficient cutting with intermediate grit laps and less than complete pre-polishing. What you are seeing is the subsurface damage that was there all along, but which sadistically lay in wait for the fine polish before making its appearance.

You have two options. First, you can go back to the previous lap and make sure the job is done before proceeding. Alternatively, you can carry on polishing and get rid of the darn scratches by brute force and time. This is not a bad option, since somehow going back to a coarser lap seems like, well, going backwards. Try to look through the haze of your frustration to see if you are really making NO progress. If things are getting better, even slowly, painfully, better, it's probably best to carry on. Besides, the time and effort spent at this stage will encourage better practice next time. In other words, you are not only becoming a faceter, you are becoming a *good* faceter.

Seeing is Believing...

Half the struggle for beginning faceters is actually seeing what is going on. The final tiny scratches can be quite difficult to discern. This is both good and bad. On the one hand, if you can't see them under your loupe, the casual observer admiring your gem at arm's length will certainly not either. On the other hand, you want your work to be (literally) a cut above commercial quality, and believe me, there is true satisfaction in producing a visually perfect polish.

Proper lighting is the key to seeing fine scratches as you approach the final, mirror-like finish. I find that a bright (75-100W) unfrosted incandescent bulb is the only way to go for seeing the last, tiny imperfections. Try working in an otherwise darkened room, and place the light so that you are just to the side of a direct reflection from the filament into your eye. Any scratches or haze will scatter the bright light and become visible against the rest of the facet, which should be reflecting the darkened room (Figure 5-51).

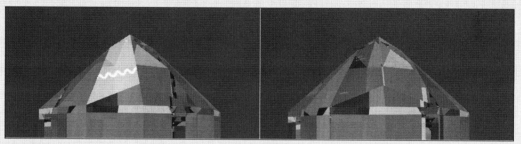

Figure 5-51 Seeing scratches. Try to look at the facet at a slight angle to the reflected image of the filament of an unfrosted light bulb. Filament reflected in the facet (left). Slight head motion moves the reflection off the facet, highlighting scratches (right).

Describing the ideal lighting arrangement is harder than finding it yourself – play around with your lamp and ambient lighting until you are satisfied. Also, don't be confident that there are no residual scratches just because you can't see them. Try twisting the stone around and changing your viewpoint with respect to the lamp – sometimes, problems show up under unexpected lighting conditions.

As during the previous stage, you need not polish the entire P2 facet, since the final girdle will be less than half a millimeter wide (refer to Figure 5-47). Set the cutting angle to 89.9° and the index to 8 for the first girdle facet. As before, you will use only the outer part of the lap. Adjust the location of the water drip as necessary to prevent drying.

Lower the stone and begin polishing the first girdle facet. Again, you should check immediately and often to see that all the angles are correct. And, as before, aim for about 1 mm of polish adjoining the P1 facets. The remainder will go down the drain when you cut the crown.

Complete the polish on the remaining P2 facets, then set up for P3. The end (at least of the pavilion) is in sight!

With two successful facet tiers under your belt, you may feel empowered to charge ahead with the P3 facets. Over enthusiasm is not a good idea at this point, however. First of all, this is how mistakes happen (see "Intelligent Consistency" on page 313). Also, recall that the P3 facets are similar in angle and index to the P1 tier. This means that even the polishing lap can move the meet points around a little. Take your time and do it right.

Check your meet points after polishing a couple of the P3 facets. Are they coming in well? If not, you can try adjusting the facet angle and cheater settings to bias the polish in a certain direction. This has the effect of shifting the corresponding facet vertex, thereby helping you "make your meets" (see Figure 5-52). Such fine tuning is an essential skill: experienced

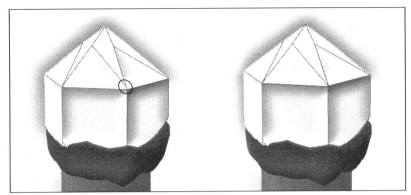

Figure 5-52 Biasing the polish to adjust meet points. The P3 facet in the left figure has missed the girdle meet point (circled). A slight increase in cutting angle can correct this (right hand figure), although be warned: you have very limited ability to move meets around at the polishing stage (see also Figure 5-48).

faceters routinely perform on-the-fly angle and cheater tweaks to match things up. Until you gain such experience, however, "on-the-fly" is probably not the way to go. Keep careful notes of what you did and what happened as a result.

Help! I keep getting new scratches!

This can be due to a couple of effects. First, the lap may be too dry. Ensure that there is always a film of water in place before lowering the stone. Alternatively, the lap may be contaminated, either by some external grit or a piece of the stone itself. Contamination is usually quite localized and hence appears at a distinct radius on the lap. Try washing the surface thoroughly with a substantial water flow to clear things away.

Some gem materials, for example beryl, can have crumbly zones that easily break apart, releasing fragments onto the lap that subsequently cause scratches. Such zones are particularly problematic if they occur near a facet edge. Examine the stone carefully, and if you have such a crumbly area, go easy with the pressure and polish it as best as you can.

Finally, you may just have a stubborn facet – there are no easy explanations for these, but they undoubtedly occur. See Chapter 8.17 for some possible solutions.

Passing Inspection

When you have completed polishing all of the P3 facets, step back, take a break, rub your neck, whatever. As with many of life's activities, the more you stare the less you see. Come back with a fresh eye and examine your handiwork.

Are there a couple of facets that could use a little extra work to perfect the polish? How about shifting a meet by a fraction of a millimeter? If so, don't go immediately back to the lap. Mark the facets with your waterproof pen and then examine their neighbours. Is the mismatch problem really on the facet you suspect? Is there an easier / better way of solving the problem? Will correcting this difficulty create others?

Help! I've been polishing forever - How long should this take?

As you gain experience as a faceter, you will discover that the speed of polishing is inversely proportional to the size of the facet – large facets take a long time, whereas tiny facets seem to take a polish almost instantaneously.

The polishing speed is also inversely proportional to the amount of material that needs to be removed, and this relates directly to the depth of pre-existing scratches and cracks. Again, the best way to reduce polishing time is to increase fine cutting and pre-polishing time.

Finally, there is an unavoidable uncertainty in assessing polishing speed. For example, some gem materials exhibit radically different polishing properties along different directions. Also, individual facets may have individual problems, such as crumbly zones and tiny voids that need to be polished out. Finally, the prevailing conditions at the lap-stone interface – factors such as the amount of water and polishing compound – can have a significant influence.

Despite all this, if you find yourself spending fifteen minutes of hard work per facet, you are very likely on the wrong track. Review the material in this section and in Chapter 8.17 for possible solutions. Properly prepared, a typical, modest-sized quartz or beryl facet should polish out in less than a minute on an Ultralap.

Return to the lap only when you have a clear strategy. Consult your notes and use the ink test (page 172) to ensure that you are doing what you think you are doing. After each adjustment, check that what you thought would happen actually did happen.

Incidentally, like mine, your gem may look backwards. Compare Figure 5-53 with the upper right drawing in Figure 5-2. This phenomenon is due to the way that different manufacturers label their index wheels (see page 303). Don't worry about it for now. Your gem will sparkle just as much, and unless you are entering a faceting competition, no one will notice or care.

Figure 5-53 The completed pavilion.

All the facets are faceted, all the tweaks are tweaked, and you are satisfied in every way. At this stage, you can safely remove the dop and half-completed gem from the faceting machine. Don't forget to store your polishing materials and do a general clean-up.

Congratulations! The pavilion is complete!

5.6 Going End to End...The Dop Transfer

You are half way to the finish line. Having helped you cut and polish the eighteen facets of the pavilion and girdle, your original dop stick is about to go into temporary, but well-deserved retirement. The remaining facets must be placed at locations that are currently inaccessible, either under the wax or protected by the dop stick itself.

The flat dop has one final duty, however. It must help you execute a *dop transfer*. This involves handing the gem over to another dop which holds the stone from the other side. Sort of like the father of the bride at a wedding. As with real weddings, however, the dop transfer can be a bit complicated, placing unwelcome strain on your nervous system, to say nothing of my metaphors.

The complication arises because you have spent a great deal of time establishing an accurate center point and rotational reference, then took care to transfer this frame of reference to the girdle facets. If you just randomly attach a new dop to the stone, all of this effort will be lost, and cutting an accurate, matched crown will be a minor nightmare.

Therefore, the goal of the dop transfer is twofold: you want to (1) transfer the stone to another dop on the other side – i.e. attached to the completed pavilion; and (2) you want to do so without disturbing the orientation and centering of the gem.

Luckily (actually, by design), you have an excellent tool in your armory to accomplish this task: the transfer jig, the same device that helped with the original dopping procedure. Although their design varies considerably from manufacturer to manufacturer (see Chapter 4.16), all transfer jigs share a few common properties, the most important of which is their ability to bring two dops together with accurate centering. This is the key to preserving all of your accuracy and alignment efforts so far.

A Perfect Fit – Selecting the Correct Cone Dop

Before starting the transfer process, you must of course identify a suitable target dop, that is, the one that will receive the stone. This dop must accommodate the pavilion, which has a quite different shape from the rough-ground table facet used for the initial dopping procedure. Due to its symmetric pavilion structure, you will use a cone dop for GeM101.

But which cone dop? As with the initial flat dop, selecting the wrong size can lead to problems later. You will want a dop that covers most, but not all of the pavilion. An undersized dop will prevent strong adhesion due to the small contact area, while an oversized dop will interfere with the first tier of crown facets. Figure 5-54 illustrates the problem and Figure 5-55 shows an appropriate choice for the citrine being cut here.

Executing the Transfer

The cone dop that you have selected will need some preparation. Begin by cleaning the dop with alcohol and examining it for damage and surface contamination.

As before, you will use wax to attach the stone to the dop, again with the help of the shellac-alcohol mixture. Place the cone dop in one block of the transfer fixture and the half-com-

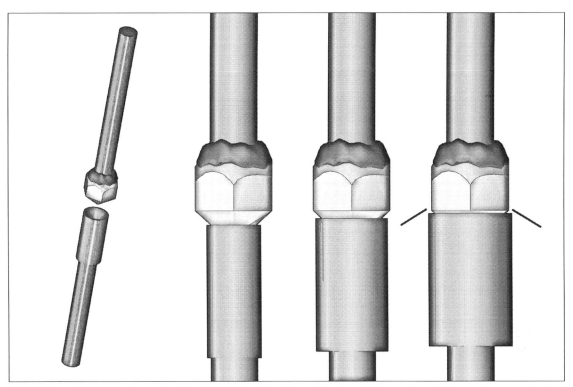

Figure 5-54 Selecting the correct size of cone dop. The three side views illustrate from left to right an undersized dop, the correct dop, and an oversized dop. Note in the rightmost figure that cutting some of the crown facets (black lines) may cut into the dop itself.

pleted gem in the other. Then, using a cotton swab or fine brush, paint the pavilion facets and cone dop liberally with the shellac-alcohol mix (Figure 5-56). Allow everything to dry thoroughly before proceeding.

Now for the fun part. Start by pre-filling the cone dop with wax. Fire up your alcohol lamp and begin gently warming a stick of dop wax. When it starts to flow, bring the cone dop up to the wax to fill it up to the brim (Figure 5-57). Don't overfill the cone: this will cause problems (and possibly burned fingertips) at a later stage.

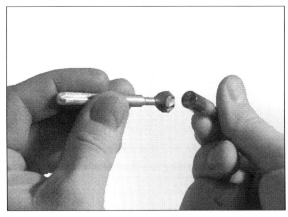

Figure 5-55 Pick a cone dop that covers much of the pavilion but still leaves room to cut the crown facets.

When things have cooled down, your should ensure that both dops are firmly seated in their respective blocks and facing the correct direction for transfer. This means some reversing and re-clamping after the operations shown in Figure 5-56 and 5-57. On my transfer jig, only one of the two blocks moves during transfer – the other remains fixed at one end. If your jig is like this, I recommend placing the cone dop in the fixed block. Also, if you plan to use keyed dops, you may have to check for proper rotation. Consult the instructions that came with your faceting machine and transfer jig.

Figure 5-56 Coat both the pavilion and the cone dop with shellac mixture.

Figure 5-57 Warm the stick of wax over the alcohol flame and fill the cone dop.

Note that you will be fusing the pavilion of the stone to the cone dop while retaining a solid bond on the crown. This requires substantial heat on the pavilion side, while avoiding any softening of the wax on the crown side. To prevent partial melting and potential shifting of the gem, wrap the existing crown-side wax bond with a piece of paper towel soaked in water. This should keep things cool (Figure 5-59 and Figure 5-60).

Everything is now in place. Using a small butane torch or the alcohol lamp, gently warm the outside of the cone dop (Figure 5-58). As the wax approaches melting temperature, it will swell and become somewhat shiny. You have probably already begun to recognize these signs of imminent fluidity.

As before, avoid direct contact between the flame and wax, and try not to let things boil. When the wax is completely fluid, carefully slide the two dops together until the gem is embedded in the wax (Figure 5-59). Don't let the gem contact the dop itself, since this can potentially chip the completed pavilion. Aim for a gap of a little less than a millimeter.

You probably now have another classic cold joint. Look for the telltale convex bulge of wax. If left as is, the stone could pop out of the cone dop, and the nature of faceter's luck is such that this will probably happen at the worst possible time. To ensure solid adhesion, you should add additional wax (Figure 5-60) and warm things through until that wonderful smooth "flowed" appearance indicates a proper bond (Figure 5-61).

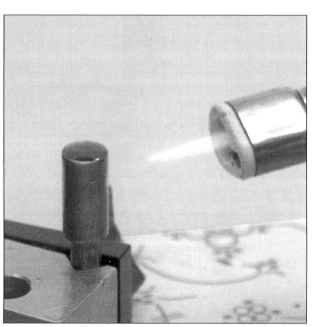

Figure 5-58 Melting the wax in the cone dop. I prefer a butane torch for this step, but it is also quite easy with an alcohol lamp. Note the level of wax in the cone dop.

When you are satisfied with the joint, set the transfer jig aside to let the wax cool completely. Dops and wax can retain heat for a surprisingly long time, and there is no sense in rushing things.

Breaking Old Bonds

The final step in transferring the stone is to break the old bond with the flat dop without disturbing the new. As before, heat is both your friend and enemy. To preserve the new bond, wrap it with a piece of wet paper towel before proceeding.

The standard procedure for breaking the crown-side bond is to heat the flat dop until it falls away from the stone (Figure 5-62). I actually prefer to use an X-ACTO type knife heated in the flame to cut the bond directly.

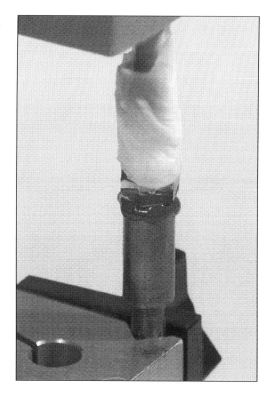

Figure 5-59 Press the stone into the cone dop. Excess wax should flow out from the joint. Make sure that the pavilion doesn't hit the cone dop.

Figure 5-60 Melt additional wax onto the joint between the cone dop and stone. Note the wet paper towel to keep things cool on the crown side.

What happens if – or more precisely, when – you end up breaking the wrong bond? Actually, this situation is not nearly as awful as it is embarrassing. If you think about it, you are just back at the starting line with a stone dopped on the crown side. Simply smile ruefully, clean up the cone dop that you removed, and start again. Of

Figure 5-61 Additional wax and heat will produce a smooth, strong bond. The wax on the left side still shows the characteristic convex bulge of a cold joint.

Whichever technique you use, make sure that you don't cut the bond on the wrong side. Seriously. This can happen more easily than you want to know. Double check. Mark one of the dops. Do whatever it takes.

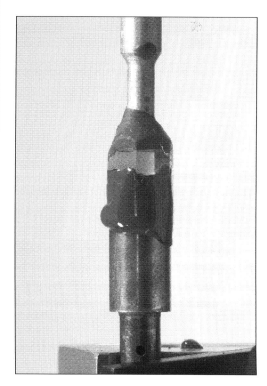

course, if you use a heated knife as I like to do, you can all too easily chip the polished pavilion. Short version: Yick. Don't make this mistake.

After it has cooled, you can drop the original flat dop into a jar containing alcohol. This should dissolve any wax remaining on the dop and leave it as good as new. Don't let the dop soak in the solvent for too long however, since some alcohols can stain some metals over time.

Finally, there will almost certainly be a few blobs of wax adhering to what will be the crown of your gemstone. You can try to remove these with a fingernail or (carefully) with a heated knife blade, or you can just leave them in place. The cutting lap that you will use on the crown is made of steel and diamonds, and the residue is made of wax. Do the math.

The dop transfer is now complete, and you are ready to embark on the final stage of faceting your first gemstone: cutting and polishing the crown.

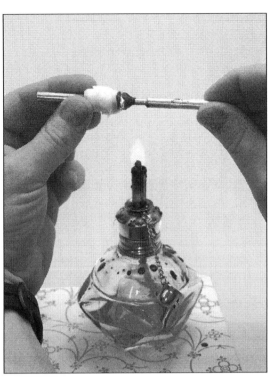

Figure 5-62 Heating the original, flat dop to break the wax bond. Note the wet paper towel on the cone dop to prevent softening of the new joint. This image also clearly demonstrates the value of using a heat (and drip) proof working surface.

5.7 Cutting and Polishing the Crown

The finish line is in view. You have successfully polished the pavilion of your first gemstone and executed a flawless transfer to a cone dop. Now you must literally crown your achievements by completing the top half of the stone.

Begin by installing the cone dop and gem in the quill of your faceting machine. If you have been paying attention, you will notice a problem almost immediately: which way does it go in? The smart-aleck response is "metal end first, stone last" but there is a real and serious point here. You have expended considerable effort establishing the symmetry and centering of the pavilion and accurately transferring this information to the girdle facets. Now you must preserve this accuracy by getting the proper dop rotation for cutting the crown.

Many faceting machines use keyed dops in an effort to maintain the rotational orientation of the facets after transfer. There are also clever jigs that you can build yourself to help with this (see Chapters 7.6.3 and 20.6). These mechanical contrivances do a reasonable job of getting you close to the correct rotation, but in my experience, they do not work sufficiently well on their own to produce competition quality results. In other words, even if you have used the keying system, you will probably want to adjust the index offset, or *cheater*, to get the crown to line up exactly with the girdle facets. In still other words, you will need to learn the mysteries of the *transfer cheat*.

5.7.1 The Transfer Cheat

The goal of the transfer cheat is pretty straightforward: by adjusting the cheater, you make sure that a certain index wheel setting actually corresponds to that setting on the half-finished gem. For example, you have already placed girdle facets at indices 8-24-40-56-72-88. If you were to re-cut the girdle facet at index 8, you need to be certain that it will correspond exactly to the facet already in place.

What happens if there is a rotational offset between the two? Figure 5-63 shows the answer. Actually this picture shows the effect of cutting a slightly mis-indexed facet at 89°, not 90°. If there is a slight offset in rotation, the new cut produces an angled line where the new girdle facet meets the old. Clearly cutting the whole crown under such circumstances would produce a bit of a mess.

Good News! You can actually use this mismatch phenomenon to get everything right. Because the test cut is so similar in angle and index to the girdle, the tilted line is very sensitive to the index error. The goal, then, is to adjust the cheater setting until this line is parallel to the existing girdle. A better option is to cut an entire tier of facets, for example the first tier of crown facets, and make sure that the last facet lines up with the first. In other words, you could test cut the C1 facets and adjust the cheater until any trace of a spiral cut disappears. Note that Chapter 7.7 provides more information on this technique.

It is a good idea to be pretty close to the correct cheater setting before cutting the test tier of facets. Not only will this save time, but also if you have a limited amount of gem rough left to produce the crown, you will waste less of it on test cuts.

There are a number of strategies for getting the initial guesstimate of the cheater setting. For example, proper use of keyed dops will get things close. Another option is to find the correct rotation using the existing girdle facets. Begin by setting the index to 8 and the cutting angle to 90°. Loosen the dop in the quill and carefully lower the gem to the edge of the lap (Figure 5-64). You should now be able to feel the right orientation by rolling the gem back and forth against the lap. Clamp the dop in place when you are happy.

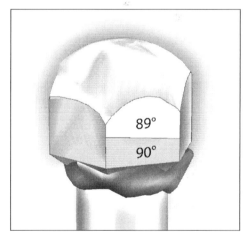

Figure 5-63 Cutting a girdle facet at 89° with the wrong transfer cheat produces an angled line. This line will be parallel to the existing girdle when the cheater adjustment is correct.

A couple of warnings about this method...You should be gentle or use a master lap to avoid scratching the polished girdle. Also, note that this technique relies on a clean edge on the gem. If necessary, scrape away any extra blobs of wax left over from the transfer or try a different girdle index.

There are other schemes for getting a good start on the correct transfer cheat. Chapter 7.6 discusses a number of options, ranging from toothpaste on a mirror to mechanical aids to laser beams. All of these approaches are interesting, and some of them even work. In fact, they may work well enough to completely eliminate the need for cutting a test tier. At this stage, however, the safest and most educational way to proceed is by making a good first guess and doing a test cut.

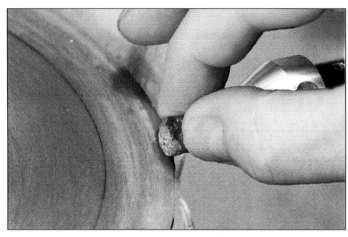

Figure 5-64 Find the correct dop orientation by rolling a girdle facet against the edge of a lap.

Cutting a Test Tier

As explained above, the strategy is to cut a full tier of facets at the same indices as the girdle to check proper alignment. This automatically gives you the index wheel settings, but which cutting angle should you use? In principle, any angle would work. Previous sections emphasize how facets with similar angles are very sensitive to index errors. You could therefore ensure accurate alignment by cutting the test tier at 89°, very close to the angle of the existing girdle (see Figure 5-63).

There are a couple of good reasons not to do this. First of all, it can be difficult to cut consistently at such a steep angle. A tiny change in depth, which would be of no consequence under normal circumstances, can produce a huge shift in the position of the facet intersection. In other words, cutting at 89° would be too sensitive a test. The second reason is that no faceting machine is perfectly square and perfectly aligned. As you gain experience, you will notice that your machine cuts somewhat differently at low angles versus high angles. For example, you may notice that the ideal cheater setting changes a bit with angle. Given this inevitable variability, it's probably best to cut the test tier at angles close to the crown angles.

In fact, why not pick exactly the crown angles? The first crown tier of GeM101 calls for facets at 31.5° at the exact same indices as the girdle (this is no accident – the design wouldn't work otherwise). You can therefore use the C1 facets as the test tier.

Note, however, that it may take several iterations to get the cheater setting correct. Each successive cut will bring the girdle closer and closer to its final thickness. Therefore, it is best to start by cutting the test tier to a very thick girdle (Figure 5-65). Once you establish the proper cheater setting, you can cut the C1 facets to their final location.

Perform a quick "pre-flight" check of your machine (Section 5.5.2), and then install the 1200 grit bonded cutting lap. Note that there may be considerable material to remove, in which case you may also want to pre-form the crown (see Section 5.5.4 and "Pre-forming the Crown ?" on page 185). Nevertheless, laps coarser than 1200 produce very rough surfaces and indistinct meet points, so even if you pre-form, you should cut the test tier with the finer lap.

Set the cutting angle to 31.5° and the index to 8. Start the water drip and gently lower the stone onto the lap. As soon as the gem makes contact, raise it again and examine what happened. Mistakes often occur at this stage, so a quick sanity check is in order. The new facet edge should be parallel to its partner on the pavilion side of the girdle.

Continue cutting until enough material has been removed to establish the first facet of a complete tier – remember the goal here is to get the cheater setting with a generous margin on girdle thickness. Move on to index 24 and cut to the meet point produced in the previous step. Continue around the stone until index 88, and then examine your results.

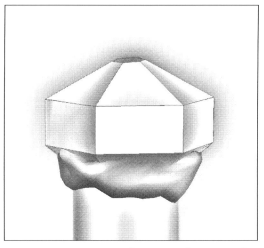

Figure 5-65 Leave enough room so that, even after a few iterations of the test tier, you have sufficient remaining gem material for a proper girdle.

There will almost certainly be a slight (or even a significant) mismatch at the last facet meet. The nature of this mismatch, either under-cut or over-cut, tells you about the direction, and, with experience, the amount of adjustment for the cheater. Figure 5-66 explains how. If you don't know which way to turn the cheater, note the current setting and do a quick experiment. You should be able to produce a visible rotation of the dop after a turn or two of the cheater knob. Just don't forget to set it back to where you started before continuing your cut.

Adjust the cheater accordingly and start over at index 8, cutting the facet slightly deeper than before. Work your way around the stone and again examine the outcome. Hopefully, your correction improved things. Based on the amount of change, estimate a new cheater setting and repeat the entire tier, again slightly deeper than before.

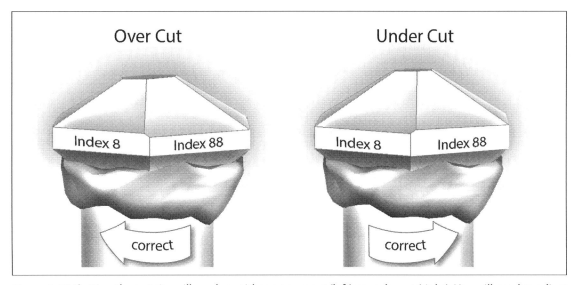

Figure 5-66 Cutting the test tier will produce either an over cut (left) or under cut (right). You will need to adjust the cheater as shown to correct the situation. Note the facet indices. Some index wheels go the opposite way (see page 303), but the sense of the correction remains the same.

After three or four iterations, you should end up with a complete tier of facets that meet well all the way around. Congratulations! You have solved the mystery of the transfer cheat. Don't forget to note the cheater setting in your log, since you may make adjustments to the individual facets during the polishing phase.

With the transfer cheat complete, you are finally ready to cut the crown in earnest.

The Transfer Cheat with Mixed Breaks

GeM101 is a very simple design with a complete tier of crown break facets – that is, the first facets above the girdle are cut at a single angle and height setting.

This is by no means always the case. Many gem designs have "mixed breaks," in which alternating facets with different angles form the crown (or pavilion) girdle line. The Briar Rose design described in Chapter 18 is one example. How do you test the transfer cheat in such a case?

The answer is quite straightforward: always work with the highest facet angles, since you can always cut a facet to a lower angle. Cutting a facet to a higher angle is like going to the barber to have your hair lengthened. Chapter 7.7 discusses this further.

5.7.2 Cutting the Crown Facets

If you have just completed testing and adjusting the transfer cheat, everything should be in place to cut the actual C1 facets. Set the index to 8, check the angle and cheater settings, and then begin. This time, you will want to take the girdle thickness down to close to its final value.

Of course, this raises the question: "how thick should the girdle be?" This turns out to be another of those conundrums that faceters seem to be able to discuss without end. A too-thin girdle may chip or fracture when set into a piece of jewelry. On the other hand, a very thick girdle is aesthetically unpleasing, and may also be difficult to set. Turn to "Weight Gain and Girdles…" on page 44 of Volume 2 for more musings on this issue. For now, you should leave the girdle a little more than half a millimeter thick (Figure 5-67).

Move on to the facet at index 24, cutting it down to the meet point created by the previous facet and the girdle (circled in Figure 5-67). As with the pavilion, you should try to hit the meet point as close as possible, but recall that the 1200 Nubond will set the final facet locations. With the second C1 facet in place (Figure 5-68), you have a new meet point to target for the third. Continue around the stone, completing the C1 tier (Figure 5-69).

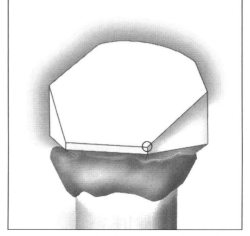

Figure 5-67 Cut the first of the C1 facets down to its final location, leaving a girdle a little more than half a millimeter thick.

Pre-forming the Crown ?

Depending on the size and shape of your original rough, there may be considerable excess gem material left over for the crown. This is a fine situation to be in for a first stone, since you may get a second chance in the event of a serious cutting error. On the other hand, cutting away a lot of expensive gem rough is not the best long-term strategy. In general, being left with a lot of extra material indicates a mismatch between the gem rough and the design.

To save time, you can pre-form the crown much as you did the pavilion. The approach is identical: select the highest angles – in this case 31.5° – and work your way around the stone at the appropriate indices.

Pre-forming the table at this point doesn't make sense, since for most faceting machines, this would force you to remove the dop from the quill, thereby losing the rotational reference from the transfer cheat. Also, you may already have a reasonable table area from the initial dopping procedure, and you can always start with a more aggressive lap when you get to the table in due course .

Whatever you decide to do, remember that you will still need to cut a test tier when the pre-form is finished. In other words, you should leave at least a couple of millimeters of girdle for the finer lap.

If all went well with the transfer cheat, there should be no under or over cut for the last facet at index 88. If you see a problem, examine all of the C1 facets for accuracy and touch things up as necessary. There isn't much girdle thickness left at this stage for experimentation and error, so once again, cut a little and look a lot.

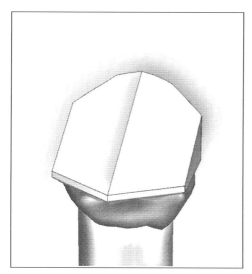

Figure 5-68 Cut the C1 facet at index 24 down to the meet point between the girdle facets and the C1 facet at index 8.

Adjust the cutting angle to 22.2° and the index to 5 for the C2 facets. A word of warning: some faceting machines don't like cutting at very low angles, that is, with the quill almost vertical. You will encounter this phenomenon later when you cut the table at a very small angle – zero degrees. The C2 angle of 22.2° is not that extreme, so you probably won't notice much difference. Nevertheless, it is a very good idea to proceed slowly until you get a better feel for your machine.

Cut the first of the C2 facets until the girdle meet point (Figure 5-70), and then move on to index 21. Proceed through the entire tier as before. When you are done, the stone should look like Figure 5-71.

With the C1 and C2 tiers complete, you have now finished cutting the crown.

But wait, you ask...the crown includes the table facet, and you haven't even started that one. This is perfectly true, but as the next section explains, you will probably need to remove the

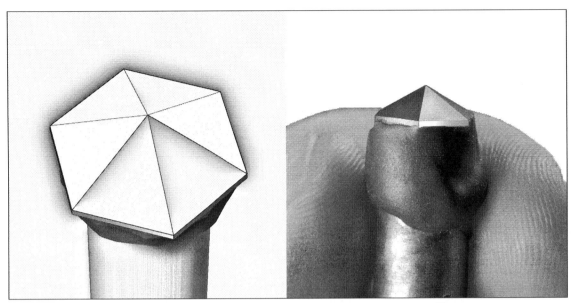

Figure 5-69 The completed C1 tier defines the gemstone's girdle.

dop from the faceting machine to cut the table. All that effort in getting the correct transfer cheat would have to be repeated if you cut the table at this stage. Instead, you will complete the fine cutting and polishing of the C1 and C2 facets before embarking on the table.

The pre-polish follows the same procedure as for the pavilion. Remove the steel 1200 lap and do a general clean-up, including your hands. Install the 1200 NuBond with master lap and re-set the machine for the C1 facets.

Pre-polish the C1 and C2 facets, again taking care that each facet receives a uniform finish. You may have to adjust the angles and cheater settings somewhat to produce a good pre-polish and clean meet-points. As with the pavilion, keep a record of your actions to prevent surprises in the polishing phase.

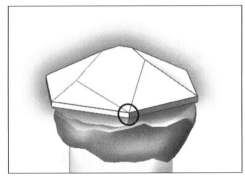

Figure 5-70 The first C2 facet hits the girdle meet point (circled).

5.7.3 Polishing the Crown Facets

When you are satisfied with the crown pre-polish, remove the NuBond lap and perform your clean-up ritual. Install the Ultralap on the master, and polish the C1 and C2 facets until all traces of scratches and haze disappear. As before, examine the polished surface with intense, oblique lighting in order to spot and eliminate those last, pesky scratches.

Recall your experience with the P3 facet tier. You were able to move the meet points around slightly at the polishing stage. This was particularly true of the girdle meet point, due to the similar cutting angle and index wheel setting between P3 and P1 (see Figure 5-48 and 5-52). You can do the same with the crown, although the substantially different angles and indices give you much less leverage.

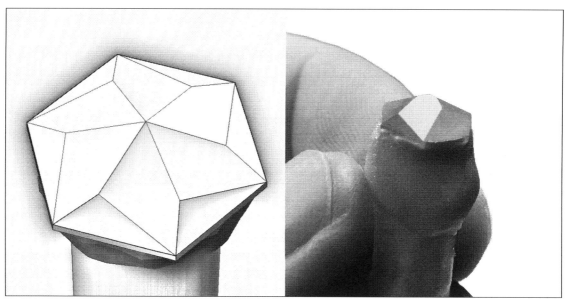

Figure 5-71 The completed C2 facet tier.

Polishing the second half of your gemstone probably went better than the first. Not only are you more experienced and efficient, but also you probably recognized that effort spent at the pre-polish stage more than pays for itself.

At this point, you should have a beautiful, almost complete gemstone on your hands (Figure 5-72). The finish line is now definitely in sight. All that remains is cutting and polishing the table.

Faceter-Induced Oscillation

There is a curious phenomenon among beginning flyers known as "pilot-induced oscillation." This occurs when the neophyte chases the instrument readings, reacting to where the plane currently is, rather than to where it will be in the future. The result is slow but endless oscillation about the desired altitude or heading.

Shifting meet points around can produce a similar effect. Correcting one problem too hastily can produce others, which when corrected cause more problems. You may even end up back where you started.

GeM101 is a simple design and is fairly resilient to such cascading difficulties. Later on, however, you will attempt more complex gems and inevitably encounter more complex interactions between facet placement and the location of meets. Establishing good planning practice now will help reduce your own oscillations in the future.

5.8 Cutting and Polishing the Table

The table facet is the last of the 31 facets in the GeM101 design. As you will learn, however, the table facet can take much more time to complete successfully than any other individual facet on a gemstone. This is not necessarily a bad thing. After all, faceting is fun!

There are a number of very good reasons why the table takes extra time and care. First of all, it is usually the largest facet, sometimes by a considerable margin. And, as you learned with the pavilion P1 and P3 tiers, larger facets take longer to cut and (especially) polish.

Another reason why tables can be problematic is that they frequently have multiple meet points. For example, the table of a standard round brilliant must accurately meet 8 different facet intersections. The accumulation of minor errors toward the top of the crown can present a real challenge for the SRB, since all those problems come together on the last, most visible facet. Luckily (actually by explicit design), the table in GeM101 has exactly zero meet points.

Figure 5-72 The crown is complete, except for the table facet.

Accumulated Error and the Anti-Culet

Depending on the amount of material you had left for the crown, the C1 or C2 facets may have created a center point at their apex, a sort of "anti-culet." Have a quick look at this center point (Figure 5-73). Did all the C1 or C2 facets intersect at a single location? If they did, you have done an excellent job.

More than likely however, there will be small offsets and errors between the facets. This is not really a problem, since the entire apex of the gem will be cut away by the table. On the other hand, it is worth thinking about how this happened. Recall that you initially established a reference point using the TCP at the base of the pavilion. Accurate placement of the subsequent pavilion facets shifted this reference to the girdle, and the careful dop transfer process brought it, in turn, to the crown.

In other words, creating this gemstone has been a steady progression of shifting accurate reference points upward from the culet through the girdle to the crown. Inevitably, errors build up in this process, and the missed meets at the "anti-culet" are the result.

There is a deeper lesson here. By continuously shifting slight errors from a place where they cause difficulty to another location where they don't, you can effectively sweep problems under the carpet (or down the drain of your splash pan). You will learn to appreciate and exploit this strategy as you gain experience as a faceter.

Figure 5-73 The C2 facets have created a new center point at the apex of the crown. Note the slight errors.

Wobbly Tables

GeM101 has no table meets – the simplest possible table, right?

Actually, maybe not.

Think about the geometry of the situation for a moment. Two points define a line. In other words, you can always draw a straight line between two points. Similarly, three points define a plane, and you can always fit a plane through three points. Put another way, you can always place a facet at three meet points. And you can sit on a three-legged milking stool on any surface without wobbling.

What happens with more and more points? Four points over constrain a plane. If the four meet points are actually in a single plane, fine. But if they are not, you cannot place a single facet through all of them. This is why that old picnic table wobbles, even on a flat balcony, and it is why hitting 4 or more meet points with your gem's table can be a challenge. This is also why a standard round brilliant, with eight table meets, is a terrible first gemstone to cut (refer back to the first section of this chapter for more opinion on this).

It seems, then, that tables with zero, one, two, or three meet points should be easy, and they are. I would argue, however, that zero is harder than one (or two or three), since you must eyeball the relative position of the facet edge, rather than hitting an exact vertex.

The final cause of table trouble is the fact that most mast-type faceting machines hate to cut at very low angles, and the table is as low as it gets: zero degrees. The reasons for the difficulty have to do with angles and forces. Basically, for intermediate angles, the force you apply to the gem pushes it efficiently down into the lap. When the quill is almost vertical however, these forces are transverse to the lap (see Figure 5-74). Slight variations in cutting depth or machine flexure then translate more directly to differences in cutting angle, and the situation rapidly goes downhill.

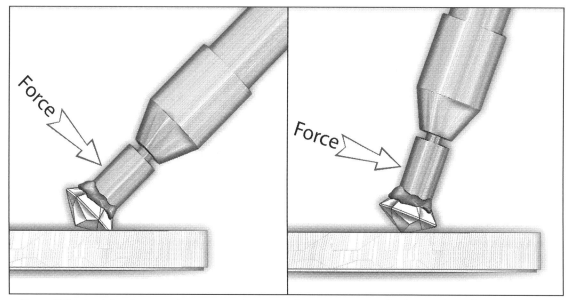

Figure 5-74 Applying force to the stone produces good cutting action at higher angles (left). Near vertical, however, the applied force is largely parallel to the lap (right).

In addition to the increased likelihood of cutting errors, operating the quill near vertical raises the risk of the stone jamming against the turning lap and digging in. Trust me, you do not want to experience this.

The low cutting-angle problem has prompted manufacturers to supply a solution: the 45° table adapter (Figure 5-75). This device comes in many forms (Chapter 4.15), but its function is very straightforward. The table adapter allows you to cut a 0° table with the faceting head at a much more modest 45°.

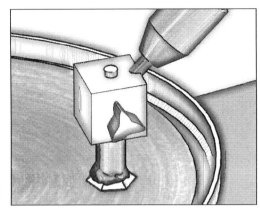

Figure 5-75 A 45° adapter for cutting tables. The knob clamps the dop and gem into the rectangular block, and the 45° shaft goes in the quill.

Begin by removing the gem and dop from the quill. Yes, this will throw away your careful rotational alignment from the transfer cheat, but hopefully, you won't need it from here on. Install the 45° adapter in the quill and make sure that it is square with the lap. The variety of available adapter configurations means that there are several ways of doing this. With my adapter, I set the cutting angle to 45° and place the adapter loosely in the quill. I then lower the faceting head until the block of the adapter lies square on a flat lap. Tightening the quill clamp then locks everything in place (Figure 5-76).

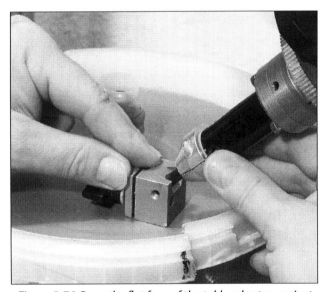

Figure 5-76 Press the flat face of the table adapter against the lap to square things up before tightening the quill.

After you have squared the table adapter, raise the faceting head and install the gem and dop (Figure 5-77). At this stage, the rotational orientation is irrelevant. Gently lower the quill and adjust the height until the stone is just clear of the cutting surface. With the 1200 grit bonded lap in place and the water dripping, you are ready to begin.

Lower the stone onto the lap and begin cutting (Figure 5-78). After a moment or two, raise the quill and examine the result. You should see the beginning of a hexagonal table facet appearing on the tip of the crown. This facet should be close to being exactly centered on the stone.

Consult the faceting diagram (Figure 5-2) one more time. Note how the table facet cuts the C2 facets approximately halfway between the tip of the C1 facets and the center of the gem. You need to cut the table facet until you are close to the correct depth. The NuBond lap will take care of the final fraction of a millimeter.

As you cut the table facet, note carefully whether it is symmetric and well centered. If the distances from the hexagon to the tips of the C1 facets are not equal, you will need to adjust the cutting angle or cheater setting. Figure 5-79 clarifies how this is done.

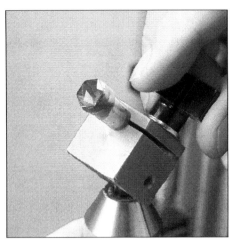 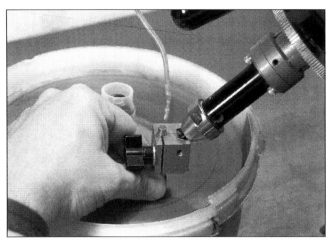

Figure 5-77 Insert and lock the dop in the 45° table adapter. The rotational reference doesn't matter here.

Figure 5-78 Cutting the table with the 45° adapter. As always, you should apply force directly to the stone, not to the dop, quill, or adapter.

Continue cutting a little and looking a lot, making adjustments to the angle or cheater as necessary. Take your time at this stage and make sure that everything is correct – that is, the table is centered and symmetric – long before you reach the final cutting depth. There will be no opportunity (nor stone) to do it later.

When you are satisfied with the depth, remove the cutting lap, clean things up, and install the NuBond with the master lap. Pre-polish the table facet to remove the damage done by the cutting lap. As before, you may have to adjust the cutting angle and cheater to ensure a uniform pre-polish. The table is the largest and most visible facet on the crown, so you really want to get the pre-polish right.

You're almost there. Remove the NuBond lap, do a clean-up, and install the Ultralap. Polish the table like any other facet, until all scratches and haze disappear. Again, you should examine your work under intense, oblique lighting to reveal any previously unseen uglies. Don't worry if the table seems to take longer to polish out. This is a natural result of its being the largest facet (see "Performance under Pressure" on page 317), and of course your eagerness to finish the stone.

When the last imperfection has disappeared, lean back, take a deep breath, and then examine the gem with your loupe. Are you really done? Tiny scratches often lurk in the corners of the table facet, where slight angle mismatches are amplified. Change the position of your lamp and look again.

It's finished. It's really finished! Time to declare victory!

The Table Song

Did your faceting machine sing to you when you polished the table? Actually, it's more like squeaking. Working with the table adapter and polishing a large facet at 0° tends to set up resonances in the quill and mast. My machine positively shrieks sometimes. This is not a problem, unless serious vibration sets in. If the noise bothers you, try adjusting the water flow and your hand pressure.

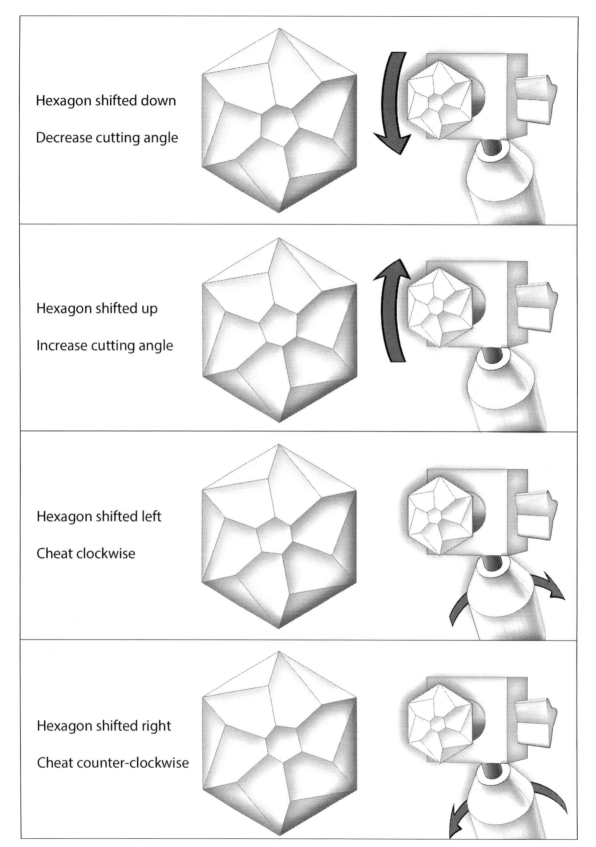

Hexagon shifted down

Decrease cutting angle

Hexagon shifted up

Increase cutting angle

Hexagon shifted left

Cheat clockwise

Hexagon shifted right

Cheat counter-clockwise

Figure 5-79 Watch carefully as the hexagonal table facet develops. Each corner of the hexagon should be the same distance from the tip of its corresponding P1 facet. Adjust the cutting angle or cheater setting as shown to ensure a symmetric, centered table

5.9 Finishing Up

Your first gemstone is finished, but it probably doesn't look like much, all bound up in a brownish coat of wax. To release the final beauty of your gem, remove the dop from the quill and hold it over the alcohol lamp on a heat-proof surface. Place the flame about two thirds of the way from your fingers to the stone (Figure 5-80 – see also Chapter 7.3.3).

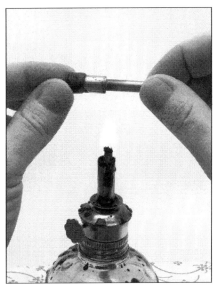

Figure 5-80 Heating the dop to release the gem. You should twist and pull on the stone just as the dop starts getting uncomfortably warm.

After a few seconds, you will feel the dop warming up in your hand. Grasp the stone with your other hand, and gently work the gem free of the wax. You should be able to twist and pull the stone out before the dop gets too hot to hold. If you have difficulty, hold the dop with a wet paper towel, although this will make it harder to sense the right moment. In any case, you will want to put the dop down on the heat proof surface as soon as the gem is free. Try not to drop the stone – it shouldn't be hot.

Your gem still doesn't shine, since a substantial amount of wax remains attached to the pavilion. Because of the way gemstones work, the pavilion must be absolutely clean for top performance. Your first gem will require a bath before its grand debut.

Wait until the stone has cooled completely, and then drop it into a small jar containing alcohol (Figure 5-81). Seal the jar and swirl the solvent gently to begin dissolving the wax.

The entire clean up shouldn't take more than ten minutes. You can speed things up somewhat by swirling the jar every few minutes. You can also pull the stone out and work on some of the larger blobs of wax with your fingernail (but nothing harder!). After a few minutes, the liquid will become clouded with dissolved wax, but this just builds anticipation…

When all the wax is gone, remove the stone and place it on a clean paper towel. Rinse the gem with clean alcohol and dab away any remaining wax. I like to perform a final wipe-down with a microfiber cloth to remove the last traces of alcohol, fingerprints, and lint residue from the paper towel.

Place the gem on a clean surface with good lighting, particularly from behind your head, and admire your work.

I hope you said wow. I sure did after completing my first gemstone, and after most of them ever since.

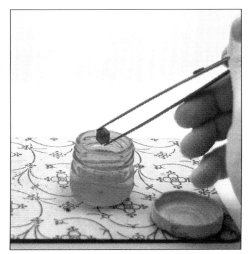

Figure 5-81 Place the gem in a jar of alcohol to remove the dop wax.

Congratulations! You are done!

You have a number of options for storing and displaying your gem. At a bare minimum, you should place it in a small glass or plastic display box (Figure 5-82). This will allow you to pocket the stone and show it off to your friends and family. It will also prevent others from covering the gem with fingerprints. You will grow to hate fingerprints.

Figure 5-82 Protect your pride and joy in a small plastic or glass display box.

Actually, you have one final duty. Put away the polishing materials, and do a general clean-up of your faceting machine. If you don't plan to start with another gemstone immediately – you have to show off, after all – put a dust cover over your work area. You should also drop the cone dop into a jar of alcohol for ten minutes to remove the dop wax residue.

Once again, congratulations on completing GeM101, your first of hopefully many gems.

6

Gem Rough

Finding, selecting, and orienting gem rough presents a daunting challenge to the beginner. From paying the right price at a gem show to evaluating internal inclusions and flaws to determining the best orientation at dop time, the deck seems stacked against the neophyte faceter.

It doesn't have to be so. This chapter provides practical, real-world advice on navigating the tricky waters of gem rough acquisition and management. It begins with several suggestions on where to find rough stones, including sections on working with lapidary dealers, attending gem shows, trading with friends, and even digging your own out of Good Old Mother Earth.

A short section on organizing your rough collection helps you forestall the inevitable chaos that a large drawerful of rocks will engender. This is followed by two crucial discussions of selecting the best piece of gem rough from a pile and paying the right price for it.

Synthetic and simulant gemstones offer the opportunity to cut large, essentially flawless gems without mortgaging your house. The chapter provides an overview of manufacturing techniques and the variety of materials available. A final section gives tips and tricks for orienting gem rough for maximum visual impact and weight retention.

6.1 Gem Rough

The first gem that I cut on my new faceting machine was a murmellite. What is murmellite, you ask? Well, "Murmel" is the German word for a child's glass marble, and there seems to be a tradition of baptizing a new faceting machine with a marble. By happy coincidence, my two young sons had a large and appealing collection of transparent marbles at the time. You can see where this is going. It wasn't too difficult to coax a prize green specimen out of their hoard, and marbles are well-shaped and chunky by design.

The upshot? My first attempt at finding, selecting, and orienting gem rough was easy and successful.

It got more difficult.

Oh boy, did it get more difficult. I don't need to bore you with war stories of failed attempts to track down and usefully exploit decent gem rough. That is what your friends at the lapidary club are for. Nevertheless, a few general guidelines on finding, selecting, and orienting raw gem materials will hopefully make your experience more pleasant and at least as educational as mine.

Figure 6-1 The first gem from my new machine, cut from top quality murmellite.

6.2 Finding Gem Rough

Unsurprisingly, the first step in managing your gem rough situation is finding some of the darn stuff. Depending on where you live and how much you can travel, the best source may be a local dealer, a virtual shop on the Web, booths at a large gem show, or even Mother Earth herself. The following sections should help you on your way to locating good gem rough at a good price.

6.2.1 Buying from Shops

Is there a real bricks and mortar rock shop in your area that carries faceting rough? If so, consider yourself lucky and get to know the proprietors. An established, trusting relationship with a reliable gem dealer will make your faceting life easier, more enjoyable, and considerably less financially risky. In all likelihood, such dealers will value your commercial relationship almost as much as you do. After all, satisfying regular customers means regular income and an expanding business. You may also find a kindred spirit, since many local lapidary dealers are in it for the love of the hobby.

Of course in this digital age, a good rock shop doesn't actually have to be made of bricks and mortar, and relationships established over the Web can be every bit as personal and trusting as the "real" thing. Because of the enormously larger potential market, gem rough dealers, both bad and good, are all over the Internet. Identifying the good ones can be a bit of a risk, although the online forums are an excellent source of information and experience (see Chapter 15.1.3).

Needless to say, you should have both your Internet and human behaviour antennae fully deployed in this exercise. And, as in any "real" commercial establishment, the dealer-customer relationship can also be both bad or good. On the one hand, our connected world has enabled robbery at the speed of light, and online comment often emphasizes complaint over satisfaction. On the other hand, bad actors can be identified almost instantly to a wide community, and hence an online dealer's motivation to preserve his or her commercial reputation is correspondingly strong.

Note that cultivating a mutually beneficial relationship with a gem rough dealer may occasionally involve some compromise on your part. Yes, the maxim that the customer is always right may apply to most commercial establishments, but individual gem dealers are a partial exception to the rule. They often provide rough parcels *on memo*, which means that you can examine the stones at your leisure and select which ones you want to keep. You will not continue to enjoy this service if you return every stone every time, however. Having gem rough out on memo costs the dealer time, money, and commercial availability of the product. In the interest of preserving and strengthening your relationship, you may find yourself occasionally purchasing a piece of rough that is below your expectations. It is perfectly reasonable and appropriate to express your dissatisfaction, but absent a ridiculous consignment, it is in your best long-term interest to buy *something*. Note also that gem dealers talk to each other and they will soon determine whether you are the type of customer who asks to examine dozens of stones from several sellers, but never seems to buy anything.

Whether your chosen shop is real or virtual, shopping for gem rough in this way holds a huge advantage over the other options listed below: you have the luxury to examine the stones properly and at your leisure. The bricks and mortar rock shop will permit you to do this on site, and if you are a regular customer, you should be able to take the stones home overnight for careful study. This allows you to conduct the full range of nondestructive testing on the rough before committing to a purchase. Obviously, home delivered material from an online dealer offers the same opportunity.

Note the use of the word "nondestructive" in the previous paragraph. Unless you have an explicit agreement with the dealer beforehand, you should in no way modify the stones before purchase. This includes the common practice of polishing a small window into the surface of the rough to examine the interior. Dipping the stones into Refractol or other immersion liquid should be kosher, provided you clean up afterward, but the rule of the road in the rough business is "you modify it, you own it." See Chapter 4.5 for more on immersion fluids.

6.2.2 Attending Gem Shows

Gem and mineral shows are like Disneyland to hobbyist faceters. There may be hundreds or even thousands of exhibitors displaying and selling an amazing variety of wares, ranging from jade sculptures to petrified dinosaur poop. Scattered in among the chaos, you may even find a few gem rough dealers.

Actually, depending on the show, you may find dozens of rough dealers from around the world, all in the same place at the same time. This has the wonderful side effect of built-in price competition and variety, but the show environment is considerably more hectic than your local rock shop. In other words, you will probably encounter better selection and value, but you simply won't have the opportunity for comprehensive evaluation of the rough prior to purchase. As with buying from real or online shops, your examination cannot physically alter the stone in any way, and few show dealers will allow you to use immersion fluids without prior arrangement. A flashlight, magnifying loupe, and the occasional discretely deployed drop of spit should all be Ok (see "What to Bring below).

Figure 6-2 The picturesque French mountain village of Ste. Marie aux Mines hosts a large gem and mineral show each midsummer.

The transitory nature of the show booth changes the sales experience compared to your storefront or online purchases. Cash transactions are the norm, receipts are rare, and you should consider all sales as final. A booth is clearly less permanent than a brick and mortar shop or even a web presence, and I have seen the same individual return to successive shows under a different company name. The short version of all this is that, when you walk away from the table, the deal is done.

On the positive side, show sales are mercifully – and perhaps not always legitimately – free of tax. It is also possible to establish and cultivate relationships in this environment. Many dealers return to the same show year after year, and a couple of purchases should make you a recognizable and welcome client. You can help nurture this relationship by talking with the dealer, as long as things aren't too hectic. Ask about the origin of the gem rough. Explain what you do and what type of material you like. Request a business card and if you have one, offer yours. Inquire about private salesroom viewing options, and if you know a favourite dealer is going to be in town, send an e-mail a week in advance to set up an appointment.

Here's a useful tip in the form of a (hopefully) hypothetical question. If you could grab a fistful of premium gem rough off a display table and run, what would that cost the dealer? Note that, given the hectic, crowded circumstances of many gem shows, you might not even have to run. The answer, I am sure you will agree, is a great deal of money, perhaps thousands of dollars.

The message (and the tip)? The quality of the gem material will get better and better as you look from your side of the table toward the dealer's. In fact, many sellers will not have their best rough on open display at all. It pays to stop and ask if there are "special items" behind the counter. Dealers will be more than happy to show you the good stuff.

The Big One

If your typical gem show is like Disneyland, then the Tucson gem show is faceter Nirvana.

Each January and February, what seems like the entire gem and mineral world gathers in this Arizona town, transforming many hotels, several parking lots, and a great deal of open space into a giant gemstone marketplace. The Tucson gem show has been growing for almost sixty years, and it is now more like 20 simultaneous large shows at almost 50 locations scattered throughout the Old Pueblo. Many of these are open to the public, although attending some of the "premium" events may require a commercial license or tax number. The whole affair attracts tens of thousands of participants and contributes something like 100 million dollars to the local economy.

Figure 6-3 Big sky, big shows, big crowds. The Tucson gem and mineral show is a must-see for any hobbyist gem cutter.

The Tucson show is unquestionably bigger, but is it better?

In my experience, no. At least not in terms of purchasing raw gemstones. It is a sad fact that the huge scale of the Tucson show does not alter the economics of the gem rough trade, and it certainly doesn't change human nature. The breadth of quality and selection may be greater than at other shows, but you are not going to find a free lunch in terms of price. In fact, quite the contrary in my experience: I have found lower prices and struck better deals at the smaller shows.

Nevertheless, the Tucson extravaganza is a one-of-a-kind event, and a January pilgrimage to the Desert Southwest should be on every gem-cutter's calendar at least once in their lifetime.

What to Bring

As emphasized in previous paragraphs, the environment of the gem show offers better variety and price at the expense of limited opportunity for careful examination of the rough. How do you make the most of this situation? Any Boy Scout knows the answer: Be Prepared.

You want to get the best possible impression of your potential purchase under the difficult circumstances of a busy gem show. This means bringing the following at a bare minimum:

- Penlight for examining gem rough and illuminating inclusions
- Spare batteries for same
- Loupe or other magnifier
- Small plastic ruler for measuring rough

In addition to these items, my gem show kit (Figure 6-4) includes small Ziploc-type bags for the rough and an indelible marker to label them with the dealer's name, cost per carat, and country of origin of the rough. I use bags that are just large enough to contain the stones and the dealer's business card, and I bring a small stack of my own business cards to hand out as a way of establishing a potential long-term relationship. I also tend to pack a few sheets of white paper to evaluate colour saturation (see Chapter 12.3.4).

Here are some things that you should *not* bring to the gem show: Portable scales are a no-no, because every dealer will have a means of weighing the rough, and you will hardly initiate a trusting commercial relationship if you insist on using your own scales. For what it is worth, I have bought hundreds of pieces of rough over the years from dozens of gem show dealers, and I have yet to encounter a single instance where the seller tipped the scales. You also shouldn't bring any additional inspection aids, such as immersion fluid. Gem show etiquette simply does not permit you to break out messy and smelly fluids at the dealer's table without prior agreement (see "Immersion Etiquette" on page 100).

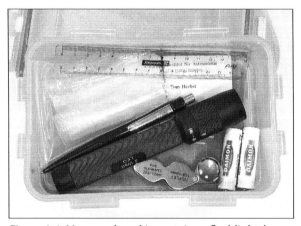

Figure 6-4 My gem show kit contains a flashlight, loupe, small Ziploc bags, ruler, pen, spare batteries, white paper, and a packet of business cards. A small plastic Tupperware box keeps everything together and provides safe transportation for new acquisitions.

Figure 6-5 One of the four giant halls hosting the annual München Mineralientage in Munich each October. This is the largest gem show in Europe, with over 1,000 exhibitors from all over the world.

Premium Gem Shows

While I like nothing better than mucking about in a pile of gem rough, hunting for that special bit of rock, not all of the gem faceting community operates this way. There are, in fact, specialized gem shows for the serious high rollers of our world.

I have been to only one such event, the InterGem show in Idar-Oberstein, Germany (www.intergem.de). The show was a bit overwhelming, with only top-drawer rough and cut gemstones on display. For example, I held a case containing a couple of dozen large blue-green tourmalines, each of which would fetch more than my annual salary (see page 213). Definitely interesting, and like Tucson, worth a try at least once in your life. And no, I didn't come away with anything other than envy.

Figure 6-6 The hushed, carpeted confines of a premium gem show. No spitting on the gem rough here. Note that you will almost certainly require some sort of commercial license or identification to get into these affairs.

A Peek Behind the Veil...

How can you possibly examine gem rough for internal flaws under the frenzied conditions of a gem show?

The answer is you can't, at least not as thoroughly as you'd like to. Chapters 4.5 and 5.3.1 explain how to search for inclusions using immersion fluid, which is unfortunately in short supply at the gem dealer's table. You will just have to muddle along as best you can given the tools at hand.

The first step is to illuminate the piece of gem rough from the side using your portable flashlight. The goal is to pick out internal bubbles, veils, and cracks, which should appear as bright flashes against the surrounding material. If you can, try both dark and bright backgrounds with this test, and you should certainly illuminate and examine the stone from all sides. Depending on the circumstances, you may be able to use some water or saliva to help see through frosty surfaces.

Any internal feature that lights up is probably an inclusion. If you find something suspicious, you should be able to rock the stone back and forth slightly to determine its depth. Confirm the existence of the flaw by examining the affected region from another direction. Veils, twinning planes, and internal fractures often appear as a two-dimensional surface embedded within the three-dimensional body of the gem. Look from the opposite side to confirm the geometry of the structure.

Finally, you shouldn't necessarily give up and put the stone back down if you find a flaw. For example, most inclusions near the surface can be removed at the pre-forming stage using a judicious choice of gem design and rough orientation. Such strategies can also place deeper flaws at an unobtrusive location in the final cut gem, such as near the junction of small crown facets or near the girdle.

Note, however, that problems near the culet will get optically multiplied, potentially turning that single, small inclusion into a bouquet of ugly. As with every "however" in faceting, this however has its own however: in some circumstances, such as the tourmalinated quartz in Figure 6-11, a flaw near the culet can increase the value of the gem considerably. Turn to Chapter 12.12 for more on the wonderful world of inclusions.

6.2.3 Trading with Friends

Your friends and colleagues at the local lapidary club can be more than just a wellspring of advice and endless discussion of wax versus epoxy. They can also be an excellent source of gem rough.

Faceters tend to be hoarders. A glance into our workshops tells the awful truth. We hate to throw things away, because somehow, somewhere, that chunk of wood or broken pair of pliers will come in useful. A glance into our rough boxes tells a similar story. Good gem rough is hard to come by, but when you find it, you have to buy an extra piece or two (or three). For example, at my current rate of cutting, I have at least twenty years of raw stones moldering, albeit in a well-organized way (see Section 6.3 below), on my workshop shelf. Of course, given the steady rise in the cost of gem rough, all of these purchases were very reasonable and justified…honestly.

Burdened or blessed with all those extra chunks of aquamarine, most gem cutters are willing to sell or trade on reasonable terms with fellow faceters. Ask around. Some clubs even organize swap meets to facilitate this type of exchange. An additional benefit of trading with fellow cutters is that you are (hopefully) less likely to get cheated on the value of a piece of gem rough, particularly if you agree that wax is the only way to go…

Note also that when faceters give up their hobby, whether willingly or not, more than just their machines become available (see "Faceting for Eternity" on page 42). An ill or departed colleague would almost certainly appreciate their rough collection falling into the hands of a kindred spirit, but as always, exercise due respect when circumstances demand it.

6.2.4 Dig Your Own!

Nothing beats the satisfaction of producing a gemstone from start to finish: digging the rough out of the ground, evaluating its form, selecting an optimal design, and finally cutting and polishing a perfect gemstone.

In a word, Wow.

Despite the fact that a substantial fraction of gem rough comes from parts of the world that are troubled in one way or another (see page 216), there are opportunities for digging your own. Whether it is sorting through mine tailings in California (Figure 6-7) or fossicking in the renowned sapphire fields of Australia, the amateur gemstone polisher can experience the start-to-finish gemstone journey.

The Internet is an excellent source of information on current mine operations. Many locations have their own websites, and the online forums regularly feature extended discussion threads on the topic (see Chapter 15.1.3).

Bounds of reason have to apply to your expectations, of course. The economic forces of the gemstone trade do not lead naturally to fee (or free) digging operations. The increased profit associated with cut goods, to say nothing of liability issues associated with mining, tends to discourage such activity. The net effect is that dig-your-own sites are few and far between, and the quality of gem rough that you can expect to extract will be lower than your initial hopes. Nevertheless – and having done it myself – Wow.

Digging My Own

Given the enthusiasm expressed in the adjacent paragraphs, it will come as no surprise to you that I have succumbed to the attractions of the dig-your-own philosophy. I have sifted gravel in North Carolina for corundum. I have sorted through piles of mine tailings in California for tourmaline (see below). I have wandered off-road trails in Arizona in search of all kinds of pretty rocks. I have even done some pretty serious hard rock mining in upstate New York for quartz crystals. Don't get me started about my fossil hunting adventures…

On a recent July business trip to San Diego, I ditched my colleagues and the air-conditioned comfort of the city to go get dirty in the tourmaline mines of the Pala region. Pala is a lovely place, carpeted with rolling pine forests and dotted with lakes, all in the shadow of historic Palomar Mountain (see Figure 3-1). For gem aficionados, it is also known as the discovery site of morganite beryl and kunzite, as well as the source for distinctive, hot pink tourmaline.

There are several fee-dig sites in the area, and on the basis of a friend's recommendation, I selected the Himalaya mine near Lake Henshaw.

I heeded the advice on the mine's website, arriving fully equipped with food, water, sunblock, and the type of clothes that I wouldn't mind throwing away afterward (a depressingly large fraction of my wardrobe fits this category). The mine operation supplies all the necessary sieves, water sluices, shovels, and buckets.

After a brief introduction by a friendly staff member, I set about moving as much of the mine tailings as I could through my sieve. After three or four hours toiling in the hot California sun, I had a decent handful of tourmaline crystals interspersed here and there with transparent quartz (Figure 6-8).

Was it worth it?

Well, that's a complicated question. Let's break it down a little.

Would I have done better spending the same money at a gem show?

In terms of finding gem rough, the answer is undoubtedly yes. The entrance fees at these dig sites, coupled with a bit of careful negotiation, should get you a fistful of nice citrine or amethyst at any gem show and could even finance a couple of grams of pretty decent tourmaline.

Did I find anything worth cutting?

Absolutely. While none of the pieces in my haul would stop me dead in my tracks at a gem show, I did manage to extract a few cutters from the pile. Note also that there are

Figure 6-7 That's me on the left hunting for tourmaline at the Himalaya mine in the Pala region of California. The operators transport a pile of mine tailings down from the mountain, and eager rockhounds sift through buckets of the stuff, searching for that elusive gem.

Figure 6-8 My haul after spending close to four hours sifting through rubble from the Himalaya mine. All of the stones on the left, including the large quartz point, are potential "cutters." Tourmaline from the Pala region is mostly pink and green, although I did find a few colourless pieces and a single, small, blue crystal.

at least two possible approaches to sifting for gemstones this way. You can use several different sieve meshes, taking the time to sort the material down to a size where smaller but more likely perfect crystals occur. On the other hand, you can use a single, larger sieve, expediting buckets and buckets of tailings through the thing, looking for that rarer, bonanza stone. I adopted the former approach, largely because I couldn't imagine letting a single potential gemstone slip through my grasp. In retrospect, and given the couple of large, beautiful crystals pulled from the pile by my fellow sifters, I would probably adopt the high-speed, high-reward option next time.

Would I recommend this type of rock hounding to others?

Again, absolutely. In fact, despite the hard work, long hours, and ruined clothes, I tried to re-jigger my schedule to allow a stab at another of the area's mines before the end of my trip. Sadly, things did not work out. This time. Maybe it's the fresh mountain air. Maybe it's miner's fever. Maybe it's the fact that a big, beautiful tourmaline crystal is just waiting for me in the next bucket. In any case, I will be back.

6.3 Organizing Your Gem Rough

Hard as it may be to believe when you first start out, you will one day be overwhelmed by your rough collection. Trust me.

I, too, was skeptical when I encountered the real-world prices of gem rough. Unlike others, I would buy only as much as I could cut, and I would of course cut everything I bought.

Ahem.

Just in case that doesn't happen, you should make an effort to organize your collection from the beginning. This means storing your gem rough in a way that you can rapidly lay your hands on a particular type of material, or even an individual stone that you remember buying last year at the local show. It also means recording and maintaining information about the price per carat, dealer name, and the locality of the rough.

Such organization and record keeping has several advantages. First and foremost, you can actually find what you want without ransacking your workshop. Second, you can maintain a decent overview of your rough collection and, for example, know for certain that you don't need a single, extra piece of zircon, except perhaps that lovely honey-coloured one that isn't really that expensive…

Accurate records let you keep an eye on the rough market as well. Although gemstone prices have been rising across the board (see Section 6.5 below), supply and demand pressures may place certain materials at a premium, impacting your purchasing strategy and, if you sell your cut gemstones, your asking prices. Finally, it is nice to know – and relate to others – the country and region of origin of your gems.

Order from Chaos

There are many ways to go about organizing your rough, and you should tailor your method to suit your needs. For what it's worth, here is what I do…

When I return from a rock shop, gem show, or prospecting trip, I make a visual record of all the material I acquired. The simplest way for me is to place the stones on the glass of a flatbed scanner and cover them with a sheet of white paper. A standard scan produces a 1:1 image of each stone, showing size and (more or less) accurate colour (Figure 6-9).

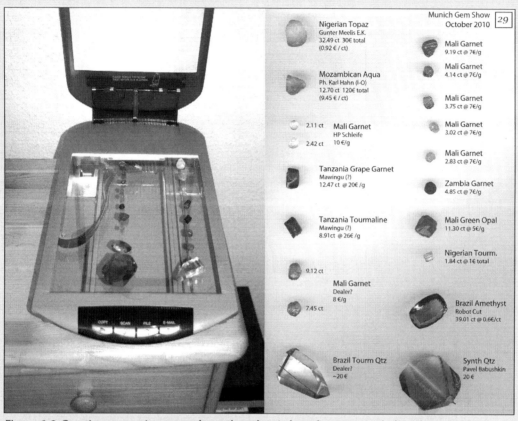

Figure 6-9 Creating a page in my rough purchase log. I place the gem rough directly onto the glass of a flatbed scanner and capture a full-page size image. In the computer, I add information about the weight, cost per carat, and dealer name. Note the page number in the upper right.

Next, I add the date and information about the location of the shop, show, or mine. Beside the image of each piece of rough, I record the weight, cost per carat, and dealer name. This can be done within the computer or by writing on a printout of the scan. Finally, if and when I cut a certain piece of rough, I record on the sheet some identifying information on the resulting gemstone, including a number, the gem design, and final yield.

So much for paper. All the printed records in the world won't help if you then dump the gem rough into a drawer. How do I organize my rocks?

There are numerous options out there for organizing small bits and pieces, whether they be nuts and bolts, sewing equipment, or resistors and capacitors. I have seen gem cutters use cardboard boxes, envelopes, and all sorts of compartmented cases. The best solution may be transparent organizers sold by electronics shops (Figure 6-10). These clever trays pop open, giving you access to a couple of dozen individual pockets ideally sized for gem rough. When closed, they slip easily into a standard office binder. Different configurations offer flexibility in terms of the size and/or amount of gem rough in each tray, and as a final benefit, they are crystal clear. Drop the tray onto a sheet of white paper, and you can make an instant comparison of the relative colour and saturation of your stones. You can also quickly tell whether a certain piece of rough might match your target design without popping it out for a measurement.

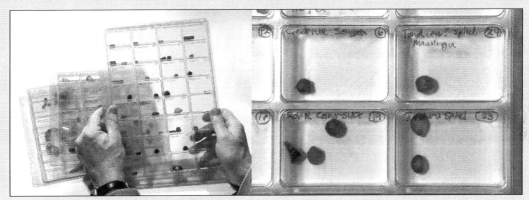

Figure 6-10 Electronic component shops sell organizer trays that are ideal for gem rough (left). This particular type contains 10-32 individual pockets and fits easily into a conventional office ring binder. Even better, you can easily record individual information on a tray cell (right).

I record identifying information using an indelible marker on the top of each cell of the tray. This information includes the locality of the material and, critically, a number corresponding to the page in my rough log recording the weight, dealer name, cost per carat, and so on (see above).

Note that I actually enjoy this organization process. While your experience and methods may be different, the benefits of organizing your rough collection are clear. My advice? Do it sooner rather than later.

6.4 Selecting Gem Rough for Purchase

You've finally made it to that big gem show, or managed to spare a few hours on a business trip to visit a lapidary shop or local swap meet. How do you actually select the best pieces of rough to buy? Gerald Wykoff, the great gemologist and author, memorably characterizes the process of selecting and purchasing gem rough as "common sense – with a slight touch of the Riverboat gamble." The whole operation can be intimidating, particularly for the beginner. Faced with dozens of tables of rough, each holding dozens of individual stones at perhaps dozens of dollars per gram, the neophyte will be justifiably nervous, particularly since in most circumstances, all sales are "as-is" and final.

6.4.1 What to Look For

There are some general guidelines which can help. In particular, there are four characteristics of gem rough that should enter your decision making process: colour, clarity, size, and shape.

Colour refers to the overall chromatic appearance of the stone and includes colour zoning (local regions of more or less intense saturation), as well as direction-dependent colouration or pleochroism (see Chapter 12.4). Look for pleasing and vibrant coloured samples that stand out from the rest of the lot. Beginners often make the mistake of evaluating colour by holding the rough up to a source of light. The white paper test (see page 90 of Volume 2) is a much more reliable means of assessing the final gemstone colour and will prevent you from accumulating (as I have) a distressingly large amount of distressingly dark garnet.

Clarity measures how well the gem rough transmits light. Clarity is impacted by all kinds of internal flaws, ranging from diffuse cloudiness to individual inclusions, bubbles, and veils. Note that some of these flaws, such as individual needles in quartz (see "Clearly Superior" below) and horsetail inclusions in demantoid garnet, can actually increase the value of the gem rough substantially.

Clearly Superior

When is less more? Particularly when it comes to gem clarity?

The answer lies in unique inclusions and flaws, which either unquestionably identify a gemstone as authentic or provide unique visual impact.

The case of a single tourmaline needle in quartz provides an arresting example of the latter. I cannot count the number of bins of transparent quartz I have sorted through, looking for that elusive piece with just the right geometry (Figure 6-11).

Why chase down such an oddball piece of rough? Well, if you arrange things right, with the needle exactly down the axis of the stone, you can produce some pretty remarkable gems (Figure 6-12). The striking reflectance pattern results from multiple reflections, particularly near the culet.

Note that Chapter 12.12 contains more advice on identifying and managing inclusions.

Parenthetical remark #1: The optical multiplication evident in Figure 6-12 carries an important lesson for gemstone orientation: except in extraordinary circumstances such as this, you will want to keep internal inclusions and flaws well away from the optical axis of the gem. Section 6.7.1 discusses this further.

Figure 6-11 A single needle of tourmaline in an otherwise (mostly) perfect quartz crystal.

Parenthetical remark #2: The gemstones in Figure 6-12 do not exist in the real world. Finding a suitable piece of quartz proved so challenging that I did not want to experiment with different gem designs on actual stone. These are three dimensional computer renderings which include the actual gemstone and needle geometry, as well as the optical properties of quartz. Turn to Chapter 15.5 to learn how it was done.

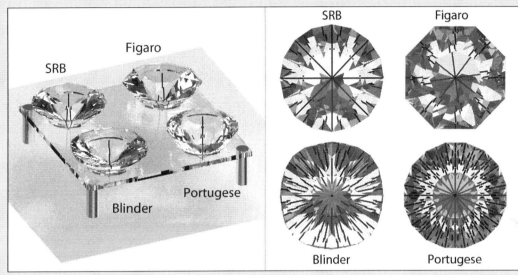

Figure 6-12 A single needle of tourmaline oriented perpendicular to the table of several gemstone designs cut in colourless quartz (left). Seen from above, the facets produce a dynamic, kaleidoscopic effect (right). These computer renderings allow a direct comparison of the optical effects of a needle in various gemstone designs.

Size has a very strong influence on the cost of finished gemstones (see Figure 6-14 in the next section), and this influence naturally appears at the rough stage as well. Beginners should count on losing up to 80% of the initial weight of the stone during the cutting process. Don't let this get you down, however: 20% retention is fairly respectable, and experienced faceters rarely reach 35% in final yield.

Shape is perhaps the most difficult of characteristics to judge for beginning cutters, since it involves visualizing the final gemstone in 3D while accounting for internal flaws, cleavage planes, crystallographic axes, and so on. Generally, rounder, more "chunky" shapes will provide the best match to common gemstone designs and hence produce higher yield. A small plastic ruler or brass caliper can be a real help in assessing the overall shape of a stone prior to purchase. Note that the shape is particularly important for smaller pieces of rough, since accounting for an internal flaw or surface divot will require removal of a proportionately larger fraction of the stone. Sadly, smaller rough usually means the more expensive gem materials.

Governing all these evaluations of colour, clarity, size, and shape is the target gem design. Note, however, that in some circumstances, the gem cut will drive the choice of stone, while in others, a unique sample of gem rough will dictate the best design. See "Cutting to the Rough or Cutting to the Design?" on page 211.

In Perfect Shape

There is a category of gem rough that has guaranteed good shape: pre-forms. These are stones that have been ground to the approximate final outline at the source, accounting for initial shape, internal flaws, and so on. For some mysterious reason, topaz seems to be available as pre-forms more than other materials (actually, I suspect it has a great deal to do with the unique colour treatment of topaz – see page 157 of Volume 2).

Although pre-forms will undoubtedly produce higher yield, there are at least two down sides to purchasing this type of gem rough. The first is the fairly obvious point that someone else has made the decision on gemstone design for you. Not only does this limit your flexibility, but also it short-circuits one of the more important and rewarding aspects of the hobby: establishing a relationship with the raw gemstone and arriving at the perfect, matching design (see opposite page).

The second potential pitfall with pre-forms derives from the economics of the gem cutting industry. Section 6.5 explains that there is a financial benefit to producing finished gemstones at the source, thus leading to shortages and higher prices for rough. Why, then, would there be an active market in pre-forms, which command little or no premium above raw stone from the ground?

The answer is that there isn't, and you almost always see gems in two forms: rough and finished. The danger for the neophyte purchaser is that unscrupulous firms will begin to cut and polish a particular stone, only to discover a fatal internal flaw. The partially completed gem then somehow finds its way onto the pile of material to be sold as rough. Short version: if you find a partially pre-formed gem in a lot of raw rough, watch out.

Turn to "Buy the Bad Stuff" on page 215 to learn about a safer, more reliable source of pre-formed gems.

6.4.2 Interactions between Colour, Clarity, Size, and Shape

The characteristics of colour, clarity, size, and shape are important enough on their own, but it is the management of their *interactions* that separate the true master cutter from the pack.

How do these various characteristics interact? Well, some things are obvious. For example, the shape of the raw stone influences its effective size, at least in terms of cutting a particular gem design. The size and shape of a piece of rough may also force a less than optimal orientation for colour. Similarly, poor clarity – for example a bad veil – can mean an effective change of size or shape. The colour saturation may conceal clarity problems, such as deeper inclusions. Finally, a few visits to a gem show – or a single dig-your-own expedition – will provide a vivid demonstration that good clarity becomes increasingly rare with increasing rough size.

Other aspects of the interaction of colour, clarity, size, and shape are less straightforward. For example, it can be very difficult to assess how the different colours of a pleochroic gem will interact, given a particular orientation of the design with respect to the crystallographic axes of the rough. Some gemstone materials can exhibit a remarkably different colour once cut, due to the removal of outer material and the exact location of colour zones and layers. Experience can be a great help here, but expect to be surprised, at least occasionally (and see page 232).

Cutting to the Rough or Cutting to the Design?

Should your piece of gem rough dictate the design you select, or vice versa?

This is a bit of a chicken and egg question, since your available material limits the range of possible designs, and your inclinations in terms of gem shape will inevitably influence which rock you pick up from the dealer's table.

There may be external constraints. For example, you may be cutting the stone for a friend, who absolutely cannot stand rectangular gems, or you may be confronted with a damaged stone or a piece of jewelry with a missing gem that needs replacement.

Absent such constraints, and with the gem rough already in hand, you can pick your own design path. Faceting a stone represents a substantial investment of time, so there is no reason to rush the selection. Sometimes, I let the gem rough itself suggest a design. It is not unusual for me to carry around a raw stone for days, taking it out of my pocket in free moments to let my imagination work on it. Will this stone shine in one of my standard gem designs, or will I have to find something new? (or create it? – see Chapters 16-18). With experience, you will know when the stone and design are right for each other.

Of course, economics comes into the equation. You can pretty well cut any design out of any piece of rough, but it may be accompanied by an unacceptable loss of yield. Internal flaws and inclusions play a role as well. They may eliminate certain shapes or force a difficult choice between a larger flawed gem and a smaller, perfect one.

The best situation is to have a range of possible designs and raw materials. That way, the choice of cut and stone becomes a synthesis arising out of your relationship to both the gem rough and your library of designs.

6.4.3 Other Considerations

A couple of final words on selecting gem rough…While considerations of colour, clarity, size, and shape should be foremost in your mind, intangibles count as well. For instance, your dealer may have a piece of marginal rock crystal that was mined in your home town, or you may finally track down a less than perfect sample of that one shade of beryl missing from your collection. As with most aspects of the hobby, inspiration guided by experience is the best approach.

I leave the very final word to Wykoff, whose riverboat gambler analogy began this section. His advice, which I follow to this day, is to be conservative with most acquisitions of gem rough, interspersed with the occasional gamble. This ensures a steady supply of high quality material, while occasionally providing a spectacular bargain that you can boast about at the local lapidary club. And no, you don't need to mention the gambles that go bad...

6.5 Paying the Right Price

Are you feeling overly buoyant and optimistic? Do you need a good solid kick to the shins of your exuberance? Here's a fact that ought to set you straight: the great masters of our craft, the ones who wrote the classic textbooks (see page xvii of the Foreword), made pointed remarks about how gem rough had gotten rarer and more expensive.

That was in the 1970's and 1980's. Yikes!

If you have been following the gem rough market since then, you know that the situation has not improved (Figure 6-13). How could this possibly be?

There are several very good reasons why gemstones in raw form are expensive and hard to find. First and foremost among these is the profit motive. The current gem market, coupled with labour costs and automation, places a clear economic imperative on the mines: finished goods are more profitable, and the greatest windfall comes from cutting at source. As a result, very little top quality gem rough trickles out to the amateur faceting market, and prices are correspondingly high.

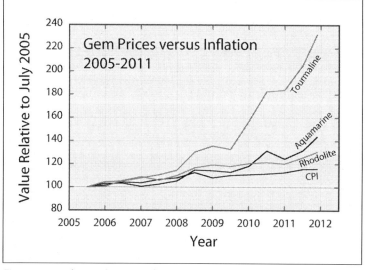

Figure 6-13 The evolution in finished gem prices over the period 2005-2012. No surprises here: everything has gone up, even outstripping the consumer price index (CPI), a measure of inflation. Data from gemval. com, an online gem appraisal site and the US Bureau of Labor Statistics (see Chapter 15.8.13 for links).

Other factors influence the price and availability of gem rough. For example, the cost of the diesel fuel needed for mining operations and the current exchange rate can affect prices significantly. Many gemstone types arise from localized, episodic finds, which can rapidly be exhausted or abandoned. Supply and demand pressures then drive the price up accordingly. The popularity and extreme value associated with Paraiba tourmaline is a textbook case of this phenomenon (see "Tulips and Tourmaline" opposite).

Export restrictions and political difficulties can also place upward pressure on the price of gem rough. It is an unfortunate fact that much of our raw material comes from places in the world that are either economically or politically challenged (or both – see "Faceters for Social Responsibility" on page 216). In these circumstances, the gem cutting trade can be an avenue to economic development, or rough gemstones may be a readily transportable currency in a large, illegitimate economy (or both). These two factors can drive up rough prices and drive down availability.

Finally, Adam Smith's "invisible hand" is at play: market forces determine retail prices and availability. Put more simply, dealers charge more because we will pay more. There is no moral judgment associated with this statement – they are merely honest businessmen and women. Here are a couple of questions to ask yourself the next time that the bile of outrage rises in your throat at the asking price for gem rough: 1. Do you know any rough dealers who are actually *rich*? and 2. How many thousands of dollars have you already invested in what is essentially a pleasant pastime? Any reader who sells cut gemstones for a living is exempt from the second question. Besides, you probably already understand that business is business.

Tulips and Tourmaline

Have you heard of "tulip mania"? The term refers to a wild and woolly period of free market capitalism in the Netherlands in the early 17th century. During the winter of 1636-7, speculation in the market for tulips drove prices up by a factor of twenty within a month, at which point the market abruptly collapsed.

Yep, you read that right. Tulips.

What sets tulip mania apart from other economic bubbles before and since is the apparent detachment of the market forces from the actual intrinsic *value* of the product. Yes, our Dutch friends dearly love tulips – a drive through the Netherlands countryside during high bloom will prove that – but please… At its peak, prices for *individual bulbs* of the recently introduced flower exceeded the average Dutchman's annual income by a factor of more than ten. Ten years of hard work for a single flower? Mania may be too gentle a word…

Actually, modern thinking has revisited the tulip mania of the 1630's, and more accurate sourcing of information is changing opinion of exactly what happened. Whatever the economists now think about the speculation and futures contracting that took place that fateful winter, you should probably take exception to the notion that any beautiful product of nature has limited intrinsic value.

The case of Paraiba Tourmaline provides another instructive example that is presumably closer to our hearts than a tale of 17th century Dutch floriculture. In the early 1980's, a Brazilian prospector or *garimpeiro* named Heitor Dimas Barbosa was bewitched by the vivid blue-green colour of some small tourmalines collected by a friend. Convinced that something truly special lay beneath his feet, Barbosa spent more than five years searching for the mother lode. Finally, in 1987, he found pay dirt, and a couple of years later at the Tucson Gem Show, Paraiba tourmaline burst on to the world gem market, enchanting visitors and experts alike with its electric blue-green glow.

Even at the time of its discovery, it was clear that the supply of Paraiba tourmaline would be limited. In a faint echo of tulip mania, asking prices at the show began at $900 per carat and rapidly shot up to $3000 per carat. Unlike with the tulips, however, the Paraiba market has never looked back. Those early stones from the original mine can fetch $10,000 per carat or more today.

Subsequent finds of similarly coloured tourmaline in Nigeria and Mozambique have not really cooled the market that much. The Nigerian material is not quite as vivid as the original Brazilian gem, and although the Mozambican stones can be larger and equally eye-popping, they just don't carry the mystique of that original Paraiba find.

Tourmaline mania? Perhaps. After all, there are single Paraiba gemstones out there whose value exceeds ten times an average worker's salary. Perhaps it is the ghost of Adam Smith whispering in my ear, but somehow it strikes me that the right price for something is exactly equal to how much people are willing to pay.

For gemstones, that is. Those flower people were nuts…

Given all these market forces, how can you be sure that you are paying the right price?

The answer is experience and preparation, and unsurprisingly, the two build on each other. For example, preparation involves researching current and historical prices for gem rough, knowledge that will help you when dealing with individual retailers. Similarly, your negotiations at the gem dealer's table will help you prepare and manage expectations for future transactions.

You can track down approximate current prices online (see Chapter 15.8.13). There are numerous sites which sell gem rough, and you can also get a reasonably good idea based on the cost of finished gemstones. Simply divide the per-carat price of commercial cut gemstones by ten to get an estimate of the cost of the rough. Note that this works for real, retail pricing, not initial bids on eBay! Finally, the best indicator of future pricing is the past. Keep a record of what you have previously paid for a certain gem species and quality. Prices keep rising (Figure 6-13), so don't forget to adjust your estimates accordingly.

At this point, it should go without saying that the desirable characteristics you should look for in raw gemstones – specifically, colour, clarity, and size – are exactly those which drive the price as well (see Figure 6-14). Beautifully coloured, flawless, and large gem rough commands premium prices. Eagle-eyed readers may have spotted a missing characteristic. For reasons of efficiency, shape usually plays a minor role: it takes a lot less time for a dealer to weigh a sample of tourmaline than it does to consider possible gem designs that can be cut from it. Recognizing this fact may lead to your greatest cost savings. A piece of rough which permits 40% final yield is effectively half the price per carat compared to another stone whose less favorable shape will yield only 20%.

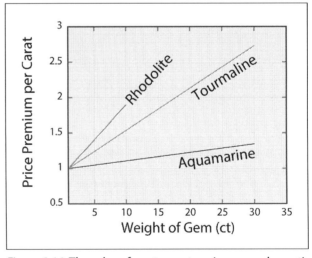

Figure 6-14 The value of a cut gemstone increases dramatically with its size. This plot shows the per-carat price relative to a one-carat stone as a function of the overall gem weight. For example, a ten-carat rhodolite will command almost double the price per carat, compared to a one-carat gem. Data from gemval.com, November 2011.

A few final words on paying the right price…You will find that there are multiple levels of costing, depending on the amount of rough you purchase. Clearly, large lots will go for a lower per-carat price than individual, handpicked stones. Incidentally, any lots you purchase may have already been picked over or "high graded." It is entirely appropriate to ask whether this is the case, and reputable merchants will be honest about high grading and charge a correspondingly lower lot price.

Dealers may also quote you a lower initial price if you show them a commercial license or present a business card, since this indicates that you are knowledgeable and potentially a valuable, repeat customer. Negotiation is the norm, and you should be able to knock down the initial quoted price. Nevertheless, you must exercise judgment and recognize that you are unlikely to teach the dealer his or her own business. Finally, be prepared to walk away from what you consider a bad deal.

Buy the Bad Stuff

Go ahead. Admit it.

You have cast aspersions on the quality of mall-outlet gemstones. You have heaped abuse on the wares of questionable eBay vendors. I daresay you have sneered at the all-night shopping channels hawking "genuine high quality gemstones."

What if I told you that some of these "once in a lifetime" opportunities are a good buy after all? Yes, the cut quality of the gemstones on offer is almost always uniformly poor, but they may represent a fairly reasonable way of acquiring rough.

How can this be?

Well, to begin with, pre-cut stones have already been sorted for internal bubbles, inclusions, and veils, and the admittedly poor surface polish will still let you see any remaining problems. Unlike with "raw" gem rough, you can return an obviously flawed cut gemstone or simply put it back on the dealer's table. You can also get a very good impression of the final stone colour before opening your wallet.

However, by far the greatest advantage of pre-cut stones is in the area of *yield*. You should consider such material as very high quality pre-forms, with an obvious location for the table, girdle, and pavilion. Given a reasonably well-matched target design, yields of 80 to 90% and more are possible.

Here's a real-world example: you should be able to pick up loose "commercial cut" amethyst or citrine gemstones for well under a dollar a carat (see the amethyst in Figure 6-9). I have seen decent, clean finished topaz gems for a couple of bucks a carat. With guaranteed internal clarity and colour, the three to four times higher yield possible with these stones compared with less well-formed rough makes this option very competitive. It can also be very instructive to purchase two identical commercial gems. Re-cutting one and performing a side-by-side comparison provides a clear example of the value of your craftsmanship.

Faceters for Social Responsibility

Stop an average person on the street and ask them what the following countries have in common:

Nigeria, Tajikistan, Bolivia, Pakistan, Burma/Myanmar, Tanzania, Russia, Madagascar, Columbia, Afghanistan, Brazil, Zambia, South Africa, Uruguay, Mozambique…

Unless you are in Tucson in February, I am willing to bet that the response will be that these countries are the location of past or present wars, political unrest, dictatorships, and so on. And I bet that no one would say that they would want to vacation there.

Of course, the list refers to the great gem producing localities of the world, and having visited at least a couple of them, I can say that general opinion is often wrong. Also, to be fair, other nations, such as Australia, Canada, and the USA belong on the list of gem producers, and they have some fine vacation spots.

Nevertheless, the question remains for the socially responsible faceter: am I helping or hurting the situation for the average person in country X by purchasing gemstone rough?

The answer is obviously complex, and it varies dramatically from country to country and year to year. Conditions for miners are rarely ideal, although for some, digging for gems represents the only viable economic opportunity in a region. Gemstones also clearly provide a means for quietly and compactly transferring wealth, which in itself can be a force for both good and evil.

I am not going to tell you whether or not you should indulge in gem rough from troubled areas of the world. As with many aspects of modern life, that is a personal moral decision that should be illuminated by knowledge of the true conditions on (and in) the ground.

And if in doubt, Norwegian peridot should be a safe bet…

Gondwana Reunited?

I have a distinct childhood memory of seeing a bumper sticker on a VW microbus that read "Reunite Gondwanaland." Growing up in the midst of the nationalist awakening of Quebec, Canada in the 1970's gave this mysterious message an unusually evocative power.

Reunite what? Reunite where?

I later learned in geography class that Gondwanaland, now conventionally shortened to Gondwana, was one of two supercontinents – the other is Laurasia – that resulted from the breakup of the original granddaddy of supercontinents, appropriately named Pan-

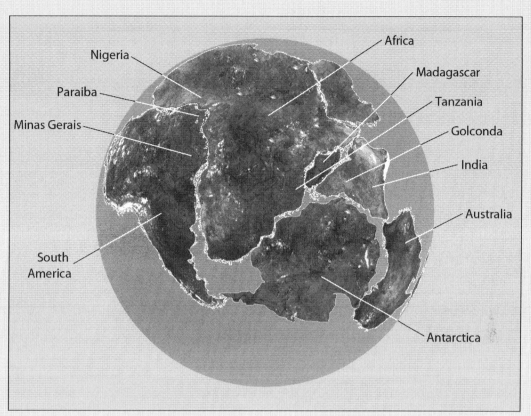

Figure 6-15 The southern supercontinent of Gondwana some 200 million years ago.

gea, some 200 million years ago. To place that all in some context, the monsters from Jurassic Park originally roamed the temperate forests and jungles of Gondwana, which was roughly centered on the South Pole of our planet (Figure 6-15).

The newly formed supercontinent did not have a long and happy run as such things go. Approximately 160 million years ago, Gondwana itself began to break up, and by the time the curtain fell on the dinosaurs 100 million years later, the various land masses that formed Gondwana – Africa, South America, the Indian subcontinent, Australia, and Antarctica – were well on their way to their current locations.

Another pointless diversion you say? Not really, because the gemstones we dearly love were formed in those ancient times, and their current geographic distribution has a great deal more to do with Pangea, Laurasia, and Gondwana than it does with modern cartographic conventions. Have you ever wondered why seemingly diverse places such as Minas Gerais Brazil and Nigeria are such rich sources of gemstones? Well, a quick look at the world of 200 million years ago shows that these regions were next-door neighbours (Figure 6-15). In fact, the "surprise" discovery of Paraiba tourmaline in Nigeria in the 1990's should have surprised no one (see page 213).

The Jurassic distribution of other rich gem fields, such as those in Tanzania, Madagascar, India, and Australia also suggest a relationship. Kind of makes you wonder what is under all that ice in Antarctica…

6.6 Synthetics and Simulants

Have you ever dreamed of finding a large, perfect chunk of gem rough?

I have. Several times. For some reason, it's usually tourmaline, either an intense blue green or a vibrant pinkish purple. I discover it lying on the ground, or purchase it for an absurdly low price at a gem show. Weird, I know, but wonderful.

Sadly, Nature is somewhat less than cooperative in fulfilling our dreams. Beautiful, clean, large rough gemstones are few and far between, and are more than likely priced out of range for most hobbyists. You can, however, experience the joy and wonder of working with large, essentially perfect crystals by entering the world of *synthetics* and *simulants*.

A **synthetic** material is chemically identical to the gemstone it is trying to imitate, and it can be quite difficult, even with modern analysis equipment, to distinguish natural stones from the lab grown versions. In the early days, experts could use the presence of characteristic growth patterns and inclusions to separate the two, but manufacturing processes have improved to the point where this is becoming more and more challenging.

Simulants are not chemically identical to the material they imitate. Instead, the manufacturers focus on matching the optical properties of the natural gemstone material. Simple physical tests, such as hardness, density, or thermal conductivity, can identify these materials. Examples include cubic zirconia and moissanite, which are diamond simulants.

This is not merely a didactic exercise: the exact terminology can be terribly important, and the history of naming and declaring artificial gemstones has a rich and often tangled history. Given the opportunities for misrepresentation, the US Federal Trade Commission has an understandably strong view of the issue:

> "There are natural gemstones, and there are laboratory-created stones. Laboratory-created stones…have the same chemical, physical and visual properties as natural gemstones, but they aren't as rare and often, are less expensive. By contrast, imitation stones look like natural stones, but may be glass, plastic or less costly stones. Laboratory-created and imitation stones should be clearly identified as such."

> - from the FTC website www.ftc.gov (search for "all that glitters"

Needless to say, names like "imitation" are less than ideal for marketing purposes, so the FTC permits some latitude in nomenclature, provided that the alternative name clearly distinguishes the product from natural material. The terms "created", "lab-created", or just "lab" seem to be particularly popular these days.

Incidentally, you can track down a great deal more information and guidance on commercial jewelry practices by searching for "synthetic gemstone" at the FTC site. Part 23 of Title 16, in particular, contains guidelines on everything from what the word "flawless" means to methods for ethically rounding off fractional carat weights. There are also regulations regarding gem treatments (see Chapter 13.5).

For natural gemstone purists, the catalog of synthetics and simulants has become depressingly long. Table 6-1 lists the most common varieties. A comparison with the compendium

Doublets and Triplets

Note that the category of simulants includes *assembled* stones, gems that are literally put together from two or more separate mineral components. Perhaps the most common of these in the past was the soudé emerald, which in its modern form is a triplet consisting of a slice of green glass at the girdle, sandwiched between a crown and pavilion of transparent synthetic spinel. Although relatively easy to detect when viewed from the side or using immersion fluids, well-made assembled gemstones can fool even the experts when mounted in jewelry. Identification can be particularly difficult if the only exposed part of the gem, the crown, is actually the real thing.

Should you worry about assembled gemstones?

Probably not. First of all, there appears to be zero economic incentive to assemble fake gem rough, and your pre-purchase visual examination would almost certainly reveal any trickery. Second, in a development that can only be termed ironic, assembled gemstones are disappearing from the market, outfoxed by "true" synthetics, which can now be produced economically for most gemstone species (see Table 6-1).

of gemstone types in Chapter 14 demonstrates that there are very few materials that lack a commercially viable synthetic or simulant. Tourmaline is a prominent, current example of a valuable natural gemstone without a marketable imitator, although it has been synthesized using the hydrothermal method (see "Keeping it Fake" on page 222). Given the history of the trade, this situation is almost certainly temporary. Peridot is another instructive example. Synthetic forsterite doped with cobalt is a common simulant for tanzanite. Replacing the cobalt with iron would yield synthetic peridot, yet it seems that economic forces are not driving this innovation…yet.

Table 6-1 Common gemstone varieties and their corresponding synthetics and simulants. Chapter 15.8.10 contains information on suppliers of artificial materials.

Species	Type	Comment
Beryl	Synthetic and Simulant	Hydrothermal emerald and aquamarine synthetics; Assembled emeralds; coloured synthetic spinel simulants
Chrysoberyl	Synthetic	Alexandrite type - lab grown chrysoberyl doped with chromium and vanadium
Corundum	Synthetic and Simulant	All colours available; Red spinel is a ruby simulant
Diamond	Synthetic and Simulant	Diamonds synthesized using HTHP and CVD methods (see page 226); Moissanite, CZ, clear spinel, rutile, strontium titanate, YAG, white zircon, white topaz, leucosapphire, glass, etc. are simulants
Garnet	Synthetic	Including "real" synthetics YAG and GGG. See page 221
Opal	Simulant	Chemically identical except for water content
Quartz	Synthetic	Hydrothermal, including colours not found in nature
Spinel	Synthetic	All colours; flame fusion and flux processes
Tanzanite	Simulant	Many simulants: synthetic olivine (forsterite) doped with cobalt, synthetic coloured corundum, synthetic coloured garnet, etc.
Topaz	Synthetic	Not widespread, due to low cost of natural material

Despite the implied gloom of the previous paragraphs, it must be said there is nothing intrinsically "bad" about synthetics and simulants, provided that the true nature of the material is explicitly declared.

Of course, that last clause in the previous paragraph is the key, and it is a sad fact that a great deal of synthetic gemstone material is not declared. Some sources claim that up to 80% of commercially cut amethyst and citrine are in fact undeclared synthetics. Diagnostic techniques have improved, but the forgers have more than kept pace.

6.6.1 Identifying Synthetics and Simulants

Given the potentially huge difference in price, how can you spot synthetic or simulant rough gemstones before laying down your cash? Here, once again, experience and market knowledge play a key role.

The specific manufacturing process can leave hints that a particular gemstone was born in a lab, not Mother Earth. For example, the synthetic amethyst and citrine that has been flooding the market has a distinctive rippled surface (Figure 6-16). Any hint of such surface "pebbling" in a dealer's "natural" quartz selection should put the entire lot (and the dealer) under suspicion. Manufactured citrine and amethyst also have unrealistically uniform body colour and tone. If every sample of dozens of pieces of rough shows identical saturation and no banding or zoning, watch out.

Other indications of artificial origin include curved internal striae or stress lines. These result from forces which build up during manufacture, particularly for the flame fusion process (see Section 6.6.2).

Size and shape can provide clues to artificial origin. Manufactured materials tend to come in larger sizes, at least originally, so a preponderance of sawn surfaces may be a strong indica-

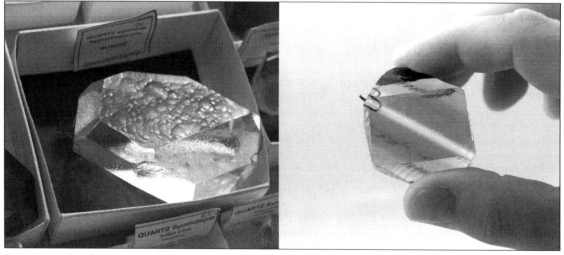

Figure 6-16 Synthetic quartz has a characteristic "pebbled" surface (left) and unrealistically uniform colour and tone. Viewed from some angles (right), you can spot the transparent seed plate used to grow the material. The right-hand sample even includes the wire loop used to hold the seed plate during production. The manufacturers add iron, cobalt, potassium and aluminum to achieve orange, blue, green, or purple body colour, respectively.

tor of lab origin. You should also check for natural crystal faces and points. Your knowledge of crystal systems and habits (Chapter 12.10) will be invaluable here.

Unfortunately, however, there is no one-size-fits-all solution to identifying artificial gemstones. The steady improvement in synthesis technologies and the unfortunate economic incentive to be less than honest has lead to a correspondingly rich and rapidly evolving range of indicators and tests. You can keep up with this fascinating field by following online gemology resources, in particular, the forums (see Chapter 15.8.1).

Finally, you should have your realism radar fully deployed when considering the purchase of gem rough. Material that is too large or clean or (especially) inexpensive to be natural probably isn't. Short version: dreams rarely come true.

Real Synthetics

If a typical synthetic gemstone is an exact copy of a material that occurs in nature, what would you call a synthesized natural material that has no corresponding stone outside the lab? I propose the term "real" synthetic, not only because it represents a true synthesis of a new natural material, but also because it will add to the rich history of confusing terminology in this field.

There are a handful of manmade gemstone materials that are real synthetics, in the sense that no corresponding material occurs in nature. Prominent among these are the synthetic garnets, such as yttrium aluminum garnet (YAG), and gadolinium gallium garnet (GGG). You could also argue that cubic zirconia – our old friend CZ – is also a real synthetic. Naturally occurring zirconium oxide does exist as the rare mineral baddeleyite, but baddeleyite is a monoclinic, not cubic, crystal (see Chapter 12.10). In the 1930's a pair of German mineralogists discovered microscopic inclusions of true cubic zirconia in larger crystals of metamict zircon. Needless to say, this did not represent a commercially interesting source of CZ.

While we're creating a whole new category, I would also include synthetic gemstones that occur in nature, but not in the particular colour produced. This means material like blue quartz and white spinel are also real synthetics.

6.6.2 Synthetic and Simulant Gemstone Manufacturing

With the exception of a few amorphous types, all gemstones are crystals. This means that they are solid masses of elements and molecules arranged in ordered, three-dimensional structures, known as *lattices* (see Chapter 12.10). Constructing such a perfect, microscopic lattice is difficult: you need to allow the component building blocks to move about freely, tumbling around until the tiny inter-particle forces coax them into the proper crystal form.

How can you encourage atoms and molecules to move about freely? By ensuring that they are in the *liquid* or *gas phase*, and in fact, there are two basic ways of building an artificial gemstone: by crystallization from a liquid, like freezing water, and by crystallization from a gas, like snow or frost forming in damp air.

Keeping it Fake

Long before I reached the age of maturity, and certainly long before I thought it was a good idea to drink *anything* with a whole olive in it, I knew from watching James Bond movies that there were two ways to make a vodka martini. And although I have no direct memory of having done so at the time, I am almost certain that I annoyed my elders by ordering my lemonade shaken, not stirred.

Beyond the vodka and vermouth, the critical ingredient in preparing 007's favourite beverage is the ice, and even at that tender age, I knew that there were at least two distinct ways of making ice as well. Most ice we encounter has crystallized out of the liquid phase, a fancy way of saying it is frozen water. Snow and frost, on the other hand, are ice crystals that form by water molecules transitioning directly from the gas to the solid phase, a process known as *desublimation* or *deposition*.

Why the dipsomaniacal digression on the making of ice? Well, ice, like the gemstones we love, is a naturally occurring crystal. We choose to synthesize ice in large blocky forms in our refrigerators. Gemstones, it turns out, can also be synthesized in useful shapes by crystallization out of the liquid or gas phase, just like good old H_2O.

Crystallization from Liquid

By far the majority of synthetic gemstones are produced by crystallization in a liquid. This liquid can be the molten form of the solid material, just like the water in your ice cube tray. There is another way of crystallizing solid out of a liquid, however: *precipitation*. This is again a fancy way of saying a simple thing, which is "un-dissolving" something. If you ever made rock candy on a string suspended in sugar solution, you know exactly what I am talking about. There are three commercially viable ways of producing solid crystals from melted material and two ways of accomplishing precipitation from solution. Here's an overview:

Melt Processes

Flame Fusion is the oldest commercial technique for producing synthetic gemstones. Developed by Auguste Verneuil over a century ago (see "Musings on a Synthetic Ruby" opposite), flame fusion involves trickling finely powdered material through a hot hydrogen-oxygen flame in a sealed furnace. In Verneuil's original experiments, the powder was Alumina (Al_2O_3), in effect, powdered sapphire. Given appropriate conditions, the temperature in the flame can exceed 2200 °F (1200 C), sufficient to melt even the most refractory materials such as corundum. The droplets fall to the bottom of the apparatus, where they freeze, crystallize, and collect on an earthen or ceramic rod. Adding additional chemicals to the powder can produce an astonishing array of colours: for example, chromium dioxide added to alumina produces synthetic ruby (Figure 6-17), while adding titanium or iron oxides results in blue synthetic sapphire.

Common Flame Fusion synthetic gemstones: Ruby, Sapphire, Spinel

The **Czochralski Pulling** process arose from an industrial need for larger, stress-free crystals in the production of lasers. In this method, the raw material sits in a small container or crucible. Due to its high melting temperature and very low chemical reactivity, platinum is the

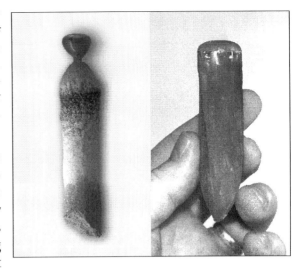

Figure 6-17 A small flame fusion ruby still attached to the top of its earthen rod (left). A larger boule of flame fusion spinel (right). The flame fusion process often produces crystals with large internal stresses, forcing the manufacturers to split the boule lengthwise. These boules have not yet been split (synthetic ruby image by Aram Dulyan from wikipedia.org).

material of choice for these containers. The operator pumps intense radio energy into the crucible, melting the material, and then lowers a seed crystal into the liquid. Slowly extracting and rotating the crystal produces a large, stress-free boule. The relatively long processing time, coupled with the fact that platinum pots and microwave generators can be a wee-bit costly, results in a relatively high cost per carat for this type of synthetic gemstone. Incidentally, all modern semiconductor chips, such as those in mobile phones and computers, are fabricated from silicon boules produced via the Czochralski process.

Common Czochralski Pulling synthetic gemstones: Alexandrite, YAG, GGG, Corundum

No, **Skull Melting** does not describe one's mental state two hours into a Grateful Dead concert. Instead, it refers to a clever solution to the production of gemstones whose melting temperature exceeds even that of platinum. Rather than trying to contain a superheated material within a metal or ceramic pot, the manufacturers of skull melt gemstones use the material itself as a container. They effectively build a multilayer spherical oven, with the molten gemstone material at its center surrounded by unmelted gemstone and finally an externally cooled container. Focused radio energy melts the core, and after cooling and crystallization, the outer unmelted "skull" can be broken to reveal the synthesized crystalline "brains." Clever? Yes. Creepy? Definitely.

Common Skull Melt synthetic gemstones: Cubic Zirconia

Musings on a Synthetic Ruby

One chilly autumn evening found me again sitting in front of my faceting machine, again charging up my polishing lap with diamond bort. I was truly "in the zone" – what we used to less charitably call being "zoned out" – pressing the tiny diamond crystals into the lap with my chunk of synthetic corundum.

Looking down at the split boule of flame fusion ruby, I mused about its being real, not synthetic.

What would it be worth? Time to take a break from the machine and do a little research…

Figure 6-18 Musings on a synthetic ruby.

Lots, it turns out. Large, flawless rubies with the colour and tone of my embedding tool sell for hundreds of thousands of dollars per carat. At about an ounce total (28 g or 140 carats), my synthetic ruby, if it were real, would fetch in the neighbourhood of thirty million dollars.

Wow! I paid something like four dollars for that split boule of synthetic ruby. Do the math. That works out to a bit under three cents per carat. A simple conversion of my ruby from synthetic to a chemically identical natural stone would increase its value by a factor of something like ten million. Again, wow! Kind of makes you want to re-investigate all that alchemy business…

Actually, a couple of hundred thousand per carat is probably a wild underestimate, since per-carat prices increase rapidly with gem size, and flawless natural rubies over one hundred carats simply don't exist. For comparison, 100-carat class flawless D-type diamonds fetch about half as much per carat…and they do exist.

My research interlude produced more than just surprising numbers. It turns out that Auguste Verneuil, for whom the modern flame fusion process is named, was not the first person to create artificial corundum in the lab. That honour belongs to Marc Antoine Augustin Gaudin, who labored for more than thirty years on ruby synthesis during the middle of the nineteenth century, eventually giving up when all efforts to produce large, transparent crystals failed. The mantle was taken up by Edmond Frémy at the Museum of Natural History in Paris, where young Verneuil served as a laboratory assistant.

The appearance of synthetic "Geneva Rubies" on the marketplace in the late 1880's prompted Verneuil to explore the possibility of re-crystallizing alumina powder after melting it in a hot flame. Within six years, he had perfected the process, and by 1907, his furnaces were producing five million carats (1 tonne) of rubies per year.

These synthetic stones were a remarkable hit with the public. Far from being viewed as "fake," Verneuil's rubies were seen as desirable in high-end jewelry as a sign of scientific progress and modernity. Kind of like the choice of material for the tippy-top of the Washington Monument (if you don't know the story, ask Mr. Google…).

Incidentally, this widespread appeal has made for a nasty surprise to many collectors, who having found or inherited a piece of high quality antique jewelry, naturally assume that the age and pedigree of the piece guarantee that the mounted gem is natural. Oops.

Of course, synthetic ruby has found many uses beyond jewelry and embedding tools. Its hardness and stability make it an excellent choice for precision bearings, including those in mechanical watches, compasses, and analog meters. In fact, it was the importance of ruby for use in precision bearings that caused a flowering of research into synthetic gemstones during World War II.

Nowadays, synthetic rubies are everywhere and in everything, ranging from lasers to precision measuring machines (Figure 6-19). Current commercial production exceeds one billion carats (200 tonnes), about three quarters of which is for industrial purposes.

Now imagine if all *that* ruby were real...

Figure 6-19 A precision ruby sphere makes an accurate, durable probe tip for a three-dimensional coordinate measuring machine.

Solution Processes

Students of ancient Greek will have already guessed that the **Hydrothermal** process involves both water and heat. It also involves considerable pressure. The material to be synthesized is dissolved in hot water inside a thick-walled pressurized steel cylinder known as an *autoclave*, or in the business, by the more colloquial and unsettling term, the "bomb". Crystallization occurs when a local region containing a seed crystal is cooled with respect to the surrounding liquid. The solution becomes locally supersaturated – just like with the rock candy – and crystal growth occurs. Due to the high equipment costs and its relative slowness, synthetic gemstones produced by the hydrothermal process tend to be relatively expensive. Figure 6-16 shows examples of hydrothermally synthesized quartz.

Common Hydrothermal synthetic gemstones: Quartz, Emerald, Corundum, Alexandrite

The **Flux** process is essentially identical to the hydrothermal technique, except the solvent is not water but rather a "flux" such as lead fluoride, lithium molybdate, or boron oxide. These materials are quite nasty – the chemists say "reactive" – and hence everything must take place in an expensive crucible under controlled atmospheric conditions. Heating a mixture of flux and raw gemstone powder causes the flux to melt, which has the effect of lowering the effective melting temperature of the gem material. After a period of time, the two are thoroughly mixed and the fun can begin. Carefully lowering the temperature of the solution allows the gemstone to crystallize out while the flux remains liquid. Some manufacturers introduce seed crystals to encourage growth, while others permit the gemstones to form randomly. At the end of the process, the excess flux can be poured off if still molten or cut away from the fully formed gem crystals. As you can guess, the flux process is slow and expensive.

Common Flux synthetic gemstones: Corundum, Emerald, Quartz, Spinel, Alexandrite, YAG, and Chrysoberyl

Crystallization from Gas

The gemstone synthesis equivalent of snow and frost is gas phase crystallization, or desublimation. There is currently only one commercially successful technique and one type of gemstone produced.

The **Chemical Vapour Deposition** (CVD) method of diamond synthesis involves the conversion of the component atoms of the gem into a plasma, which is subsequently deposited on a suitable substrate, eventually producing a layer of crystal. For diamond, this basically means taking a gas rich in carbon – methane, for example – and zapping it with a powerful source of energy, such as an arc discharge, microwave generator, laser, or electron beam. The actual chemical and physical processes which take place as the layers of diamond develop are poorly understood, or an industrial secret, or both. Currently, CVD techniques produce relatively small diamonds of high clarity and purity. Note that the more traditional technique of diamond synthesis is the High Temperature, High Pressure or HTHP process. This involves crushing a solution of graphite or diamond grit in an anvil at very high temperatures (2700° F or 1500 C) and pressures (50,000 atmospheres), a neat feat pioneered by the General Electric Corporation in the 1950's. HTHP results in larger gems, but cannot easily produce the most valuable, colourless diamonds.

Common CVD synthetic gemstones: Diamond

Keeping it Real

Innovation never ceases in the world of synthetics. Confronted with negative consumer reaction to the notion of "artificial" gemstones, several companies are promoting hydrothermal emerald and ruby grown from real gemstones. They purchase scrap beryl and corundum from cutting houses. This is badly included rough or surplus generated during trimming, but it is unquestionably "real." The companies simply recrystallize this material into high quality rough using relatively standard hydrothermal processes. At tens of dollars per carat, these finished gems are expensive by synthetic standards, but they are far cheaper than the real, real thing.

Figure 6-20 Recrystallized ruby gems sell for a tiny fraction of the cost of "natural" stones. This company also offers cubic zirconia gems with a surface layer of "real" diamond, applied via chemical vapour deposition (see above).

6.7 Orienting Gem Rough

Having made it this far into the chapter, you have no doubt found, organized, and selected your target piece of gem rough. What next?

Orientation.

Orientation is the process of identifying the optimum location of the gem design within the piece of raw stone. This almost always means visualizing the final gem (Figure 6-21). Mathematically stated, orientation means maximizing the yield from the gem rough, given the particular dimensional ratios of the design. As with many things couched in pure mathematical terms, however, the previous sentence is dead wrong, or at least incomplete. Practically stated, orientation means finding the best way to glue the rough onto your dop, where "best" means ending up with the largest, prettiest gem possible.

Ah. The pretty factor. Some may call you shallow and superficial, but visual impact is, in fact, one of the goals of the game here. This is not to understate the importance of weight retention, but ask yourself, would you rather have a huge unattractive gem or a somewhat smaller one that is an absolute knockout?

I thought so. Large as possible, as long as it's pretty. Getting there will be a challenge, however. The variety of factors to consider in orienting gemstone rough for maximum yield and visual impact can prove daunting to the beginner. Fear not. The following paragraphs should help point you in the right direction – errr, orientation.

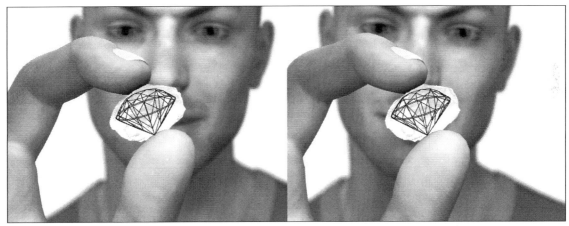

Figure 6-21 Examine your gem rough from all angles, and try to project the gem design inside the stone. This is a three-dimensional image. See Chapter 11.9.2 for tips on viewing it correctly.

6.7.1 Things to Consider in Orienting Rough

Yield

Yield is defined as the ratio of final to initial weight of a cut gemstone, and it is the single most important factor driving the orientation of the rough, at least for commercial operations. You are not a commercial operation. These days, robots can produce large unattractive gems at a rate with which you simply cannot compete. You should therefore consider yield among the mix of other factors with appropriate priority. Nevertheless, if you find that it will be impossible to fit your target gem cut within the existing rough with at least 20% final yield, it is probably time to consider another design.

The actual process of assessing this yield involves careful measurements and some simple calculations. You can extract the target dimensions from the gem design. Specifically, the header of most modern cutting prescriptions will provide the ratio of length to width, crown to width, and pavilion to width (see Figure 5-4). Chapter 10.8 contains a complete description with examples of how to use these values to orient rough for maximum yield.

If you find the examples in Chapter 10.8 intimidating, or if you are working with inexpensive rough, you can make a pretty good stab at optimal orientation using a simple geometric guideline. Most gemstones have a depth about two-thirds of their width at the girdle (see Figure 6-22 and "The Science of Art" on page 264 of Volume 2). For non-round gems, use the shortest girdle distance across the stone in your assessment.

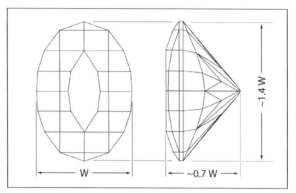

For example, if you plan to cut an 8 mm Standard Round Brilliant, you will need a piece of rough about 6 mm deep. For a 10x5 mm emerald design, count on needing approximately 3.5-4 mm of depth. If your chosen rough has a nice clean volume of the appropriate shape, you are good to go.

Figure 6-22 Most gemstones have a depth about 2/3 of their shortest width. This is the Topo design, available online at boghome.com. See also Figure 16-23.

Gem Rough and Holistic Sofas

First impressions can often be mistaken impressions, and nowhere is this more true than in the art of gemstone orientation.

Consider for a moment the case illustrated in Figure 6-23, which presents a seemingly simple problem: cut a rectangular gemstone design, namely Fritz15 from Chapter 19.2.1, given a suitably rectangular piece of rough from which to cut it.

Yes, the gem rough in the figure looks like a half-melted stick of butter, but that is beside the point. It seems to be a perfect match. Simply glue the dop stick to the top surface and have at it. Figure 6-24 shows the obvious, best orientation.

Figure 6-23 A simple problem: Cut a rectangular gemstone from a rectangular piece of rough.

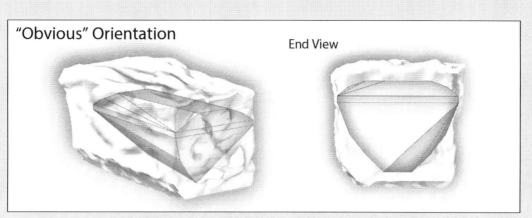

Figure 6-24 The "obvious" best orientation of Fritz15 within the gemstone rough.

Not so fast.

Although the orientation in Figure 6-24 is reasonable and will produce decent yield, there may be a better way. Recall that you are trying to maximally fit one geometric volume (the gem) inside another (the rough). Nothing forces you to stick to conventional notions of up, down, left, and right, however. This is the three-dimensional world, after all. Given the shapes shown here, it is an entirely appropriate metaphor to say that you should think outside of the box.

A short but relevant literary diversion is in order. In his time traveling suspense novel, *Dirk Gently's Holistic Detective Agency*, Douglas Adams writes of a peculiarly appropriate conundrum. The problem is as follows: the main character, Richard MacDuff, a young computer programmer, has taken delivery of a sofa, which has become irretrievably stuck in the staircase up to his apartment. Richard spends a great deal of time and some company resources on constructing a computer graphics simulation of the situation, including three dimensional rotations in all possible directions to either get the sofa upstairs, or failing that, back downstairs and out the door. After much hard work, the conclusion is inescapable: both options are impossible.

We learn later in the novel that an accident with a time machine during delivery of the sofa is at the root of the problem, but you should take inspiration from young MacDuff nonetheless. His efforts to solve his furniture problems are exactly the sort of thing that you should be doing in orienting gem rough. No, I am not talking about writing a computer simulation, although such a program would be very cool. Instead, as you examine your gem rough, imagine the design spinning and rotating in all possible ways and ask yourself which orientation permits the largest possible gem.

Figure 6-25 shows another possibility. Here, the gem has been rotated around its long axis by 3/8 of a turn, placing the keel into the upper right corner of the rectangular rough.

Is this orientation better? Unquestionably yes. In fact, a little work with a ruler and calculator shows that this "unconventional" orientation will produce a gem which is about 9% larger in each dimension. That in itself is nothing to sniff at, but in terms of yield, this

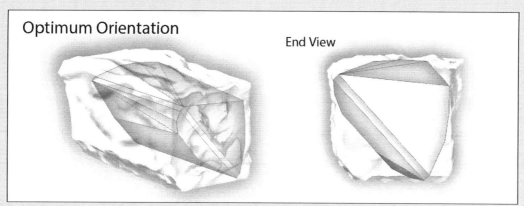

Optimum Orientation

End View

Figure 6-25 A better way, with the deep keel projecting into a corner of the rectangular rough.

corresponds to an improvement of more than 30%. That could translate to hundreds of dollars in final value, depending on the size of the final gem and the type of material. Definitely worth some mental spinning of sofas…

By the way, Figure 5-25 shows another example of how different rotations can have a significant impact on yield.

Finally, here's an almost unbearably nerdy footnote: In the early 1990's, a computer screensaver program called HolisticSofa reproduced Adams' fictional simulation, rotating sofa, staircase, and all (look for Holistic Sofa on YouTube…everything is on YouTube). And here's an almost unbearably nerdy admission: I personally witnessed this screensaver in action at the time and thought it was pretty neat.

A very final and well-deserved credit: a "Just Ask Jeff" online tip by the late great gem designer Jeff Graham inspired this look at unconventional orientation.

Serious Orientation Issues

In July 1986, the DeBeers company unearthed what would end up being the single largest faceted D-type flawless diamond ever discovered. How it all came about is a fascinating lesson in corporate secrecy, public relations, and above all, careful planning and orientation of the gem rough.

The Centenary diamond in its initial raw form weighed a hair under 600 carats, which places it in the top 20 of all rough diamonds ever found. With the company's centennial celebration looming, DeBeers officials decided to keep the find a secret, setting up a team of experts to examine the best possible way of cutting it.

The great rough gem was unveiled in front of four hundred entranced guests at the centennial dinner celebration in May 1988, and planning began in earnest to facet the stone. The honour of leading the design team fell to Sir Gabriel Tolkowsky, renowned gem cutter and great nephew of diamond expert and mathematician Marcel Tolkowsky (see Chapter 16.4). Together with other master cutters and a team of engineers, Tolkowsky began the arduous task of assessing, orienting, and finally cutting and polishing the stone.

You see, the Centenary rough had a problem – several problems actually. While the gem was of unquestioned quality and size, its shape was far from ideal. A large horn-like protrusion on one side would almost certainly have to be removed, and there was a deep concave divot on the largest flat surface of the stone. When Tolkowsky first saw the Centenary, he was deeply impressed by its clarity and purity, but expressed concern that the shape suggested no obvious design.

For over a year, the great gem lay untouched while the master cutter and his team examined and mapped every detail of its surface and interior. Preparation of special tools and the construction of an underground faceting laboratory went on in the meantime. Eventually, Tolkowsky and DeBeers officials decided to attempt to cut a single large gem from the rough, and over a period of five months, the team laboriously removed the protrusions and surface flaws from the stone.

Tolkowsky prepared a total of thirteen different possible gem designs, and the DeBeers board accepted his strong recommendation to produce a modified heart shaped stone. With the official go-ahead in hand, the Tolkowsky team finished the gem in ten months, revealing the completed Centenary Diamond to the world in early 1991.

Yes, it took them only ten months to cut and polish the gem – "only" is a relative term here, since the planning and evaluation occupied the remainder of the almost five years between discovery of the rough and the public unveiling of the 274-carat flawless faceted gem. Talk about serious orientation issues. During that time, Tolkowsky memorably observed that he "…became another man. A strange man. I was looking at the stone in the day, and the stone was looking at me at night."

The yield? Well, you can do the math as well as I. Even without 100 million dollars on the line, it takes serious attention and serious care to achieve a yield in excess of 45%. Imagine what Tolkowsky can do with less problematic rough.

Surface Features and Internal Flaws

Figure 6-21 shows an earnest young fellow heroically trying to imagine a possible gemstone design within the three-dimensional body of a piece of rough. While this is certainly an essential step, the figure tells only part of the story. The visualization process must account for both surface and internal features which can affect the appearance and value of the final gem. Concave faces and divots may diminish the yield unacceptably (see "Serious Orientation Issues" above), while inclusions, bubbles, and veils should be avoided or placed in optically acceptable locations in the gem (see "A Peek Behind the Veil…" on page 201). Such considerations may very well make the difference between a usable gem design and one that must be discarded, and they will certainly be decisive in determining the best location for dopping the table.

Colour

Many beginners are surprised at how different the colour of a cut gemstone can be compared to the original rough.

Correction. All beginners are surprised at how different the colour of a cut gemstone can be compared to the original rough.

Correction. All faceters of all skill levels are surprised at how different the colour of a cut gemstone can be compared to the original rough.

The fact is that colour is one of the great mysteries and attractions of gemstones. Chapters 11 and 12 explain the origins and effects of colour, and a brief perusal of that material will make it clear that gemstone orientation can have a very strong effect.

Pleochroism

Many materials are pleochroic, showing different colours along different directions with respect to the crystallographic axes of the gem. Often, the long or "c" axis shows the purest and most desirable colour. Tourmaline can be a prominent exception: you almost certainly have a nice little chunk of tourmaline in your rough box which shows a lovely blue-green colour when viewed from the side, and an awful olive-green to brown shade down the optical axis (Figure 6-26). Some tourmaline is completely opaque, or "closed," along the c-axis.

Corundum is another interesting example where pleochroic colour strongly drives the choice of orientation. For ruby and sapphire, the most desirable hues, red and blue, respectively, require orientation of the table perpendicular to the c-axis. Failure to do so will result in distinct pink tones for ruby and less valuable greens for sapphire.

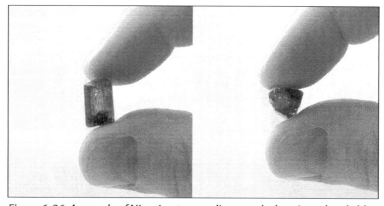

Depending on the orientation and gem design, pleochroism can be your best friend or worst enemy. This is definitely an area where experience helps, but there are a few general guidelines to turn this physical phenomenon to your advantage.

Figure 6-26 A sample of Nigerian tourmaline rough showing a lovely blue green in the side view (left), but a more muddy olive green along the c-axis (right). For most gemstone designs, the best final colour will result from orienting the rough so that the left panel corresponds to looking down on the table.

First and foremost, closed c-axis rough should be cut in elongated quasi-rectangular designs that emphasize colour, not brilliance. The reason for this is that brilliant designs tend to scatter light in all directions through the body of the stone, including the opaque black direction. Elongated rectangular designs channel the light in directions perpendicular to the long axis, a highly desirable situation if that long axis is closed (see Figure 6-27).

A second general guideline for pleochroic success is to orient the table of your gemstone perpendicular to the direction of most pleasing colour. In other words, if you hold the piece of gem rough so that it has the best colour (don't forget your piece of white paper here – see "When is Too Much Too Much?" on page 90 of Volume 2), you are looking di-

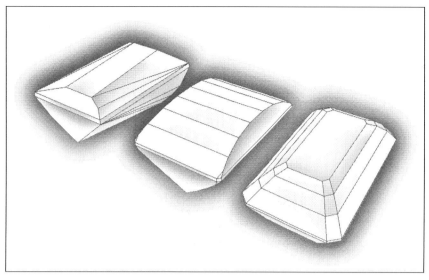

Figure 6-27 Elongated rectangular designs with steep end facets are a good choice for closed c-axis rough. Shown (left to right) are: Fritz15 (see Chapter 19.2.1), Jeff Graham's Smith Bar (online – see Chapter 15.8.4), and a classic emerald cut.

rectly down at the future table (see Figure 6-26). A word of warning, however: Given the complexity of light paths through a gem, there is no guarantee that what you see is what you will get in terms of overall body colour. Re-read the first three sentences on the opposite page to understand what this means in terms of predictable outcomes.

Also, locating the future table this way can get you into trouble when there is a conflict between orientation for best colour and cleavage planes. Luckily, one of the most cleavage-prone gemstone materials, kunzite, usually has the best colour along a direction that keeps the table safely away from cleavage.

Finally, you can make a reasonable guess about how the various pleochroic colours will mix for a given gemstone design and orientation. For example, a round brilliant should be dominated by the table-view colour, with the perpendicular directions mixed in approximate equal proportion. An oval oriented along the optical axes of the crystal will show one colour concentration at the ends and the other around the belly.

You can exploit pleochroism to produce some interesting and appealing effects. This is a common practice in orienting andalusite. Figure 12-15 shows a square reflector cut along the optical axes in tourmaline. This gem is a seafoam blue in two quadrants and a yellow-green in the other two.

Additional Colour Considerations

Other colour effects will influence your decisions on gemstone orientation. For multi-colour stones such as ametrine (Chapter 12.3.8), the classic emerald or bar cuts emphasize both colour intensity and separation. It is even possible to deliberately recombine the separated hues of a multi-colour gem (Figure 6-28). Note that some gemstone species, such as tourmaline, can have a "skin" of outer material with a qualitatively different colour. Removal of this layer during faceting can produce a strikingly different final hue.

Figure 6-28 (left) Orienting the colour split of ametrine perpendicular to the long dimension of a reflector cut will produce a clean separation of hue. This is the Slice design from Chapter 19.3.3. (right) A different ametrine reflector that deliberately blends the colours of amethyst and citrine by orienting the split lengthwise. This grayscale reproduction cannot show the interesting result – "interesting" in the sense that half the people who have seen it love the effect, while the other half hate it.

Colour spots and zones are also a consideration when orienting rough. Conventional wisdom dictates that you place small spots of desirable colour in the culet, since a large fraction of light rays pass through this region (see "Clearly Superior" on page 208). This can significantly improve the colour and saturation of an otherwise marginal gem (Figure 6-29).

For similar reasons, you should orient planes or zones of colour perpendicular to the viewer's sight line. This helps to avoid obvious and undesirable banding (Figure 6-29).

Soudé emeralds, which consist of a slab of green glass sandwiched between a transparent crown and pavilion, perfectly demonstrate this strategy (see "Doublets and Triplets" on page 219). Orienting the glass parallel to the table makes the trickery hard to spot, particularly if the gem cannot be viewed from the side.

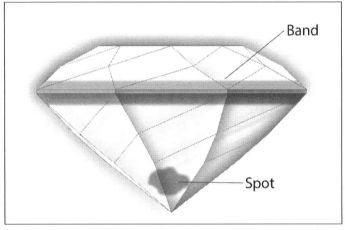

Figure 6-29 You can minimize the visual impact of colour planes and bands by orienting them parallel to the table. Conversely, placing a spot of desirable colour in the culet can enhance the tone of the entire gem.

Other Factors

Additional physical or optical material characteristics will enter your selection of gemstone orientation. For example, cleavage planes can be a nightmare if they lie parallel to a large, highly visible facet like the table. The rule of thumb is to orient materials with strong cleavage (topaz, kunzite, fluorite, etc.) with any such facets at least 7°-10° off such planes. Chapter 12.11.1 provides further information, including tips on how to locate the cleavage plane.

Birefringence can also be an issue. As Chapter 12.4 explains, birefringence causes the light rays entering a gem to split in two, resulting in fuzziness and "facet-doubling" when the stone is viewed from certain directions. The aesthetic value of this optical multiplication of facets is a matter of taste. Some cutters insist on orienting a gem to minimize the effect, while others (myself included), find the effect appealing or not worthy of concern.

6.7.2 A Final Word on Orientation

All of these orientation strategies are definitely the conventional wisdom, and – guess what? – the conventional wisdom can be wrong. For example, placing spots and zones as shown in Figure 6-29 will help ensure uniform body colour throughout the gem, but is uniformity always best? Heck no! In fact, some of the most spectacular gemstones I have ever seen worked their magic by the explicit separation of colour. Once again, use your judgment and don't be afraid to roll the dice with a unique piece of gem rough.

7

Dopping

This chapter describes dopping techniques, specifically the multitude of strategies that faceters have developed to attach their valuable gem rough to a dop.

A whole chapter on gluing a rock to a stick? Are you surprised? You shouldn't be, since dopping represents one of the most challenging aspects of gem faceting, particularly for the beginner.

Of course, there is a lot more to dopping than merely gluing a couple of things together. In fact, achieving precision and accuracy in this process is the secret to increased yield from valuable rough. Proper dop transfer procedure can also spell the difference between a well-proportioned gemstone that is a pleasure to cut and the frustrating, cheater-bedeviled nightmare that inevitably follows an inaccurate transfer.

The chapter begins with a general discussion of traditional dopping practice, including the idiosyncrasies of wax, epoxy resin, and cyanoacrylate glue. For a detailed tutorial, turn to Chapter 5. It then goes on to argue in favour of a hybrid technique that combines the best aspects of wax and epoxy. A photographic tutorial shows you the way to hybrid happiness. The final sections explain several strategies for ensuring accurate dop transfer, as well as cutting a test tier of facets to make sure you did everything right.

7.1 Dopping Techniques

Dopping can be a pain. Literally.

Whether it is fingers burnt by hot wax or that beautiful tourmaline which flew off the dop while you were touching up the table, the process of reliably attaching gemstones to dops can be one of the most difficult, frustrating, and unreliable aspects of faceting.

Given that we have spent thousands of dollars on precision machinery and hundreds of hours gaining experience in using it skillfully, it seems almost psychotic to entrust our precious gem rough and our even more precious sanity to a tiny, misshapen blob of wax that we have crudely dribbled over the stone.

But there it is. Despite countless efforts to develop alternatives, most faceters are attaching their gemstones to the dop in essentially the same way that their forebears did half a millennium ago. Whether they use traditional wax or a more modern adhesive such as epoxy or cyanoacrylate glue, the typical hobby cutter glues the stone to the stick as well as he or she can and hopes for the best.

Yes, you have guessed my secret. I have "issues" with dopping, as do most faceters. In fact, even a brief visit to one of the several online faceting discussion groups will unearth a treasure trove of discussion, both pragmatic and dogmatic, on the relative merits of wax (green versus brown versus black), epoxy (five minute versus slow setting), and cyanoacrylate glue (normal versus gel). Other discussions focus on tools and procedures, including the pros and cons of various transfer fixtures, dop types, and alignment aids.

How can you keep your own dopping issues to a minimum? As with selecting a faceting machine, your personal habits and taste should dictate which dopping technique you adopt. Keep an open mind and try alternatives.

7.2 Wax versus Epoxy versus Cyanoacrylate Glue

So. In living tribute to the pioneers of our field, modern faceters attach their gemstones to their dop sticks using a variety of adhesives, including dopping wax, epoxy resin, and cyanoacrylate glue (see Figure 4-1). Which adhesive is best? The short answer is all (or none) of the above. Each has its own benefits and difficulties, as Table 7-1 tries to summarize.

7.2.1 Dop Wax

Wax is the traditional adhesive, and every faceter should know how to use it. Unfortunately for the beginner, however, it is the most difficult to work with, at least in terms of getting accurate centering of the stone on the dop. Sustaining the proper wax temperature for even flow and good bonding is hard enough. Doing so while opaque, burning-hot wax is dripping everywhere adds a new dimension of difficulty and pain. For smaller (read expensive) rough, a de-centering of a quarter of a millimeter (approximately 0.01 inch) can result in a yield reduction of 30%. See Section 7.8 for more on the importance of accurate dopping.

This disadvantage is offset by wax's wonderful ability to be warmed up, in other words softened, over and over again without loss of strength. Experienced faceters take advantage of

Table 7-1 The pros and cons of various dopping adhesives.

Adhesive	Advantages	Disadvantages
Dop Wax	fast and reliable bond	difficult to get accurate centering, very short working time
	can re-center stone slightly after dopping	heat buildup can cause stone to shift after dopping
	easy release and cleanup	unsuitable for heat sensitive stones
		opaque – cannot see for fine positioning
Epoxy Resin	long working time and transparency allow very accurate positioning	relatively slow setting
	reliable bond, excellent shock resistance	difficult release, no fine tuning after glue sets
	suitable for heat sensitive stones	more difficult cleanup
Cyanoacrylate Glue	very accurate	very short working time
	fast, reliable	release can be difficult, no fine tuning after setting
	suitable for heat sensitive stones	poor gap filling properties
		water weakens some glues

this property, tweaking the position of the stone repeatedly as they make their initial cuts. The masters swear by wax, and you should take their allegiance very seriously.

Dop wax comes in several varieties and melting temperatures, usually distinguished by colour. Green or red wax has the lowest melting temperature, typically 160° F (70° C) and is often used for bonding cabochons. Black dop wax has very similar properties and requires somewhat higher temperatures, approximately 170° F (77° C). Finally, brown "diamond setters" wax melts at 180° F (82° C) and provides the firmest, most heat-resistant bond. As usual, opinions vary, but I always use the brown variety. Chapter 4.1.1 provides more information on dop wax.

7.2.2 Epoxy Resin

Epoxy is a relatively recent invention, with the first commercial resins appearing in the United States and Europe in the 1930's. This "miracle" adhesive is now used in such diverse applications as integrated circuit manufacture and the bonding of carbon fiber for the chassis of Formula 1 racing cars. Epoxy is available in multiple formulations for many different applications. The types most applicable to amateur lapidary work are the fast-setting "five-minute" type and the extra strength general-purpose epoxies.

As mentioned in Chapter 4.1.2, there is an inverse relationship between the setting time and the ultimate bond strength: the slower-setting epoxies produce a much stronger bond. This difference is somewhat academic for the faceter, since even the weakest, fastest-setting epoxy is plenty strong enough. Note, however, that you should select a transparent variety to allow a clear view of things as you align the stone to the dop.

Epoxy's great strength actually turns out to be its weakness. Although the gem never flies off the dop, it can be very difficult to release the stone when you are done. This is especially true for cone dops (see page 259). A variety of solvents can help, but the safe ones, such as acetone, can take a very long time to work, while the effective ones, such as methylene chloride, are very nasty indeed (see "Serious Solvents" on page 93).

7.2.3 Cyanoacrylate Glue

The cyanoacrylate (CA) adhesives are truly a product of the television age. Although initially developed at Eastman Kodak during the Second World War, CA glues entered the cultural mainstream through mass marketing and television advertising. Anyone over forty years old will remember the construction worker lifted off the ground by a single drop of "Krazy Glue" on his helmet.

CA's reputation for rapid setting and great strength is well deserved, and has resulted largely from instances of skin bonding, both intentional (as in those pranks from college) and accidental (as in when you tried to attach that tiny sapphire to a dop). In fact, CA is occasionally used instead of suture for some surgical operations.

Cyanoacrylate's major disadvantage for the hobby faceter is its short working time. Bonding can occur in seconds, so you better get it right the first time. Also, even though CA dissolves readily in acetone, this does not necessarily mean that bonded stones are easy to release. Strong CA adhesion depends on a very small gap between the two parts being glued. This also means that it can be difficult for the solvent to work its way into the cracks to release the full, bonded surface.

7.3 Standard Dopping Technique

Whichever adhesive you select, the technique of attaching a gemstone to the dop remains essentially the same. This section describes standard dopping in general terms, with procedures that are specific to a particular adhesive highlighted when necessary. Note also that Chapter 5 presents a detailed dopping tutorial with plenty of photographs.

Of course, every stone must be dopped twice, once for the pavilion and once for the crown. These steps are known as the initial dopping and transfer, respectively.

7.3.1 Initial Dopping

The conventional cutting order in modern faceting is pavilion-girdle-crown-table. There are excellent reasons for this (see page 304), but inevitably an unusual design or piece of gem rough may force some alteration. Nevertheless, in almost all instances, the *initial dopping* procedure attaches the stone to a (usually) flat dop for the pavilion cut.

The steps involved in the initial dopping procedure are:

- dop selection
- orientation and preparation of the dop and rough
- alignment to the table
- application of adhesive and gluing together
- setting and curing

Full Disclosure

This section provides detailed explanations of techniques that I never actually use.

I include descriptions of standard wax, cyanoacrylate, and epoxy dopping simply because I wish that I had this information as I made my own personal journey down the bumpy dopping road. I learned the hard way that none of the standard methods, with the possible exception of wax, is of any real use to a beginner. In fact, the standard dopping techniques suck.

There. I said it. I feel better.

In fact, I now feel great about dopping, since I started using a hybrid technique which combines the advantages of wax and epoxy with very few, if any, of their shortcomings. You, too, can make dopping a breeze. Turn to Section 7.4 to learn how.

Of course, in fairness to the traditional methods, it may be just my incompetence that led to my frustration, my "issues." And in fairness to the following sections, much of the material, such as cleaning and alignment, apply to all dopping techniques, both traditional and hybrid.

Dop Selection

With the pavilion-first approach, the first dopping must obviously occur on the crown side, and there will usually be a flat spot, either natural or purposely ground, where the future table will be located (see next page). A flat dop stick provides maximum mechanical support and adhesion to this flat surface.

Selecting the correct diameter flat dop involves a compromise. On the one hand, a larger diameter will provide greater support and more gluing area. On the other hand, a too-large stick may interfere with cutting the girdle. You should aim for a dop about two-thirds of the *minimum* diameter of the completed stone. For example, if your gem rough will allow you to cut a 6x9 mm oval, select a 4 mm flat stick for the initial dopping.

Beginners often select an oversized dop, particularly if they have had a recent experience with a stone coming loose during cutting. Proper dop bonds are plenty strong, and such mishaps are usually the result of incorrect gluing procedure, not undersized dops. Turn to page 157 for hints and advice on how to deal with a too-large dop. Figure 4-10 shows a potential outcome.

Orientation and Preparation

You should have a very clear idea of where the future gemstone lies within your piece of rough before even considering dopping. The cutting lap is not the place to make design decisions, particularly for the beginner. Carefully examine your rough and identify exactly where the pavilion, girdle, crown, and table will be. Chapter 6.7 provides some guidelines.

Depending on the size and shape of the rough, you may want to pre-form it prior to faceting. This could involve attaching the stone temporarily to another dop stick, or you can pre-form it in place, that is, roughing in the pavilion immediately prior to cutting the pavilion and pre-forming the crown immediately after transfer to the cone or vee dop. Chapter 8.3 describes the pre-forming process, and there is a detailed tutorial in Chapter 5.5.3.

Whether you pre-form or not, you should ensure that there is a relatively flat region near the location of the future table for attachment to the dop. This region can be a natural flat spot on the rough (but beware of cleavage planes – see Chapter 12.11.1). If no suitable surface exists, grind a temporary table on a coarse lap. Experienced faceters hold the rough in their hand to do this, but there is no reason not to temporarily dop the stone for this procedure. Chapter 5.4 explains how.

Standard cyanoacrylate adhesives work best when the surfaces of the two pieces being glued together match very well. Any gaps should be small, perhaps less than 0.5 mm. A temporary flat is therefore essential if you use CA glue. Reports differ on the gap-filling effectiveness of gel-type cyanoacrylates. See also "Bridging the Gap…" on page 249. Wax and epoxy have excellent gap-filling properties, so a roughed-in table may not be necessary.

With the gem rough properly shaped, you can begin the final preparation for dopping. This generally means a thorough cleaning of the dop and stone with alcohol or acetone. Skin oils are the enemy of essentially all lapidary adhesives. Once the bonding areas of the stone and dop are clean, don't touch them!

The final preparatory step is to mark the location on the stone where the center of the dop should be. Note that this is not necessarily the center of the gem! Some designs, such as pears, have an offset between the center of rotation – that is, where the dop attaches – and the center of the stone. The Green Flash design in Chapter 19.2.9 is another example. The following paragraphs explain how to identify and mark the sweet spot for the dop.

Alignment to the Table

The stone is ready. The dop is ready. All you have to do is bring them together with some glue, right?

Wrong. It's actually a little more complicated than that. Section 7.8 emphasizes the importance of accurate alignment. Even tiny errors can make a significant difference in yield, and hence the value, of the final gem, so it is worth getting the alignment right.

This generally means using some sort of alignment aid in the gluing process. This can range from a simple blob of putty to a sophisticated mechanical device. The goal is to hold the stone firmly in place while the adhesive – wax, epoxy, or cyanoacrylate – sets and can take over the job of maintaining alignment. This is particularly important if you have to work fast, as is the case with dop wax and CA glue. Also, if the adhesive is opaque, it may be difficult or impossible to see what is going on once the glue is in place. It is always best to get the alignment right in advance and have confidence that it won't change.

Modeler's clay or putty is the simplest alignment aid. Begin by placing a blob of clay on one arm of your transfer fixture (Figure 7-1). The exact procedure will vary depending on the geometry of your jig (see Chapter 4.16). If you do not have a suitable surface on which to place the putty, use the face of a large, flat dop as the mounting surface. Also, some modeling clays liquefy at very low temperatures. If you are using wax, make sure that your putty

doesn't get gooey when things heat up. Dux Seal and similar brands can withstand brief exposure to high temperatures and hence will work well.

Push the gem rough into the modeler's clay, table side up, and work around the edges of the stone, pushing the putty into the gap between the gem rough and transfer jig. The goal here is to have the stone "floating" in the clay for easy adjustment.

You need to get both the centering and the tilt right. For the math geeks out there, this means four separate parameters: x-position, y-position, pitch and roll (Figure 7-2). If you are using keyed dops, yaw, which corresponds to index wheel setting, can also be important. For example, if you are cutting a long rectangle, make sure that the long direction of the rough will line up with the correct index wheel setting when the dop and stone are locked into the quill. Consult your machine's instruction manual for further details.

Figure 7-1 A blob of putty will hold the gem rough in place during the dopping process.

Luckily, there are a few additional alignment aids immediately at hand: dops. A small diameter dop installed on the other arm of the transfer jig can show you how accurately the stone is centered – when you bring the two sides together, the dop should hit the exact center of your reference mark on the table (Figure 7-3). This fixes x and y.

Getting the tilt – that is, the pitch and yaw – of the stone right can be a bit trickier. If you have ground a temporary table, a larger diameter flat dop brought carefully into contact with the stone can reveal tilt errors. If there is no appropriate flat surface on the future table, you will have to eyeball it.

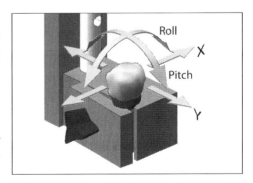

Figure 7-2 For accurate alignment of the gem rough, you need to get four things right: the X-Y position and the pitch-roll angles.

Note that shifting the centering can change the tilt and, similarly, adjusting the tilt can change the centering. Look at the stone from a number of different directions, repeat your checks with the small and large dops, and finally, make sure that you are happy with both centering and tilt before proceeding.

Gluing the Stone

When the stone is properly centered, you can install the flat dop on the other side of the transfer jig. The exact gluing procedure depends on the type of adhesive: dop wax, epoxy

resin, and cyanoacrylate glues all have their idiosyncrasies. Proper accommodation of these "personality traits" is the key to dopping success.

Note, however, that you won't get anywhere with any of these adhesives if the stone and dop are not absolutely clean. Before proceeding, perform a last gentle wipe of all mating surfaces with alcohol. This may erase any alignment marks on the stone, so make sure you are happy with both the orientation and stability of the stone beforehand.

Figure 7-3 Use a smaller dop to get accurate centering on your marked stone.

Stone Alignment Gadgets

This section began by highlighting the importance of maintaining accurate alignment during dopping. In fact, accurate centering and tilt is so critical that a number of mechanical devices have appeared on the market to assist with this procedure.

The mechanical GUIU dop from Ultra Tec is one such alignment aid (Figure 7-4). It uses a system of screws to allow fine position adjustment, and these screws hold the stone rigidly in place for gluing. Other manufacturers offer similar screw-based alignment hardware. The Magdop takes a somewhat different approach, using a powerful rare-earth magnet instead of screws to prevent shifting of the stone. The Sticky Dop provides yet another alternative based on heat resistant silicone putty.

These and other alignment aids are readily available by mail order. A quick search of the Internet should turn up suitable vendors. It will also turn up some surprising prices: you can easily spend tens or even hundreds of dollars on such devices.

Do you really need fancy stone alignment hardware? Probably not, at least initially. Give putty a try – you may never look back. On the other hand, the loss of yield for a single, poorly aligned but valuable gem can dwarf the cost of a commercial device. See page 123 for more on stone alignment gadgets.

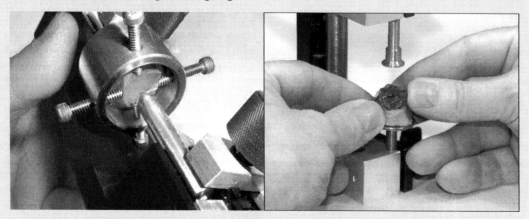

Figure 7-4 The GUIU (left) and Sticky Dop (right) dopping alignment aids.

Dop Wax

Note: Chapter 5.4.1 contains a detailed description, including pictures, of the wax dopping procedure for the initial bond. To prevent unnecessary repetition, this section provides only a brief overview.

Before trying to glue a gemstone to a dop using wax, you need to be aware of the most important open secret about this type of adhesive: hot wax will not, in general, adhere well to a cold stone. The result is the classic, convex "cold joint" appearance of a poor wax bond (See Figure 7-5 and page 148). The outcome of trying to cut such a poorly bonded gem involves ballistics, impact physics, and psychic stress. Note that warming the stone can help "tighten up" a cold joint, although it is rarely a good idea to apply heat directly to gem rough. In fact, you should always apply heat (and cold) to gemstones slowly and carefully. Even less-sensitive materials can have inclusions and incipient fractures that are just waiting to surprise you.

You can improve adhesion by coating the gemstone and dop with a layer of shellac prior to dopping. You will need some shellac-alcohol solution and a cotton swab or small brush. Chapter 4.3.1 explains how to prepare the solution. Paint the bonding areas of both the stone and dop with the mixture and allow them to dry completely before proceeding.

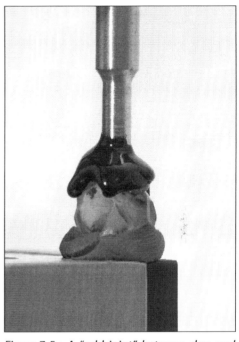

Figure 7-5 : A "cold joint" between dop and stone. Note the convex bulge of wax. Figure 5-23 shows another example of a cold wax joint.

Install the flat dop stick facing upward in your transfer jig and then begin warming wax above the flame of an alcohol lamp. Frequently turning the wax will ensure gentle heating. Once the wax begins to flow, transfer a drop or two to the prepared surface of the flat dop. When the wax has cooled, re-install the dop stick in the jig facing downward (see Figure 5-17 and 5-19). Again, differences in transfer jig geometry may force an alternate approach.

With the stone facing upward in the transfer jig, heat the shaft of the dop until the blob of wax becomes liquid. A small butane torch can be a real help here.

Press the stone and dop together and clamp the arms of the transfer jig in place. The dop should be close to, but not touching, the gem. A small amount of wax should have squeezed out between the dop and stone. You almost certainly have a cold joint, and will need to add wax and heat to ensure a strong bond.

Melt additional wax over the alcohol lamp and apply it to the area between stone and dop. Steadily build up a fillet that will give both volume and strength to the joint. Gently heat the dop and wax, rotating the transfer jig to prevent dripping. Eventually, the wax will be heated through and will flow smoothly over both stone and dop.

Set the jig aside and allow everything to cool completely. The result should be a strong wax bond ready for the cutting lap (Figure 7-6).

Epoxy Resin

Dopping with epoxy is straightforward. Simply mix up the glue, apply it to the stone and dop, squish them together, and then wait for the epoxy to cure.

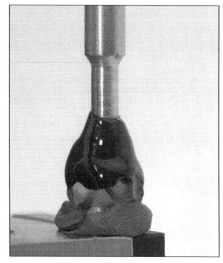

As always, it is a little more complicated than that. For example, some epoxies are quite sensitive to mixing proportions, so you should take extra care in following the manufacturer's instructions. Also, outdated epoxy almost never works well, particularly if the tubes have been opened and the contents exposed to air. Check the "Best Before…" date on the container before beginning.

Begin by preparing the stone as usual: careful cleaning, followed by alignment in the transfer jig using putty or your favourite mechanical aid (see "Stone Alignment Gadgets" on page 244). You will need a clean surface and mixing tool to prepare the epoxy. For the surface, I usually use a small piece of aluminum foil, folded over several times for strength (breaking through makes a mess of the tabletop – see Figure 7-7).

Figure 7-6 The completed wax bond.

A cotton swab cut in half serves as an excellent disposable stirrer. I bias-cut the swab (like green beans) to generate a point. This can be a great help in adjusting the distribution of resin at the dop-stone interface.

Squeeze separate blobs of the resin and hardener onto the mixing surface. Most five-minute epoxies require equal volumes of each. Note that this does not necessarily translate to equal

Which Epoxy?

Your local hardware store no doubt offers a wide array of epoxy resins tailored to every possible purpose. Which one works best for dopping?

The short answer is "Try and See…" The required bond strength for dopping is relatively modest compared to most applications. Therefore, the nominally "weaker" five-minute epoxies are a good choice, offering rapid setting time in an easy to use product. Needless to say, it is no fun waiting 36 hours for that Herculean glue to set, and you should avoid epoxies which generate or require high temperatures during bonding.

The "See" part of "Try and See" is actually pretty important. One of the great advantages of epoxy is that transparent formulations are available. This lets you examine the stone-dop joint for uniformity, bubbles, etc. It also lets you see things after the glue has dried.

The range of manufacturers and brands will vary from region to region. Local lapidary clubs or participants in online message boards may have a recommendation (Chapter 15.1.3). Failing that, just try a general-purpose transparent five-minute epoxy. Follow the directions carefully, and you will almost certainly be satisfied.

diameter drops, since one of the two components may be more viscous, resulting in a more spherical, and hence larger, blob for the same apparent diameter. Note also that mixing proportion errors will be greater for smaller amounts of epoxy, so you may want to prepare a little more than you need, particularly for smaller stones.

Mix the two components thoroughly with the stirrer. You should note a changed appearance of the resin as it combines and reacts with the hardener. Try to mix the glue thoroughly without introducing too many bubbles. Place a few drops of epoxy on the flat dop and bring the stone and dop together. A small amount of excess epoxy should squeeze out of the gap. Lock the stone and dop in place with the transfer jig before proceeding to the next step.

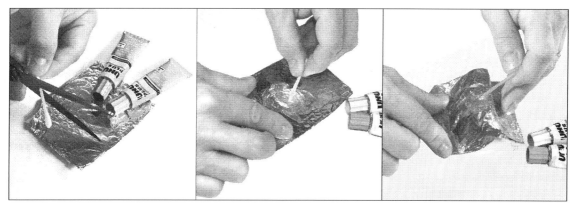

Figure 7-7 Cotton swabs and aluminum foil make excellent disposable tools for mixing epoxy. Check the residue on the foil to determine when the epoxy has set (right).

The job is almost done. There should be enough glue between the stone and dop to ensure a strong bond. As additional insurance, add a few extra drops of epoxy around the stone-dop interface. Smooth this extra adhesive to form a continuous fillet between stone and metal. This material will provide additional lateral support when working the stone against the cutting or polishing lap.

Clean up any extra epoxy on the dop or rough. I usually use the other half of the cotton swab for this purpose. As you work around the stone, you will notice the epoxy flowing slowly downward with gravity. Rotating the jig will help keep the glue in place (Figure 7-8).

Five-minute epoxy typically requires (surprise!) about five minutes to set. Note that there is a big difference between setting and curing. After the setting period, the glue will no longer flow, but it is nowhere near ready for the lap. Consult the packaging material for curing times. I typically lay the transfer jig aside to cure overnight. A warm (but not hot) location, such as the top of a radiator, may increase the ultimate strength of the bond.

A final word of advice: don't use too much glue. There should be enough epoxy on the stone and dop to fill the gap completely and create a smooth fillet. Any excess will end up on the shaft of the dop stick, the floor, your fingers, the cutting lap, etc.

Note that epoxy resins are chemicals and should be treated with respect. Avoid direct contact with the skin and consult the packaging materials or Material Safety Data Sheets. An online search of the product name and "MSDS" should get you started.

Five Wonderful Long Minutes...

The great advantage of epoxy resin over other lapidary adhesives is its long working time. You should have at least three to five minutes to get things right before the material begins to solidify. Once the glue has started to set, it will get increasingly difficult and messy to make any changes.

Until then, you can adjust the alignment, but be careful, since the epoxy will continue to flow with gravity. Epoxy resin's great advantage therefore comes at a cost: you have to make sure that the glue stays in place until it sets. This may mean rotating the

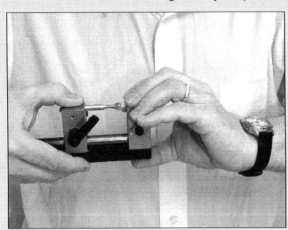

transfer jig continuously for several minutes (Figure 7-8). Of course, you should take advantage of this time and the continuously varying perspective to double check that everything is Ok. Epoxy dopping may be leisurely, but it is also permanent. If you are unhappy with how it turned out, you essentially have to start over from the beginning.

Figure 7-8 Rotating the transfer jig ensures an even distribution of epoxy. It also lets you check your watch.

Cyanoacrylate Glue

The procedure for dopping with cyanoacrylate glue is very similar to that for epoxy, with a couple of prominent exceptions. First, CA adhesive has a very short working time, typically tens of seconds, so it is doubly important to have everything in place and aligned before starting.

The second major difference is that cyanoacrylate glues generally do not work well if there are significant gaps between the surfaces to be bonded. Granted, so-called "gap-filling" CA adhesives exist, but reports from faceters have been mixed on their effectiveness. Of course, if you began by grinding a temporary table, you have already ensured a good match between dop and stone.

Prepare the gem rough and dop as for the other adhesives. Clean surfaces are particularly important for cyanoacrylate glue – a stray fingerprint or a bit of putty residue can spoil your whole day. Place a drop or two of adhesive on the dop, and then bring the stone and dop together. Cyanoacrylates set quickly, so do a final check that everything is in place before beginning.

Like epoxies, CA glue does not immediately reach its final bond strength. Consult the manufacturers instructions for optimal curing times and conditions. Some faceters have reported that water can weaken a CA bond. If you experience this difficulty, try sealing the dop-stone interface with transparent nail polish after the glue has cured. Another option is to add a thin ribbon of dop wax over the bond. This not only protects the CA glue from water, but it may also provide useful wax clues for re-aligning the stone should it become detached (see Section 7.5).

Bridging the Gap…

You can still ensure a strong cyanoacrylate bond, even if your gem rough is irregular and gaps are inevitable. The trick is to custom fit your dop to the stone. You can do this by applying a blob of hot wax to the dop and creating an impression of the gem rough in the wax before it has cooled. You can then glue the stone to this wax impression. It's a lot easier than it sounds…

Begin by coating the flat dop with shellac-alcohol mixture as described on page 146. Warm a stick of dop wax over an alcohol burner and apply several drops of wax to the flat face of the dop. The exact amount will depend on the size and irregularity of your stone. Once the wax has cooled, place the flat dop in one arm of your transfer fixture and affix the stone to the other with putty. Hold the transfer jig with the dop uppermost and apply heat until the wax softens and begins to sag (Figure 7-9).

Figure 7-9 Heat a small blob of dop wax.

Do not let the wax melt completely and do not heat the gem rough. Bring the dop and stone together briefly and then separate them. This creates an impression of the stone in the wax. Voilà! A custom-fitted dop ready for successful gluing with cyanoacrylate (Figure 7-10). Note that for some rough shapes, a cone dop will work better.

Incidentally, this is a "hybrid" dopping procedure, one that uses both wax and glue to achieve the desired result. Such mixed approaches can offer the best of both worlds, while avoiding the shortcomings of each. In fact, I always use a hybrid dopping technique. See Section 7.4 below.

Figure 7-10 Squeeze the stone and dop together briefly to produce a wax impression. This eliminates gaps for dopping with cyanoacrylate glue.

There is one final rule for successful dopping with cyanoacrylate adhesive: don't glue your-self to anything. This admonition is only half in jest. If you are not careful, you really can glue your fingers together, or your hand to your transfer fixture, or your eyeballs shut. If the worst happens, you can loosen a cyanoacrylate bond with nail polish remover or acetone. Do not, repeat, DO NOT use these solvents if you have glued your eyeballs shut. Read – or in this case, have someone else read – the manufacturer's instructions and consult your physician.

Setting and Curing

For all types of lapidary adhesive, the maximum achievable bond strength depends on a number of factors, such as the temperature and humidity in your workshop. Time is also a vital factor. Attempting to cut a stone too soon after gluing will almost always end in heart-break (and perhaps even stonebreak).

Wax bonds offer by far the easiest and quickest post-gluing phase. You should be able to grind away at the stone as soon as the wax is cool to the touch. Note that for larger stones and brass dops, this can be many minutes.

Epoxy resin and cyanoacrylate glue have considerably longer setting and curing times. You should typically allow five minutes for setting and overnight for curing. See the manufactur-ers instructions and the previous paragraphs for further details.

7.3.2 Dop Transfer

Standard faceting procedure calls for the pavilion and girdle to be completed before moving on to the crown. As Chapter 5 makes clear, much of the work in cutting the pavilion involves establishing reference locations, especially the center point or culet and the girdle facets. A symmetrical, pleasing gemstone depends on accurate alignment of the centering, tilt, and rotation between the pavilion and crown, and this, in turn, depends on proper *dop transfer*.

You will use a transfer jig for this procedure (see Figure 7-11 and Chapter 4.16). These devices allow *co-axial* clamping of the two dops. Co-axial means that the two dops share the same axis. In other words, the long dimension of the two dops form part of a single line. This means that they have the same centering and tilt. Dop *keying* systems can help preserve the rotational informa-tion (see page 94). Alternatively, various transfer cheat strategies allow you to recover the rotational reference after completing the transfer. See Section 7.6 for more.

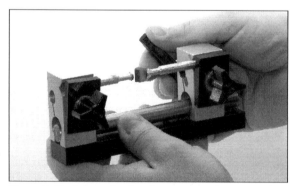

Figure 7-11 A transfer jig clamps two dops together, preserving centering, and tilt. With keyed dops, you can preserve the rotational reference as well.

The dop transfer procedure involves several steps:

- selection and preparation of the second dop stick
- preparation of the pavilion
- mounting and alignment of the dops in the transfer jig

- application of adhesive and gluing
- setting and curing
- removal of the initial flat dop

Note that Chapter 5.6 contains a detailed tutorial with pictures of the dop transfer procedure. As before, this section provides an overview highlighting the differences between dop wax, epoxy resin, and cyanoacrylate glue.

The Key to Transfer Success?

In principle, a keyed dop properly inserted in the quill will contain the rotational reference information. In other words, the appropriate notch, surface, or groove will bear a known, fixed relationship to the index wheel numbers. Transferring the stone to another keyed dop in an appropriate jig imprints that information on the second dop, and, in turn, installing that dop properly in the keyed quill should make everything work out: the crown facets should line up with the pavilion.

That is the principle, but it is not necessarily the reality. There are a number of possible causes for disappointing results with keyed dops. For example, executing a keyed dop transfer involves at least four installation steps, each of which requires attention and care: two installations into the quill and two into the transfer jig. Small errors can build up, ruining the alignment. Some keying systems use an adjustable-depth pin and groove arrangement. If set too shallow, the pin may allow some play in the dop rotation; if set too deep, the pin can push the dop sideways and alter the overall orientation. Note also that some types of rotation alignment difficulties cause index errors to double on transfer.

Whatever the cause, opinion among experienced faceters on the benefits of keyed dops is mixed to say the least. For what it's worth, I gave up on keyed dops after my first couple of gems and have never looked back. Chapter 4.4 contains further information and opinion.

Selection and Preparation of the Second Dop Stick

The second dop stick must provide the same mechanical support and large gluing area as the first. Here, however, the bonding surface is not flat, and the gemstone shape guides the choice of dop stick.

Use a cone dop for round or near-round stones. Emerald, navette, and other long designs get better support from a vee dop. Chapter 4.4.2 describes each of these types in detail, and provides information (and opinion) on custom specialty dops.

The girdle should be complete at this stage, and crown angles tend to be lower than those of the pavilion. Hence, there is less danger of cutting into the dop, and in principle, you can use a larger diameter dop stick than before. Nevertheless, there are several good reasons not to.

First, a cone or vee dop has more gluing area than a flat dop of the same diameter, so even the same diameter may be overkill. Also, if the second dop reaches nearly to the edge of the gem, excess adhesive near the dop-stone interface may obscure your view of the girdle reference points. Third, a larger cone dop is harder to release once the stone is completed. Don't dismiss this as a trivial concern, for you, too, may one day encounter the Nightmare Stone from Hell™ (see page 259).

There is a final, important reason for not selecting an oversized dop for cutting the crown. Some post-transfer alignment techniques actually require you to polish a small portion of the girdle facets (see Section 7.6.2 below). An oversized cone or vee dop will just get in the way. Short version: pick a cone or vee dop of the same diameter as, or slightly smaller than, the initial flat dop.

Preparation of the Pavilion

To revive a tired metaphor, cleanliness is next to adhesiveness. Wipe the completed pavilion with a lint-free paper towel soaked in alcohol. If you are using wax, coat the clean stone with a layer of shellac-alcohol mixture and let it dry (Figure 7-12). If your adhesive of choice is epoxy or CA, you are already good to go.

Figure 7-12 For transferring with wax, apply a layer of shellac-alcohol mixture to the new cone or vee dop (left) and the completed pavilion (right). The transfer jig makes an excellent holder for drying dops.

Mounting and Alignment

Install both dop sticks in the transfer jig and check for proper centering by sliding the completed pavilion gently into the cone or vee dop. Not only does this provide a sanity check that everything is ready, but also it guarantees that the sliding mechanism has sufficient travel to seat the pavilion into the target dop. As always when bringing gem material and metal into close proximity, take extra care to avoid chipping and scratching.

If you plan to use a keying system to help preserve rotational alignment, you should also tighten and check any locking mechanisms at this time.

Gluing the Stone

The actual gluing procedure during transfer is very similar to the initial dopping step, and as before, the details vary somewhat between adhesives.

Wax

Note: Chapter 5.6 contains a detailed tutorial showing dop transfer with wax. This section provides only a brief overview.

For wax, prepare both the pavilion and second dop with a thorough cleaning and coating with shellac-alcohol mixture (see opposite page). You should protect the initial wax bond from heat to prevent softening and possible loss of orientation – your cherished centering, tilt, and rotation. The easiest protective measure is to wrap the initial bond with a strip of moist paper towel (Figure 7-13).

Slowly warm the stick of dop wax over the alcohol lamp until the wax begins to liquefy. While holding the jig with the target dop pointing upward, transfer a few drops

Figure 7-13 Wrapping the initial bond with a strip of moist paper towel will keep things cool during transfer.

of wax into the cone or vee dop until it is approximately two thirds full. This will allow good coverage of the pavilion without too much spillover. Set the stick of wax aside and apply heat to the target dop until the wax becomes liquid. You may also wish to warm the completed pavilion to help ensure a strong bond. Do this very carefully, however, since both the gemstone and previous wax bond may be susceptible to heat. When the wax is liquid, bring the pavilion and dop together, gently squeezing the joint until the wax completely fills the stone-dop gap. Don't force things too far: bottoming out increases the risk of chipping your lovingly polished pavilion.

Fingertip Flambé

Try to avoid boiling the dop wax, since this can weaken the material. Also, overheated wax tends to liquefy quickly, leading to uncontrolled dripping, tabletop messes, and burned fingertips. You should take the last point seriously: the melting temperatures of green, black, and brown dop wax are 160°, 165°, and 176°F (71°, 74°, 80°C), respectively (see Table 4-1). A quick look at your favourite cookbook will inform you that these are exactly the "done" temperatures of beef, pork, and chicken, respectively. My cookbook doesn't list human flesh, but I would bet good money that it's in that range somewhere. Watch out.

Oh. One more thing. Dop wax is also flammable. You will not soon forget your first burning, smoking, and dripping stick of dop wax. Make sure it's your last.

A small amount of wax should spill out of the joint, forming the classic "bead" of a cold wax bond (Figure 7-5). Further indirect application of the alcohol lamp should heat the area sufficiently to allow the wax to flow smoothly over the stone and dop to form a strong joint.

This bond should suffice in most circumstances, but for additional insurance, you can create a fillet to surround and support the pavilion. This involves alternate applications of dop wax and heat, steadily building up supporting material around the pavilion. This stage of the process carries the greatest danger of overheating and shifting the initial bond. If transferring takes longer than expected, unwrap the strip of paper towel, check that the initial bond is still cool, and then re-moisten the paper with cold water before re-wrapping and proceeding.

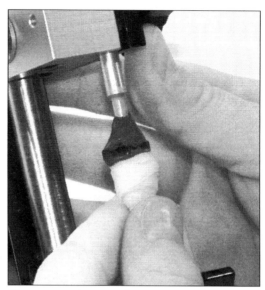

Figure 7-14 The completed wax bond between the pavilion and cone / vee dop. Note the moist paper towel protecting the initial bond.

The final wax bond should be smooth and continuous from stone to dop (Figure 7-14). Any discontinuities or bulges may indicate a cold joint, which may fail under stress. Apply heat until the wax has flowed over the surface of both stone and metal.

Epoxy

Executing a dop transfer with epoxy seems as easy as the initial dopping: just make sure that both the pavilion and cone/vee dop are clean, mix up the adhesive, apply to the dop and stone, squeeze together, and wait.

Actually, as before, there are a few subtleties. Epoxy is a very robust adhesive, and releasing the completed gem may be problematic without taking a few precautions at this stage. At a bare minimum, you should place a tiny ball of putty or crushed tissue paper in the base of the dop before gluing. This prevents adhesion to the culet, which might otherwise break off when parting the stone from the dop. My most recent re-cutting and repair job was the direct result of forgetting this step. I also apply epoxy only to the upper part of the cone or vee dop, near the rim.

Some faceters mix a small amount of cornstarch with the epoxy. This gives the hardened resin some porosity, aiding the penetration of acetone or other solvent during the release phase. It may also prevent culet damage. Other cutters suggest placing a single layer of tissue paper between the dop and stone for the same reason.

The variety of available adhesives and solvents makes a single recommendation difficult. Try straight epoxy (with the culet protection), and modify your technique as needed. The online discussion groups (see Chapter 15.1.3) are an excellent source of information and experience with epoxies available in your area.

Whatever epoxy and technique you adopt, there should be a smooth continuous bond between stone and metal. Also, various transfer cheat procedures (see Section 7.6 below) may require access to or visibility of the girdle facets – try to keep the glue on the pavilion facets only.

Cyanoacrylate Glue

The gluing procedure for dop transfer with CA adhesive is almost identical to that for the initial dopping. The only difficulty lies in the fact that some cyanoacrylates require essentially zero gap between the two mating surfaces. Grinding a temporary table ensured a good match for the initial bond, but unless you have a (very large) selection of faceted concave dops, there will inevitably be significant gaps when it comes to cutting the crown.

There are two possible approaches. The most straightforward is to select a gap-filling cyanoacrylate for the transfer. Although some users claim that the gap-filling CA produces a weaker bond, the increased contact area and mechanical support that cone and vee dops provide should more than compensate. Also, even the harshest critics of gap-filling cyanoacrylate concede that the normal CA that they prefer simply cannot bond non-mating surfaces.

The obvious alternative to gap-filling glue is to make a hybrid bond using a wax impression of the pavilion as described in "Bridging the Gap..." on page 249.

Note that there is a nonzero risk of damage when releasing the completed gem, and as with epoxy, you should protect the culet with a small ball of putty or tissue paper prior to gluing. A thin coating of transparent nail polish will again protect the bond against possible weakening due to contact with water.

Setting and Curing

As explained at the end of Section 7.3.1, you should allow sufficient time for the new bond to set and cure. Do not adjust the transfer fixture during the setting period, which is typically several tens of seconds for wax, and several minutes for epoxy and cyanoacrylate glue. For epoxy, you may have to rotate the transfer jig during setting to keep the resin in place (Figure 7-8). Follow the manufacturer's instructions regarding curing times.

Releasing the Original Dop

The wax is cool, or the glue has cured, and all is well. You have successfully transferred the centering, tilt, and (possibly) rotation information from the first dop to the second. It is time for the initial dop to depart the scene.

Releasing the original dop is usually not problematic. If the initial bond is wax, you will want to wrap the new bond in moist paper towel to prevent unwanted heating and shifting. A combination of warming of the original dop (not the stone) and gentle sideways pressure should cause the dop to fall off. For larger stones or more stubborn wax, try cutting the bond with a heated scalpel blade (see also page 179).

Breaking epoxy and cyanoacrylate bonds is usually more difficult. Both adhesives can be dissolved in acetone, for example by wrapping the initial bond in a strip of paper towel soaked in the solvent. Avoid cross contamination and possible weakening of the new bond during this step. Gentle heating of the original dop over the alcohol lamp can also help. However, if you value your eyebrows, don't use the acetone-soaked towel and the alcohol lamp at the same time.

See the next section for additional tips if you have difficulty with releasing the original dop.

Open Transfer

A good friend and colleague of mine rarely bothers with transfer jigs, preferring instead to execute an *open transfer*.

What is an open transfer?

An open transfer simply means removing the partially completed gemstone entirely from the first dop before attaching it to the second.

Why on earth would you want to do this? The adjacent text has taken great pains to explain that proper alignment of the crown and pavilion facets requires you to control the centering, tilt, and rotation of the gem as you transfer it from one dop to the other. A combination of precision transfer jigs, dop-keying mechanisms, and strategies for determining the transfer cheat can help.

The idea behind an open transfer is to depend solely on the geometry of the partially cut gemstone to maintain this control. For example, a round pavilion can only fit one way into a cone dop. This takes care of centering and tilt, provided that the pavilion can settle accurately into the machined cup of the cone dop. A temporary table facet can help define the perpendicular, so even diehard open transfer mavens occasionally use a flat dop and a jig to get things right. Establishing the rotational reference with open transfer is identical to that with conventional dop transfer, if you, like me, have little faith in dop keying systems. In other words, the standard techniques of determining the transfer cheat laid out in Section 7.6 work fine.

That's all well and good, but again, why on earth would you want to do this?

It turns out that open transfer offers significant advantages for some faceters. First, it is very quick and in skilled hands, more than accurate enough for most purposes. Open transfer allows you to immediately free up the dop from a half completed gem, so you can, for example, cut a sequence of identical pavilions before moving on to the crowns. It also permits you to completely clean the stone after the pavilion polish, providing a better opportunity to examine progress and search for inclusions and flaws that may alter your cutting strategy. Finally, becoming comfortable with open transfer is an excellent way to train for the challenging task of repairing damaged gems.

Of course, there are definite disadvantages to this technique as well. It requires more skill, and any errors in centering, tilt, and rotation mean more work with the cheater later on. Open transfer is also unsuitable for many gem designs with more complicated symmetry, since the technique requires that the completed pavilion "settle" into a cone dop with the correct centering and tilt. I am not entirely sure how or even whether open transfer would work on those designs requiring a vee dop.

Do I recommend open transfer?

Definitely not, at least not for the beginner. Dopping is enough of a challenge as it is, and you should take advantage of any tools which can help. Nevertheless, wise and experienced gem cutters, like my friend, cannot all be wrong. As you progress and gain confidence, you should give open transfer a try.

7.3.3 Releasing the Completed Gem

You have invested hours at the lap producing a valuable, near-perfect gem, and you cannot wait to release it from the dop to admire the results. Well, you can and should wait, since rushed and improper procedure at this stage can easily ruin the stone. Trust me…I have done it more than once.

Releasing a gem glued with dop wax could not be easier. Simply hold the end of the dop stick in your fingers, heat the shank of the dop over the alcohol lamp, and twist the stone free. You will soon discover the "sweet spot," about 1/3 of the way from the stone to your fingers, where application of the flame makes the metal uncomfortably warm just as the wax gives up the ghost. Let the stone cool thoroughly before placing it in a jar of alcohol to dissolve away any remaining wax, and you are done. Admire away.

Despite their other advantages (see Section 7.2), the epoxy and cyanoacrylate adhesives can put up a vexing fight when you try to release the completed gem. The problem lies in the fact that, in most instances, both of these glues must be at least partially weakened with a solvent, typically acetone, before any mechanical efforts to dislodge the stone can bear fruit. Cone and vee dops provide a significant and well-shielded bonding surface, making penetration of the solvent difficult. An extended soak in acetone should be enough, however.

Place the dop and stone in a sealed jar with sufficient acetone to completely cover the bond and let it sit on your bench overnight. The following morning, remove the dop, dry it, and then try to pull the stone free. If it pops out, great! Place the freed gemstone back in the acetone to help dissolve any remaining glue, and you are again home free.

Unfortunately, experience dictates that the stone will almost never just pop out. In fact, it was persistent difficulty with stubborn glue bonds that prompted me to abandon standard dopping procedure and start using a hybrid technique (see Section 7.4 below).

If the initial acetone soak didn't bring success, you should try to scrape away any softened adhesive with your fingernail, return the dop to the acetone, and give it a few more hours. Gentle heating, as with the wax release, can also weaken epoxy and CA bonds. Just seal the jar and double check that there is no stray acetone on your dop, stone, or fingers when using an open flame.

Releasing the Impossible Gem

Is your lovely gemstone still stubbornly stuck in the cone dop, despite your soaking, heating and praying? Sooner or later, you will encounter the Impossible Gem that simply refuses to let go of its dop. The only counsel here is to have patience and keep soaking, scraping, heating, and pulling.

Extreme cases may require extreme measures, however.

If you are truly desperate, you could try a more aggressive solvent, such as methylene chloride (*Attack* is one commercial product in this category). Note, however, that methylene chloride is a profoundly nasty chemical that should only be used with proper protective gear in a well-ventilated environment. Read the manufacturers instructions carefully and see "Serious Solvents" on page 93. Note also that in some jurisdictions, methylene chloride based products are either restricted or outright banned. I cannot in good conscience recommend it.

If all else fails, you can try drilling or grinding away the dop stick, in order to allow the solvent to gain access to the adhesive bond. Needless to say, this should be a last resort, and you must take extra care not to damage the stone. See the opposite page for a truly sad story of a gem that simply refused to let go...

7.4 A Better Way?

The table of comparisons in Section 7.2 lists the pros and cons of dop wax, epoxy resin, and cyanoacrylate glue. Although many experienced faceters loudly defend and adhere to their favourite adhesive (sometimes literally in the case of CA), there is no clear winner in my opinion. In fact, a cursory scan of the earliest sections of this chapter will tell you that I think that there are only losers. The ideal faceting adhesive simply does not exist.

The combination of advantages and shortcomings of wax, epoxy, and CA has led to the development of several *hybrid* dopping strategies, that is, techniques that use the best properties of two or more adhesives at once. The wax impression method described on page 249 is one such hybrid dopping technique, since it exploits the gap-filling property of wax, coupled with the reliability and low working temperature of cyanoacrylates.

Here is the short version of my bumpy journey from wax to a Better Way. I began with the traditional "pure" wax technique, but it has the serious shortcomings of very short working time and reduced visibility of the dop-stone interface. This leads to less than optimal stone alignment. The epoxy adhesives offer enormous advantages over traditional dop wax in both these areas, but, as the previous sections make clear, problems may arise in breaking the bond during transfer and especially when the gemstone is complete.

Frustration with pure wax, and near disaster with epoxy and CA (see "The Nightmare Stone from Hell™" opposite) led me to seek an alternative. This section describes my favourite dopping method, which is a hybrid combining brown "diamond-setters" dop wax with five-minute epoxy. Simply put, the technique is a modification of epoxy resin dopping using a thin layer of wax between the epoxy and the dop. The wax layer allows easy separation during transfer and on completion of the stone, while the epoxy provides a strong bond, longer working time, and improved visibility of the girdle area. This method also works great with heat sensitive gem materials.

7.4.1 Initial Dopping

This description assumes the traditional (and highly recommended) pavilion-girdle-crown cutting order. Hence, the initial dopping will be to the future table area. You should consider grinding a temporary flat area for bonding if no suitable surface exists on the gem rough. See page 242 and Section 5.4.1 for further details.

Since the general goal is to establish a thin layer of dop wax as a buffer between the epoxy and the dop stick, the preparation for initial dopping is very similar to that for the traditional wax technique.

The Nightmare Stone from Hell™

As a gem cutter, you will never forget your first sapphire.

I know I never will, for that lovely, cornflower-blue chunk of prime Montana rough transmogrified itself into the Nightmare Stone from Hell™. This is the story of how less than a gram of gem rough almost ended my faceting career before it started. It's not easy to recover from a Nightmare Stone from Hell™, but perhaps hearing a fellow cutter's tale of woe will prepare you for your own encounter. Steel your nerves, dear reader, and carry on if you dare…

It all started well, as such things usually do. Based on a tip from a friend, I had ordered a five-carat piece of Montana sapphire rough, and the package had arrived without incident. The stone itself was magnificent, showing a pale turquoise-green along one axis and the classic cornflower blue along another. Best of all, the shape of the rough would let me cut a Standard Round Brilliant with pretty decent yield in the blue-up orientation. As a final bonus, this orientation placed a zone of more intense colour near the culet, allowing me to hope and plan for a deeper, richer blue in the final gem (see Chapter 6.7.1).

I was a wax dopper at that point, and I had not yet realized the benefits of hybrid techniques (Section 7.4). I knew that polishing sapphire could lead to excessive heating and the consequent softening and shifting of dop wax, but I was prepared. I would take things slowly and easily – it was expensive gem rough after all – and I would use a higher temperature, diamond-setter's wax (Chapter 4.1.1).

As it turned out softening dop wax was the least of my problems.

The first sign of trouble came swiftly and terribly into my life. I was happily cutting the pavilion with a 1200-grit steel lap when I heard and felt an awful crunch. I blinked a couple of times, swallowed hard, and then raised the quill for inspection.

My initial concern about a fractured stone proved unfounded, or at least unsupported by the evidence. More precisely, I could not evaluate the presence of damage to the gem rough because the gem rough was gone. In its place were the ragged remains of the wax bond, which had just failed in spectacular fashion.

"Alright," I told myself, breathing easier. "At least that sound wasn't the gem being destroyed."

I had read advice online about broken wax bonds, and knew that it was possible to recover from the situation by gluing the jigsaw puzzle of the broken wax back together (see Section 7.5). All I had to do was locate the stone, buy some cyanoacrylate adhesive, and glue the gem back in place.

"No problem," I thought, "…just switch off the machine, lower the quill, and find the detached stone."

Easier thought than done, as it turned out. The quill lowering and power switching went well, but I was at a loss as to where the sapphire ended up.

I did all the right things, by the way. I checked the area of the lap and in the splash pan and even in the waste water bottle on the floor. I searched my work area and the general direction a ballistic gemstone would take if flung away by a spinning lap. I even tried the flashlight trick on the floor (see Section 7.5.1).

Nothing. It was as if the stone had simply winked out of existence.

That was an unmistakable sign to give up and move on to another gem, and I should have heeded the warning, since worse was yet to come. Nevertheless, I doggedly and systematically searched my entire work area, discovering several tools and doodads that I thought were lost forever and eventually finding the stone. It had pathologically come to rest just behind the base of a desk lamp, invisible unless you stood up and searched from the other side.

With relief, I noted that substantial wax still adhered to the gem rough, and that the ragged fracture area seemed to match that on the end of the dop. A short foray to a local hardware store for Krazy Glue, and I was in business…

Gluing the gem back into place seemed to go well, although don't believe them when they say that a clean fracture should produce a perfect match. I note in the interest of fairness that "them" includes "me" – see Section 7.5.2 below.

The match was much less than perfect, as it turned out. Whether there was some plastic deformation of the wax before it failed, or perhaps some damage to the delicate jagged remains of the bond as it flew across the room, or even the common error of using too much adhesive, the facets did not quite line up as they did before. Close, but not close enough.

"Not a problem," I asserted through gritted teeth…"Look at it as an excellent pre-form and just re-cut the pavilion facets."

This I set out to do, and all seemed well with the world. The pavilion breaks came in fine, and I was just starting in on the mains.

"Crunch," exclaimed the gemstone, as it once again broke loose and flew across the room.

This time, the sapphire was easier to find, but the fractured bond seemed to be in even worse shape.

"Really not a problem," I whispered, knowing full well that I was back at square one.

I had read on the Internet that cyanoacrylate glue can weaken in the presence of water, and I had taken no extra precautions to keep the stone-dop junction dry. The standard recommendation is to seal the bond under a layer of transparent nail polish (see page 248). It was time for another pleasant foray to the local shop. Several hours later, I had a re-fitted and sealed cyanoacrylate bond ready to go.

This one didn't even survive the light test cut I tried on the first facet. It didn't even produce a sickening crunch. The stone just folded over and fell off.

"That's interesting," I stated flatly. I cannot be sure, but I think that a small amount of steam came out with the words.

The next day found me again at the hardware store, standing in front of an array of epoxy cements. Given my tribulations and state of mind I should be forgiven, but I asked the clerk for the strongest epoxy on the planet. Not a good idea, as will be clear presently.

The clerk knitted his brow and seemingly reluctantly handed over a cardboard blister package containing two small tubes.

"Twelve hour work time. Seventy-two hour curing time. Really strong." The clerk hesitated, as if he was trying to build up the courage to ask me what on earth I needed that stuff for. In the end, discretion won over curiosity and he kept his silence. I paid up and headed home with my Herculean glue.

Three days later, I was once again ready and eager to cut stone. Due to its viscosity, fitting the jigsaw together with the epoxy did not go as well as with the cyanoacrylate, but at that point, I was already resigned to the fact that I would once again be starting over.

Incidentally, at this fourth cutting of the pavilion facets, the gem rough was not getting any bigger, and my dream of producing a one-carat sapphire had faded away.

Guess what? The epoxy held, and I was able to cut and polish the pavilion without further incident. Things were back on track.

In fact, things went so swimmingly, that I decided to use the super epoxy for the dop transfer as well. Why not? I carefully aligned the completed pavilion with a cone dop, mixed up and applied the epoxy, and then squeezed the two together.

Another three days went by, and the epoxy had cured. It was time to break the initial bond with the flat dop. As usual, I prepared a heated scalpel and began to cut away at the epoxy.

"Oops," I gulped as I tried to push the heated blade into the resin.

It was as hard as iron and wasn't going anywhere. Not willing to be defeated at this point by some stupid glue, I examined the epoxy bond. Sure enough, there was a slight mark where the red-hot scalpel had made contact. This will work! It will just take time and effort. I continued sawing away with the hot scalpel for several minutes. Eventually, the stone broke free and I was once again on the path to sapphirine pleasure.

Cutting and polishing the crown were completely uneventful, at least on the scale of how things had gone so far. Even polishing the table went well, and I was looking forward to popping the stone out of the cone dop to admire the outcome of my long and difficult journey.

"Oops," I repeated, realizing that my difficulties in breaking the initial bond at dop transfer meant that "popping the stone out of the cone dop" might not be as easy as I had imagined.

That recognition was about the only thing I got right. With little hope of success, I attempted to free the stone using a hot scalpel and an extended soak in acetone.

No success. No surprise.

You can probably guess the next part of the story. I tried more heating and soaking. No luck. I tried placing the dop and stone in the oven at 500°F (260°C) for several minutes and then pulling and prodding on the stone. Nope. A longer sojourn in the oven produced nothing more than singed fingertips and an evil look from the wife. I even tried a methylene chloride based solution that I promised myself that I would never use, since it is such a nasty chemical (see page 93 and page 257). Zip.

Approaching the end of my rope, I consulted a colleague at my workplace. This worthy fellow is a true expert on epoxies, and buys methylene chloride by the drum, not the small jar. He took one look at the sticky mess of sapphire, epoxy, and aluminum dop stick and shook his head.

I had seen him express his viewpoint this way in the past, and I knew that it did not bode well for the sapphire, nor for his opinion of my alleged lapidary skills.

"You're going to have to drill it," he grunted, pointing with a stubby finger at the junction of the shank and cone of the dop, "...to let the solvent in."

"Errr. Can you help me?" I asked. At that point I had lost all faith in my ability to deal with that tiny chunk of sapphire.

"Nope. But I can lend you the drill bit." He crossed to a cabinet in his workshop and returned with the tiniest drill bit I had ever seen. "One millimeter. We use it for circuit boards...Be careful."

Again, you can probably guess the rest of the story. I carefully chucked the bit and drilled through the aluminum at a point that I reckoned was safely below the tip of the culet. I figured that a second hole halfway around would ensure better solvent flow.

I was half right in my reckoning and figuring. A two-day soak in more methylene chloride eventually did release the gem, so the solvent flow was fine. To my grim surprise, the drill location was not.

Why was I surprised? This was, after all, the Nightmare Stone from Hell™. Why shouldn't it be perfectly formed, except for a ragged wound where the culet should be?

Believe me, I stared at that sapphire for a long time. Although qualitatively smaller than originally planned, the colour was magnificent, and the facets – at least those untouched by the drill bit – were flawless. With a determination that can only be called pigheadedness, I decided that I should repair the stone.

Re-cutting the pavilion was out of the question: I knew that my spirit would not survive that, and I would then probably have to re-do the crown and end up with an even smaller gem. But I had an idea. Most old-style cuts actually have a tiny culet facet parallel to the table. I could convert this Standard Round Brilliant into an Old European Cut brilliant, and even pretend that it was intentional! Turn to Figure 16-20 to see what I mean.

Another bright idea! I attached the table to a flat dop (using wax…the epoxy was at that point somewhere outside the window of my workshop), and it was a cinch to place a tiny culet facet on the bottom of the gem.

In the end I won. Figure 7-15 shows the Nightmare Stone from Hell™ At 0.42 ct, it is considerably smaller than intended. Nevertheless, the stone is truly lovely, and as I said at the beginning, unforgettable.

Figure 7-15 A lovely Old European Cut sapphire.

Select a flat dop that is approximately two-thirds the size of the completed stone. See page 241 and Chapter 5.4 for further guidance on dop selection. A thorough cleaning of both dop and gem rough with alcohol will ensure good adhesion. Coating the dop with shellac-alcohol mixture will also help (see Figure 7-16). Chapter 4.3.1 explains how to prepare this solution.

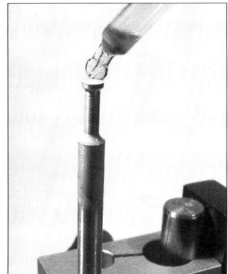

When the solution has dried, warm a stick of dop wax over the alcohol lamp and apply a drop of wax to the tip of the dop. Try to make a small bead or lens of wax on the tip, without letting it overflow down the shaft (Figure 7-17). I prefer the brown "diamond setters" wax, which has a slightly higher melting temperature than others, although for this technique, any faceter's dop wax will do. Chapter 4.1.1 gives information on the characteristics of various types of dop wax.

Install the flat dop in one arm of your transfer fixture, and select a larger flat dop for the other side. I prefer the 1/2-inch Graves dop, since it has a textured face (see below). To prevent drips, I usually place the wax-coated dop facing upward as shown in Figure 7-18.

Figure 7-16 Clean the dop thoroughly and then apply a drop or two of shellac-alcohol mixture. When dry, the coating should leave a faint brown patina on the dop stick.

Heat the bead of wax until it is melted, but not boiling. Gently bring the larger flat dop into contact with the wax, and then withdraw it. The goal is to "freeze" and mold the wax into a thin, flat, textured disk suitable for epoxy bonding (Figure 7-19). The two dops should never touch, and you should avoid wax overflow. You can clean up any excess "ears" of wax sticking out using a scalpel or razor blade. I typically aim for a disk of wax a little less than a millimeter thick.

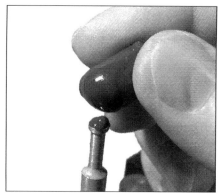

Figure 7-17 Apply a blob of wax to the prepared tip of the flat dop.

Now comes the important part: aligning the stone with the dop. Remove the waxed dop and attach the gem rough to the lower side of your transfer fixture using putty (Figure 7-20). Not all transfer jig geometries allow this, so you may have to modify this approach somewhat. Adjust the location of the stone for optimum high yield. A second, smaller diameter dop on the top side should help you get things centered up, while a larger flat dop can reveal any errors in tip and tilt (see Section 7.3.1 for further tips). Take your time here, since poor alignment means poor yield.

When you are completely happy with the location of the stone, remove the alignment dop from the top half of the transfer jig and replace it with the waxed dop prepared earlier. You are now ready for the epoxy.

Figure 7-18 With a larger flat dop in the other side of the transfer fixture, gently re-melt the blob of wax.

I use UHU brand five-minute epoxy, which is available worldwide. This two-component resin is a very high quality product that allows several minutes working time after mixing. It hardens within a couple of hours, creating an extremely durable, transparent bond. Chapter 4.1.2 and Section 7.2.2 give further information on epoxy resin adhesives.

As you probably know (or will soon find out), epoxy can be messy. To avoid problems during mixing, I use a disposable surface (a small sheet of aluminum foil) and a disposable mixing stick (half of a cotton ear swab – see Figure 7-7). Section 7.3.1 contains more information and tips on using epoxy resin.

Figure 7-19 The thin disk of wax provides a buffer between the epoxy resin and the dop stick. A textured flat dop creates a larger surface area for gluing.

Apply a drop of the mixed epoxy to the gem, and then gently lower the dop until it nearly touches stone. Excess epoxy should squish out the sides. Don't crunch the dop into the gem:

this will damage the wax and possibly the rough as well. It may also mess up your careful alignment if the stone is embedded in soft putty. Aim for an epoxy layer somewhat less than a millimeter thick between the wax and the gem. Lock the dop in place.

Before proceeding, do a sanity check on the alignment. Is the stone where it should be? If not, you can still nudge the gem slight-

Figure 7-20 A blob of putty and various dop sticks can help with alignment to the future table. Here, a smaller diameter flat dop assists with centering. The design of your transfer jig may require a slightly different strategy.

ly before the epoxy sets. Unlike with wax, you have several minutes to get the alignment perfect, and transparent epoxy lets you see where everything is.

Figure 7-21 After squeezing the dop and stone together, apply additional epoxy to create a smooth fillet that will support the gem during cutting.

When you are satisfied with the centering, pitch, and roll of the gem rough (Figure 7-2), apply additional epoxy to the dop and stone to create a smooth bond and fillet (Figure 7-21). I continuously rotate the transfer jig during this phase to prevent drips from running over the rough (Figure 7-8). After a few minutes, the epoxy will have set, and you can place the whole rig aside for curing.

Allow the bond to cure for several hours. Depending on the brand of epoxy, it may help to place the transfer jig in a warm place, such as on a radiator. With UHU, this definitely speeds the hardening process and produces a better bond.

After a few hours, or better overnight, the epoxy should be hard enough to begin faceting the pavilion. You can use your fingernail to see how things are going: even determined, firm pressure with the sharp edge of your thumbnail should leave no indent or impression in properly cured epoxy resin.

The initial bonding is complete and you are ready to start cutting the pavilion. Remove the dop and stone from the transfer fixture, put away your precious blob of putty, and admire your handiwork (Figure 7-22).

Figure 7-22 The completed hybrid bond. Note the disk of wax embedded in the epoxy to allow easy release after dop transfer.

7.4.2 Dop Transfer

The transfer process is very similar to the initial dopping. Again, you want to place a thin layer of wax between the stone and dop to allow the comfort of using epoxy while retaining the easy release properties of wax. This technique also prevents accidental chipping of the pavilion from contact with the metal dop stick.

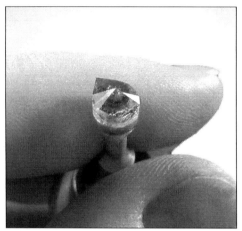

Figure 7-23 Clean the completed pavilion with alcohol prior to transfer.

Begin with a thorough alcohol cleaning of the completed pavilion (Figure 7-23). This is also your last chance to check that all is well with the half-completed gem, or just to marvel at your excellent meet points and perfect polish.

Select a cone or vee dop of the appropriate diameter to receive the pavilion. As explained on page 251, you should use a dop that is similar in size to the original flat dop (Figure 7-24).

Clean the chosen dop with alcohol, and as before, apply a drop of the shellac-alcohol solution to ensure good adhesion of the dop wax. Let the thin layer of solution dry completely.

When the shellac is dry, clamp the cone or vee dop into your transfer fixture, and melt a small amount of wax into the dop. Try to fill the cone or vee groove, without having too much sticking above the rim (left side of Figure 7-25).

As with the hybrid wax-CA technique described on page 249, you will need something to form and solidify the melted wax into the desired shape. Clearly, a flat dop, even a nicely textured one, will not do. I use homemade brass "anti-dops," which are the mirror image of actual cone and vee dops (Figure 7-25).

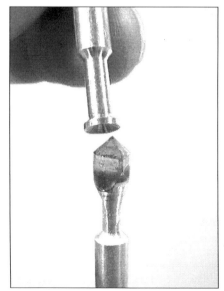

Figure 7-24 Select the correct size of cone or vee dop.

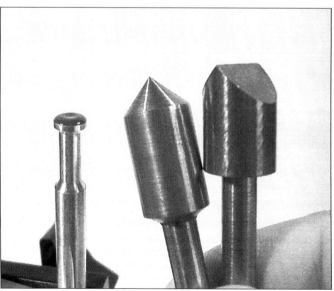

Figure 7-25 Simple "anti-dops" can be used to form the wax layer for cone and vee dops.

These anti-dops are very easy to fabricate with simple shop tools, and they do have the virtue of being large brass blocks that can readily "freeze" wax (see below). Nevertheless, they are, admittedly, totally unnecessary. Just use the stone itself to make an impression, as explained in "Bridging the Gap..." on page 249. Alternatively, you can fabricate anti-dops on your faceting machine, using inexpensive rough (i.e. glass) permanently attached to a dop stick. The anti-cone dop is essentially a 45° free-wheel pavilion pre-form (see Section 8.3.2), and the anti-vee dop is two simple facets. Sticklers for completeness will note that flat dops are their own anti-dops.

I considered texturizing my anti-dops to increase the surface area for bonding, but did not do so in the end. Cone and vee dops already have a larger bonding surface, and my difficulties in the past with these types of dop were uniformly due to epoxy bonds that were too strong, not too weak.

Back to the transfer. Clamp the wax-filled cone or vee dop into the transfer fixture facing upward and mount the anti-dop (or half-finished gem) on the other side. Gently warm the cone / vee dop until the

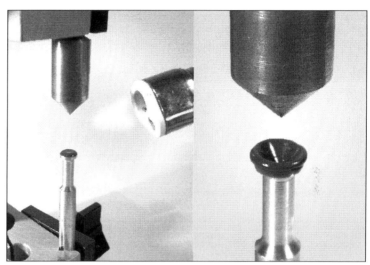

Figure 7-26 *Molding a thin layer of wax using an anti-dop. You can also use the cut pavilion to shape the wax. Just make sure to withdraw the upper dop before the wax has a chance to heat the gem and stick to it.*

wax is molten, but as before, take care not to boil it. Bring the two dops together carefully and then withdraw the anti-dop. Make sure that you don't squeeze out all the wax. As before, aim for a thickness of slightly less than a millimeter. If all went well, the cone or vee shape should be "frozen" and molded into the second dop (Figure 7-26).

Figure 7-27 *Do a final fit check before mixing up the epoxy.*

You are now ready for the epoxy stage. Replace the anti-dop with the dopped gemstone (if necessary), making sure not to touch the cleaned pavilion facets. Gently lower the stone and check for good alignment and fit (Figure 7-27). This step is of course unnecessary if you used the pavilion to form the wax.

Mix up a small amount of five-minute epoxy as before. In order to protect the culet during release, I place a tiny blob of putty or balled-up paper towel in the base of the cone or vee dop (see page 254).

Using the mixing stick, distribute a small ring of epoxy around the rim of the cone dop, or at the outermost edges of the vee dop. The goal here is to ensure a decent bonding surface without filling the entire dop. Of course, this is easier said than done, particularly if you are working on a small diameter stone. Note that the epoxy will spread somewhat when you insert the completed pavilion.

Carefully lower the gemstone until it is well seated and epoxy flows out of the gap. If you plan to use the girdle facets for mechanical or optical alignment of the stone after transfer (see Section 7.6), you should take care that no excess epoxy flows over the girdle facets. Having the gemstone on top certainly helps, as does a light touch and the right amount of glue.

Lock the dop in place, and, using additional epoxy, form a smooth joint and fillet as before. Rotate the transfer jig until the epoxy sets in order to prevent asymmetries and dripping. When

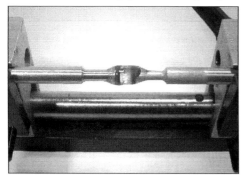

the epoxy has set – you can test this with the residue on your mixing surface – place the transfer jig aside to allow the glue to cure. As before, a warm place may speed up the process and strengthen the final bond (Figure 7-28). Allow the epoxy to cure completely before attempting to break the initial bond.

Figure 7-28 Setting and curing of the epoxy bond. Note that there are now wax layers on both sides of the stone.

Separating the stone from the original flat dop is straightforward. This is one of the beautiful aspects of hybrid dopping. For smaller stones, I use a heated scalpel to cut through the epoxy and wax disk separating the stone from the original flat dop (Figure 7-29).

A couple of friendly warnings…first, avoid breathing the vapours created by your heated scalpel: a web search for the hazards of burning epoxy fumes is rather alarming. Also, please don't cut the wrong bond at this point. It is distressingly easy to do.

For larger stones, you may have to begin with the hot knife treatment to get through the epoxy "skin" and then use the standard wax release explained in Section 7.3.2. Here's a brief recap: remove the joined dops from the transfer jig and then heat the shank of the original, flat, dop over the alcohol lamp. By the time that the end gets uncomfortably warm to the touch, you should be able to bend and break the wax bond holding the flat dop to the table area. At this point, very little heat has

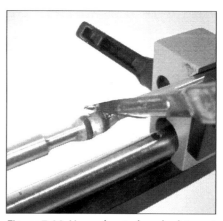

Figure 7-29 Use a heated scalpel to cut through the skin of epoxy on the initial bond.

been transferred to the gem, so you needn't worry about melting and shifting on the other side of the stone. For that extra feeling of security, you should wrap the gem and second dop in a wet paper towel.

Figure 7-30 The completed transfer.

Dop transfer accomplished! In all likelihood, some epoxy and wax remained on the crown area of the stone after separation (Figure 7-30). You may be able to remove this with a fingernail, or just let it fall off while cutting the crown.

Now back to the faceting machine to cut and polish the second half of the gem!

7.4.3 Releasing the Completed Gem

Releasing the completed gemstone from the cone or vee dop is almost as straightforward as for the flat dop during transfer (see previous section). In principle it should be easier, since you are no longer concerned about preserving alignment. On the other hand, the larger bonding area with the cone or vee dop can make for a slightly greater challenge.

Begin by removing the dopped stone from the faceting machine and take a moment to ogle those crown meets (Figure 7-31). The only thing separating you from your gem is a fraction of a millimeter of wax and epoxy. Nevertheless, now is not the time to rush. The hybrid dopping technique allows almost effortless release of the stone, but it is neither instantaneous nor immune to recklessness.

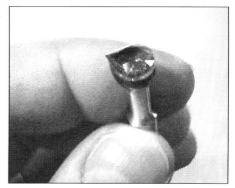

Figure 7-31 The completed crown.

As before, cut through the thin skin of epoxy using a heated scalpel (Figure 7-32). Take extra care at this stage. The epoxy can provide some resistance to a hot knife, while the underlying wax provides very little. Cutting too deep can allow contact between the knife and gem, and possibly chip the pavilion. Again, avoid breathing any epoxy vapours.

Figure 7-32 Cut through the skin of epoxy, taking care not to damage the gem.

With the epoxy layer severed, you can now heat the shank of the dop with the alcohol lamp and work the stone free. This should happen long before the end of the dop or the gem itself gets too warm to touch. For heat sensitive materials, you may opt for an extended soak in alcohol rather than an open flame. In these cases, you should still cut through the epoxy to allow the alcohol to work its solvent magic on the wax.

There will almost certainly be residual wax and epoxy on the gem. A good soak in acetone will allow easy clean-up. This may take a few hours in the worst case. You can also use your fingernail to remove residual clumps of wax and epoxy, but take care not to place excess stress on the stone, particularly near the culet.

Note that alcohol seems to dissolve dop wax quickly and epoxy not at all, whereas acetone dissolves both wax and epoxy relatively slowly. If there is a lot of residual wax, I occasionally use the one-two combination of alcohol then acetone to speed things up.

Free at last! Your gemstone is done (Figure 7-33). There is nothing to match the excitement of seeing your wonderful handi-

Figure 7-33 Your gemstone released from its prison of wax and epoxy.

work emerge from an ugly brownish-gray mess of wax and epoxy. Perform a final check for small specks of stubborn epoxy (your loupe can help here), eliminate any residue with your fingernail, and then clean the gemstone with alcohol and a lint-free cloth. Enjoy...

7.5 Re-attaching a Lost Stone

In terms of ego management, nothing beats the disheartening "crunch" of a dop bond breaking prematurely on the lap. If you have not yet experienced this soul-crushing event, don't get complacent. Sooner or later you will. Inevitably, a combination of heavy handedness, sloppy dopping practice, or just plain bad luck will cause a bond to break, sending your lovely gemstone flying into the void (turn to page 259 to hear my story).

7.5.1 Search and Rescue

The first step in recovering from this minor disaster is to find the gem. If you are lucky, it is still between your fingertips. You were, after all, applying pressure to the stone while cutting and not to the dop or quill, right? (see page 153). The next best – and most likely – location is in the splash pan. If you are not sure where the stone went, check there first.

Still missing in action? Check your workbench, including under the faceting machine, then on the floor. The spin direction and speed of your lap should give you a good clue where to start. Crawling around on your hands and knees will give you a healthy new perspective on the importance of keeping your work area clean, as well as on the unsuitability of shag carpet.

For smooth flooring, you can also try switching off the lights and sweeping a flashlight beam parallel to the floor. Even a small transparent gemstone will cast a prominent long shadow under these circumstances.

Whatever you do, don't give up. Despite all evidence, solid objects such as gemstones do not simply vanish. You may have better luck in the morning with daylight and less-tired eyes. Just don't forget to put up the "Do not vacuum" sign...

7.5.2 A Perfect Fit

When you have (finally!) recovered the loose gem, examine the region of the bond carefully. You will almost always see an irregular fractured area of wax or epoxy (or both – see Section 7.4). The mirror image of this area lies on the tip of the dop stick back in the faceting machine. The secret of re-attaching a lost stone is gluing these two pieces of the jigsaw puzzle back together. With luck, you should be able to retain the correct gem orientation and carry on cutting.

By the way, you should also examine the gem itself for damage. The action of breaking free and tumbling across the lap surface may have produced uglies that will need attention later.

Begin the re-attachment procedure by doing a careful test fit of the stone to the dop. Do not remove the dop from the quill, since this will erase its carefully-achieved alignment with respect to the index wheel (see Chapters 5.6, 5.7 and 7.6 below). Check the stone-dop joint for missing pieces of wax or epoxy, but do not touch the area of broken adhesive. Not only could this damage the matching faces, but also skin oil is the enemy of all waxes and glues.

If there is a good, tight, unambiguous fit, you can probably re-attach the gem successfully. If not, you might have to clean up the stone and dop and start from the beginning. The silver lining to this dark cloud is that gem detachment almost always occurs early on while you are cutting the pavilion. If you manage to break a half-finished gem out of a cone dop, it might be time to switch to decaf.

If all seems well, prepare your favourite cyanoacrylate or epoxy adhesive. Wax is not really an option here. Apply the glue sparingly to the joint and press the stone firmly against the dop. Allow the adhesive to set completely per the manufacturer's instructions. You should probably keep firm pressure for several minutes to prevent creep in the bond. Thereafter, place the quill pointing vertically upwards and allow the glue to cure completely – you probably need a few hours away from the machine at this point anyway. When you return, you should be able to pick up where you left off.

7.6 The Transfer Cheat

You should by now be convinced of the importance of retaining gem orientation during transfer from the initial flat dop to the cone or vee. If not, turn to Sections 4.16, 5.6, 5.7, and 7.3.2. A properly aligned faceting machine, coupled with undamaged dops, a high quality transfer jig, and a bit of care should lead to satisfying results.

Satisfying, but not perfect.

Transferring a half-completed stone to a new dop will produce some rotational misalignment of the pavilion and crown facets. The cause is straightforward: removing the dop from the machine breaks the fixed relationship between the rotation of the dop and the settings on the index wheel. Transferring the stone to a second dop introduces additional rotational uncertainty, as does inserting the second dop and gem back into the quill to cut the crown. Dop-keying schemes built into the machine and transfer jig attempt to keep things together, but in my experience, such devices are of limited worth. Chapter 4.4.1 contains more punditry on this issue.

The bottom line is that, after transfer, the gem will invariably be somewhat rotated with respect to the index wheel, requiring some cheat to bring things into alignment.

Faceters have developed a variety of schemes to counter this difficulty. The generic term "transfer cheat" refers to strategies aimed at ensuring rotational alignment between the crown and pavilion facets after transfer. These strategies range from doing nothing (not recommended), to the elaborate tests and tweaks necessary to produce a competition quality gem.

Correcting imperfect rotation involves adjusting the "cheater" or index splitter, which is a device that allows re-centering of the zero point of the index wheel (see page 23). Determining the direction and amount of cheater adjustment is the goal of all transfer cheat strategies.

This section describes four different ways of measuring and establishing the transfer cheat. Why four? Well, as with many aspects of faceting, personal cutting style and temperament can determine the best strategy. The methods below are ordered in increasing complexity and accuracy. If you plan to complete ten stones a day for commercial sale, the toothpaste test or even your dop-keying scheme should suffice. On the other hand, if you are a perfectionist, or plan to enter a competition whose judges are perfectionists, you will want to pursue a more careful and accurate means of establishing the transfer cheat.

Incidentally, before trying any of the methods described below, make sure that you understand which way the quill rotates when you turn the cheater a certain direction, say clockwise. This may sound condescending or even ridiculous, but there is nothing worse than figuring out how to fix a problem, and then making the situation twice as bad by turning the cheater the wrong way. I speak from personal experience on this.

Note also that the gem cutting tutorial in Chapter 5 contains additional information and advice on the transfer cheat process. See in particular Section 5.7.1.

7.6.1 The Toothpaste Test

Not only does regular application of toothpaste ensure a shiny white smile, but also it can help you line up your gemstones. This transfer cheat technique exploits the fact that even a thin film of toothpaste is opaque. Therefore, squeezing a small blob of your favourite dentifrice between a reference facet – on the girdle, for example – and a reference surface on the faceting machine – such as a mirror placed on a master lap – will reveal any tilts between the two.

This one is a lot easier to do than it is to explain. Begin by mounting a master lap securely to the spindle of your faceting machine. Place a small flat mirror on the lap. The mirror must lie perfectly steady with the top surface exactly parallel to the lap. A fragment of broken mirror is therefore superior to a fancy mirror in an irregular frame.

Most household mirrors are the so-called "rear-surface" type, in which the reflecting surface is on the back side of a piece of flat glass. This arrangement protects the delicate reflective coating from mechanical abrasions and damage. It also means that if you angle your eyeball correctly, you can see the underside of objects lying flat on the glass. See page 278 for more.

The trick should be obvious now. Place a small blob of toothpaste on the surface of the mirror. Adjust the cutting angle to 90° and the index to a girdle facet. Gently lower the gem into the toothpaste and watch the reflection of its underside in the mirror (Figure 7-34).

When the gem and glass make contact, the opaque whiteness of the toothpaste disappears. More than likely, this will be along one edge of the girdle facet. Adjust the cheater and cutting angle until the toothpaste film disappears uniformly. Voilà, you have the correct transfer cheat!

Figure 7-34 A small blob of toothpaste between the gem and mirror will reveal any tilts between the girdle facet and the lap surface.

It whitens. It brightens. It solves all your problems...

There are several other circumstances in which you may want to use toothpaste and a mirror to line up a gem with the index wheel. For example, you can check that you have preserved alignment after re-attaching a lost stone (see Section 7.5). Of course, in this instance you can use any convenient facet, not just the girdle.

Hobby cutters frequently want to touch up a few facets and improve meet points after completing the table (see "Shooting Stars" on page 345). Most faceting machines require a 45° table adapter, which means pulling the dop out of the quill and losing rotational alignment. The toothpaste and mirror trick will help you re-install the gem reasonably close to where you should be.

Finally, the toothpaste technique can also help you line up with unknown facets when repairing a damaged gem.

7.6.2 Test Polishing the Girdle

Here's a simple question: If the goal of the transfer cheat is to achieve proper alignment between the facets cut before and after transfer, why bother with all these keying systems and toothpaste? Why not just use what you're after – the facets themselves – as the reference?

Test polishing a girdle facet is the classic technique for checking and adjusting transfer cheat. In *Faceting for Amateurs*, Vargas suggests leaving the girdle facets at the pre-polish stage before transfer. Wiping a girdle facet across the polishing lap after transfer will then reveal any slight errors in rotation, just as in conventional polishing (see also page 332). Adjusting the cheater brings the gem into alignment, letting you get on with completing the girdle facets before starting in on the crown.

A slight variant on this technique is to polish the girdle facets, transfer the stone, and then cut into a girdle facet using a fine grit lap and a cutting angle less than 90° (see Figure 5-63). This will produce a clean edge, whose angle to the existing girdle line will guide the direction and magnitude of any corrections. Note that the intersection line between two facets with nearly the same orientation is very sensitive to their exact angles, so using something close to 90° will be very accurate. Yes, this is a variant of cutting a test tier of facets (see Section 7.7).

7.6.3 Mechanical Jigs

A simple mechanical jig can help you preserve rotational alignment after transfer. Figure 7-35 shows a homemade version, and Chapter 20.6 gives detailed plans for building it.

By now, you have probably noticed that I go on and on about preserving orientation and references during the dop transfer. I tend to go on

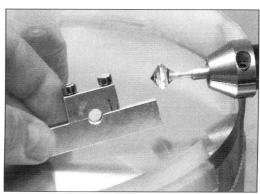

Figure 7-35 A simple mechanical jig for preserving rotational alignment after transfer.

and on about a lot of things, but this one is important, and it is the explicit design goal of this simple device.

Here's the idea: a clamp mechanism with a reference flat surface can tie the rotational alignment of the original flat dop to another fixed reference plane, such as a master lap. After attaching the second dop to the stone, this relationship can be used to transfer this alignment back to the quill. It's a lot easier than it sounds, and a few photographs should make the procedure clear.

Begin by setting the index wheel to zero, the cutting angle to 90°, and the cheater to the setting you used to cut the girdle. Install a master or other flat lap on the platen of your

faceting machine, and loosely attach the jig to the exposed part of the flat dop protruding from the quill (Figure 7-36). Yes, this requires a bit of planning, since you need to have left sufficient exposed dop shank when you started.

Now here's the clever part. Lower the cutting head gently until the underside of the alignment jig lies flat on the master lap. The bolts must be loose enough to allow the jig to self-adjust to the surface of the lap. Get down to lap level and eyeball the jig-lap interface. There should be no gaps along the quill rotation or cutting angle directions. Adjust the bolt tightness, quill height, or cutting angle if necessary.

Figure 7-36 Mount the alignment jig to the exposed portion of the original, flat dop, leaving the bolts somewhat loose to allow rotation.

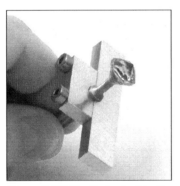

Figure 7-37 The jig locked to the original flat dop.

When you are happy that the jig is exactly square with the lap, tighten the bolts to lock it to the flat dop. You have now effectively transferred the rotation orientation of the index wheel to the dop itself, and the dop plus jig can now be safely removed from the machine (Figure 7-37).

Execute the dop transfer as usual. Sections 7.3.2 and 7.4.2 explain how. Note that you may need extra care and planning to work around the alignment jig, particularly if you use your machine's dop keying system, (Figure 7-38). After completing the transfer, do not immediately break the original bond, since the flat dop still holds the jig and its valuable rotation information.

Now it is time to transfer the rotation alignment from the dop plus jig back to the quill. Check that the faceting machine is in the exact same configuration as before: reference lap installed, index zero, cutting angle 90°, and the cheater at its

Figure 7-38 Perform the dop transfer with the alignment jig in place on the original dop stick.

girdle reference location. Raise the cutting head a millimeter or two, and then carefully slide the cone or vee dop into the loosened quill (Figure 7-39).

As before, the trick is to have things loose enough to allow the jig to settle squarely against the lap when you lower it into place. Of course, at this point, it is the quill clamping mechanism and not the jig that should be loose. Take extra care not to lower the cutting head too far, since this will apply significant forces to the stone and dops, potentially breaking a bond and ruining the alignment.

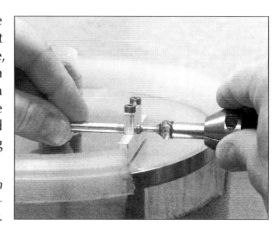

Figure 7-39 Install the cone or vee dop in the quill with the machine configured exactly as it was when you originally clamped the jig in place.

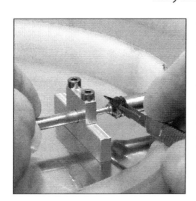

When everything is in place, tighten the quill to the cone or vee dop. Make a final check that the jig is still square with the lap and adjust if necessary.

The rotational alignment information is now back in the quill where it belongs, and you can safely break the initial bond to the flat dop and jig (Figure 7-40). If all went well, you should be able to proceed happily with cutting the crown.

Figure 7-40 Break the initial bond after clamping the cone or vee dop. A hot scalpel can release this hybrid wax-epoxy bond (see Section 7.4.2).

7.6.4 Optically Aligned Transfer – A Better Way to Cheat?

Appreciating a beautifully cut gemstone is fundamentally an optical process, so it seems fitting to use an optical technique to ensure an accurate transfer cheat. As with the toothpaste method (Section 7.6.1) and the wipe test described on page 332, this technique can be used to replace a dop in the machine under other circumstances, for example to touch up the star facets after completing the table. Unlike some of the other strategies, optically aligned transfer does not require any further cutting or polishing of facets, and it can be used at any time to restore the desired cheater angle, provided that a polished girdle facet is available. The entire procedure takes approximately 5 minutes, and it is very accurate.

Why Go Optical?

I initially tried all the "standard" transfer cheat techniques, but was unsatisfied with the results. I followed all the recommended procedures faithfully, but inevitably a tiny error would creep in, resulting in an imperfect match between pavilion and crown facets. My dissatisfaction was largely persnicketiness, the result of working with truly accurate and repeatable machinery in my "day job," and the high expectations for quality inculcated in me by my faceting teacher (you know who you are).

The method outlined here is based on a standard optical technique known as *retro-reflection*, in which a beam of light returns exactly to its source after reflection off the surface being aligned.

The Retro Look Comes to Faceting

The left panel of Figure 7-41 illustrates the basic principle. A mirror placed on a flat reference lap bounces light back along its incoming path. By the laws of geometric optics, the reflected beam will return precisely to its source only when the light path is exactly perpendicular to the mirror (and hence to the lap). This is the retro-reflection condition. Retro-reflection lets you use the beam of light to define the plane of the lap with very high accuracy.

Inserting another reflecting surface, such as a polished girdle facet, into the beam will also produce a reflection, and the new surface will be exactly parallel to the lap only when that reflection also goes exactly back to its source (right panel of Figure 7-41). When that condition occurs, the gem facet and lap are by definition parallel. Pretty neat trick, eh? It also happens to be exactly what you want. When a girdle facet is exactly parallel to the lap, you have the correct transfer cheat. You also get a perfect, 90° cutting angle in the bargain.

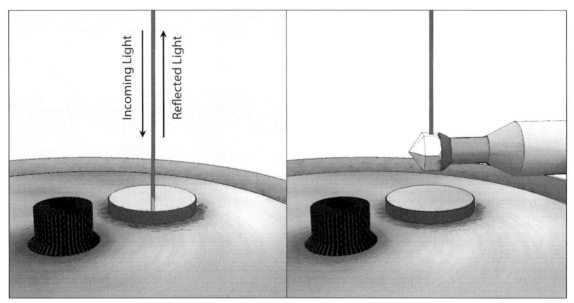

Figure 7-41 A retro-reflected beam of light is by definition exactly perpendicular to the mirror (left). If both the mirror and gem facet retro-reflect (right), then the two surfaces – mirror/lap and facet – must be parallel to each other.

So much for the theory. The implementation is actually fairly simple (Figure 7-42). My arrangement uses light from an inexpensive laser pointer, since they are bright, easy to use, and provide a compact spot over a distance of many yards. A second mirror held several inches above the lap at 45° allows the incoming and outgoing beams to be horizontal, a configuration better suited to the layout of typical rooms (no cathedral ceiling in my workshop!). Also, adjusting this 45 degree mirror is easier than positioning the laser for perfect retro-reflection.

You should be able to convince yourself that the presence of the 45° mirror changes nothing. If the light goes exactly back to the laser pointer, the optical path between the two mirrors is exactly perpendicular to the mirror on the lap, and also to the girdle facet.

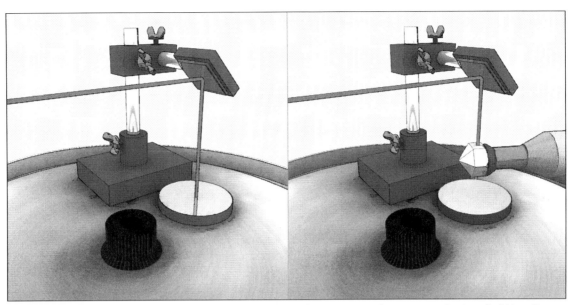

Figure 7-42 A real-world implementation of the retro-reflection principle, using a 45° mirror held in a jig to allow horizontal beams.

What You'll Need…

In order to set up your own optical alignment rig, you will need a laser pointer, a pair of small mirrors, and a mechanism for holding and adjusting the 45° mirror

Laser

I use a cheap laser pointer purchased at a discount house for less than $20. The only requirement here is that the laser stay on continuously. My pointer has a recessed momentary-on switch, which I hold down with a breath mint and an elastic band (Figure 7-47). Yes, my middle name is kludge, and yes, a Fisherman's Friend can be a Faceter's Friend. You can place the laser on any convenient surface, such as a shelf, although having some means of adjusting its location will help (Figure 7-46).

Mirrors

Almost any mirrors will do. The one lying on the lap should provide an accurate reference. This means it should either be a first surface mirror face down, or at least a rear surface mirror that is reasonably parallel. Watch out for edge burrs and projections on the back that will spoil the alignment. You should be able to judge how well your mirror performs by rotating it by 90, 180, and 270 degrees and checking that the spot stays put after retro-reflection.

Jig to Hold 45° Mirror

This may be the hardest part to find. I began with a hobbyist's "third hand" – the gadget with alligator clips and wing nuts. This was difficult to control, so I rigged together a simple mirror holder with a screw adjustment. Eventually, and for the ultimate in ease, I scrounged some old surplus hardware from an optical bench (Figure 7-45).

A Look Below the Surface

What's all this about first-surface versus second-surface? Optical mirrors come in two varieties: those with the reflecting material directly exposed to the environment and those with the reflecting surface on the back side of the glass substrate. With the former type, light strikes the mirror surface first, and it is unsurprisingly known as a first-surface mirror. In the second type, the incoming photons must first pass through, and be partially reflected by, the front-most glass surface. With their usual flair for imaginative names, opticians call such a configuration a second-surface mirror (Figure 7-43).

Figure 7-43 A first-surface mirror (left) produces a simple reflection, while the second-surface mirror (right) produces a more distant reflection and faint double ghosts.

Why two types? The first surface mirror provides the best performance, at the cost of exposing the delicate metallic reflecting film to the environment. A first-surface mirror is depressingly easy to scratch and notoriously difficult to clean. A rear-surface mirror, on the other hand, is very robust but suffers from a pair of faint ghost images due to partial Fresnel reflection at the first glass surface (consult Chapter 11.8 to learn why this happens).

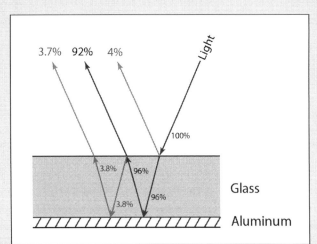

Figure 7-44 Second surface mirrors produce a pair of faint ghost images bracketing the primary reflection.

Why two ghost images? Figure 7-44 provides the explanation. You can do the photon accounting yourself, assuming 4% reflection at each glass-air interface and perfect reflection off the mirror. A little math leads to the conclusion that the primary reflection will have approximately 4% ghosts on either side. Yes, the ray bouncing in Figure 7-44 goes on forever, but again, you should be able to convince yourself that any further ghost images are very faint indeed.

All domestic mirrors are second-surface type. Look carefully the next time you are gazing admiringly at yourself in front of a mirror at home. You should be able to spot the ghost images. A dark background can help.

You can pick up usable pieces of second-surface mirror material at your local hardware store. Science and educational suppliers such as Edmund Scientific, offer suitable inexpensive first-surface mirrors (see Chapter 15.8.11 for links).

Optically Aligned Transfer – Detailed Instructions

The optically aligned transfer technique is straightforward and makes a great deal of sense once you have tried it once or twice. The following paragraphs provide further detailed instructions that should get you up and running.

1. **Place the reference mirror on a clean lap.** I use a first-surface mirror approximately 30 mm in diameter with the reflecting surface facing downward on a master lap. Almost all faceting machines have minor misalignments and inaccuracies that may be radius-dependent. Also, some laps may become worn or dished with use. For these reasons, it is a very good idea to place the reference mirror at the radius on the lap where you usually polish. The contact surface of the mirror will rest on top of any small hills on the lap, averaging any variations over the area it covers.

2. **Set up the 45° mirror and laser.** The exact technique will depend strongly on your mirror holding jig. Mine sits directly on the lap, with the 45° mirror above the lap mirror and pointing across the room to the table where the laser sits (Figure 7-45).

3. **Align the laser pointer to the lap mirror.** Turn on the laser and adjust it so that the beam strikes the 45° mirror. If you have trouble getting it to line up and stay put, try embedding the laser in some modeling clay (Play-Do). You can also try a small photographer's tripod (Figure 7-46).

Figure 7-45 Surplus hardware from an optical bench allows easy control of the 45° mirror.

Laser Safety

Read the warnings supplied with your laser pointer and obey them. The manufacturers are not joking. All lasers, including the inexpensive diode devices found in laser pointers, will do serious and potentially permanent eye damage if misused.

Adjust the 45° mirror so that the spot of light returns to the laser. This does not have to be exact, as long as you send the laser back to the same spot in step 4 below.

Can't see the spot clearly? Try rigging a small index card with a hole punched in it to the front of the laser pointer (Figure 7-47).

4. **Align the gem to the lap.** Once you have established perfect retro-reflection with the reference mirror, try to do the same with a girdle facet. I usually cover the reference mirror with a tissue to prevent distracting reflections. Dial in a 90° cutting angle and set the index so that a polished girdle facet faces upward. Do this from the design, not by eyeball!

Figure 7-46 Configuration of the laser pointer and the two mirrors. When properly adjusted, the laser beam should return exactly to its origin. Note the white index card attached to the front of the laser.

Note that in this configuration, the correct index is exactly opposite that of the cutting index (the facet is facing upward, after all). For instance, if you are targeting a girdle facet at 16 on a 96-tooth gear, set the index to 80.

Adjust the position of the quill and stone so that the downward-traveling laser beam strikes the girdle facet. A small, handheld index card can be a great help for following the beam. Reflection off the facet and then the 45° mirror sends the light back toward the laser pointer. You might get additional confusing reflections from other facets. Inking unused girdle facets can help here. Adjust the cutting angle and cheater settings until the spot returns exactly to the laser or the location it was before. Figure 7-48 illustrates the procedure.

Figure 7-47 A simple white index card taped to the front of the laser will help you find and center the returning spot of light. Just don't forget to punch a small hole to let the light out in the first place! I use some more spare optical bench hardware to hold the laser pointer, but a standard tripod (Figure 7-46) works just as well.

That's it! Your girdle facet is aligned with the reference mirror and hence with the surface of the lap. Do some reality checks (step 5) and then start cutting!

5. **Do some reality checks.** Just to be sure, you should re-verify the alignment between the laser pointer and the reference mirror. Just shift the stone out of the laser beam and remove the tissue covering the reference mirror. The reflected spot should stay put. There are some additional useful checks. For example, you should verify the spot location using different girdle facets. If the spot moves around slightly, repeat step 4 using the facet which represents the approximate middle position. How much variation is acceptable? Estimate the amount of cheat you have to apply to bring the spots to the same point. If this is small compared to the amount of cheat you apply during normal faceting, you should be all right. The following paragraphs contain some additional comments about accuracy.

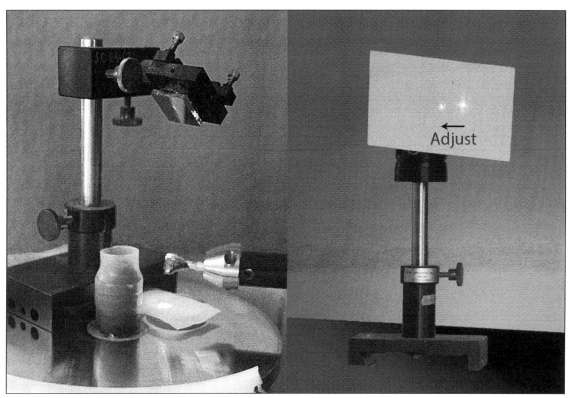

Figure 7-48 Adjust the cheater and cutting angle until the beam reflecting from the girdle facet (left) returns to the center of the white index card (right). Note the piece of paper covering the lap mirror to avoid spurious reflections.

Some Remarks about Accuracy

This optical alignment technique is very accurate. You can estimate the cheater angle error using some simple geometry. For example, with my setup, I can usually retro-reflect the laser to within 1 mm or so of its original location. With a total path length from the gemstone to the laser pointer of about 3 yards, this corresponds to an angular accuracy of 1 part in 5000. Note that when you rotate a mirror – or a gem facet – by one degree, the reflected light is rotated by two degrees. One part in 5000 corresponds to approximately 0.01°. For a 96-index gear, it is about 1/300th of an index.

Is this accurate enough? The short answer is yes, for at least two simple reasons. First, you will likely find as I did that aligning this way produces no discernible error when checked with a test tier of facets (see Section 7.7 below). Second, you will notice that cheater adjustments that you would normally consider minute during faceting produce significant shifts of the laser spot.

A longer path length would allow greater accuracy, although it becomes harder and harder to judge the center of the spot of light, particularly with an inexpensive laser pointer. Yes, physics geeks, a HeNe gas laser with less beam divergence would improve things, and how many angels can you get to dance on a girdle facet?

A Final Word of Caution

This technique should simplify the procedure of finding the correct cheater setting, but it is subject to error. Obviously, referencing to the polished girdle facets in this way presumes that you have an accurate girdle. Bumping or moving the lap, mirrors, or laser during the measurement can cause problems as well. As a matter of practice, I usually cut a test tier of facets to confirm accuracy (see next section), but I rarely have to cut more than one.

7.7 Cutting a Test Tier of Facets

All of the techniques described in the previous section will get you very close to the correct transfer cheat setting. I know that "very close" may sound close enough, but you will want to do better if you are a stickler for accuracy, or if you finally give in to temptation and enter a gem cutting competition. The real proof of an accurate transfer is in the stone itself.

As mentioned at the outset of Section 7.6, the transfer methods described later on are more accurate than those discussed earlier – that is, optical alignment is better than a mechanical jig, which is in turn better than test polishing a facet or using toothpaste.

Whichever technique you employ, it is an excellent idea to cut a test tier of break facets after transfer. This means cutting all the way around the stone at the same angle, placing each successive facet at the meet point created by the previous one. Incorrect cheat angle will show up as a slight spiral cut, producing an offset between the last and first facets in the tier (see Chapter 5.7.1 and especially Figure 5-66). A slight tweak of the cheater should improve things, and a few iterations should produce an even row of facets and hence the correct cheater setting.

7.7.1 The Down Side of Test Tiers

Although pretty much guaranteed to produce great results, cutting and iterating a test tier of facets has a number of disadvantages. First of all, it can be slow, since accuracy depends on adjacent facets being cut to exactly the same depth. Any over-cut of a facet halfway through a test tier forces you to compensate or start over. Also, maximum yield from expensive rough often means having very little extra gem material for a few test tiers.

A less obvious problem arises with gem designs that do not have uniform crown break facets. Briar Rose (Chapter 18) is an example of this. The design calls for 33° crown breaks at 14-18-46-50-78-82 and then another set of 31.15° breaks at 02-30-34-62-66-94. In order to check the cheater setting, you have to test cut the facets in increasing (or decreasing) index order, *i.e.* 02-14-18-30… and so on. This is because each test facet must establish the meet point for the next one. Given the mixed angles, doing this would involve alternating the cutting angle between 33° and 31.15° after every second facet. Believe me, after a couple of test tiers, this becomes very old, very fast.

The Sakhir design in Chapter 19.3.4 provides an even more extreme example. In order to achieve the effect of parallel lines on a shield form, Sakhir has seven (!) different sets of crown break facets with angles ranging from under 19° to more than 40°. Doing a test cut once around this series of break facets to confirm a good cheater setting would require twelve separate angle and height adjustments, an arduous task indeed, with no small risk of making a disastrous error.

There is a better and easier way: simply test-cut all of the crown facets adjacent to the girdle at the largest break facet angle. In the case of Sakhir, this means 42.36° for all facets (Figure 7-49). This will test for proper cheat and a good girdle line, while ensuring that you can later cut away the excess material at the lower-angle indices. Note that, depending on the gem design, you may have to alter the height (but not the angle) of the quill between adjacent facets.

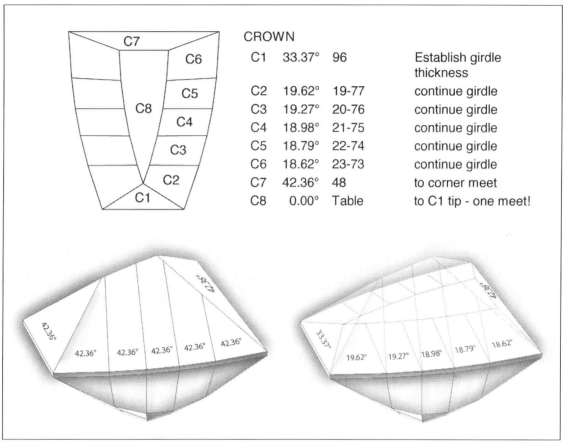

CROWN			
C1	33.37°	96	Establish girdle thickness
C2	19.62°	19-77	continue girdle
C3	19.27°	20-76	continue girdle
C4	18.98°	21-75	continue girdle
C5	18.79°	22-74	continue girdle
C6	18.62°	23-73	continue girdle
C7	42.36°	48	to corner meet
C8	0.00°	Table	to C1 tip - one meet!

Figure 7-49 When cutting a test tier on a design such as Sakhir with varying crown break angles (top), simply cut all test facets at the largest angle (bottom left). When you are satisfied with the cheater setting, cut the final crown break facets at the correct angles (bottom right). Note that the bottom left figure is for illustration only. Unless it was unavoidable I would never cut test tiers so close to (or at) the final girdle thickness.

7.8 Dopping Accuracy and Yield

Whew! Forty-seven pages on dopping, to say nothing of the dozen or more pages on the topic scattered elsewhere throughout this book.

Why?

I have said it multiple times, but I am going to say it again: accurate dopping is important.

How important?

Great question. The table on the next page tries to demonstrate how important. It will help you evaluate the amount of rough lost when cutting a smaller gem (while maintaining the same design). I originally made this to help judge whether cutting out a certain fault is worth it in terms of lost carat weight, but it also gives a measure of loss of yield if you dop inaccurately.

Incidentally, the calculation is a trivial one: the fraction of material remaining after a change in gem size is simply the cube of the final to original size ratio. For example, if you reduce a gemstone's dimensions by a factor of two, the weight goes down by a factor of eight. Yikes!

7.8.1 Using the Rough Loss Chart

Locate the current (or maximum possible) dimension of the gem across the top of the chart. This can be the length, width, or any linear scale of the stone. Scan down the column until you reach the entry corresponding to the final, corresponding dimension, for example, after accounting for that inaccurate dop job or cutting out a nasty veil. The table entry will give you the fraction of the current (or maximum) carat weight that will remain.

For example, you are working on a piece of garnet which should yield a round 6 mm in diameter. By not carefully following the last forty seven pages of advice, you dop the stone half a millimeter off center, something that is disturbingly easy to do. This will produce a gem only 5 mm across (0.5 mm smaller on both sides!). The chart indicates that the resulting stone will weigh 57.9% of the original. Double yikes!

Did I mention that accurate dopping is important?

Table 7-2 Rough loss chart. This table shows the remaining fractional percent of gem material in going from an initial linear dimension to a final one. Find the initial size in millimeters across the top of the chart and then read down to the appropriate final size. See text for an explicit example.

Starting Stone Size (mm)

Final Stone Size (mm)	10	9.5	9.0	8.5	8.0	7.5	7.0	6.5	6.0	5.5	5.0	4.5	4.0	3.5	3.0	2.5
2.5	1.56	1.82	2.14	2.54	3.05	3.70	4.56	5.69	7.23	9.39	12.5	17.1	24.4	36.4	57.9	100
3.0	2.70	3.15	3.70	4.40	5.27	6.40	7.87	9.83	12.5	16.2	21.6	29.6	42.2	63.0	100	
3.5	4.29	5.00	5.88	6.98	8.37	10.2	12.5	15.6	19.8	25.8	34.3	47.1	67.0	100		
4.0	6.40	7.46	8.78	10.4	12.5	15.2	18.7	23.3	29.6	38.5	51.2	70.2	100			
4.5	9.11	10.6	12.5	14.8	17.8	21.6	26.6	33.2	42.2	54.8	72.9	100				
5.0	12.5	14.6	17.1	20.4	24.4	29.6	36.4	45.5	57.9	75.1	100					
5.5	16.6	19.4	22.8	27.1	32.5	39.4	48.5	60.6	77.0	100						
6.0	21.6	25.2	29.6	35.2	42.2	51.2	63.0	78.7	100							
6.5	27.5	32.0	37.7	44.7	53.6	65.1	80.1	100								
7.0	34.3	40.0	47.1	55.9	67.0	81.3	100									
7.5	42.2	49.2	57.9	68.7	82.4	100										
8.0	51.2	59.7	70.2	83.4	100											
8.5	61.4	71.6	84.2	100												
9.0	72.9	85.0	100													
9.5	85.7	100														
10	100															

8

Cutting and Polishing

It is almost miraculous how the straightforward action of simple spinning disks can change a shapeless rock into a hypnotically sparkling gemstone. Of course, experienced faceters will argue with the term "straightforward action," and the manufacturers of cutting and polishing laps will claim that their wares are much more than "simple spinning disks."

Whether straightforward or carefully controlled, simple or precision-manufactured, words don't matter. Getting the job done and enjoying it does. This chapter explores a range of issues associated with the cutting and polishing of gemstones. This includes basic instructions for pre-forming gem rough, as well as tips and tricks for improving your experience at the lap. It is not, however, a tutorial on cutting and polishing. Turn to Chapter 5 for that. Also note that Chapter 17 addresses advanced methods for establishing the gem outline, while Chapters 2, 3, and 4 discuss faceting machines, laps, and additional equipment, respectively.

8.1 Cutting vs Polishing

Let's begin with a simple question:

Both cutting and polishing remove gem material. What's the difference?

Again the word "simple" (see previous page). As you shall see, this is hardly a simple question, and as with many aspects of our hobby, asking a group of faceters about cutting versus polishing is a good way to initiate an evening full of vehement and occasionally enlightened jawboning.

On a fundamental level, cutting and polishing are the same process carried out at different scales of surface roughness. Both exploit the abrasive properties of some agent to remove gem material in an efficient yet controlled manner. The exact microphysical nature of this abrasion has been somewhat controversial, however, particularly for polishing.

For example, in the mid-20th century, some material scientists (and gem cutters) argued that there were fundamental physical differences between cutting and polishing and that, in polishing, some sort of melting process takes place at the microscopic scale. These theories have been largely discarded based on subsequent experimental testing and theoretical developments, but true mysteries remain as to what exactly takes place on the polishing lap. Section 8.11 delves further into this conundrum.

Ok. I can wait for the theory. What is the practical difference between cutting and polishing?

On a practical level, machinists distinguish between cutting and polishing based on the relative hardness of the lap. In the machine shop, cutting or grinding takes place with a loose abrasive and a lap that is generally harder than the work piece. Subsequent polishing uses powdered agents and a considerably softer lap.

Two Body Versus Three Body Abrasion

Want to stop all conversation at a party sometime? Declare openly that you are a tribologist.

What, you may ask – although probably no one at the party will – is a tribologist? A tribologist is an investigator who studies the science and technology of friction, lubrication, and wear.

Still pretty quiet at the party, eh?

Actually, the field of tribology is extremely important, for it is the study of the interaction and wear of solid bodies that enables the gears of our modern industrial world to turn without breaking down all the time. Tribology also has something to say about how our cutting laps work.

Specifically, your friendly, neighbourhood tribologist distinguishes between two-body and three-body abrasion. Both occur when a harder, rougher substance removes material from a surface. In the two-body mode of abrasive wear, the hard particles are fixed in place, usually on the surface of a tool or lap. This case corresponds to the action of sandpaper. In three-body abrasion, the hard particles are free to tumble and roll between the tool and surface. This can change the nature of the resulting wear. For example, in the machine shop, two-body abrasion tends to produce scratching, while the three-body mode introduces denting as the grit particles impact the work surface.

What does all this have to do with faceting? A great deal, as it turns out. Despite the fact that we may use loose abrasives on our laps, we are almost always in the two-body mode of abrasion. This is because the grit particles embed readily into the relatively soft surface of the lap. In fact, we often assist this process using a hard roller or a piece of scrap gem material (see Chapter 3.2.2 and Section 8.14.3 below).

There is a very good reason for our two-body bias: loose grit is simply more difficult to work with. Not only can it agglomerate into larger particles than we intend, but also clean-up between mesh sizes becomes a critical, disaster-prone process. Nevertheless, the two-body mode is not universal. Polishing with diamond on ceramic is an obvious exception.

Despite our desire to be two-body cutters, Nature doesn't always play fair. Two-body abrasion turns into three-body abrasion when a grit particle or a fragment of the gem itself breaks loose and starts tumbling around. This is not usually a problem at the rough cutting phase, unless of course, the renegade particle causes contamination between laps. Random bits of grit tumbling around during fine cutting or polishing is a different matter, however, and nasty scratching is often the result (see Section 8.17.3 below).

At this point, any self-respecting tribologist is probably spluttering words like "outrageous" and "unfair," since an instance of detached grit or fragmented work surface is hardly well planned three-body abrasion. The tribologist is right, and deserving of that self-respect, despite what the others at the party think…

In the optics shop, where precision lenses and mirrors are fabricated, the practical distinction between cutting and polishing lies largely in the testing method. Rough cutting requires contact testing of the lens or mirror with mechanical devices. Once the surface has improved to the stage where it transmits and reflects light, optical testing takes over. As with their machinist friends, opticians use loose abrasives for cutting and powdered agents for polishing.

These distinctions between cutting and polishing do not carry over easily into the faceter's workshop. For example, we routinely use cutting laps whose base material is softer than the gems they cut, and we rarely, if ever, do any kind of optical testing, beyond enjoying our handiwork, of course. Finally, with the advent of a new generation of diamond bonded laps, loose abrasives are rapidly becoming a thing of the past, at least for cutting (see Chapter 3.2.3).

What, then, is the real practical difference between cutting and polishing from a faceting perspective? One obvious answer is that cutting moves facets around, while polishing just gives them a nice luster. In other words, you better have all the facets in place with clean meet points before you install the polishing lap. While this is excellent advice, it is by no means all-encompassing – experienced faceters routinely make small adjustments to meet points while polishing.

Cutting and polishing therefore seem to be a continuum, and while it may seem that separating the two is a distinction without a difference, let me offer one observation based on experience. Polishing occasionally produces surprises, sometimes good sometimes bad, while cutting rarely does. A stubborn facet that refuses to behave may miraculously take on a fine polish simply by changing hand pressure or the rotation direction of the lap. Other facets may require more extreme measures, such as a switch of polishing agent from diamond to cerium oxide. These unexpected twists in the road are part of what makes polishing polishing.

8.2 Cutting Technique

The following sections discuss cutting technique, a collection of methods for transforming a raw piece of rough into a very close approximation of the final gem that is ready for polishing.

An earlier great worker of stone, Michelangelo, was supposedly asked how he could possibly produce a masterpiece such as the sculpture of David, which has amazed visitors to Florence for over five hundred years. Michelangelo apparently replied that he simply starts with a big block of marble and then chips away everything that doesn't look like David.

While almost certainly apocryphal, this story has direct relevance for the cutting of gemstones. Chapter 2.1 explains that a gemstone is a piece of transparent mineral whose volume is defined by the intersection of many flat planes. The process of cutting gemstones, then, involves removing any material that doesn't look like the gem, in other words, any material not within those intersecting planes. This essentially means cutting flat facets into the surface of the stone at specific angles and depths. If done properly, what remains should look like a gem.

Figure 8-1 Michelangelo's famous sculpture, the result of removing all of the marble that didn't look like David. Image courtesy of Rico Heil.

8.3 Pre-Forming Technique – Passive Aggression

The term pre-forming refers to strategies for getting the original piece of gem rough reasonably close to its final form. Here, "reasonably close" means establishing the correct dimensions and approximate shape. It does not involve precision cutting and meet points. Instead, the goal is to remove unneeded stone effectively and quickly. You should regard pre-forming as a time-saver. It is almost never a stone saver.

Note that there is some confusion in terminology regarding pre-forming. Some faceters refer to the process of establishing the gem outline using precision cuts as "pre-forming." This book will (mostly) stick to the classical definition in the previous paragraph. See Chapter 17.1 for more.

You have a variety of options for removing large amounts of unwanted stone, ranging from hogging out the material on a grinding wheel to performing mathematical calculations coupled with careful cuts on the faceting machine. The choice will depend most strongly on the size and value of your faceting rough. Taking a 10-gram piece of clear quartz, worth perhaps two bucks, down to size on the faceting machine is hardly worth your time, to say nothing of the wear and tear on your expensive laps. On the other hand, knocking the rough edges off several tens or hundreds of dollars worth of sapphire requires a little more consideration and care.

The fundamental problem with aggressive pre-forming techniques is that they can be very wasteful of rough. A slight miscalculation can have serious consequences on a coarse grinding wheel or rock saw. Also, such crude instruments can cause significant subsurface damage in the crystal, resulting in a usable volume of stone which is considerably smaller than anticipated. Similar warnings apply to the aggressive "channel" or "ripple" type cutting laps.

For valuable – and therefore typically smaller – gem rough, you should do the pre-form on the faceting machine. This allows greater control and provides an excellent opportunity for you to become familiar with the idiosyncrasies of the gem design and your particular piece of rough. More than once, I have discovered a "feature" within a stone early enough during the pre-forming process to take corrective action.

Is Pre-Forming Cutting or Cabbing?

Many faceters consider the pre-forming process as completely distinct from cutting. This is partly due to the fact that traditional pre-forming *is* different, with the stone often hand-held against a grinding wheel or rock saw. Also, there are a number of accessories, such as offset dops and motorized jigs, which purport to add pre-forming capability to your existing faceting machine (see "Commercial pre-forming devices" on page 293 and Chapter 4.11.2 for more).

Actually, I do almost all my pre-forming on an unaccessorized faceting machine, and I do not view the pre-forming process as distinct from cutting. This is mostly due to the fact that (a). I usually cut more expensive types of gem rough and hence take greater care, and (b) I am cheap, and every extra doodad means less money spent elsewhere. Nevertheless, for larger pieces of low-cost gem rough, I will adopt a more aggressive approach.

8.3.1 Grinding and Sawing

Nothing beats a grinding wheel or rock saw for making large amounts of stone disappear in a small amount of time. Which one you choose will depend on availability and how sensible it is to save the cut-away material. With a rock saw, you may be able to salvage sufficient gem rough from the scraps to cut additional stones. The superfluous gem rough removed by a grinding wheel is, needless to say, somewhat harder to work with.

Commercial grinding wheels and rock saws suitable for pre-forming are widely available and range in price from a few tens to a few hundreds of dollars. If you only occasionally need to use a grindstone or saw, the tools at your local lapidary club may be the best option (see also page 128). Ask one of the locals for proper operating instructions.

The most important aspect of grinding and sawing is safety, for both you and the stone. These machines can be dangerous and destructive if used improperly. Simple grinding and sawing safety tips include:

- If at all possible, do not hold the gem material directly in your hand. Consider dopping the rough temporarily to a piece of wooden dowel, such as that used by cabochon cutters (Figure 8-2).

- In order to avoid overheating and potential damage to the stone and machine, make sure that you are using the correct type and amount of lubricant.

- Wear safety glasses and avoid loose clothing that can become entangled.

- Consult the manufacturers instructions and / or your local expert before switching on.

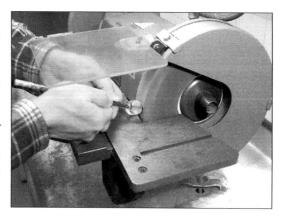

Finally, you should keep in mind that these crude pre-forming devices are exactly that: crude. You should always stop well before the stone reaches its final shape and size. This will give a safety margin to allow removal of any subsurface damage while bringing the gem to its proper final outline on the faceting machine.

Figure 8-2 A grinding wheel (shown) or trim saw (Figure 4-29) may be an excellent choice for pre-forming. Note the safety precautions: a shield to protect the face and a dowel rod (here a pencil) to protect the hands.

8.3.2 Facet-Machine Pre-Forming

For modest-sized gems or expensive material, you already have all the equipment you need for pre-forming: just dop up the rough and get going with a coarse lap on your faceting machine.

There are two main approaches to facet-machine pre-forming: free-wheeling and standard cutting.

Free-Wheel Pre-Forming

Some authors recommend "free-wheeling" for pre-forming. This essentially involves disengaging the index wheel and freely rotating the stone against the coarse lap. The result is a cone (or series of cones) approximating the pavilion, and a cylindrical form for the girdle (Figure 8-3).

Although it is quick and easy, I do not use the free-wheel pre-form technique for a variety of reasons. First, and most obviously, free-wheeling will not work on non-round gem designs –

you can hardly free-wheel an emerald pre-form. Also, even so-called "round" designs are not really round. A cone or cylinder may not be a good approximation, leading to lost yield or extra effort at the next stage (see "Cone Loss" below for more on this). Finally, going through the process of roughing in a couple of facet tiers using conventional cutting techniques and a coarse lap forces you to become familiar with the piece of rough and the sequence of initial, critical cuts.

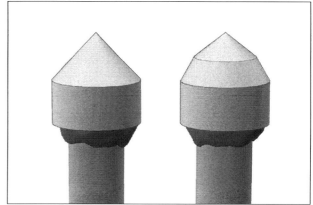

Figure 8-3 Free-wheel pre-forms. Choosing several cutting angles (right image) may allow a closer approximation to the final gemstone.

Pre-Forming by Cutting

Here is where the procedures of pre-forming and facet cutting merge. The "standard cutting" approach to pre-forming involves cutting some of the gem facets in the usual way on a coarse lap. This usually means working directly from the initial cuts of the gem design, such as the main and girdle facets. Clearly, it makes no sense to rough in the gem shape using the finer details, and meet points should serve only as approximate guideposts.

Chapter 5.5.3 provides a detailed tutorial for pre-forming in this way. The advanced techniques explained in Chapter 17 for establishing the gem outline may also help at the pre-form stage.

A final word of (oft repeated) caution: although considerably more refined than a grindstone or rock saw, the coarser laps – say, grit 260 and lower – can cut surprisingly aggressively on a faceting machine. They also can create every bit as much subsurface damage as a grinding wheel or saw blade. As always, you should halt the pre-form process well before you reach the final gem shape and size.

Cone Loss

Free-wheel pre-forming implicitly assumes that gemstones look more or less like cones – or perhaps more accurately, a couple of cones stuck base-to-base (Figure 8-4). Yes, truncating the crown-side cone certainly improves things, but how good is this assumption?

Clearly, this question translates directly to the issue of whether free-wheel pre-forming is wasteful of gem rough. In other words, if you execute a conical pre-form, do you end up with a smaller gemstone than you otherwise would?

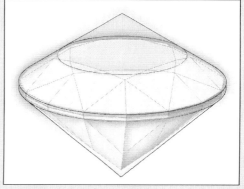

Figure 8-4 Free-wheel pre-forming assumes that the gemstone resembles a pair of cones.

I think that the answer is yes, and here's why. If you grind away gem rough until a perfect cone emerges, then clearly the final gemstone must fit inside that cone. Put more mathematically, the cone must *circumscribe* the eventual gem.

One way to measure how well the gem fits inside the cone is to compare the volume of the cone to that of the pavilion (Figure 8-5). Simple mathematics and the volume calculation of GemCAD make this comparison fairly straightforward (see Chapter 15.3.1 for more on GemCAD).

For a standard round brilliant with classical angles, the pavilion fills approximately 90% of the volume of the cone. Pretty good, I suppose, but then again, with sixteen sides, an SRB is very close to a circular shape. For a gem with fewer girdle facets – for example, GeM101 from Chapter 5 – the fit will be considerably worse. In fact, for this hexagonal design, the pavilion occupies less than 80% of its cone. This means that if you free-wheel pre-form GeM101, you will still have to cut away about a quarter of the remaining gem material to make the pavilion (Figure 8-5).

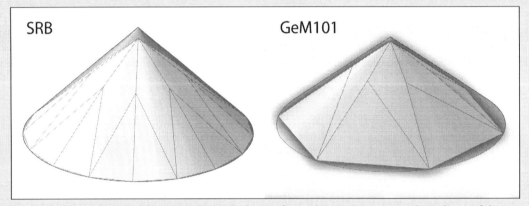

Figure 8-5 The final gemstone must fit inside the pre-formed cone. Comparing the volume of the pavilion to the volume of the circumscribing cone gives a measure of how good a match this type of pre-form actually is. An SRB (left) is a better match than a hexagon (right).

Free-wheelers may argue at this point that life is tough, and that you would have had to cut away that material anyway. Not so. In fact, I always try to match projections and divots in the rough to the rotation of the gem design in order to maximize yield. A cone has no preferential rotation. Figure 5-25 shows an example where a more thoughtful choice of orientation – in other words, not immediately grinding a cone – leads to an improvement in yield of about 50%. Chapter 17.3.3 takes this strategy one step further.

Perhaps an extreme example will make it even clearer. Imagine that you are cutting GeM101 and have a more or less hexagonal piece of rough, in other words, a pretty good match to the gem outline. Would you free-wheel pre-form a cone and then begin cutting another hexagon? Of course not. Needless to say, not every piece of gem rough matches the design right out of the ground, although hexagonal crystals are fairly common (see Chapter 12.10). In any case, you should be guided by the raw stone in selecting both the gem design and rough orientation. It makes no sense to throw away half that guidance – and significant gem rough – by always pre-forming a cone.

Note also that free-wheel pre-forming is closely related to the practice of grinding rather than cutting and polishing the girdle. You can see how I feel about ground girdles in Section 8.18.

Commercial pre-forming devices

There are commercially available devices that can assist in the pre-forming process. These include so-called "offset pre-formers," which allow you to shift the center of the stone with respect to the center of the dop very accurately. This permits you to free-wheel the girdle outline of a non-round gem design, such as an oval or marquise. Note, however, that any pre-forming accessory is by definition crude, and you will probably have to use more advanced techniques to get an accurately dimensioned girdle (see Chapter 17).

Commercial pre-forming devices are not absolutely necessary, and they can be surprisingly costly. Most modern faceting diagrams give explicit "pre-form" instructions, if needed, for establishing the girdle outline. With a little experience, you should be able to generate just about any gem shape without additional mechanical assistance. Turn to Chapter 4.11.2 for more on pre-forming accessories.

8.4 Lap Selection and Sequencing

As explained on page 288, the process of gem cutting involves placing flat planes, or facets, at specific locations on the rough stone. Faceters use abrasive flat disks, known as laps, to achieve this goal. Cutting laps come in a variety of types, ranging from home brewed, diamond-impregnated copper disks to high tech sintered steel laps (see Chapter 3.2). While individual cutting lap construction and composition may vary, there is one underlying strategy that is essential to successful gem cutting: proper lap selection at the proper time.

Cutting laps are available in a range of grades ranging from coarse to ultra fine, and they are normally used sequentially on the stone as it approaches its final shape. These grades are typically measured in traditional "grit" or "mesh" sizes, with low numbers representing coarser grit and high numbers denoting a finer abrasive. Section 3.2.1 explains the cutting lap numbering system.

8.4.1 The First Cut is the Deepest

Given the information in the previous paragraph and Section 3.2.1, a beginner's first intuition would be to start with his or her coarsest lap, and then work steadily to finer and finer grades until the gem is ready to be polished.

That intuition would be wrong. Not wrong-headed, just wrong.

The reason is that every gem material and every piece of gem rough is individual. For example, some materials are very soft and can be cut efficiently with a relatively fine lap, while others, such as those with cleavage plane problems, may not take kindly to a coarse lap at any stage. The gem rough may also exist as a pre-form or be fortuitously close to its final shape right out of the ground. In such instances, lap choice should be driven by the current state of the gem shape, not by any rigid, chronological sequence.

Additional factors driving the selection of the initial cutting lap include the size and cost of the gem material. Cutters who ignore these factors will soon learn that an aggressive lap can grind away a tiny or expensive stone at a horrifying rate. Always err on the side of caution: any change of initial cutting lap should arise from a recognition that things are progressing too slowly rather than too fast.

For typical gem materials, I begin with a 1200 grit bonded steel lap on smaller stones – those with a final cut weight below a couple of carats – and a coarser 600 lap for larger rough. For really large pieces, which for me are by necessity also inexpensive on a per-gram basis, I may go with a 260-grit lap to hog out the basic shape.

Sawing Rough on Your Faceting Machine

Do you want the speed of a rock saw and the precision of a faceting machine? Why not combine the two?

Standard diamond-impregnated rock saw blades can easily be adapted to the spindle of your faceting machine. These blades come in a variety of thicknesses and standard diameters of 4 and 6 inches (10 and 15 cm). The thinner blades – 0.01 inch (1/4 mm) and thinner – produce a very small cutting width or "kerf," resulting in less wasted stone.

Mount the blade on the spindle just as you would any lap. Thinner blades will benefit from additional support. This is where your collection of discarded CDs can help (back in the day, I use to say, "Thank you, AOL!"). Saw blades are obviously thinner than conventional laps, even when sandwiched between CDs. Depending on the geometry of your lap locking nut, you may also need to add some large diameter washers to ensure good mechanical contact (Figure 8-6).

Clamp the dopped stone in the quill and adjust the cutting angle and index settings as needed. For example, you may want to pre-form by cutting the pavilion mains. You should always select the fastest possible rotation speed, particularly for thin blades, and ensure a steady flow of cooling water.

Figure 8-6 Sawing a boule of synthetic sapphire on a faceting machine. You should support thinner blades between a pair of old CDs, and large flat washers can help if the sandwich is too thin for your clamping mechanism.

Trimming rough with a saw blade on your faceting machine is much like standard cutting, with the obvious exception that you need to work with the stone moving from the outside in, rather from the top down. The gap between the outside edge of the blade and the inside wall of your splash pan must be at least as large as your gem rough, plus some buffer, so a four inch blade may be the best choice.

All set? Start a generous water flow and then carefully lower the stone into the gap between the spinning blade and the splash pan. Double check that you have the correct height. If this is your first attempt, make a test cut with plenty of margin. You may be surprised at how thick the kerf is, particularly if the blade is bent or imperfectly clamped.

When you are ready to go, bring the stone gently against the edge of the blade and start the cut. You should pull the stone back every few seconds to inspect your progress and allow the water to wash away any debris in the gap. Reduce your finger pressure as you get close to completing the cut.

Inevitably, the last fraction of a millimeter of stone will give way in a hard-to-predict fashion, but of course, you have left plenty of margin for such vagaries of fate, right? The waste stone should drop into your splash pan, and you can raise the quill to examine your efforts.

When the first cut is done, move onto the next angle, index, and height setting. Each machine, blade, and stone combination will produce slightly different results, so take notes and learn from your experience. You will probably find as I did that using a saw blade this way becomes much more difficult as the angle between the blade and stone surface gets far from 90° (Figure 8-6 shows the ideal situation of perpendicularity).

After your final cut, rinse everything thoroughly and store the blade in a clean container. Most rock saws use oil-based lubricants, so I usually give the blade a good spray of WD-40 before putting it away.

Finally, be careful. Be really, really careful. Diamond saw blades, particularly thin, rapidly spinning ones, display an alarming propensity for slicing flesh. The gap between the blade and your splash pan is a no-man's land, or perhaps more appropriately, a no-finger's land. Respect it, and keep any body parts you want to retain well away.

8.4.2 Subsequent Lap Choice

Given a good selection of initial cutting lap, the principle of using finer and finer grit should produce satisfying results. The basic idea is to proceed through each lap grade, re-cutting and refining the shape as the surface approaches a smooth, pre-polished state.

For most gem materials, the overall sequence, including the initial rough cut, will be something like 260-600-1200-1200 NuBond (Figure 8-7). Note that the NuBond laps cut at a considerably finer effective grit than their numbering indicates (see page 69). As explained above, for softer, smaller, or more expensive rough, the sequence will start with a mesh finer than 260. Some harder materials, such as corundum, CZ, or chrysoberyl, may also benefit from a final pre-polish "cut" with 3000 grit, using either a bonded lap or loose diamond embedded in a traditional metal polishing lap (see Section 8.14.3 below). These gem materials do not, in general, react well to NuBond laps (see page 71 and page 341).

These sequences will almost certainly work, but experienced cutters recognize that some steps can be skipped for an individual stone. For example, a particularly well-behaved piece of gem rough may allow the leap from a 600 steel lap directly to the 1200 NuBond. Nevertheless, hidden subsurface damage is the number one bugbear for beginning faceters, and the best cure is careful and complete cutting at each step in the sequence.

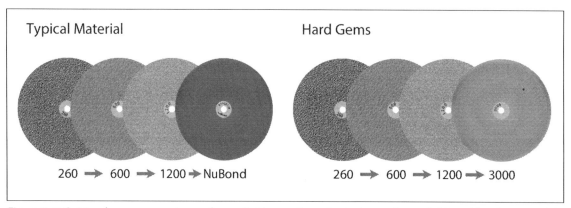

Figure 8-7 Cutting lap sequence to produce reliable results on typical gemstones (left) and harder materials, such as corundum (right). These particular orderings will be effective in almost all cases. Note however, that in many circumstances, you should start with a finer grit than 260, and it is very reasonable to skip some steps (see text for more).

8.5 Putting Stone to Lap

Enough with the lectures on lap types and selection…how do you actually cut the gem?

The short answer is that you lower the stone to the lap and have at it.

The longer answer is not that much more complicated. With careful preparation and a few straightforward precautions, cutting is easy and fun. Note that the next few paragraphs provide an abbreviated overview of cutting procedure. As mentioned earlier, the tutorial in Chapter 5 examines the process in detail, and has lots of nice pictures to boot.

First, you should have a cutting diagram and understand how to read it. Such diagrams are available for an amazing variety of gem designs at little or no cost, and the advent of computer programs such as GemCAD (see Chapter 15.3.1) means that essentially all modern designs have been test-cut, at least on the screen. Consult Section 5.1.1 if you are unfamiliar with modern cutting diagrams.

Second, you should insert the already dopped stone into the quill (Chapter 7 expounds in great detail on the theory, practice, and metaphysics of dopping). You will almost certainly have to use the cheater at some stage, so make sure that it is set to somewhere near the middle of its range. Adjust the rotation of the stone (Section 5.5.1), and then lock the dop in place.

The next step is to pick the appropriate initial cutting lap and mount it on the faceting machine. The previous section gives advice on initial lap selection. Always remember to err on the side of a finer lap.

Dial in the cutting angle and index wheel settings for the first facet. Adjust the cutting height so that the gem rough just touches the surface of the lap. Your very first test cut will reveal any serious problems, so you shouldn't aim too deep.

Note that with conventional mast-type machines, you should always adjust the height after the angle and index. Many faceting machines will cut happily with the height set too low: the stone rides a little higher – in other words at the wrong cutting angle – and you realize too late that disaster has struck. My sequence is always:

1. set gem height well above the contact point

2. adjust cutting angle and index

3. lower gem to touch the lap

Section 8.9.2 provides more wisdom on this issue. See also page 153.

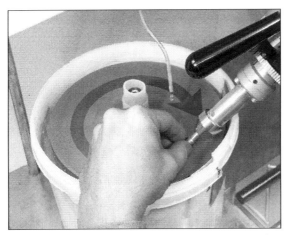

Figure 8-8 The lap should turn in the direction that the quill is "pointing." This prevents jamming and possible damage to the stone, machine, and operator.

Raise the quill and then start the lap rotation. Select a medium speed if the controller allows it. Some machines have reversible motors. If yours is one of these, double-check that the lap is turning in the proper direction (Figure 8-8). Getting this wrong and having the gem dig into the cutting surface is not pretty.

Adjust the water drip until the lap stays completely wet while spinning. Too little water will produce scratching, excessive heat, and, in the worst instances, damage to the stone or lap. Too much water can lead to hydroplaning and wet neckties (This is a joke. Needless to say, you should never facet while wearing a necktie – see Chapter 4.13).

As a final step before lowering the stone, verify that your faceting machine is ready to go, with all appropriate mechanisms, such as quill, mast height, etc., locked down and tight (see Chapter 5.5.2). After this sanity check, grasp the gem between your fingers and lower it to the lap. Apply light pressure on the stone for a few seconds to do a quick test cut and then examine the result. A sweeping motion back and forth across the lap will ensure consistent cutting and allow the water drip to remove any stone residue.

As emphasized on page 153, you should always hold the stone, not the dop, quill, or (if present) handle. Doing so gives you a better tactile sense of what is happening between the gem and lap and should alert you sooner to problems. This includes overheating of the stone, which can lead to all kinds of trouble. Grasping the gem also ensures steady cutting pressure and minimizes mast flexure and other effects which can ruin accuracy. Heavy handedness can even break the stone right off the dop. This will happen to you sooner or later, and while it makes for amusing war stories at the lapidary club, digging around in the shag carpet for

Lube Job

Lubrication is essential to successful cutting and polishing, and amateurs have used a surprising variety of substances to help achieve that perfect balance of smooth aggressiveness on the lap. The faceting literature and online resources are replete with tales of experimentation with various types of soap, anti-freeze, acids, and even kerosene (see "True Grit" on page 63 and "Doing Acid" on page 322).

My opinion? Water works fine. Set up a steady drip and cut away…

Although I have had my share of cutting and polishing problems, the culprit has always been something other than the choice of liquid lubricant. Poor technique, insufficient fluid flow, crumbly gemstone rough – you name it, I've seen it. What I haven't experienced is a desire to fill my drip tank with a substance of dubious utility and which may be harmful to me or to my machine. Yes, this is a strong opinion expressed strongly, and it may rub some experienced cutters the wrong way. A steady flow of fresh, pure water should cool things down…

a tiny wayward sapphire is simply no fun at all (see "The Nightmare Stone from Hell™" on page 259). As an added bonus, gripping the gem reduces the chance of impacting the central retaining nut or falling off the side of the lap (see "Cutter Beware" opposite). Short version: push on the stone.

Your initial test cut should help you select the appropriate height to continue with the first tier of facets. When they are complete, proceed with the second and subsequent tiers. Chapter 5 provides considerably more detailed advice on these steps, while Section 8.6 discusses the actual cutting order for facet tiers.

A Comfortable Cut

On a recent family vacation, we did a two-hour highway stint under difficult conditions: weather, traffic, music selection – the works. When we finally took a break, I was surprised at how difficult it was to get up and out of the driver's seat. My legs were stiff, my arm hurt, and turning my head left and right produced some alarming sounds and senses.

I shouldn't have been surprised, given the increasing profile and importance of ergonomic issues to workplace health and safety. In fact, my office had recently instituted regular reviews of seating, lighting, computer monitor placement, and so forth. I knew that sitting hunched over the wheel in a state of nervous agitation (not that song, again!) for two hours would produce some bad symptoms.

The same can happen when you cut. Yes, yes, traffic is not an issue and unless you have a very unusual workshop, weather should not play a role. Nevertheless, the opportunities for stress abound, and it is very important that you not worsen this situation with bad ergonomics. You will spend a great deal of time in that chair in front of that machine and under those lights. Make sure the experience is a good one.

I am not a doctor – at least not that kind of doctor – and it would be wildly inappropriate bordering on irresponsible to give medical advice here. Nevertheless, you should pay particular attention to proper body position, the height of your workbench, the adjustability and support of your chair, and the lighting, to name just a few. Unsurprisingly, faceters are also susceptible to repetitive motion disorders. Take regular breaks away from the faceting machine. Heck…do what I do and go wash your hands every time you switch laps (see "Keep Things Clean" on page 158).

There are plenty of online resources and recommendations regarding workplace ergonomics. Consult your physician, particularly if you experience discomfort during or after a cutting session.

8.5.1 Knowing When to Stop

Grinding away valuable gem rough is such fun that it can sometimes be difficult to know when to stop.

A particular cut is finished when the facet has both the correct surface roughness and location (or depth). Clearly, maximum yield will occur only when these two factors come together at least approximately at the same time. Such synchronicity is the ultimate aim of the experienced gem cutter.

Surface Roughness: As a general rule, you should always cut until the surface looks uniform and smooth, and then go a little further. This is to ensure complete removal of subsurface damage caused by the previous lap.

Depth of Cut: Most cutting diagrams will give some indication of the appropriate depth of cut for a facet. This may be a pre-existing meet point or a specified length-to-width ratio. Modern faceting machines have either a hard or soft stop to indicate when cutting is complete (Chapter 2.4). Add-on devices, such as the depth-of-cut indicator, can provide additional clues (Chapter 20.7)

When you are done with a particular lap, store it in a sealed container to prevent contamination (Chapter 4.9.2). Perform a general clean-up of the machine and work area before switching to a finer grit. In most instances, you should re-cut all of the tiers in order with the finer lap, but see the next section for more complete advice on facet sequencing.

Cutter Beware

Your innocent piece of gem rough confronts many dangers as it travels across the surface of your cutting lap. Two of these dangers lie at the edges of its little world: the central locking nut and the outer edge of the lap.

The Nutcracker

You will not soon forget the first time that you smash a partially completed gemstone against the locking nut that holds the lap to the platen. If you are very lucky, nothing serious will happen, beyond a brief heart-stopping moment of panic. More than likely, however, the impact with the lap nut will send your gemstone flying across the room. In the worst instance, part of your gem will go flying, and part of it will stay put.

Depending on the exact configuration of your faceting machine, you can take some preventive measures. For example, after my first inadvertent lap-nut smash (and after locating the gemstone), I forced a short length of rubber tubing over the locking mechanism to soften any possible future impacts (Figure 8-9). Note that there will inevitably be a small crevice between the tubing and the nut in such an arrangement. Liquid and cutting residue seeping into this area may lead to cross contamination between laps, so keep things as clean as possible.

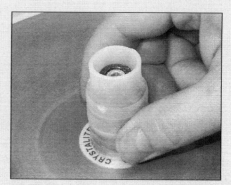

Figure 8-9 A short piece of rubber tubing acts as an excellent lap-nut bumper.

Here Be Dragons…

Legend has it that mapmakers of past centuries denoted areas off the edge of the known world – the *terra incognita* – with the words "here be dragons."

Although the legend is more likely due to the practice of drawing sea-serpents and other fanciful creatures in blank areas of their maps, the ancient cartographers have much to teach modern faceters about the dangers lurking at the edge of the world.

Figure 8-10 Avoid the dangers lurking beyond the edge of your lap.

Because of its more aggressive cutting characteristics, the edge of the lap is a seductive place to work (see "Your Lap's Sweet Spot" on page 72). Beware, however, that having your stone fall off the edge during cutting can be truly disastrous. You will almost certainly produce deep gouges on the stone, which will require significant back-pedaling and re-cutting to correct. You may even hurt yourself.

The bottom line is that you should use the edge of the lap judiciously, and take care not to venture too close to the precipice. Here be dragons indeed…

8.6 Cutting Sequence for Facets

The diversity of gem designs makes it difficult to establish general rules for the cutting sequence, that is, the order in which the various facet tiers should be executed. Nevertheless, you will find that almost all modern gem cuts are "bottom-up" in their philosophy. More specifically, the cutting sequence almost always begins at the culet or keel, working its way through the pavilion and on to the girdle and, after transfer, upwards through the crown to the table. See "The Great Debate: Pavilion-First or Crown-First?" on page 304 for more on this bottom-up approach.

Seeing the Facets

It can be quite a challenge to see and hence control the exact facet intersections, particularly early on when the coarser laps are in play.

Establishing a comfortable workspace with good lighting is the best remedy here. Try to adjust the location and direction of your eye and lamps to maximize contrast. Switching between bare and frosted bulbs may also help. Chapter 4.8 provides further hints.

If you still have difficulty, grab your trusty waterproof indelible marker and paint the offending facets. I find that the medium-point viewgraph pens work best. As the outer layer of stone is ground away, the ink also goes down the drain, revealing your facet edges and vertices in all their glory (Figure 8-11). A bit of alcohol on a paper towel will clean things up when you are done – just don't get any of the solvent on the dop wax or you will have a sticky mess.

Figure 8-11 Ink coarse-cut facets to see what's happening.

A combination of lighting and ink should get you through the early phases of cutting when the facets are particularly hard to see. The good news is that, early on with coarse laps, precise facet placement is not particularly important. You will have to cut away the frosted surface anyway, in order to eliminate subsurface damage. The finer and finer cutting laps will produce a more and more reflective surface, which in turn will allow you to see the facet intersections better and better. Sometimes, the world can be a kind and gentle place.

Beauty is Not Only Skin Deep...

"HELP!" you declare, "My fine cutting lap is producing deep scratches!"

No it isn't.

More accurately – No, it probably isn't.

Welcome to the awful world of subsurface damage. While it is possible that your fine lap has been contaminated by coarser grit, the overwhelming likelihood is that you have subsurface damage. Every single faceter will encounter this phenomenon and be baffled and frustrated by it. Knowledge and preparation are your best weapons against this insidious enemy.

What exactly is subsurface damage? As Chapter 5.5.5 explains (see page 157), a coarse lap can cause microscopic stress fractures and flaws to propagate deeper into the stone, creating damage that only appears later as the outer layers are smoothed away. Coarser laps inevitably cause more and deeper subsurface damage, but all cutting laps display the effect. In fact, optical shop experts – the guys who produce lenses and mirrors – will tell you that a depth approximately five times greater than the previous grit size must be removed before moving on to the next grade of abrasive. After using a coarse, 260 mesh lap, this corresponds to cutting away about half a millimeter of subsurface damage.

A little reflective chin scratching should lead you to the realization that there are two reasons for sequencing cutting laps. First and most obviously, the finer and finer grades produce a smoother and smoother surface finish in preparation for polishing. The second and less obvious reason is that the finer and finer laps do less and less subsurface damage. Polishing would be a singularly lengthy and frustrating task were this not the case.

Unless you have a very good reason to do otherwise, you should execute the cutting sequence as laid out in the prescription. In modern designs, this usually means following a list of cuts from top to bottom on the page, or through a numerical or alphabetical sequence of labeled tiers in the diagrams. Beware! You may occasionally find a design where the listing and labeling order don't agree. Generally, the list order will take priority in such cases, but when in doubt, consult the designer or do a test cut in the virtual world of GemCAD (see Chapter 15.3.1).

Following the prescribed sequence is particularly important for beginning cutters and/or well-established designs. Nevertheless, there are good reasons for going off the plantation in terms of sequencing the tiers of facets. For example, optimizing the order may reduce the number of mast height and cutting angle changes. It could even save you valuable gem rough, (see "Saving Stone with Clever CAM" on page 282 of Volume 2). Be warned, however: if you ignore the suggested sequence, awful things might happen, such as the sudden absence of key reference meet points. Short version: verify your plans in GemCAD before going rogue.

The one exception to this rule is the rough cutting of tiny facets, such as the stars on a Standard Round Brilliant. It simply makes no sense to attempt to place such small facets with a 260 lap. Over cutting is almost inevitably the result, leading to even more re-cutting of the larger facets and a smaller final gem. In these instances, you should view the sequence of cutting laps as a continuum between pre-forming and final polishing. It is acceptable – and even recommended – to skip the finer details with the coarser laps. The true final shape and meet points arise at the later stages.

Reversed Gemstone Syndrome

Do your gemstones turn out backwards? Are they the mirror image of what you expect?

Figure 8-12 shows what I mean. You follow each step in the cutting instructions carefully, and you end up with a reversed gemstone. Not that it isn't pretty and all, but what the heck is going on?

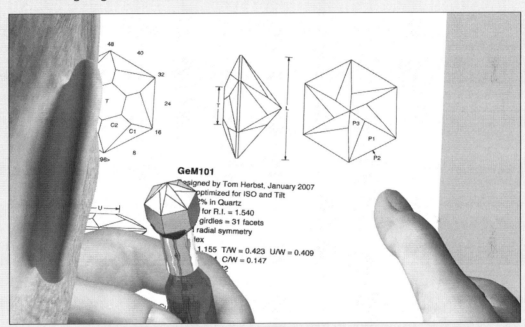

Figure 8-12 Depending on your faceting machine, you may find that the gems you cut are the mirror image of what you expect. See also page 175.

The answer lies in the manufacturers' choice of index wheel numbering. Some machines use clockwise numbering, in which the index values increase clockwise as you look at the gear. Others have chosen a counterclockwise arrangement. There is no "correct" choice in this regard, but needless to say, the two types of machine will produce different gemstones from the same prescription.

For what it's worth, the GemCAD design program (see Chapter 15.3.1) assumes counterclockwise index wheels, although there is an option to reverse this. My machine happens to have clockwise gears, so yes, I suffer from reversed gemstone syndrome. A careful examination of the photos in Chapter 5 (especially Figure 5-53) will reveal the symptoms.

And for those who have skipped ahead to Chapter 10.7, the answer to your question is yes, gemstones with mirror symmetry will turn out the same, independent of index wheel numbering direction.

The Great Debate: Pavilion-First or Crown-First?

If you have read any significant fraction of this book, you have already realized that there are a number of contentious issues which faceters debate, seemingly without end. The wax versus epoxy controversy is a classic, along with the mast versus platform discussion. The standoff between advocates for pavilion-first versus crown-first cutting order is yet another, but unlike those other issues, this one seems to have an unambiguous answer.

Pavilion first.

The reasons are straightforward and compelling. Chapters 10.4 and 11.7 explain that the pavilion angles drive the ultimate optical performance of a gemstone. Cut them too shallow, and you end up with the dreaded "fisheye," a gem which allows light to leak directly out of the pavilion. Cut the pavilion too deep and you have a similar problem with the second internal reflection. The solution? Get the pavilion right.

Getting the pavilion right means getting it done first. If you end up a little short of gem rough, you can always adjust the crown somewhat – either lowering the angles or increasing the size of the table – with lesser impact on gem performance. Similarly, if a serious cutting error or previously invisible inclusion forces a re-cut, you can usually use these strategies to fit the crown into the remaining material. To summarize, here is The Reason to go pavilion first: If you don't have the material to cut a proper pavilion, the rest doesn't really matter.

There is a second, less obvious reason to start with the pavilion. As Chapter 5 makes clear, successful gemstone cutting involves transferring accurate reference locations from one side of the gem through the girdle to the other. The process of establishing a center point for the pavilion, even if it is only as a "pre-form," can be very accurate when executed correctly (Step 1 in Chapter 5.5.5 explains how). However, unless you have a lot of extra gem rough, you will not have sufficient material to begin with a center-point reference on the crown. If you do have enough, you probably have the wrong design or the wrong piece of rough or both. Yes, you can try to cut an accurate initial crown by outlining the girdle first, but this leads to greater error, largely due to mast flexure and the fact that operating the quill at 90°, quite far from its usual orientation, amplifies machine alignment problems (see Chapter 17.2). So here is Reason Number Two: center points are an easy, accurate basis on which to build your gem, and pavilions are built on center points.

Much as I hate to see a good argument come to an end, I fear that the pavilion-first versus crown-first debate has a clear winner. One down, thirty-seven to go...

8.7 Meet Point Faceting

Meet point faceting is a method for cutting gemstones using the intersection points – the *meet points* - of previous cuts as a target for placing subsequent facets (Figure 8-13). Because these targets are physical locations on the gem, rather than estimates made by a person looking at dials and gauges on an imperfect machine, meet point faceting can be very accurate.

Amateur faceters owe a great debt of gratitude to Thomas J. Ricks, Robert Long, and Norman Steele, who developed, formalized, and promulgated the meet point technique during the mid 1970's. Their series of books, particularly "Introduction to Meetpoint Faceting," should be on every serious amateur's bookshelf (see Chapter 9).

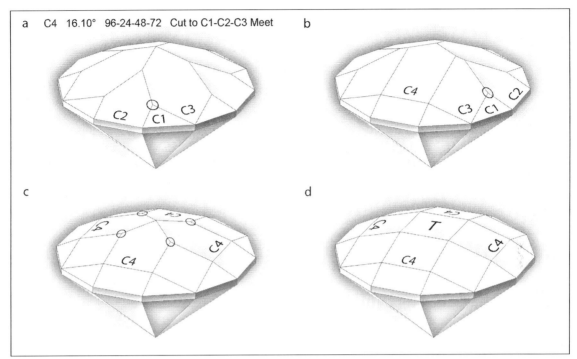

Figure 8-13 Placing a new facet at the target meet point formed by the intersection of existing facets. (a) Facets C1, C2, and C3 intersect at the target meet point (circled). (b) The first C4 facet is in place...time to move on to the next meet point (circled). (c) The four C4 facets are done, and they have created four meet points for placing the table. (d) The completed crown.

8.7.1 Why Meet Point?

A little experimentation with some inexpensive gem rough will demonstrate vividly that working to a facet intersection is easier and more accurate than working to a less well-defined location on the stone. For example, you will find an instruction such as, "cut facet C4 to the intersection point of C1-C2-C3" much easier to execute accurately and repeatably than, say, "cut P6 to 1/3 the width of the gem." Try it. You'll see.

What is less obvious is that meet point faceting is a great way of cutting non-round gem designs without needing an accurate pre-form. In fact, the CAM, CLAM, and OMNI techniques (Chapter 17) are essentially methods for creating a gem outline using meet point faceting. Its almost universal application in modern gem designs is an acknowledgment of the enhanced accuracy possible with the meet point technique.

Despite its great strengths, the meet point method does suffer from a few limitations. Perhaps the greatest of these is the fact that some classic and important gem designs are simply not amenable to the meet point technique. For example, the traditional emerald or step cut (Chapter 1.3) does not produce well-determined facet intersections, and a pleasing, symmetric gem will ultimately depend on your judgment in placing the step tiers.

My meets meet better than your meets…

Sooner or later, you will either witness or take part in a head-to-head comparison of gemstones produced by two or more cutters. You will then learn that meet point accuracy is second only to polish quality when faceters compare their work. Hunched over, gemstone in hand and loupe in eye, they will mumble to themselves about how this facet missed that meet, or how a less-than-scrupulous cutter has curved a facet edge to fake a good meet (see "Throwing a Curveball" on page 333).

To the outside world – that is, normal people – this may seem like the ultimate case of not seeing the forest for the trees. How can anyone criticize such a beautiful gem? And in many ways, they are right. A reasonably well-cut gemstone will sparkle just as well as a perfect one.

Nevertheless, among faceters there is an undeniable motivation – some may call it a creed, others an obsession – to produce a gem that is as perfect as possible. In fact, meet point quality is a decisive factor in judging competition gemstones.

A second drawback of meet point faceting is that it depends on accurate and known cutting angles. Stated another way, it may be easy to hit an existing meet point, but that meet point won't be in the right place if you have the wrong angles. This limitation is becoming less and less important as high quality faceting machines permeate the hobbyist world. Also, modern gem designs are usually worked out on a computer, ensuring accurate angles and a reproducible cutting sequence. The days are rapidly fading when the faceting instructions called for a range of possible angles, as long as things looked more or less correct.

Incidentally the emergence of complex and interesting meet point gem designs coincided with the home computer revolution. This is no accident. It is now possible for amateurs and professionals alike to produce meet point gem designs that are straightforward, deterministic, and (mostly) foolproof. Chapters 16-18 contain much more information to help you get started.

Ultimate Accuracy

How accurately can you make your meets?

This is a great question. In principle, the size of the atoms and molecules of the gem rough set the ultimate accuracy. Not even the fanciest faceting machine in the world is going to split an atom to make the perfect meet. Hard core physics geeks will point out at this stage that lattice vibrations and the Heisenberg Uncertainty Principle are the real limits here, but perhaps if we ignore them, they will go away…

Returning from the ridiculous back to the sublime, there is a more practical limit set by the fact that a gemstone is essentially an optical instrument which refracts and reflects visible light, albeit in an extravagantly pleasing way. The physics of light and waves tells us that structures smaller than the wavelength of light are indiscernible. In other words, you cannot actually "see" something smaller than the wavelength of light used to observe it.

Presumably, then, the ultimate meet point is one for which the actual intersection points of the facets fall within a circle approximately one wavelength across (Figure 8-14). For those keeping score, this accuracy is several thousand times worse than the one suggested in the first paragraph. However, at one fifty-thousandth of an inch or about one half of a thousandth of a millimeter, such meets would still be pretty good.

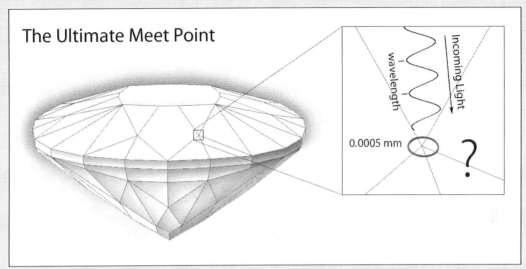

Figure 8-14 The ultimate meet point. If the facets come together within one wavelength of visible light, the meet point will be indiscernible from a perfect one.

Is this ultimate accuracy achievable? Yes, in principle. Technologies and machines currently exist which can create sub-wavelength structures in quartz and other optical materials. Be prepared to mortgage your house, however, if you want to play with one of these machines.

What is the ultimate accuracy achievable with amateur equipment? I actually had the opportunity to test this, thanks to a request to produce an optical component for an astronomical instrument. The design called for a four-sided glass pyramid with very shallow angles, approximately 1° (see Figure 8-15).

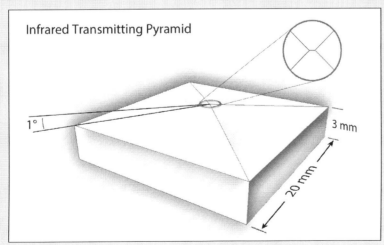

Figure 8-15 The design for a very accurate glass pyramid for an astronomical instrument. The pyramid is essentially a very shallow apex crown, cut in a special glass that transmits infrared light (Figure 11-2). Sharp edges and an accurate center point were a strong requirement. A "roof line" produced by missed meets (inset) was simply unacceptable.

The performance of the overall instrument depended on an extremely accurate intersection of the four faces of the pyramid. Any errors would show up as a "roof line" and would affect the measurements made on sky.

How well did I do?

After a few trial cuts with less expensive glass, I would have to say pretty well. Using a special tabling adapter and a microscope, I was able to produce and measure a meet point approximately 0.0002 inch (5 microns) across, using otherwise conventional amateur equipment (Figure 8-16). This is approximately ten wavelengths of visible light, so yes, there is room for improvement, and yes, it looked pretty good with a 10x loupe…

Figure 8-16 The glass pyramid mounted vertically for edging (top left). Ink dots identify the four apex crown facets. The pyramid dopped on the special tabling adapter for polishing (top right). The entire pyramid through the microscope (bottom left). High magnification image showing a sharp, accurate meet point at the 5 micron level (bottom right).

How can I tell if a gem is a meet point design?

This is another great question. Here's an easy answer: look at the diagram. If the cutting instructions say things like "cut to P1-P2 meet" then the design is meet point.

Unfortunately, the easy answer isn't exactly correct.

The problem is twofold. First, there is no convention out there among designers to include such additional information in the cutting instructions. I think that it would be a great idea to have such a convention, but then again, so would getting the manufacturer's to agree on which way index wheels should go 'round (see page 303).

The second difficulty is more insidious. Some ostensibly meet point designs are simply not meet point. In other words, the prescription may claim that a facet can be cut to a certain meet point, but in the real world, that meet doesn't yet exist. This may be due to carelessness on the part of the designer or more commonly, by taking shortcuts in GemCAD. Before releasing them to the wider world, I always test cut my designs twice: once in the computer and once with real stone.

So. What's an honest faceter to do?

Here's a foolproof solution: cut the design in GemCAD first. Chapters 15.3.1 and 18 can help you get started. Make sure that you set the gem symmetry to 1-fold, non-mirror. This forces you to cut one facet at a time, just like on your machine (see page 258 of Volume 2). If you can execute the design by locating facets at existing intersections, then the design is meet point.

8.7.2 Meet the Future of Faceting

The number and variety of meet point designs now available would keep an amateur busy for a lifetime. Unless there are very good reasons to do otherwise, such as requiring a classic emerald, I see no reason to cut anything other than meet point designs. Given this arguably iconoclastic viewpoint, it should come as no surprise that all of the cuts in Chapter 19 use meet points. If a particular gem strikes your fancy but is not meet point, look around (see Chapter 15.1 for tips). Some intrepid amateur has probably worked out a way to execute the design using the meet point technique.

Designing at the Machine

Does the advent of meet point faceting, accurate amateur machines, and the home computer signal the end of the era of the master cutter, who sits at his or her machine and designs new cuts in living rock?

Absolutely not. We mere mortals will always have enormous respect for these individuals, and there will always be designs and unique pieces of gem rough that call out for their special skills. Modern techniques and hardware have simply made the hobby more accessible to those of us without the talent and experience to match the masters.

8.8 Keeping Track

One of the most valuable outcomes of my admittedly lengthy and overpriced education was learning how to take notes. I have notebooks for everything, ranging from the lab activities in my day job to fuel consumption and maintenance of my car. Nevertheless, the most used and treasured notebook in my collection is the dog-eared, water-sprayed volume that is my faceting log. Not only does it capture the history of all of my lapidary activities, including occasional forthright remarks, but also it serves as a vital reference both during and after cutting the gem.

The advent of portable computers has somewhat diminished the role of pen and paper in everyday work, but as Chapter 4.10 makes clear, the faceter's workshop has remained and will continue to be the domain of jotting, sketching, and logging.

To prevent disaster and frustration, you need to keep track of what you are doing. You really do. All it takes is a single instance of "touching up" the polish on a facet at the completely wrong cheater setting to convince you of the value of this advice.

Organizing your faceting notes is, of course, very much a matter of personal preference. For what it's worth, Figure 8-17 shows an extract from my notebook devoted to the Scrambler design (see Chapters 17.3.3 and 19.2.7).

I assign one page to each gem, recording standard information such as initial rough weight, final yield, starting date, gemstone design, and so forth across the top. Below this general information block, a small table records cutting progress of the pre-form. Because the design corresponded so closely to the rough (see Chapter 17.3.3), I was able to generate this pre-form with a 1200 Crystalite lap. For each pre-form tier – PF1-PF4 plus the girdle – I recorded the exact angle setting for later reference. The numbers under "1200" for each tier correspond to micrometer settings on my home-cooked precision angle device (see Figure 20-17).

Immediately after the pre-form data, a larger table collects information on the cutting and polishing of the pavilion. This table organizes the facet tiers in rows and the various laps across the columns. At each step, I recorded the angle setting, as well as any important remarks. For example, I noted a change of angle on facet tier P2 with the NuBond (single asterisk) and a shift in cheater setting to 5.5 on tier P5 at index 80, also with the NuBond (double asterisk – I circle cheater settings to distinguish them). There was also an inclusion breakout on the girdle with the 50k diamond polish ("+" symbol). This breakout forced me back to the NuBond to re-cut things, hence the extra two columns. The task was considerably eased by the careful record of angle and cheater settings. That's the whole point of this exercise.

The next section of the log includes notes from the transfer cheat process. In this instance, I was able to establish the cheater setting (1.3) after cutting a couple of test tiers. Chapter 7.7 explains what is going on.

The final element in the cutting log is another table of angle and cheater settings for the crown and table. Compared to the difficulties with the pavilion, it seems that completing the second half of the gem was more or less uneventful.

I am the first to admit that this particular scheme for keeping track is far from ideal, and it certainly won't work with every faceter's personal style. Nevertheless, maintaining a careful record of angle and cheater settings literally saved my butt when that breakout occurred on the girdle. Without careful notes, I would have had to re-discover the proper cutting angle and cheater values, undoubtedly miring myself in a deeper nightmare. Starting with your very first gemstone, you should develop and use your own logging procedure. Sooner rather than later, you will be very thankful that you did.

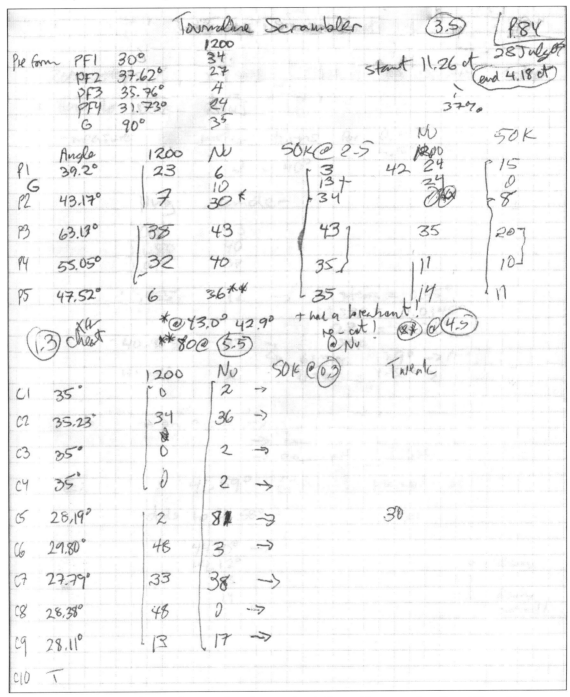

Figure 8-17 A single page from my faceting notebook. See text for an explanation of the entries.

8.9 Troubleshooting Cutting

Despite the encouraging words in previous sections about how easy and fun gem cutting can be, the process is not trouble free. You may make an actual mistake (see below) or you may just have the vague sense that the stone is just not "right." This section describes a number of ways of getting back on the straight and narrow road to cutting success, and presents a variety of strategies for avoiding trouble in the first place.

8.9.1 Making Mistakes

Face it. Sooner or later, you are going to make a mistake.

You are going to cut into a beautiful piece of gem rough at the wrong index or the wrong angle. For some of us, making such mistakes happens all too soon and all too often. What can a reasonable person do?

When the worst happens – when you have made a serious error in cutting – you should stop the machine and sit back for a moment. Take a deep breath and try to relax. Your initial feeling of despair at having destroyed the stone is almost always misplaced.

Examine what you have just done and try to understand how it occurred. Many times, a minor error is compounded by rushed efforts to correct for it: the instant cure can often be worse than the problem. This is particularly true if the cause of the mistake is fatigue or eyestrain. You should also record in your notebook all the incorrect settings and any additional factors that contributed to the error (see Section 8.8).

Once the situation is clear, you can begin to examine recovery strategies. There are always a number of possibilities, even for the most severe of errors:

1. If you have sufficient raw material for both the pavilion and crown, you can merely shift the design down the length of the rough, re-cutting the entire stone without reducing yield (see also page 166). While time-consuming, this option completely eliminates any evidence of your mistake.

2. If there isn't enough extra rough, you can always opt for the same cut in a smaller size. Such a decision should not be taken lightly, however, since the yield plunges rapidly with decreasing diameter (Section 7.8). Unless it is a competition or collector stone, other strategies are almost always superior.

3. Depending on the nature and depth of the missed cut, you can just leave it in place and polish it as though it was part of the plan. Many gem designs, particularly the brilliants, are capable of disguising fairly serious errors just by their sparkle. Examine any commercially cut stone to soothe your doubts about this. Purists would argue that the gems available in most shopping malls consist entirely of cutting errors.

4. An interesting option is to alter the gem design to accommodate your "special feature." This can be as simple as cutting the crown a little shallower to eliminate the problem. For the reasons emphasized in Chapter 11.7 and on page 304, this will not work as well with the pavilion. Note also that many designs have optimized angles. Changing them may have serious consequences for the final appearance of the gem (see Chapter 10.5). The GemCAD and BOG programs (see Chapter 15.3) can help you assess the effects of any changes.

5. Alternatively, if the cut allows it, you can place similar "errors" symmetrically around the stone (this is one reason for recording the settings). If possible, you should try your "enhanced design" in GemCAD before proceeding.

6. Finally, you can treat the damaged stone as a pre-form for a completely different gem design. Careful selection of the alternative can result in zero lost yield.

8.9.2 Avoiding Mistakes – Look Before You Leap

The best strategy for dealing with mistakes is not to make them in the first place. This is not meant to be a silly or condescending remark. There are straightforward ways to help ensure that you don't do something dumb. For example, many faceters develop a rhythm to their work, regularly checking the cutting diagram and the machine settings before setting stone to lap.

Think of it like driving: when you come to a four-way stop, you halt, look right, then left, and then probably right again before proceeding (my British, Australian, and other right-hand-steering friends may now mutter indignantly). In the same way, you can set the new cutting angle or index, check back with the diagram, and then once again verify machine settings before committing to the cut. A convenient holder for the sheet of faceting instructions, coupled with good lighting and a comfortable workplace (see page 298) makes these steps a natural and easy part of the hobby.

Wykoff's book recommends the acronym CHIA – Cheater, Height, Index, Angle – to help you remember what to check. As a continual and friendly reminder, you might even consider acquiring one of those terra cotta chia pets for your work area. Your favourite green-topped farm animal, cartoon character, or president will flourish under your well-planned lighting. Note, however, that CHIA is not the recommended order for changing your faceting machine settings (see "Angle First, Height Second" on page 153 and further advice on page 297).

Intelligent Consistency

The well-known nineteenth century essayist, philosopher, and poet Ralph Waldo Emerson famously stated that "a foolish consistency is the hobgoblin of little minds" (*Self-Reliance*, 1841).

Note that he wasn't a well-known nineteenth century faceter.

In fact, establishing a rhythm to your cutting can be one of the more relaxing and "zen" aspects of the hobby. It also prevents the most common types of errors, such as incorrect angle, index, and mast height settings.

As the well-known twentieth century faceters, Glenn and Martha Vargas, somewhat less famously stated: "orderly, repetitive operations pay in reduction of errors..." (*Faceting for Amateurs*, 3rd Edition, 1989, p. 157).

Ok, so it's not poetry, but it is great advice.

8.9.3 Look As You Leap

Even with the best preventive technique, mistakes will occur. Once again, however, there are steps you can take that will mitigate the impact of such errors. The most obvious is to do an initial, very light cut, followed by a visual inspection, whenever you change anything on the machine. You will also develop a sense for the sound and "feel" that a properly placed new cut makes. For example, if you are adding a small facet at a small angle to an existing one, the cut should feel smooth and fairly quiet. Starting a major facet on the raw rough will have a lot more tactile and audible "bite." With your antennae up, you should be able to catch an improper index or angle setting almost immediately, before serious damage occurs. This applies to polishing as well as cutting, although there may be less auditory feedback. If the stone doesn't "feel right" on the lap, there is a good chance that you are doing something you shouldn't.

8.9.4 Subtle Mistakes

Although a missed index or incorrect angle produces great drama and anguish, problems usually sneak up on you in more subtle and nasty ways. Self-important cinema critics in big-city newspapers refer to this effect as the "banality of evil." Don't let it get you.

The most common source of problems for a cutter who plays by the rules is the fact that errors accumulate. A complicated gem design is like a house of cards, each tier building on the last and sadly, carrying forward its problems. Imperfect facets produce imperfect meet points, which serve imperfectly as the reference locations for later facets, which are themselves imperfect. And the cycle builds and builds on itself until the gem is thoroughly messed up.

Unfortunately, there are no magical cures for this malaise, beyond avoiding all but the simplest gem designs and making sure that your faceting machine is well aligned. There is a treatment, however: take extra care in placing important facets and monitor your progress. When you spot a problem, try to identify the true source of the difficulty. Compensating earlier errors with later corrections on different facet rows is a notoriously bad way to deal with the situation. It is almost always better to go back to the offending tier and set things right.

It is also common to placate one's worries with the misplaced hope that all can be made good on the polishing lap. It usually cannot. Cutting errors that are obvious with a 1200 cutting lap are simply too large to compensate with 50,000 mesh diamond. It is of course possible to make slight adjustments during the polishing phase, and experienced faceters almost always move things around a tiny bit. Just don't count on fixing cutting errors this way. In short, both the surface smoothness and facet meets should be in good shape before putting away the last cutting lap.

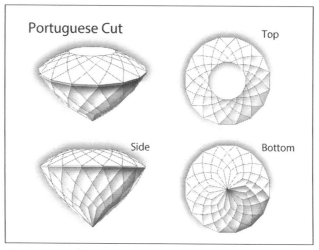

Figure 8-18 The Portuguese cut, with its many tiers built on one another, is very susceptible to accumulated error.

As the Lap Turns…

If I always use the same lap and the same rotation rate, I will always get the same cutting speed. Right?

Wrong.

Multiple effects are at play here. The cutting speed will be influenced by the conditions at the stone-lap interface, and many factors contribute to these conditions. Variations in hand pressure or facet size will have an effect (see "Performance under Pressure" on page 317), as will the quantity of water and cutting residue on the lap. Some gemstone materials offer different resistance to cutting along different crystal directions, adding yet more variation.

Even ignoring hand pressure, surface conditions, and crystal effects, you will inevitably see variations in cutting speed with a single lap. There are at least two reasons for this. The first is differential wear, which results in much more rapid cutting action at the inner and outer edges of the lap (See "Aging Gracefully" on page 316 and "Your Lap's Sweet Spot" on page 72).

The second effect is that the cutting rate depends directly on how many abrasive particles per second encounter the gem rough. You may think that the entire lap is turning at a constant rate, but the *linear speed*, and hence the number of abrasive particles per second, is a strong function of how far out on the lap you work. For a standard eight-inch lap, the difference can be a factor of five or more, with the outside rim of the lap traveling – and cutting – considerably faster. Some faceters even report having difficulty with very long, thin cuts, due to the differential speed and cutting action across a single facet!

You should learn to turn all of these variables to your advantage. Exploit the differential lap wear to fine-tune your stone removal rate, and select a lap rotation speed and cutting radius that is well matched to the job at hand. For example, you should find yourself using the most well-behaved, worn region of the lap to cut tiny facets. You may even have the motor switched off.

Cutting Variables

Fine. You understand how small errors can accumulate and how they should be dealt with promptly. What causes these small errors? Can they be avoided?

The answer to the second question is yes and no. There are some obvious and well-known sources of small cutting errors, and there are countermeasures. For example, the biggest variable is hand pressure, which is perhaps better described as head pressure. There is an unavoidable desire to force things when progress is slow. More mental pressure leads to more hand pressure, which in turn translates to more rapid cutting. It also produces mast flexure and other effects which lead to cutting errors. In the worst instance, it can even cause the stone to break loose and fly across the room. Keep that pressure inside your head and use faster rotation or a coarser lap to speed things up.

> ### Aging Gracefully
>
> As with people, cutting laps change as they get older, and as with people, in many ways they improve.
>
> A brand new 1200 bonded steel lap cuts far more aggressively than one that has seen a hundred stones. Is the older lap worn out? Definitely not. In fact, experienced faceters treasure older – let's call them seasoned – laps even more than the shiny new ones. They produce gentle, predictable results.
>
> It's nice to think that some things truly improve with age. Of course, the other way to look at this is that, like people, laps eventually get old and become dull, slow cutters. Try this theory out at your next lapidary club meeting…

Another obvious variable is stone hardness. We all know that different gem materials have different hardness, and generally, harder stones cut slower than softer ones. However, some materials, such as kyanite, can display significantly different hardness – and hence cutting speed – for different cutting *directions* (see "As the Lap Turns…" above and page 125 of Volume 2). In other words, some facets will stubbornly refuse to show progress, while others come in with disturbing ease. Such seemingly pathological behaviour can be extremely confusing and frustrating for the beginner. The message here? Know your materials and know your particular piece of stone. Note down in your logbook where the slow (and fast) facets are and adjust your style accordingly.

8.10 Polishing Technique

An older and wiser friend once told me that life throws two types of experience at you: those that build confidence and those that build character. You will find, at least initially, that polishing gemstones is a real character builder.

Polishing is also perhaps the richest aspect of our hobby in terms of lore and specialized techniques. As you will learn, the masters have developed an amazing variety of approaches for achieving that elusive perfect polish. Some of them even work.

This section should help you navigate the difficulties of polishing gemstones and avoid many of the pitfalls and mistakes that can trap the beginner. With experience, the polishing of gemstones becomes (relatively) easy, predictable, and fun. And, while following the advice in this chapter will in no way guarantee a trouble-free experience with every gem, it should smooth out the worst bumps along the road. Besides, you needed to work on your character anyway, right?

8.11 How Polishing Works

Note: this section contains a short physical and historical diversion from the business of polishing gemstones. You don't need to understand its contents to make pretty rocks.

Before embarking on an explanation of how to actually polish a gemstone, let's take a brief detour into the fascinating microscopic world of polishing physics. As you will see, this discipline has a long and distinguished history, as well as some pretty remarkable ideas about what actually happens on our polishing laps. I am indebted to a number of scholars of this subject for the material in this chapter. Direct references to their work appear in Chapter 9.4.

The introduction to this chapter implied that cutting and polishing were essentially the same physical process, with the obvious remark that they operate on different scales of surface roughness. That introduction also foreshadowed the notion that things are just a bit more complicated (are you surprised?). It is all very well and good to explain cutting and polishing as similar processes, in which a hard abrasive, applied as a sequence of ever-finer particles, scratches away the softer gemstone material until a high gloss appears. Unfortunately, this simplified view slams face-on into the common observation that cerium oxide, with a Mohs hardness of 6, is able to put a beautiful polish on quartz or beryl, which have a hardness of 7 to 8.

Oops.

It turns out that understanding how polishing works is of considerable importance in fields well beyond gemstone faceting. For example, the production of optical components, ranging from eyeglasses to camera lenses to giant telescope mirrors, relies on predictable polishing outcomes. The heart of all modern electronics, the silicon chip, also has a critical polishing stage early in its fabrication process. As a result, a great deal of theoretical and experimental effort has been invested in studying how polishing actually works.

Performance under Pressure

You probably remember your high school science teacher explaining why wide tires on racing cars make no sense. Traction depends on friction, and friction depends in turn on local pressure and contact area. If you put on a wider tire, the contact area goes up but the local pressure goes down, resulting in exactly the same total traction.

You probably also remember seeing every racing car in the world sporting wide tires.

What's going on, and what does it have to do with faceting?

Well, what's going on is the fact that traction depends on a great deal more than just pressure and contact area. If you have ever been to a drag strip, you know what I am talking about. Both the tires and the road surface are *sticky*. Chemically sticky. Like fly paper. That kind of sticky depends on molecular forces between the rubber and the road, and that kind of traction definitely increases with surface area.

Again, what does this have to do with faceting? Well, in cutting and polishing, the local rate of stone removal depends on the local pressure, just like traction. For a larger facet, the same hand force will produce less local pressure – albeit over a larger area – and hence a slower cutting rate. This is why tables come in so slowly, yet it is fiendishly easy to over cut a star. Want to learn more about the physics of pressure and lap speed in polishing? Google "Preston's Equation" to begin your explorations.

It turns out that there is a chemical, "sticky" aspect to faceting as well. Section 8.11.2 explains how molecular forces come into play on our polishing laps.

Sadly, almost none of this research has been on gemstone materials, with the exception of quartz and sapphire. There are important physical insights into gemstone polishing that can be extracted from these efforts, however, and there are good reasons to believe that many of the same processes take place on our polishing laps.

8.11.1 A Brief History of Polishing Theory

Yes, yes, they invented gunpowder and spaghetti, but did you know that the Chinese may also have come up with what we now call gemstone polishing? Approximately six thousand years ago, Neolithic farmers in ancient China were using loose abrasives to polish jade objects of transcendent beauty and startling surface quality. Interestingly, the initial analysis of these artifacts suggested that quartz sand was the abrasive of choice. More recent studies using scanning electron microscopy hint that the ancient Chinese used alumina grains. Talk about old timers sticking with their Linde A...

Figure 8-19 A four thousand year old jade axe from China.

Polishing of glass for optical components dates back to the 13th century, and over the subsequent 500 years, lenses became relatively commonplace for magnification, vision correction, and in scientific instruments such as microscopes and telescopes. And, while jewelers, opticians, and instrument builders were willing to experiment and pass on their knowledge, there is little mention of physical theories for polishing until the mid seventeenth century. Both Robert Hooke, who is best known for his pioneering work in microscopy, and Sir Isaac Newton, who is best known for doing just about everything else, finally stepped forward to fill this gap.

The Hooke and Newton theories proposed that rubbing a piece of glass or metal with ever-smaller abrasive particles replaces the initial deep scratches with smaller and smaller ones, until the eye can no longer distinguish the finely scratched surface from a perfect, liquid-like finish. Sadly, this was one of the very few things on which Hooke and Newton agreed. Their intellectual battles within the Royal Society were legendary, and allegations persist that Newton, who took over stewardship of the Royal Society after Hooke's death, was somehow responsible for the disappearance from the Society's archives of the only known portrait of his former nemesis (see Figure 8-20).

Figure 8-20 Isaac Newton (left) and Robert Hooke (right) proposed the first theory of polishing physics. The Newton portrait is by Godfrey Kneller, who painted the great scientist in 1689. The Hooke portrait is a modern historical reconstruction by Rita Greer based on descriptions of Hooke's appearance.

Early in the twentieth century, Lord Rayleigh, who also explained to us why the sky is blue, presented a more thorough discussion of the polishing process, including both chemical and mechanical effects. Specifically, Rayleigh noted that a fine polish results from steadily breaking, grinding, and scratching away the surface with ever-finer particles down to the level of the deepest initial pits.

As with a surprising number of early fundamental theories, these guys got it essentially right. Their explanation of the polishing process corresponds closely to what is now known as the brittle wear theory (see below).

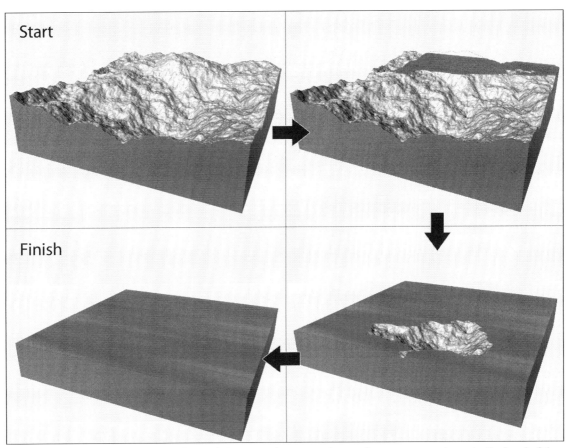

Figure 8-21 Rayleigh suggested that polishing involves removing surface structures down to the level of the deepest initial pits.

Sir George and the Magical Melting Layer

After such an auspicious start, the physical theory of polishing went seriously off the rails, only a couple of years after Rayleigh departed the scene. Observing the liquid-like surface of polished glass, Sir George Beilby suggested that the uppermost layer actually melts during polishing and flows to fill the initial cracks and imperfections. In his view, surface tension in the molten material was responsible for the flat, perfect finish:

"The polished surface on a solid substance is as truly due to the presence of a surface tension skin as is the surface of a liquid"

- Sir George Beilby, 1921

As confirmation of his theory, Beilby noted that the initial scratches on a piece of polished glass would reappear if the surface polish were etched away with acid. His conclusion? The melted then re-frozen layer of glass is more prone to acid attack and would hence disappear rapidly, revealing the underlying (and pre-existing) scratches.

Beilby's theory, enunciated in detail in his 1921 book "Aggregation and Flow of Solids," sparked a vigorous debate in the pages of the leading scientific journals of the day. Claims and counterclaims flew back and forth between partisans for the flow theory and those who clung to a purely mechanical view of polishing.

This debate raged on for over a decade until a key set of experiments, published in the Proceedings of the Royal Society in 1937, found that polishing only occurred if the melting point of the abrasive was higher than that of the material being polished. The obvious implication was that flow could not occur if the abrasive melted before the glass.

Figure 8-22 Sir George Beilby, father of the aggregation and flow theory of polishing. Image courtesy of the Society of Chemical Industry, www.soci.org

Score one for Sir George. This evidence was so convincing that the flow theory of polishing, and the eponymous Beilby layer, became accepted fact and little further research took place for another two decades.

In the 1950's, advances in experimental physics and a general blossoming of all things technological led a new generation of researchers to re-examine the classic theory of polishing. Phase contrast microscopy revealed that even the most finely polished surfaces exhibit scratching, a result incompatible with liquid flow. The reappearance of scratches after acid etching of a polished surface was explained by the vulnerability and subsequent exposure of subsurface damage from the grinding stage.

This realization, coupled with a greater understanding of mechanical and chemical processes at the microscopic level, resulted in the general abandonment of the Beilby flow theory by the scientific community in the mid-1960's.

Interestingly – and some would say not surprisingly – the faceting community was not about to let a few scientific facts get in the way of a good theory. References to Beilby flow persisted for another thirty years in the lapidary literature, up to and including relatively recent textbooks. At least one of these reference works gives advice on the selection of polishing compounds based on their melting temperature in comparison to various gemstone materials.

8.11.2 Brittle, Ductile, and Chemical Abrasion

Enough history and snarky remarks about poor old Sir George. How does polishing actually work? More specifically, how on God's Green Earth can a soft compound like cerium oxide put such a high polish on something hard like beryl?

The answer is complicated and by no means complete. The modern theory of grinding and polishing of surfaces has identified three distinct processes, called *brittle wear, ductile grinding,* and *chemical polishing.*

Brittle Wear

Brittle wear or brittle grinding is the best understood of these processes, and it corresponds closely to Hooke and Newton's original ideas about successively finer scratches. Brittle wear is a fracture process, in which the individual abrasive particles impact the surface, causing chipping and material removal. Incidentally, these impacts are sometimes called Hertzian, after Heinrich Hertz, another hero and giant of modern physics (see page 52 of Volume 2).

Clearly, cutting laps exploit the brittle wear phenomenon to remove gemstone material rapidly in the early stages of gemstone production. Finer and finer cutting laps produce successively smaller scratches and pits, resulting in a surface we call "pre-polish."

This purely mechanical process can carry through to the polishing phase in the form of a metal or ceramic lap and extremely fine diamond crystals – see *bort* in the Glossary at the end of this book. Eventually, the surface damage becomes too small to see, and you end up with a polished gem. Critics of diamond polishing will argue that this never really occurs, and that a diamond-polished surface is only somewhat less scratched-up than a rough ground one – see *curmudgeon* in the Glossary at the end of this book.

Incidentally, effective grinding requires hard abrasive particles, so this won't clarify the cerium oxide conundrum. However, brittle wear does explain how diamond can polish sapphire. Hence, it clarifies the corundum conundrum (sorry, I couldn't resist).

Ductile Grinding

A very curious phenomenon occurs in the brittle grinding of glass when the size of the abrasive grains gets smaller than a few microns (one micron is a millionth of a meter or about one twenty-five thousandth of an inch – see Chapter 3.2.1). At these size scales, fracturing and chipping of the glass no longer occur, and the abrasive particles push the surface material to the sides like a plough. The resulting lateral forces shear away some of the glass molecules along the plane of the surface and force the remainder to flow away from the path of the abrasive. This phenomenon is known as ductile grinding.

Ductile grinding leaves a fairly smooth surface, although some subsurface damage does occur. The one major difference between brittle wear and ductile grinding is the amount of residual internal forces or *stress* left in the ground surface by this process.

Rough grinding with relatively large particles – in other words, brittle wear – introduces very little stress in the ground surface. Essentially, bashing away with big, diamond boulders causes the material to shatter, and this tends to happen first and best in areas of pre-existing internal stress. When the abrasive particles get small, however, the resulting stress in the ground surface can rise dramatically. This is understood in terms of the shearing and plastic deformation that takes place when ductile grinding takes over.

You may have noticed that some gem materials seem to get harder when polished. For example, going back and re-cutting a facet seems to go much more slowly than the initial cut. Garnet and tourmaline are particularly susceptible. This apparent hardening of the surface may be related to the increased surface stress induced by ductile mode grinding. Then again, maybe it is not – to my knowledge, no studies of this phenomenon exist for materials other than glass, metals, and perhaps sapphire.

Those still concerned with the CeO_2 conundrum will have to be patient. Like brittle wear, ductile grinding cannot explain how cerium oxide polishing works.

Chemical Polishing

The final and least understood process is chemical polishing. The potential importance of chemistry in the polishing process has been recognized for centuries, and researchers have tested a wide variety of compounds in their quest for the ultimate surface finish on metal and optical components.

Hobbyists are also willing to explore new ways of achieving that perfect polish. A perusal of the faceting literature and online discussion forums will reveal a cornucopia of recommendations for additives to your polishing compound or drip tank. Note that some of these chemical agents are potentially hazardous to both man and machine, so exercise due caution and restraint (and see "Doing Acid" below).

Even pure water, which we consider to be the most neutral and benign of substances, can be very reactive. The water molecule is both physically small and highly polar – that is, one side of the molecule has a net positive charge while the other side is negative. Water can thus go places and pull on atoms better than other solvents. Pure H_2O is even able to fatigue glass surfaces and promote fracture. Adding a few nasties such as cerium oxide to the mix amplifies the chemical power of this process.

Here, then, we have the somewhat unsatisfactory answer to the cerium conundrum. A combination of mechanical action and chemical bonding weakens the gem material, and the surface is literally pulled apart at the molecular level. The fact that chemically polished surfaces, unlike those prepared with ductile grinding, exhibit very little internal stress indicates that the amount of mechanical shearing of the surface is minimal.

Doing Acid

Chapter 7 of Gerald Wykoff's classic book "The Techniques of Master Faceting" provides a fascinating glimpse into the role of chemicals in the polishing process. He describes a visit to East Asian lapidary factories, where the workers toiled in heavy protective gear in front of air exchangers, to avoid contact with strong acid fumes. In his Chapter 7, Wykoff presents a remarkable photograph of such a worker and notes memorably that "a well-dressed faceter, polishing with acid, wears: rubber gloves, long sleeved shirt, rubber apron, safety eye glasses, and a respirator because, while acids contribute to a superb polish, they are poisonous, toxic, corrosive, and caustic..."

Luckily, you don't have to go this far. Amateur gem cutters have used dilute acids such as vinegar for decades, but their effectiveness has been called into question in recent years (see "Lube Job" on page 298). Although strongly espoused by some, fewer and fewer hobby faceters see the need for such chemicals.

8.12 Laps and Polishing Agents

Polishing gemstones requires a healthy amount of art, in addition to the science discussed in the previous section. As with mixing paint on a palette, the correct combination of inputs, in this case the lap and polishing agent, can spell the difference between success and frustration. Having a decent selection of both laps and polishes will give you the flexibility to react to new gemstone materials or problem facets.

A typical amateur faceter will have three or four different types of polishing lap. Table 3-3 on page 74 lists the most popular varieties. You don't need to rush out and drop several hundred dollars on polishing laps, however, at least not right away. Most hobbyists start cutting quartz and beryl, which polish extremely well with inexpensive Ultralaps. A good choice for a second lap is one of the metal alloys such as zinc, tin, or, best of all in my opinion, a BATT lap.

While the variety of polishing laps seems to have increased in recent years, the field of popular polishing agents has narrowed somewhat. In their seminal book *Faceting for Amateurs*, first published in 1969, Glenn and Martha Vargas identify nine different polishing agents in relatively common use. These include cerium oxide, diamonds, and alumina, which are very familiar today. Also on the list were oxides of tin, iron (rouge), chrome, and zirconium, as well as more odd substances such as rotten stone (see Chapter 4.12) and barnesite, a mixture of rare earth oxides that was popular as a glass polish among amateur telescope makers in the mid-1900's.

Nowadays, cerium oxide and diamond are the overwhelming favourites, with alumina still holding its own among devotees of garnet, peridot, and beryl. These agents usually come in powdered form, although impregnated laps are also available. Chapters 3 and 4.12 contain considerably more information on the common types of lap and polishing agent, respectively.

8.12.1 The Combination is the Key…

Wonderful! There is an enormous selection of (occasionally costly) laps out there and two or three different polishing agents. Which lap goes with which agent for which stone?

The answer is simple: use whatever works.

Needless to say, the combinations are nearly endless. Table 8-1 attempts to summarize the conventional wisdom, but as the foregoing paragraphs have made clear, you will always discover new problems and new possibilities. Ultralaps may be a good way to start, but as you gain confidence and want to try more interesting and challenging gem materials, you will inevitably collect more laps and try different polishing agents with each. Keep careful track of your experiences and talk with others at the lapidary club or online. Not all combinations will work – keep notes and if you find the magical mix, stick with it and tell your friends.

One semi-obvious cautionary note about mixing polishing agents: be careful about cross contamination. The metal oxides are generally benign and can be effectively removed from a lap with gentle scrubbing. Diamond particles, on the other hand, work by embedding themselves in the metal matrix of the lap itself, and they do not easily let go. Although most users have no problem using the same metal lap for both oxides and diamond, you should consult the manufacturer or online resources for your particular lap. Needless to say, even stronger cautionary words apply to changing grades of diamond: you can re-charge an alloy lap with a coarser mesh, but don't go the other way. Buy a new lap or use the flip side.

Table 8-1 Lap and polishing agent combinations for common gemstone materials.

Material	Lap / Polishing Agent	Material	Lap / Polishing Agent
Beryl	just about any: CeO_2 or alumina on composite or metal; diamonds on metal or ceramic	Peridot	alumina on metal (vinegar can help); alumina on composite; diamond on metal or ceramic
Chrysoberyl	diamonds on metal or ceramic / alumina on metal	Quartz	CeO_2 Ultralap; CeO_2 on composite or metal; alumina on metal
Corundum	diamonds on metal or ceramic	Spinel	alumina on metal or composite; diamonds on metal or ceramic
Cubic Zirconia	diamonds on metal or ceramic; alumina on metal	Topaz	alumina on metal or composite; diamonds on metal or ceramic
Garnet	alumina on composite or metal; diamonds on metal or ceramic; CeO_2 on composite or metal	Tourmaline	alumina or CeO_2 on composite or metal; diamonds on metal or ceramic
Opal	CeO_2 Ultralap; CeO_2 on composite or metal	Zircon	alumina on metal or composite; diamonds on metal or ceramic

8.13 Pre-Polish

If you learn nothing else from this book, learn this: the best way to guarantee faceting success is to build on success. Chapter 5 emphasizes that you cannot get a nice, symmetrical stone unless you build on an accurate initial center-point and girdle. You also cannot get facets to meet unless all the previous tiers are more or less in order.

The lesson in this chapter is that you cannot get a good polish without good cutting. You can learn this lesson in a few minutes by reading and absorbing the following paragraphs, or you can do as I did and spend long, hard, educational hours on the polishing lap.

Do you remember *subsurface damage,* our deadly enemy from page 302? He's back and he's about to get even.

Subsurface damage is without doubt the leading cause of "polishing problems" among beginners. I place "polishing problems" in quotes because subsurface damage is really a cutting error, not a polishing error. There is nothing like a properly executed fine polish to bring out all the uglies left by your cutting laps. Of course, these uglies are immediately interpreted as too much diamond on the polishing lap or some other bogus polishing issue. The beginner attempts an array of corrections to his or her polishing technique, all to no avail. In fact, the better the actual polish, the worse the scratches look. The obvious interpretation is that polishing is difficult.

Wrong wrong wrong. Here...I'll say it again: wrong.

A good polish needs a properly prepared surface, and a properly prepared surface is one in which all the macroscopic cracks and scratches have been cut away by a succession of finer and finer cutting laps. The result is called a *pre-polish.*

How can you tell whether you have reached a proper pre-polish? Typically, you should be able to easily see into the body of the stone and get reflections off the surface (refer to "Seeing the Pre-Polish" below). Experience with different laps and gem materials will also be a great help, but the ultimate proof is in the pudding. If scratches persist – that is, existing scratches don't go away, but, thankfully, new ones don't appear – then you more than likely have subsurface damage. At this point it may be quicker, easier, and less frustrating in the long run to bite the bullet and go back to the fine cutting lap and get things right.

Seeing the Pre-Polish

How can you tell if the pre-polish is coming in properly?

With a good pre-polish, the surface of the gem should already have the start of a transparent glossy finish. You should be able to see inside the body of the stone, and you should also be able to see clear reflections at grazing incidence (Figure 8-23). Needless to say, there must be no significant meet point errors or surface scratches and flaws at this stage.

For most materials, you will execute the fine cut or pre-polish with a NuBond type resin lap or a very fine diamond mesh. Because they serve this important function, the Nu-Bond and fine diamond disks are often called "pre-polish laps."

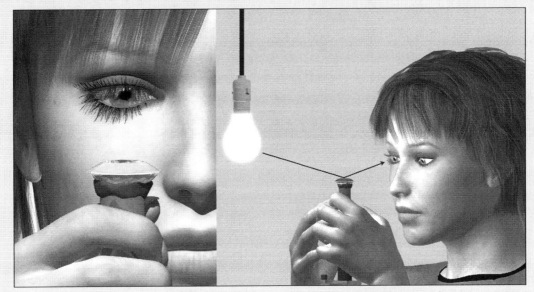

Figure 8-23 Seeing reflections off a pre-polished surface at grazing incidence.

8.14 The Charge of the Lap Brigade...

Modern diamond-bonded steel cutting laps (Chapter 3.2.3) are truly a luxury in terms of ease of use: just drop them on the spindle, fire up the motor, and go.

No such luck with polishing laps.

Most polishing laps need preparation to work properly. The exact nature of this preparation depends strongly on the type of lap, but it can range from simple cleaning to scoring the lap surface to (most commonly) charging the lap with a polishing agent. Because polishing lap preparation varies so widely, the following sections deal separately with each major lap type.

8.14.1 Prepping Bonded Polishing Laps

The combination of ease of use and polishing performance on softer stones, such as quartz and beryl, makes the bonded polishing lap an excellent choice for beginners. This category includes the popular Ultralap family of impregnated polishing sheets, as well as bonded solid laps, such as the venerable Pol-A-Gem, the Dyna Disk, and the Greenway / Creamway laps from Gearloose (see Chapter 3.3.2). Bonded laps do not need to be charged: the polishing compound, almost always cerium oxide or alumina, is pre-mixed into the plastic matrix forming the surface of the lap.

Of course, as with any lap, the abrasive particles eventually become dull and/or ineffective, resulting in significantly reduced polishing action. Luckily, the metal oxide bonded laps can be "re-charged," simply by preparing them exactly like any other lap that accepts cerium oxide or alumina (see next section).

There is one preparatory step that is unique to Ultralaps: proper mounting on the spindle. Ultralaps are thin Mylar sheets and have no structural support or strength. As such, they must be used in conjunction with a flat, supporting disk such as a master lap. You might also consider using your pre-polish lap as a support, since it should allow you to use the same height and cheater settings. Consult the manufacturer's instructions or see page 170 for detailed information on mounting Ultralaps on your faceting machine.

8.14.2 Prepping Lucite or Metal Laps with Oxide Polish

The metal oxides, especially cerium oxide and alumina, are the traditional polishing agents for quartz and beryl (see Table 8-1). Although now somewhat eclipsed by the pre-charged bonded versions, a Lucite lap charged with metal oxide can produce a fine, mirror-like polish. Popular metal laps, such as those made of zinc or BATT material, can do the same.

Charging with powdered metal oxide is relatively easy and fun, at least for those who like finger painting. The goal is to create a *slurry*, that is, a milky solution with water that can easily be spread across the lap surface. Some hobbyists have had difficulty with mineral-rich (hard) tap water and suggest distilled water instead.

You should aim for the consistency of milk, not cream. This corresponds roughly to a teaspoon of compound in a small jar. Some faceters pre-mix the oxide with water in a

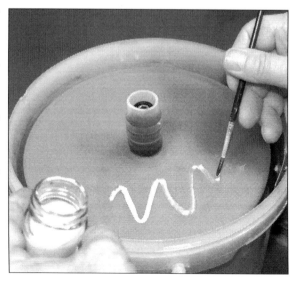

Figure 8-24 Paint a small amount of the oxide-water slurry on the lap prior to spreading it with a finger..

plastic pump spray bottle, while others blend the two in a small container and paint the slurry onto the lap using a brush. The real fun-lovers combine the powder and water directly on the lap surface.

Whichever technique you employ, make sure that the oxide is well mixed and free of any clumps. Agglomerated metal oxide particles can lead to scratches. Smear a small amount of the slurry with your (clean) finger over the entire lap surface, and wipe away any excess with a paper towel. You are ready to begin – just don't forget to use a steady but slow water drip, since over-dry abrasive can produce excess heat and lead to the dreaded agglomeration blues. As with all polishing agents, the usual beginner's mistake is to use too much.

8.14.3 Charging Metal Polishing Laps with Diamond

Metal polishing laps enjoy wide popularity, since they work well with most gemstone varieties and produce sharp, flat facets. Charging such laps is also relatively easy, particularly in comparison to ceramics.

Properly prepared, the surface of a metal lap contains countless, partially embedded diamond crystals, whose sharp edges do all of the actual work. The metal of the lap itself is very soft – Mohs hardness 3-5 – and serves only as structural support, allowing the diamonds to do their magic from a firm, flat reference plane. In the ideal case, the metal never touches the gemstone, and in fact, the appearance of metal flakes on partially polished facets is a sure sign that it's time to add more diamond.

Charging a metal lap involves getting the diamond properly embedded into the metal. The exact technique varies somewhat, since you can purchase diamond polishing agent in several different forms. These include loose diamond bort, pre-mixed paste, and diamond spray.

Begin by cleaning and drying the metal lap thoroughly. If you are using loose bort, scatter several drops of extender fluid across the lap. Alternatively, you can apply a thin layer of spray oil such as WD-40. Using a clean fingertip, rub the fluid into the lap until the entire surface is covered uniformly. Place your still-oily finger over the mouth of the vial of diamond powder and invert, allowing a small amount of diamond to adhere to the tip. Smear this diamond onto the lap (Figure 8-25). Repeat this process three or four times, and then begin working the smear marks across the surface of the lap until it is uniformly gray in colour.

Diamond paste is a little easier. Place 3-4 beads, each ~0.1 inch (2 mm) in size at several locations on the surface of the clean lap. Using a clean fingertip, spread the paste until the surface is coated uniformly.

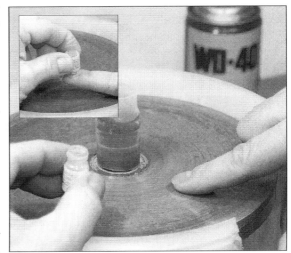

Figure 8-25 Charging a polishing lap with loose diamond bort. See text for details.

Figure 8-26 A steel ball bearing held in place on a screwdriver forces the diamond particles into the surface of the metal lap. An inexpensive piece of synthetic corundum is an excellent alternative (see "Musings on a Synthetic Ruby" on page 223).

Diamond spray is easier still. Shake the bottle to mix up the diamond and then hit the lap with 2-3 full sprays.

Let the embedding begin! The basic idea is to force the diamond particles into the surface of the slowly turning lap using something hard. This something can be a chunk of synthetic corundum (Figure 6-18), a dressing stick, or even a steel ball bearing on a screwdriver (Figure 8-26).

Work your chosen tool across the surface of the lap, applying steady firm pressure. Three to five minutes of effort should ensure a good charge. Wipe away any excess compound with a clean paper towel, and then start polishing!

To Score or Not to Score

No, dude, "scoring a lap" does not mean getting a totally excellent price on a Falcon ceramic. It refers to the practice of introducing irregular scratch marks onto the surface of a (usually metal) lap to improve its polishing performance.

The justification for this practice is threefold. First, with all the additional surface area and crevices, the lap can hold the polishing compound better and hence polish longer. Adherents also believe that the grooves supply an escape route for polishing residue to flow away from the stone and toward the edge of the lap. Less junk on the contact surface of the lap means less scratching. Finally, scorers argue that the irregular surface reduces metal to stone contact, thereby eliminating a potentially dangerous source of overheating.

Unfortunately for such wonderful theories, there is no actual evidence that scoring helps. In fact, as near as I can tell, the faceting community, from rank beginner to grand master, is about evenly split on the benefits of scoring. And, like the great wax versus glue dopping controversy, the practice of scoring stimulates endless debate, both online and at the lapidary club. You have been warned.

There is one unambiguous down side to scoring a metal lap, however. Digging into the surface of the metal raises small ridges and bumps, whose combined effect is to "soften" the lap surface. Until such features are banged flat and the damaged zone work-hardened, the lap will produce somewhat rounded facets.

If you choose to score your laps, use a commercial scoring tool or a section of hacksaw blade. Work steadily from spindle to edge on the slowly turning lap, checking regularly

that you are laying down a relatively uniform pattern of scratches (Figure 8-27).

When you are satisfied, clean the lap thoroughly under running water to remove the larger fragments of metal. It is also a good idea to burnish the surface by holding a piece of scrap quartz against the turning lap. Use plenty of water, but no polishing agent. This process should serve to knock down the largest bumps and ridges, minimizing the softening effect that scoring introduces.

Figure 8-27 Surface scoring of a metal alloy lap.

8.14.4 Charging Ceramic Polishing Laps with Diamond

Ceramic laps are highly valued among serious gem cutters for the wonderfully flat facets and sharp edges they produce. Such performance comes at a price, however, since ceramic laps are notoriously difficult to use.

Ironically, the process of applying diamond polishing agent to a ceramic lap is largely an exercise in removing diamond from the lap, not adding it. This is because, unlike with the metal variety, the diamond does not become embedded in the lap matrix. Ceramic laps are extremely hard – comparable to corundum. As a result, the diamond particles tumble around on the surface of the lap, polishing the stone (and the lap) as they go. See "Two Body Versus Three Body Abrasion" on page 286 for more. An additional consequence of this is that the ceramic lap needs to be re-charged regularly as the diamond particles break down and polishing slows. It is not uncommon to re-charge a ceramic lap after every facet tier. Finally, these laps can require a break-in period, and if the ceramic becomes glazed, a treatment with a dressing stick. See Chapter 4.9.1 and consult the lap manufacturer's instructions for more.

There are almost as many approaches to charging ceramic laps as there are advocates for their use (the wags out there might remark that in either case, this is not a large number). For example, some experienced faceters recommend using a boron carbide ("Norbide") dressing stick to both break in and charge a ceramic lap. Others simply sprinkle the abrasive on the oiled surface of the ceramic and then have at it.

All of these strategies share one common goal, however: distributing a tiny amount of diamond uniformly over the lap surface. Most users combine the diamond with oil (olive oil is a favourite), graphite, wax, or some other lubricant. Unless you like the sound of fighting cats, you should do this as well.

Begin by applying a layer of your lubricant of choice to the lap surface. This is particularly important if the lap is new. If you are using oil, place about a dozen drops around the surface of the lap. Then, with the spindle turning very slowly, carefully scrape and spread the oil uniformly over the surface using a straight razor blade. Emphasis on the word "carefully" – blood is a notoriously poor lubricant. Wipe away any excess oil with a clean paper towel.

Some cutters use a spray-type oil such as WD-40, applying a light, uniform layer before scraping and wiping the surface. Powdered graphite is another interesting option, particularly since this approach uses pure elemental carbon as both the abrasive and lubricant (see "Diamonds are Forever...?" on page 81 of Volume 2). To go all-carbon, combine about half a teaspoon (8 ml) of graphite powder with an equivalent amount of diamond extender fluid and an ounce (30 ml) of alcohol in a small plastic spray bottle. Shake well and apply a spritz or two to the lap, rub it thoroughly into the surface, and then wipe away any excess with a clean paper towel.

Figure 8-28 Charging a ceramic lap with spray diamond. Note the second bottle filled with lubricant.

With the lap properly lubricated, you are ready to apply the diamond. The standard 50k grit works well, but competition cutters tend to go for the finer stuff, either 100k or 200k. Combine half a teaspoon (8 ml) of well-shaken diamond spray, half a teaspoon (8 ml) of extender fluid and 1-2 ounces (30-60 ml) of alcohol in a small plastic spray bottle. Shake well. Aim a single short blast toward the lubricated lap from a distance of about a foot (30 cm). Wipe the surface of the slowly turning lap from the spindle outward with a clean paper towel dampened with alcohol. Repeat the wiping process with a second piece of paper towel and you should be good to go. No water drip necessary. Use slow lap rotation speeds for best results.

Actually, you will probably get scratches, and scratches from a ceramic lap are almost always a sign that you have too much diamond. Try (carefully) scraping the slowly turning lap with the razor blade and repeat the wiping process with the alcohol-dampened towel. Try diluting the diamond spray even further. If all else fails, thoroughly wash the lap surface in the sink and try again.

Keep the lubricant and diamond spray bottles nearby. If the squealing gets out of control, apply a bit of lubricant. If polishing slows, try adding a little diamond. If you see build up of cutting material on the lap, clean the surface with alcohol and re-charge with lubricant and diamond. Most of all, don't panic and don't despair. Sooner or later, you will get the hang of it, and when you do, you will be rewarded with the flattest, eye-poppingest facets imaginable.

8.15 Putting Stone to Lap

All charged up and ready to go?

In principle, polishing amounts to little more than lowering the stone onto the lap and rubbing until everything looks good. Of course there are subtleties, but they are almost always associated with reacting to problems, and naturally, you will never encounter any of those, right?

Simple statements about lap speed, amount of polishing compound, and so forth are difficult, since they will vary from lap to lap and stone to stone. Chapter 3 and the previous section give general advice, but you should take it easy until you grasp all the variables in play. By the way, in the previous sentence, "take it easy" means using lower lap speed and less polishing compound. This almost always helps.

Before taking the plunge, another regular sanity check is in order. Make sure that you have the correct index, angle, cheater, and mast height settings, and double check that all the relevant locking mechanisms are snug and the motor is turning the right way. See Section 8.9.2 for more preparatory tips. Don't learn the hard way: a serious mistake in these settings can be every bit as disastrous now as it was during the cutting phase. The polishing lap removes very little stone, but it has a correspondingly reduced ability to compensate for errors. A major misstep at this stage may force you back to the fine cutting lap.

As with cutting, you should hold the stone, not the quill, dop, or handle. Apply firm but not excessive pressure and try to get a tactile feel for the polishing process. Your fingers often recognize that there is a problem long before your eyes or ears can sense that something has gone wrong.

Polish a little and look a lot. This is particularly important when starting a new tier of facets. Slight differences in cutting angle or index are very important at this stage, and they may not represent explicit errors in the various settings. For example, you may see a slight but systematic difference in cheater value between fine cutting and polishing, due to irregularities or dishing of the lap surfaces (see "Nail that Polish" below).

Such small errors manifest themselves as localized or directional polish (see Figure 5-46), and this effect is most visible and easy to understand on a pre-polished, not fine-polished, surface. Fix the problem as early as possible on the first facet of a tier, before it becomes an enduring headache. As always, take careful and complete notes (see Section 8.8).

Finally, make sure that you read Chapter 5.5.6. It provides further wisdom and tips on getting polishing right.

Nail that Polish

Everything is going well. You have done a great job cutting and pre-polishing your gem, and you are raring to go on the polish. Everything is in place, you touch the first facet down to the lap, and then lift it up to examine what is happening…

Instead of the first sign of a nice polish coming in across the facet, you notice that one edge has been polished completely, leaving the remainder of the facet untouched.

What's going on and what can you do about it?

A number of things could be happening. You could have dialed in an incorrect cutting angle or index wheel setting, but of course you checked all that thoroughly before lowering the stone to the lap (see page 313). Pat your chia pet on its pretty green head and press on…

The more likely culprit is lap wear. Turn to page 72 to learn more about this insidious process, the effect of which is to cause a systematic difference in angle between your various laps. For example, my well-worn NuBond 1200 pre-polish lap requires a one-notch clockwise twist of the cheater to get things right. If I don't twist back after I am done, the polish ends up on one side of the facet.

Lap wear and other effects are an ever-present fact of life in front of the faceting machine, and I would in no way suggest that you replace any lap which shows evidence of dishing and wear. Instead, you can compensate for most of the effect by taking careful notes and predicting the appropriate correction, the one-notch twist that leads to uniform polishing goodness.

If that doesn't work and you are simply lost, you can experimentally determine the appropriate angle and cheater settings. Try inking the facet as described in "Seeing the Facets" on page 301 or the toothpaste test in Chapter 7.6.1. Alternatively, if you are using diamond on a metal lap, the thin coating of lubricant will leave an unambiguous signature on a clean facet. Wipe the stone completely clean – a microfiber cloth really helps here – and then rub the facet briefly on the stationary lap. A quick examination under the loupe should reveal which way to adjust things. Figure 5-46 explains what to do next.

Incidentally, these techniques are also the key to success in re-cutting damaged stones or in re-establishing rotational alignment if you have to remove the dop from the quill.

Finally, keep careful notes. Seriously. Playing around with the cutting angle and cheater can help you nail that polish, but without meticulous record-keeping, it may well lead to confusion and headaches. I'll say it again: keep careful notes. Section 8.8 suggests one scheme for doing so.

8.16 Polishing Sequence

For all of its other difficulties, the polishing phase is delightfully devoid of choices in lap sequencing. Unlike cutting, which requires a carefully chosen series of grit sizes for best results, most hobby faceters polish in a single step on a single lap.

One exception to this rule is the practice of giving a final post-polish "kiss" of metal oxide to a surface previously polished with diamond. This custom arises from the perception among many that diamond particles leave a "streaky" or "greasy" finish, which the lightest of touches with cerium oxide or alumina can clean away (see page 116). If you also feel this way, by all means go for a two-lap run when you polish.

So much for sequencing laps. Is there any other type of polishing sequence?

Actually, yes. The other important sequence during polishing relates to the facet order. Intuition may suggest that you should polish the stone in the same order as you cut it, in other words, by following the sequence in the cutting diagram. But there are other ways, some of them potentially better. For example, Glenn and Martha Vargas argue for a polishing sequence from the culet toward the girdle for the pavilion, and from the table toward the girdle for the crown (*Faceting for Amateurs*, p. 180). Are they right?

As with so many aspects of our hobby, the proper facet sequence during polishing is very much a matter of personal taste and hot debate. For example, highly qualified cutters, whom

I respect, argue that the optimum sequence is the one that minimizes angle and height changes. This both speeds the polishing process and minimizes the likelihood of gross errors.

I have essentially always followed the cutting prescription sequence for at least two very good reasons. First, the facet order may be essential to establishing meet point targets for later tiers. Since it is possible to shift meet points around a little on the polishing lap, getting the stone absolutely correct geometrically may depend on completing the meets in order.

The second reason to follow the published sequence is familiarity. By the time you get to 50k diamond or metal oxide, you will have executed a certain sequence of angles and index wheel settings several times. Doing it once more is familiar territory, and is less likely to result in a mistake.

There is a third argument for following the order in the diagram, at least to the point of doing the table last. With most faceting machines, cutting or polishing the table requires removal of the dop and gem from the quill and the use of a 45° adapter (see Chapters 4.15 and 5.8). Removing the dop loses the rotational reference between the facets on the stone and the index wheel. Keyed dops can help, but for top quality gemstones, they simply do not allow accurate replacement without a subsequent alignment check (see Chapter 7.6).

The end result of all this is that I recommend both cutting and polishing the table at the very end, after the rest of the gem is complete. With care (and a little luck), the table can float in and hit all of its meet points. In that instance, no subsequent touch-up is necessary. Executing the table earlier on would require at least one more dop removal, re-installation, and alignment step. See Section 8.19 below for further tips on polishing the table facet.

Throwing a Curveball

I hate myself a little bit for including the following paragraphs, and I hope that my faceting teacher will close his eyes and skip to the next section, because I am going to tell you how to cheat.

Not cheat in the cheater sense. That's not real cheating (see "Cheat to Win..." on page 25). This type of cheating is genuine skullduggery.

Here's the situation: You have a complex gem design, and the meet points simply aren't coming in. There is something fundamentally wrong somewhere, but you cannot find it. Yes, you could, and in an ideal universe, should, go back to the beginning, re-cutting everything carefully to eliminate the problem.

Right. Maybe in some other universe.

There is a nefarious alternative: curved facets. Chapter 2.1 defines a gemstone as a convex volume subtended by the intersection of many flat planes. What happens if some of those planes aren't exactly flat?

Figure 8-29 shows the answer. By slightly and continuously varying the cutting angle, height, and even cheater settings, you can curve the facet and extend it to make one meet point without disturbing the others. This can go a long way toward solving your problems.

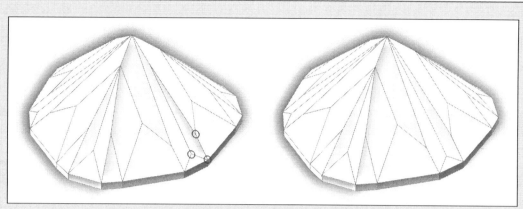

Figure 8-29 Curving a facet can help you make meet points. In the left panel, three meets came in fine (circled) long before the fourth corner of the facet reached the culet. By curving the facet slightly (right panel), you can make the fourth meet without disturbing the others. Careful examination would reveal that the facet is indeed slightly curved. This is the FanCZ design from Chapter 19.

Needless to say, there is a whole raft of warnings associated with this activity. First of all, there are definite limits. You cannot curve a facet too much before it starts looking awful – in fact, much worse than missed meet points. A corollary of this is that the method works best on facets whose neighbours are close in both cutting angle and facet index. For such facets, minor adjustments have the most effect (see Figure 5-48). Similarly, wide facets are more likely to reveal your trickery than narrow ones. You should perform any facet curving on the polishing lap only, since it would be difficult or impossible to reproduce the exact sequence of angle and height changes with two or more separate laps. Finally, don't try this if you are entering a competition. The judges are not fools, and they will justifiably skewer you for thinking that they are.

I cannot in good conscience recommend facet curving. Nor can I in good conscience state that I never do it. There. I feel a little better...

8.17 Troubleshooting Polishing

Essentially all of the comments earlier in this chapter regarding troubleshooting during the cutting phase carry over directly to polishing (see Section 8.9). As with cutting, pro-active, preventive measures at the polishing stage can reduce errors and minimize their impact when they occur. Corrective action may require repeating an earlier step in the process, although unlike with cutting, polishing errors rarely force a dramatic change in overall gem size or design.

Polishing has its own idiosyncrasies – some would say pathologies – and this section attempts to provide useful advice on preventing and reacting to them. Let's begin, however, at the beginning: how to determine whether you have a problem.

8.17.1 Finding Fault

It is a frustrating fact of faceting life that it can be very difficult to see minor scratches and other imperfections in a polished facet. Getting an accurate impression of the surface quality requires proper lighting, magnification, and patience.

Of course, it is also an encouraging fact of faceting life that it can be very difficult to see minor scratches and imperfections in a polished facet. Unless you are cutting for competition, it is often the best strategy to do the best you can and let the beauty and sparkle of the completed gemstone take care of the rest.

To reveal what you don't really want to see, experiment with a variety of lamp arrangements and loupes. I find that a single, bright, unfrosted bulb in an otherwise darkened room works best. I use relatively high magnification (10-20X) and examine the facet just to the side of the reflection of the filament in the facet. Under these conditions, scratches and imperfectly polished regions manifest themselves as whitish zones that are easy to pick out against the otherwise dark reflection. Turn to "Seeing is Believing..." on page 173 for more on seeing scratches.

8.17.2 Preventing Problems

As mentioned five paragraphs up, the best approach to dealing with polishing problems is to avoid them in the first place. Yes, the same silly and condescending advice from Section 8.9.2. Particularly silly and condescending, since you just spent over two hours on that one bleeping facet, just trying to get a decent polish to come in. Trust me, however, that a few simple precautions can save a great deal of time on the polishing lap, to say nothing of time spent explaining to the spouse the broken glass and 8-inch metal disk lying in the garden outside your workshop window.

The primary and most effective preventive measure is to ensure that you are truly ready for polish. This means that all the cutting was executed properly with accurate meet points and, most importantly, complete removal of subsurface damage caused by the coarser laps. If you have not read and absorbed the material in Section 8.13, go back and read it again. Photocopy it and mount it on the wall above your faceting machine. Consider having it tattooed on a visible part of your body.

The simple fact is that most polishing problems, especially among beginners, are not due to bad polishing technique but rather to bad – or more specifically, incomplete – cutting.

Contamination is also a leading cause of polishing perplexity and pain. The abrasive particles used in polishing are micron-sized and smaller (below 1/25,000 of an inch – see Table 3-1). The grit embedded in your typical cutting lap is a boulder by comparison. Any such particle present on your polishing lap will soon make itself known in obvious and awful ways.

The best strategy for dealing with contamination is by isolation, both before and after the fact. Always keep your laps separated, ideally in individual plastic bags or containers (see Chapter 4.9.2). Perform a general clean-up of your work area whenever you switch from coarser to finer grit, and particularly when transitioning from cutting to polishing. Note that your "work area" includes your hands. Dealing with polishing lap contamination, once it occurs, is also an exercise in isolation – see the next section.

You should complement your contamination prevention campaign with a close look at your cutting laps. Some bonded steel laps have been known to fail in an arrestingly nasty fashion, steadily releasing their payload of coarse diamond grit to the environment. If you notice persistent contamination problems and have a veteran steel lap, consider skipping it for a couple of stones to see if the problem disappears. Self-charged copper cutting laps (see Chapter

3.2.2) are also an excellent source of diamond grit contamination. Yes, the hard-core faceters love them, but ask yourself, do I really need a homemade cutting lap? Is it really worth the cost and effort of replacing the workshop window?

The final preventive measure may seem obvious, but it is often ignored: use the correct lap and polishing agent for the type of gem that you are cutting. Table 8-1 will help you get it right.

8.17.3 Polishing Problems and How to Deal with Them

Are you a beginning faceter, with perhaps two or three gemstones under your belt? If so, I am willing to bet that this is the very first chapter and section you looked at. Why am I so sure? Well, I remember polishing my first few gems. I would like to say with fondness, but I can't. Difficulty during the polishing phase is undoubtedly the most mysterious and frustrating aspect of faceting, and I suspect it leads to more people quitting than anything else.

It doesn't have to be this way. It really doesn't.

Remember. Prevention first. If this really is the first part of the book you have looked at, please turn back a page or two to the section on preventing problems. In terms of actual polishing, a few simple strategies, coupled with the experience and confidence gained by completing more and more gems, should lead you through the minefield of polishing difficulties. This section explains some of these strategies. You're going to have to build your own experience and confidence.

Scratches

I hate scratches. I really hate them. Not only can they ruin the appearance of an otherwise perfect facet, but they also have an extraordinarily nasty habit of popping up suddenly at the worst of times and in the worst of places. Like a child's jack-in-the-box, you can crank away happily, enjoying the music, but you know that, sooner or later, Jack will appear. The following paragraphs explain some of the reasons why scratches occur and what you can do to keep Jack in his box.

Lap Contamination

Surface contamination of the polishing lap may be the worst of the many possible causes of scratching, since it usually leads to multiple, deep gouges. Contamination scratches occur alone or in groups parallel to the motion of the lap. In the worst instances, you can feel or (horrors!) hear them occur. If you suspect a contamination problem, stop polishing immediately and assess the situation. Having a polished chunk of scrap quartz at hand lets you test the lap surface. If holding the quartz against the lap produces similar ugly scratches, you almost certainly have a contamination problem.

If contamination occurs, the first step is to clean the lap thoroughly with flowing water and a non-metallic scouring pad, followed by a recharge with polishing compound. Test the resurfaced lap with your scrap quartz. If the problem goes away, great! You can probably carry right on. If the problem persists after a good scrubbing, the offending particle is likely embedded in the surface of the lap. The following paragraphs explain what to do next, assuming that you have a Lucite, metal, or bonded resin lap. Embedding a foreign particle into a ceramic lap takes a rather heavy hand and is pretty unlikely to occur.

Isolating and Eliminating Contamination

The first step is to locate exactly where on the lap the problem occurs. You could use your almost-completed gemstone, experimenting with various locations to see where the truly awful scratching occurs. You could also use your skull to evaluate how hard a brick wall is.

A better suggestion is to use your piece of scrap quartz to find where the interloper is lurking. Touch your sample down on the turning lap at various radii to locate the source. At some point, you should notice that scratching occurred, and you may even be able to locate the particle itself by examining the lap surface for a whitish tail of residue (Figure 8-30).

If that fails, stop the lap and sweep the quartz from the lap nut to the edge at the six-o'clock position (i.e. closest to you). By manually advancing the lap rotation and checking regularly, you should be able to pinpoint the source. Circle the offender with an indelible marker.

Once you locate the problem, try some hard-core localized scrubbing and flushing with water. If you still experience scratching on the scrap quartz, you can try digging out the particle with a small screwdriver. Don't worry about the damage that this might cause: the

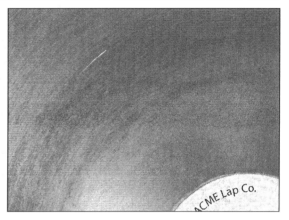

Figure 8-30 A small piece of scrap quartz can help you localize the source of contamination scratching. Large, hard, embedded particles will leave a telltale streak. Note that this photograph has been altered for illustrative purposes. I am pretty obsessive about cross-contamination, and have never suffered from buried boulders…knock on wood.

Indirect Infection

One of the darker aspects of the opening of the New World was the shameful idea of trading smallpox-infected blankets to the Native Americans. The deadly virus, only a few microns across, would cling to the fibers in the blanket, waiting to do its deadly work on the next human who came in contact with the cloth. Historians are unsure whether this disgusting plan ever came into practice, but it does convey a warning for modern faceters.

Although far more benign on the global scale of things, errant abrasive also has a nasty propensity to cling to fibers and go where it is not wanted. And, as with human diseases, the path of transmission of these micron-size particles may be somewhat indirect. For example, a piece of paper towel laid down on a workbench can pick up a piece of grit and transfer it to the gem the next time you wipe it to get a view of the polish. Working the infected stone against the lap can embed the particle in the surface, and voilà! Contamination and scratching.

You can break this chain of infection before it starts. Always keep your work area scrupulously clean and make sure that any cloth or paper wipes are fresh and uncontaminated. Wash your hands each time you switch to a finer cutting or polishing lap. Check and clean the nooks and crannies of your machine, and don't forget to give the dop and stone a quick wipe as well.

area should be quite small, and it will soon be worn flat and (for metal laps) work-hardened. Besides, the lap was largely useless with the contamination in place.

If all efforts to isolate and remove the contamination fall short, you have three options. First, you can simply discard the lap or use it for other purposes (master lap, Frisbee, etc.). Metal laps can be resurfaced by any competent machinist, although if you use diamonds, give him or her fair warning. Diamonds have a tendency to be really hard and machine tools have a tendency to be really expensive. The third option is not for the faint of heart: clearly mark the area of contamination and continue using the lap. And try not to forget what that funny ink circle is for...

Polishing Agent Agglomeration

Although not nearly as serious as lap contamination, the clumping-up or *agglomeration* of polishing agent more than makes up for it in frequency of occurrence. Luckily, agglomeration problems are very easy to avoid and remedy. Agglomeration scratches fall into two general categories: those associated with too much polishing agent and those caused by a lack of lubricant on the lap.

Here's a useful maxim for polishing that applies equally well in your wider life: less is more. Simply using less polishing agent can eliminate the lion's share of agglomeration scratching. This is true for both metal oxide polishes and diamond bort. As always, when faced with sudden scratching problems, you should try cleaning and recharging the lap first. This time, use less polishing agent.

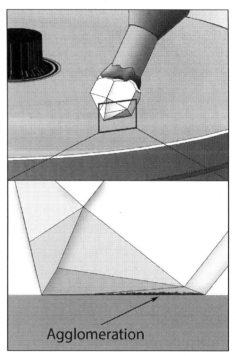

Note that certain gem shapes may be particularly vulnerable to agglomeration scratching. If two adjacent facets meet at a very shallow angle, there will be a thin air wedge between stone and lap as you polish (Figure 8-31). This geometry is particularly good at picking up (and agglomerating) any excess polishing agent on the lap.

Figure 8-31 Adjacent facets with nearly the same angle and index wheel setting can encourage agglomeration scratching. Here, the P1 and P3 facets of GeM101 (see Chapter 5) are the culprit.

Even with the correct amount of agent present, surface conditions on the lap can cause the abrasive particles to ball up and cause scratching. This is almost always due to a lack of water in the case of metal oxide polishes and a lack of oil/extender fluid in the case of diamonds. There will be other evidence of poor conditions, beyond the scratching of your beloved facets. Improper lubrication leads to a distinctly different tactile "pull" of the stone as you sweep it across the lap. With experience, you will recognize this phenomenon in time to correct the situation before scratching occurs. Of course, experience will teach you how much lubricant is enough in the first place. Everyone's a winner.

Self Scratching

When polishing goes bad, there is an unfortunate tendency to start throwing around blame. The source of the scratching is lap contamination, or agglomeration, or oversized grit in the polishing agent. Actually, in many instances, the guilty party is the gemstone itself. A number of conditions can lead to small chunks of the gem breaking away and tumbling in destructive fashion across the polished facet. To quote Shakespeare, the fault, dear Brutus, is not in our stars, but in ourselves (…this is the correct quotation from Julius Caesar. I mangle it horribly in Chapter 15.3).

As a matter of course, you should examine your stone carefully throughout the cutting and polishing stages. Are there bubbles or crumbly regions inside the gem that can come to the surface and cause problems? Often, the appearance of a tiny "crater" in the middle of a facet coincides with sudden scratching. In this case, an internal flaw has broken through the facet to cause general havoc. Quartz, tourmaline, and beryl are particularly prone to such flaws and their resulting headaches.

The sharp edges of facets are also a vulnerable location, where the exposed crystal lattice of the stone can break more easily than elsewhere. If you experience mysterious scratching and are fairly certain that none of the usual culprits is responsible, examine your gem for bubbles, flaws, and frayed edges.

What can you do to prevent this self-destructive behaviour in your gemstones? As always, the best solution to this problem is not to have it in the first place. When selecting rough, judge the location and severity of any internal flaws, since they may influence both the ultimate value of the gem and your ability to polish it. Similarly, when matching gem designs to rough, try to cut away any potential problem areas, and if that is not possible, at least make sure that they are buried deep. Chapter 6 provides further tips on selecting and orienting rough.

There are a few strategies for minimizing self scratching. Try using a lower lap speed and less hand pressure, or reverse the lap direction entirely (see next section). If the bubble or defect is small, consider polishing it out. Note that this may force you to re-polish surrounding facets to tune up meet points. In the worst case, you may have to go back to the pre-polish lap.

An exposed bubble or flaw is not the end of the world, as long it is reasonably stable and lets you polish the rest of the facet. Of course, such surface irregularities will be a magnet for dirt and potential future fractures. Use your judgment, and don't forget that the usual calculation of time versus value versus yield still applies.

Dealing with Unexplained Scratching

It would be nice if there were always a clean, clear explanation for scratching problems. It would also be nice if politicians always told the truth and toast always landed jam side up. The unfortunate fact is that, in many instances, you won't have a clue as to why scratches keep showing up. Do not despair, however, since there are a few additional tricks you can try.

Reverse lap direction. If your faceting machine has a reversible motor, give it a try. Sometimes working a facet in the opposite direction can clear up all your problems. This may be related to pushing rather than pulling on exposed cleavage planes, or it just may be that the polishing conditions are sufficiently different to sidestep the difficulty.

A couple of important notes deserve mention, however. First, polishing on a backwards-running lap can cause serious damage to the gem, faceting machine and operator. Normally, the lap rotates away from the quill axis, so that any sticking or excess friction lifts the stone off the lap (see Figure 8-8 earlier in this chapter). With the motor reversed, however, such problems can lead to the stone jamming and digging in to the lap. Take extra care and use a slow speed when polishing this way. The second point is that, even if your machine does not have a reversible motor, you can achieve the same effect by working on the opposite side of the spindle (Figure 8-32). This may be an awkward position, so double all the cautions regarding safety of stone, machine, and fingers.

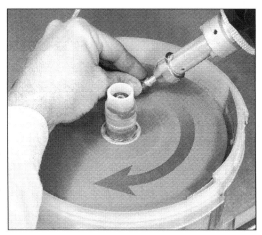

Figure 8-32 You can polish on a backwards-running lap by either reversing the motor direction or by working on the opposite side of the spindle.

Change lap speed, polishing location, and hand pressure. This one is easy, and it often works. Try slowing down the motor or speeding it up or turning it off entirely. Move to a different radius on the lap. Apply a little more or less pressure on the stone. All of these strategies change the physical conditions between the facet and lap, and shaking things up often shakes things loose.

Change the amount of polishing agent and lubricant. This is really a corollary to the section on agglomeration scratching, but it deserves emphasis. A common error among beginners is to apply too much polishing agent to the lap, and this error usually leads to scratches. If you are using diamonds on a metal lap, give the lap a good wipe with a clean paper towel and try again. If this doesn't work, rub a couple of drops of extender fluid into the surface. With bonded laps and metal oxides, try varying the water drip. Some veterans recommend adding vinegar to the water, but this can lead to machine corrosion, and I have never found it necessary (see "Lube Job" on page 298). If you are using a ceramic lap, scrape and wipe the surface with an alcohol-dampened paper towel to remove excess diamond. If you are a beginning faceter and you are using a ceramic lap, clean the lap thoroughly, mix one ounce of food-grade ethanol with your favourite sweet beverage, drink, and go look for an Ultralap.

Use filtered or distilled water. There is an astonishing range of quality and constituents in tap water from various parts of the world. I am sure that you have experienced odd or chemical-tasting water at some point in your peregrinations. Undesired constituents extend beyond mere dissolved chemicals, however. Some frustrated faceters have eventually traced down their unexplained scratching to sand (!) coming out of their water taps. If you are in any doubt, use filtered or distilled water. Chapter 20.5 shows how to convert a domestic water filter jug into a drip tank that will eliminate this problem.

Change laps and / or polishing agents. Although you may have settled on a particular combination of lap and polishing agent for a certain gem species, there is no guarantee that it will work with every stone of its type or even with every facet on a single gem. If the simpler tactics, such as changing lap speed and hand pressure, fail utterly, try changing to a completely different type of lap and / or polishing agent. The appearance of characteristic "horsehair" scratches in quartz is a classic example of when to try this. Table 8-1 can help you find alternatives.

Try a different brand of polishing agent. Some faceters have reported that they have received poorly graded polishing agent. The resulting mix of coarse and fine particles is a guaranteed but easily avoidable source of frustration. Ask your faceter friends for a good supplier, or consult the web resources in Chapter 15.8.

Repeat the pre-polish. Did I mention subsurface damage? Did I mention it three times? Oh... only twice. Ok, I'll say it again. Many unexplained polishing scratches aren't from polishing at all. In fact, the beautiful polish has only served to bring out subsurface damage and scratches from the cutting phase. In many instances, it will be quicker and less frustrating to go back to the pre-polish lap and get things right.

Surface Irregularities

This is a catchall category, including all polishing oddities that are not obviously scratches and pits. Usually, surface irregularities occur with a particular gem species or gem-lap combination. The following paragraphs list some common difficulties and how to address them.

One side of a facet polishes while the other does not. This is an easy one: there is a slight angle misalignment between the facet and the polishing lap. See "Nail that Polish" on page 331 and Figure 5-46. Note that this condition can also lead to scratching, since polishing agent can build up in the small air gap between stone and lap (Figure 8-31).

Mottled "orange peel" surface on facet. Harder materials, particularly corundum, are prone to this difficulty, which is characterized by patchy glazed regions and pitting on an individual facet. Although most commonly associated with the bonded pre-polish laps like the NuBond, the dreaded orange peel can appear during fine polish as well. To pile horror on horror, the polishing lap occasionally rips out whole chunks of the facet surface. The only real remedy is to switch to a different type of lap, and you will probably have to go back to the pre-polish stage to clear things out. For corundum, try 8000-grit diamond on a metal lap as a final pre-polish.

Shredding and splintering of the surface. This awful situation usually arises with materials such as topaz which have perfect cleavage planes. You of course oriented the rough to avoid placing these planes near the table (Figure 12-42), but a gem will have facets in all directions. Try polishing slowly and reversing lap direction. In some instances, you will have to live with a less than perfect polish.

Systematic over or under polishing. Materials such as kyanite have different hardness in different directions (see page 316 of this volume and page 125 of Volume 2). This can cause apparently inconsistent polishing behaviour. Some facets seem to take forever, while others are so fast that it is easy to go past the meet points. With such stones, you should note the problem facets and be prepared to polish less or more as necessary.

Rippled or "flow" appearance. The surface of the facet appears gently rippled, like sand under a slow moving stream. This condition occurs particularly with quartz polished with metal oxides and Ultralaps. Although less aesthetically objectionable than other surface irregularities, rippling can usually be removed by using a very light touch or switching to a different type of lap.

8.18 Cutting and Polishing the Girdle

Why a special section? Isn't cutting and polishing the girdle just like any other facet tier on a gemstone? Can't I learn everything I need to know from Chapter 5?

Three questions. If you choose to facet the girdle – as I think you should – then the answer to the second question is pretty much yes. Girdle facets cut and polish pretty much like any other facet and (question 3) Chapter 5 will help. If you decide not to facet the girdle, leaving it with the traditional rough-ground finish, then I guess the answer to the second question is no. A fairly self-evident and uninformative no, since not cutting facets is quite different from actually cutting them.

Nevertheless, I hope to convince you that cutting and polishing the girdle of your gemstones is a worthwhile exercise (and hence in answer to question 1, deserving of a special section). There are several compelling reasons to do so:

1. Cutting a well-formed crown. A significant portion of this chapter and an even greater part of Chapter 5 has tried to hammer home the point that successful gem cutting is an exercise in transferring reference points upward from the culet through the girdle to the crown and table. Messing up that process, or in the case of a non-facetted girdle, interrupting it halfway, can only lead to trouble. Presumably, you have taken great care in establishing an accurate pavilion center point and proper symmetry, and a faceted girdle serves as a means of carrying all of that fine work forward to the crown.

2. Aligning the pavilion and crown tiers. A pleasing reflectance pattern depends on accurate rotational alignment of the pavilion and crown facets. This means placing the crown facets exactly where they should be with respect to the pavilion. Another way of saying this is that you have to get the transfer cheat right. Chapter 7.6 has a great deal more to say on this issue. Suffice it to say here that a majority of the techniques used to establish the transfer cheat require a faceted girdle.

3. Greater flexibility in girdle thickness. Faceted girdles can be made thinner than ground girdles. Figure 8-33 compares the two for an eight-sided round. The intersection of the circu-

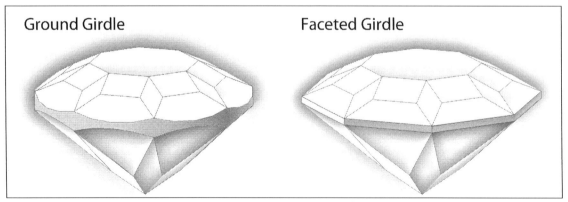

Figure 8-33 A ground girdle (left) produces a scalloped edge of varying thickness, while a faceted girdle is uniform and can be thinner overall (right). This is the Parapet design from Chapter 19.1.6.

lar ground girdle with the pavilion and crown facets produces a scalloped surface of varying thickness. The situation becomes more extreme for designs with lower symmetry, such as hexagonal gems. To avoid thin edges that are susceptible to breakage, a ground girdle must be thicker overall. In the all-too-frequent instance of having insufficient extra gem material, the flexibility to make a thinner, uniform girdle can make all the difference in the world.

4. Avoiding distracting frostiness. For materials with higher index of refraction, the photons can bounce around quite a few times before exiting the gemstone toward your eye. This means that there is a very real chance that you can "see" the girdle looking downward through the crown. You can convince yourself of this using the ray-trace feature of GemCAD (see Chapter 15.3.1). Multiple internal bounces can lead to distracting frosty patches if your gemstone has a rough ground girdle.

5. Ease in setting. This one relates closely to number 3. A faceted girdle with uniform thickness and a clear view to any internal inclusions or flaws is simply easier and safer to mount in jewelry.

Having (correctly) decided to cut and polish the girdle facets, you should be aware of a number of issues and challenges that the girdle presents.

First and most importantly, faceting the girdle requires you to put your machine in an extreme configuration, and it may not behave exactly as expected. The overwhelming majority of facet tiers lie at angles below 45°, in other words with the quill angled down toward the vertical. The girdle facets are at 90°, as far away from typical conditions as you can get. This tends to amplify any machine alignment errors. Also, cutting with the quill horizontal can lead to greater mast flexure problems. For this reason, some manufacturers offer a "girdle rest," a simple block which braces the quill when it must work parallel to the lap (see Chapter 4.11.4).

If you have left yourself substantial gem material for the crown, you may find yourself faceting a great deal of stone (and possibly adhesive and dop metal as well) when working on the girdle. Making the initial cuts at 90° and then polishing at a slightly smaller angle can help. See page 168 for more.

Finally, the layout of most faceting machines will require you to work near the outer edge of the lap. This location experiences less wear and hence tends to cut more aggressively (see "As the Lap Turns…" on page 315 and "Your Lap's Sweet Spot" on page 72). Oh yes… working near the edge of the lap also increases the chance of falling off. Turn to "Cutter Beware" on page 299 to learn of the horrors.

A final word on girdles…You can exploit the flexibility of girdles to increase yield from valuable gem rough, without materially altering the optical performance of the stone. See "Weight Gain and Girdles…" on page 44 of Volume 2 to learn more.

8.19 Cutting and Polishing the Table

We can argue whether girdles deserve their own section in this chapter, but in the case of tables, the argument should end before it starts.

Why? Because tables are problematic. I have problems cutting and polishing tables. So do you. So do all of us and we always will.

Why are tables problematic? Let me count the ways (note that Chapter 5.8 also counts the ways and moans about them a fair bit):

1. The table is usually the largest facet on a gem. Larger facets cut and polish more slowly and increase the likelihood of problems (see "Performance under Pressure" on page 317).

2. The table comes last. With the traditional pavilion-girdle-crown cutting order, the table is usually the final facet, and it sees all of the accumulated cutting errors that have built up over the previous tiers. Tables also frequently have four, eight, twelve, or more meet points, each of which is the result of cumulative error. Yuck! (see Section 8.9.4, "Shooting Stars" opposite, and "Wobbly Tables" on page 189).

3. The tabling adapter. You have to cut the table at 0°, which for a typical faceting machine forces you to remove the dop from the quill and use a 45° tabling adapter (Chapter 4.15). This means additional alignment headaches, and of course, you lose precious rotational reference information connecting the already-cut facets to the index wheel (see Chapter 7.6).

4. The table is at 0°. Most faceting machines don't like to cut at 0°. Even with a tabling adapter, you can experience jamming, skittering, and loud shrieking (from both you and the stone – see "The Table Song" on page 191).

Having counted the ways, what can you do to improve your tabling experience?

First and foremost, you should cut and polish the table together at the very end, unless extreme circumstances demand otherwise. This strategy eliminates the rotational reference problem described above, since all of the other facets are complete before you are forced to remove the dop from the quill.

Second, you should cut carefully and check your progress frequently. While tables are large and generally cut slowly (point 1 above), the consequences of an over cut are pretty serious. There is no moving the design down a little bit at this stage. A serious error will demand a re-cut of the crown at the very least.

Note also that all your thinking about gem orientation has gone out the window. Yes, the angle display may read 45°, assuming you are using a tabling adapter, but that doesn't mean everything is hunky-dory. The adapter may have an angle offset, and of course the index setting doesn't mean much with the machine configured this way. You will have to adjust things using the facet angle and the cheater (see Figure 5-79). To ensure consistency – and this may just be a foolish consistency (see page 313) – I always install and square up the tabling adapter at index zero.

You should also recognize that even the most carefully placed table may not make all of its meet points. It's not the table's fault. Rather, accumulated error on the remainder of the gem has produced a set of meet points that do not fall in a single plane. See "Shooting Stars" opposite for tips on how to proceed.

Finally, follow the instructions in Chapter 5.8. Yes, that information is for a specific gem design, but as a matter of fact, cutting a table is cutting a table. It's always problematic. I have problems cutting and polishing tables. So do you. So do...

You get the idea.

Shooting Stars

Tables are tough. No question about it. The adjacent text counts the ways…

In my experience, the real kicker is Reason #2, the fact that the last facet has to eat all of the accumulated errors of previous tiers while making multiple meet points. Tables are truly tough.

Figure 8-34 illustrates this problem for an eight-meet table on a standard round brilliant. Having cut the table down to the first meet points, adjusting the angles appropriately to keep the table centered, you realize that no single facet will hit all the meets. Argghhh!

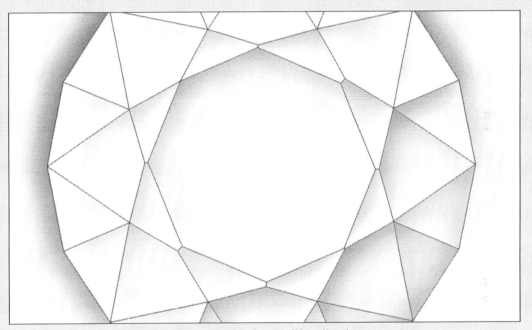

Figure 8-34 No single table facet will hit all eight meet points.

You basically have two options at this stage. The first is to do the best you can by cutting the table further. This means that some meet points will be over-cut while others will be under-cut. Try to aim for the middle and see how bad it looks.

If you remain unsatisfied, you will have to adjust some of the other facets. This is not as difficult as it sounds, particularly for designs with smaller facets near the table. The standard round brilliant, with its eight star facets, can be adjusted fairly painlessly.

It's time to shoot the stars. Here's how. Begin by cutting the table down toward the lowest meet point. In other words, continue cutting the table without adjusting the angles until you have cut through all of the meet points except one (Figure 8-35). Note that in many instances, if you had adjusted the angles to do as well as possible (Figure 8-34), you may hit two or even more meet points at this stage.

When you are happy, polish the table. With any luck, you are done with it forever. Remove the dop from the 45° adapter and re-install it in the quill.

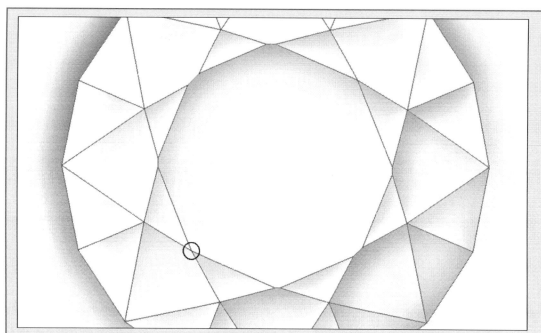

Figure 8-35 To adjust the star facets, begin by cutting the table down to the lowest meet point (circled) at the same angle and cheater setting used in Figure 8-34.

Now comes the real work: re-cutting the star facets. Adjust the gemstone to the cutting angle and index for the stars. This will almost certainly force you to re-establish the correct rotational reference between the gem and the index wheel. Refer to the top of page 332 and Chapter 7.6 to learn how to do this.

Begin at what you believe to be the star facet with the most over-cut meet points. Adjust the cutting angle to a lower value and use the cheater to re-cut the facet to the pre-existing lower meet point and to the best "eyeball" location at the table. In other words, try to produce a well centered, symmetric facet, but do not cut into any of the lower tiers. Figure 8-36 illustrates the idea.

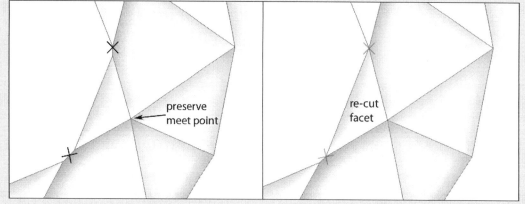

Figure 8-36 Cut to the pre-existing meet point (arrow) at a lower angle. Adjust the cheater so that the facet hits the desired target locations (x symbols). Note that these targets may already coincide with the vertex of an existing facet. In the example shown here, the tip of the upper adjacent star facet looked fairly good already.

Move to the adjacent star facets and repeat the procedure as necessary. Note that for some of these, you will have two targets: the pre-existing lower tier meet point and the tip of a neighbouring star facet that you just re-cut. Not every star facet will need adjustment, but the last one you re-cut will of course have three target meet points. This is a lot easier to do than it is to explain. Just make sure that you keep adjusting the cheater to keep the star facets centered and symmetric. You don't want to end up with an overly small or large last star. Keep careful notes of all settings, particularly if you are using a pre-polish lap. Finding all those angle and cheater values again on the polishing lap would be no fun at all.

You should end up with something that looks like a very well cut stone. If the accumulated error was really large, your new star facets might be slightly asymmetric or of different size, but hopefully, this will get lost in the sparkle. I personally find minor differences in facet size less aesthetically distracting than missed meet points.

Congratulations! You have turned a sloppy stone into a glowing nugget of meet point beauty! In most instances, it would take a very discerning examination to uncover your legerdemain. Note that this procedure should work for most gemstone designs, but it is always an excellent idea to do a sanity check by re-cutting a virtual stone with a program such as GemCAD (see Chapter 15.3.1).

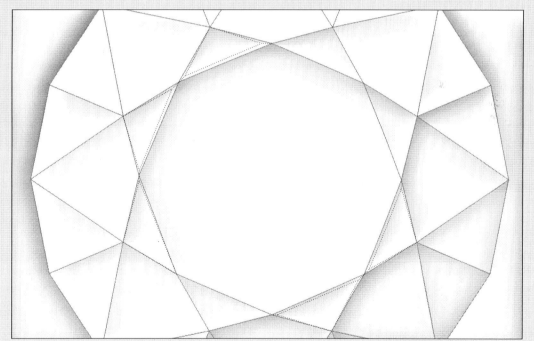

Figure 8-37 Work your way around the stone, re-cutting the star facets as necessary so that things look right. The dotted lines show the facets from Figure 8-35. For this gem, only five of the eight stars needed tweaking.

8.20 A Last Word on Polishing: Warnings and Wisdom

I began this discussion of polishing by noting that you will more than likely find it to be a "character building" experience. There will inevitably be frustrations and seemingly illogical outcomes on your polishing lap. I can only encourage you to work through these as best you can and to remain secure in the knowledge that things will get better as you gain experience.

The best advice I have heard comes from Rob Kulakofsky, proprietor of color-wright.com and the guy who taught me to cut:

The more I learn about faceting, the more I think (that) there is some kind of mysterious, and sometimes aggravating property to polishing. Maybe the stone is picking up the energy signals from the faceter, or the alignment of celestial bodies has to be just right. Whatever it is about polishing that makes it so variable, I've come to the conclusion that if a technique works for you, stick with it. That's because what works just dandy for one person is a nightmare for others.

In other words, if you find a good combination of polishing compound, lap, and technique, use it, but don't get frustrated or fearful to try something else when that problem stone comes along.

9

Further Reading

Are you a beginning faceter? If so, I sincerely hope that your adventure does not end here, at the conclusion of this book introducing you to the hobby. First and foremost, I really hope that you are cutting gemstones. All the reference books in the world cannot compare to the experience you will gain at the lap.

Having said that, there are many additional printed resources that can help you on your way, not the least of which is the second volume of this book. It's called Amateur Gemstone Faceting Volume 2: Expanding Your Horizons. It contains chapters on how gemstones actually work, as well as explanations of the properties and common treatments of gem materials. You can learn how to facet on your computer, cutting your creations on screen or producing photorealistic images of your treasures long before lowering stone to lap. Several chapters aim to launch you on your way to gemstone design, and the final part of the book contains a number of ideas for do-it-yourself projects, including a digital angle encoder upgrade for your faceting machine.

With that shameless advertisement out of the way, I am forced to admit that there are other reading materials out there to increase your enjoyment of faceting, and some of them are very good. This chapter contains a non-comprehensive list of further reading for the inquisitive cutter. The list is non-comprehensive for two reasons. First, it reflects my knowledge of the current spectrum of faceting related books, with all the limits and bias that implies, and second, more and more information material is appearing exclusively on the Web. Chapter 15.8 points you to these additional network resources. And yes, it is one more act of shamelessness that Chapter 15.8 is in Volume 2…

9.1 Instructional Books on Faceting

This section lists instructional books on faceting, organized alphabetically by author. Although some of these volumes are now quite dated, they are an excellent learning resource. At various locations in this book, I refer to the "bibles" of faceting. These are the bibles.

John Broadfoot and Peter Collins
Cutting Gemstones: A Beginner's Guide to Faceting
292 pages softcover, spiral bound
Published by Gem Info Pty,
Brisbane, Australia. First published 2001, Second edition 2003
ISBN 978-0-646-41461-5

H. C. Dake
The Art of Gem Cutting: Including Cabochons, Faceting, Spheres, Tumbling, and Special Techniques
96 pages softcover
Published by Gem Guides Book Co.,
Baldwin Park, California. First published 1938, 7th edition 1987
ISBN 978-0-9351827-2-9

Jeff Graham
Learn How to Facet "The Right Way…"
58 pages (loose-leaf binder).
Published by Jeff R. Graham,
Tucson, Arizona. First published 2000
Available at silversupplies.com (this the online home of Starr Gems, a familiar landmark to Tucson faceters) or at rockpeddler.com.

Graves Company
Fundamental Faceting
32 pages, softcover.
Published by the Graves Company as a faceting primer and manual

Robert H. Long and Norman W. Steele
Introduction to Meetpoint Faceting
126 pages softcover, ringbound
Published by Seattle Faceting Books,
Mercer Island, Washington. First published 1985

Tom Mitchell
Faceting 1
39 pages PDF

Published by Mitchell Jewelry Studio,
The Villages, Florida
www.mitchelljewelrystudio.com

Edward E. Smith
**The `411' Information Guide About How You Can Cut and Polish Gems
into Valuable Jewels**
106 pages softcover, spiral bound
Published by Secrets of the Pros,
Yuma, Arizona. First published 2005
ISBN 978-0976560302
Subtitle is : Covering 80 Major Gemstones. Cabochons Carvings Faceting
& Cabinet Specimens

Edward J. Soukup
Facet Cutters Handbook
64 pages softcover
Published by Gem Guides Book Co.,
Baldwin Park, California. First published 1962, 2nd edition 1986
ISBN 978-0910652-06-6

Glenn and Martha Vargas
Faceting for Amateurs
340 pages hardcover
Published by Glenn and Martha Vargas,
Thermal, California. First published 1969. Fourth edition 2003
ISBN 978-0917646096

Gerald L. Wykoff
The Techniques of Master Faceting
240 pages hardcover
Published by Adamas Publishers,
Washington, DC. First published 1985
ISBN 978-09607892-2-1

Gerald L. Wykoff
Master Gemcutting Tips
166 pages softcover
Published by Adamas Publishers,
Washington, DC. First published 1993
ISBN 978-0960789276

Gerald L. Wykoff
The Techniques of Master Gem Polishing
311 pages softcover
Published by Adamas Publishers,
Washington, DC. First published 1994
ISBN 978-0960789290

Subtitle is : A Comprehensive Overview of the Techniques, Tools and Knowledge Required To Apply a Fine Polish on All Types of Gemstones

9.2 Collections of Gemstone Designs

This section lists published collections of gemstone designs, again alphabetically by author.

Gram Faceting Designs

Jeff Graham published hundreds of gemstone designs, both in print and on the web. The following collections cost less than $20 each and are available online at silversupplies.com or rockpeddler.com. There are typically 42 unique designs per collection, distributed as unbound loose-leaf pages. The entire collection runs $269.

Gram 1 Faceting Designs – 63 pages, including 56 designs optimized for beryl, CZ, garnet quartz, topaz, tourmaline. Includes loose leaf binder. Mostly 96-index designs.

Additional Design #1 – 44 pages, with 42 designs optimized for quartz, garnet, and tourmaline. For 96 and 80-tooth index wheels.

Additional Design #2 – 43 pages, with 42 designs for quartz, tourmaline, topaz, garnet, apatite, tanzanite, opal, peridot, sapphire, CZ, spinel, beryl, and zircon. For 96 and 80-tooth index wheels.

Additional Design #3 –43 pages, with 42 designs optimized for quartz, tourmaline, topaz, garnet, apatite, tanzanite, opal, peridot, sapphire, CZ, spinel, beryl, and zircon. For 96 and 80-tooth index wheels.

Additional Design #4 "Money Cuts" – 44 pages, with 42 designs that are relatively fast and easy to cut. For refractive index 1.62-1.93 and with conventional length-to-width ratios for commercial sale. 96 index.

Additional Design #5 "Barions" – 43 pages, with 42 barion designs for refractive index 1.62 to 1.93. For 96-tooth index wheels.

Additional Design #6 "CheckerBoards - Money Cuts" – 44 pages with 42 designs featuring checkerboard crowns. Like the others in the Money Cuts series, this collection contains designs that are fast and easy to facet and have conventional length-to-width ratios. 96 and 120 index.

Additional Design #7 "More Money Cuts"– 44 pages with 42 easy to cut, low facet count designs for gem materials with n=1.54-1.93 and index wheels with 80, 96, and 120 teeth.

Additional Design #8 "Diamond Checker Boards - Money Cuts" – 44 pages with 42 designs featuring non-rectilinear checkerboard crowns. Fast and easy to cut, with conventional L/W ratios. Index 80, 96, 120.

Additional Design #9 "Mirages - Money Cuts" – 44 pages with 42 designs that produce floating "mirages" in the reflection pattern. Fast and easy to cut, with conventional L/W ratios. Index 72, 77, 80, 96.

Additional Design #10 "Mirages 2 - Money Cuts" – 44 pages with 42 designs. A follow-on to collection #9. Index 72, 77, 80, 96.

Additional Design #11 "Sunstone - A new approach..." – 44 pages with 42 designs optimized to get the most out of sunstone. Index 80, 96.

Additional Design #12 "Glitter - Money Cuts" – 44 pages with 42 designs optimized for "glitter" in larger gems or less saturated gem rough. This means a relatively large number of kite-shaped facets. Index 64, 96.

Additional Design #13 "Domes" – 44 pages with 42 designs featuring relatively simple, reflector pavilions and high, dome-shaped crowns. Ideal for lightly-saturated tourmaline nodules. Index 72, 80, 96.

Additional Design #14 "Gem Beads" – 44 pages with 42 designs for faceted beads. Index 96.

Additional Design #15 "More Checkers" – 44 pages with 42 additional checkerboard designs. Index 96.

Robert H. Long and Norman W. Steele Designs

The legendary gem designers Long and Steele produced a series of design collections. Each comes as a sheaf of loose-leaf pages published by P/M Marketing for less than $15. The entire series costs approximately $85. In addition to the diagrams, each shape-specific collection includes technical discussions of cutting strategy appropriate to that type of design.

Facet Design Volume 1: Ovals – 92 pages with 89 different oval cuts, 17 with detailed instructions. Contains a mix and match section for alternate crowns and pavilions. Explains the CAM technique.

Facet Design Volume 2: Navette / Marquise –104 pages with 50 different marquise cuts, 23 with detailed instructions. Includes a section on pre-forming for various L/W ratios.

Facet Design Volume 3: Heart and Pear – 117 pages with 54 pear cuts (18 detailed) and 24 heart cuts (11 detailed).

Facet Design Volume 4: Cut Corner Rectangle Emerald – 116 pages with 70 different cut corner rectangle and emerald designs, 21 with detailed instructions. Explains the ECED outlining technique.

Facet Design Volume 5: Rounds – 108 pages with 340 different round cuts, 12 with detailed instructions.

Facet Design Volume 6: Barions – 95 pages with 92 Barion designs, 52 with detailed instructions. Explains the CLAM technique.

Facet Design Volume 7: Antique Square Cushions – 69 pages with 91 designs, 20 with detailed instructions.

MDR Designs

In addition to manufacturing faceting machines (see Chapter 2.8.3), MDR Lapidary Products also produced a series of gem design collections, which retail for less than $10 each.

The Book of Gem Cuts, Volume 1 – 23 pages with 15 designs. Published by MDR Lapidary Products, 1971.

The Book of Gem Cuts, Volume 2 – 27 pages with 22 designs. Published by MDR Lapidary Products, 1971.

The Book of Gem Cuts, Volume 3 – 24 pages with 19 designs. Published by MDR Lapidary Products, 1976.

The Book of Gem Cuts, Volume 4 – 19 pages with 15 designs. Published by MDR Lapidary Products, 1976.

Finding Books

The website worldcat.org maintains a database of library holdings worldwide. You can find almost anything on worldcat. For example, from here at my desk in Heidelberg Germany, I can query the database for the nearest library copy of Marcel Tolkowsky's seminal 1919 monograph on diamond design (see page 243 of Volume 2).

The results are not always encouraging. The closest copy of Tolkowsky's work sits in the Cambridge University library in the United Kingdom. I would have to cross over 500 miles of land, to say nothing of 30 miles of water, to sample the contents of that tome (a total of almost 900 km, but see page 190 of Volume 2). The nearest library copy of a much more recent work, Broadfoot and Collins *Cutting Gemstones* (see Section 9.1) is in Canberra, Australia, some 10,200 miles (16,400 km) away. Luckily, I ordered my own copy (see "Bibliophilic Blues" on page xviii of this volume).

Jim Perkins Designs

Jim Perkins publishes a number of books of gemstone designs. He also offers individualized faceting classes and other services at northcoastlapidary.com Each of the following collections costs approximately $20, and you can order the whole bundle, with extras, for $160.

50 Diagrams Potpourri – 50 designs

Better Angle Choices Better Performance – 50 designs

Designed for Quartz – 50 designs

Designed for Garnets, Sapphires and Rubies – 40 designs

Gem Book I – 50 designs

Gem Book II – 50 designs

Gem Book III – 50 designs

Gem Book IV – 50 designs

Gem Book V – 50 designs

My Favorite Faceting Designs – 53 designs

Facetron Learning Book: Learning to Facet in the 21st Century Using the Facetron – includes 16 designs

Glenn and Martha Vargas Designs

In addition to authoring one of the faceting "bibles," Glenn and Martha Vargas produced three hardcover collections of gemstone designs, as well as a book on gem material properties (see next section).

Diagrams for Faceting Volume I – 166 pages with 160 designs. Published by Glenn Vargas, 1975, ISBN 978-0917646027

Diagrams for Faceting Volume II – 151 pages with 132 different designs from Glenn and Martha Vargas, as well as 20 from Ernst Wollert. Published by Glenn Vargas, 1983, ISBN 978-0917646058

Diagrams for Faceting Volume III – 149 pages with over 133 designs from Glenn and Martha Vargas, as well as contributions from faceters all over the world. Published by Glenn Vargas, 1987. ISBN 978-091764 6072

9.3 Gemstones and Mineralogy

This is actually a huge category, with literally hundreds of books available. Those listed here represent a good starting point for your explorations. Alphabetical by author.

Ronald Louis Bonewitz
Rock and Gem
360 pages softcover, published by Dorling Kindersley, Ltd., 2008
ISBN 978-0756633424

Gemological Institute of America (GIA)
Gem Reference Guide, for the GIA Colored Stones, Gem Identification and Colored Stone Grading Courses
270 pages softcover, published by the Gemological Institute of America
ASIN B001C8ZW3Y

Cally Hall
Gemstones (Smithsonian Handbooks)
160 pages softcover, published by Dorling Kindersley, Ltd., 2010
ISBN 978-1405357975

Walter Schumann
Gemstones of the World
272 pages hardcover, published by Sterling, fifth edition 2013
ISBN 978-1454909538

Glenn and Martha Vargas
Descriptions of Gem Materials, Third Edition Revised
159 pages softcover, published by Glenn Vargas, 2006
Available at rocksandgems.info and gemcutter.com

9.4 Miscellaneous

History of Faceting and Faceting Machines

Glenn Klein's *Faceting History* provides a comprehensive review of man's attempts to fashion diamonds and coloured stones into gems. It also contains an extensive bibliography for further discovery. He has most recently produced a volume on the evolution of faceting machines.

Glenn Klein
Faceting History: Cutting Diamonds and Colored Stones
242 pages softcover, published by Xlibris, 2005
ISBN 978-1599260822

Glenn Klein
Evolution of Faceting Machines
141 pages hardcover, availabe at www.glennklein.com

Polishing Physics

Chapter 8.11.1 attempts to explain the physics of polishing. Interested readers looking for more detail can consult the following papers and references therein. Alphabetical by author.

Stephen W. Attaway, *The Mystery of Gemstone Polish Part 1*, 1999. Available at www.attawaygems.com/NMFG/Selected_Articals.html.

M. J. Cumbo et al., *Slurry particle size evolution during the polishing of optical glass*, Applied Optics, Vol. 34, No. 19, p. 3743, 1995.

Donald Golini and Stephen D. Jacobs, *Physics of loose abrasive microgrinding*, Applied Optics, Vol. 30, No. 19, p. 2761, 1991.

John C. Lambropoulos et al., *Surface microroughness of optical glasses under deterministic microgrinding*, Applied Optics, Vol. 35, No. 22, p. 4448, 1996.

H. Lu et al. *Culinary archaeology: Millet noodles in Late Neolithic China*, Nature 437, 967, 2005. Not strictly polishing physics, but it does answer the question on page 318.

Peter J. Lu, *Scratching the Surface of Polishing Physics*, Junior Paper, Department of Physics, Princeton University, 1999.

John Sinkankas, *What is Polishing?* Lapidary Journal, Feb. 1999, p. 51.

Rosiwal Cutting Resistance

Chapter 12.9.3 refers to the following scholarly article on the Rosiwal Cutting Resistance test.

Maarten A.T.M. Broekmans, *Failure of greenstone, jasper and cataclasite aggregate in bituminous concrete due to studded tyres: Similarities and differences*, Materials Characterization 58, 1171, (2007).

The Diamond Industry

Zoellner's book provides an excellent overview of both historical and modern diamond marketing. Targeted at a non-expert readership.

Tom Zoellner

The Heartless Stone: A Journey Through the World of Diamonds, Deceit, and Desire

352 pages, published by Picador, 2007

ISBN 978-0312339708

Computer Graphics and Ray Tracing

Chapter 15 explains how three-dimensional ray tracing works, and encourages you to try your hand at photo-realistic rendering. Those who wish to dive deeper into the topic can jump off from the following references, which represent only a tiny fraction of the literature on computer imaging..

James D. Foley, Andries van Dam, Steven K. Feiner, and John F. Hughes

Computer Graphics – Principles and Practice in C

1200 pages hardcover, published by Addison-Wesley, 1995

ISBN 978-0201848403

A seminal reference on computer graphics, including 3D imaging and rendering. For the serious cutter who wants to build his or her own ray-tracing software.

Fletcher Dunn and Ian Parberry

3D Math Primer for Graphics and Game Development

429 pages softcover, published by Jones and Bartlett Publishers, 2002

ISBN 978-1556229114

A more practical, "nuts and bolts" textbook on the mathematics of three-dimensional objects and ray-tracing. Includes sample code in the C programming language.

Rod Stephens

Visual Basic Graphics Programming : Hands-On Applications and Advanced Color Development

736 pages softcover, published by John Wiley and Sons, 1999

ISBN 978-0471355991

Another excellent code-oriented textbook on graphics programming, including 3D geometry and transforms. Includes sample code in Visual Basic.

Glossary of Faceting Terms

It's often the words that get you. Yes, a particular topic might be complex or broad ranging, and hence difficult to learn for the newcomer, but why oh why do people throw up the additional barrier of terminology, of jargon? (You think I am overstating things? Turn to the "simplified" explanation of crystal systems on page 129 of Volume 2.)

Faceters are as guilty of this as anyone, and although there are very good arguments for precise terminology in a discipline, there are equally good arguments for keeping it simple. This chapter attempts to bridge that gap by providing a fairly comprehensive and precise explanation of faceting terms in plain language. It also supplies direct links to the appropriate chapter or page of this book where you can dig up more information.

This is, of course, not the only glossary of faceting terms out there. Vargas' *Faceting for Amateurs* has an excellent glossary, as does Broadfoot and Collins *Cutting Gemstones*. Perhaps the granddaddy of them all is the "Faceting Dictionary" compiled by the great gem designer, Fred Van Sant, during the period 1992-1995. The listing on the following pages builds directly on Van Sant's work.

A

absorption — The property of a material to absorb light, in particular at certain wavelengths characteristic of that material. See Chapter 12.3.1.

accuracy — A measure of how close a result is to the actual answer. See page 392 of Volume 2. Also see precision.

acetone — An organic chemical solvent that is effective in dissolving epoxy resin and dop wax. See Chapter 4.3.

adamantine — The surface luster characteristic of diamond and other high refractive index gemstones. See Chapter 12.7.2. See also luster.

adularescence — A type of iridescence in which alternating layers of mineral produce a milky glow. Moonstone is the best known adularescent gem. Closely related to labradorescence. See Chapter 12.7.4.

alcohol — An organic chemical solvent useful for dissolving dop wax and general cleanup. Alcohol is available in multiple forms, some of which are very toxic. See Chapter 4.3.

allochromatic mineral — An allochromatic mineral is intrinsically colourless and depends on trace impurities to imbue body colour. See page 85 of Volume 2. See also idiochromatic mineral.

allotrope — Allotropes are different forms of the same chemical element, such as the diamond and graphite allotropes of carbon. See page 82 of Volume 2. See also polymorph.

alumina — Shorthand name for aluminum oxide (synthetic corundum) polishing compound. See Chapter 4.12.1. See also Linde A, Linde B.

amber — An amorphous mineraloid gem formed from fossilized tree resin. See Chapter 14.2.

amorphous — A material exhibiting no long-range order at the molecular level. Examples include amber, glass, and opal. See Chapter 12.10.

angle of incidence, reflection, refraction — Angles associated with the interaction of light with matter. These angles are conventionally measured with respect to the normal (perpendicular) to the surface. See Chapters 10.3 and 11.4.

angle stop — A mechanism for restricting the cutting angle of a faceting machine. Angle stops come in hard stop and soft stop varieties. See Chapter 2.4.

angle transform — see tangent ratio transform

anisotropic — The characteristic of a mineral which displays different properties along different directions. For faceters, this usually means minerals that are birefringent and can split incoming light rays. See Chapter 12.4. See also birefringence and isotropic.

apex crown	A type of gem design which features conventional facets meeting at the top of the stone rather than a table facet. See page 21 of Volume 2.
arbor	A drive shaft held true by precision ball bearings. Used to convey motion from the motor to the platen in a faceting machine. See Chapter 2.2.1.
Arduino	A small commercial microcontroller suitable for hobby projects, including the digital angle encoder shown in Chapter 20.8.
asteria, asterism	Asteria, also known as star-stones, exhibit the property of asterism, in which aligned fibrous inclusions produce the visual illusion of a star. Star sapphire is the best-known type of asteria. See Chapter 12.7.3.
aventurescence	An optical effect produced by tiny, plate-like inclusions in a mineral. The most familiar type of aventurescence is the schiller seen in sunstone. See Chapter 12.7.5.

B

baguette (gem cut)	A rectangular step-cut, often used as a smaller accent gem.
bail	A jewelry element, usually in the form of a metal loop, used to attach a pendant to a necklace. Also spelled *bale*.
barion (gem cut)	A gemstone design featuring a brilliant-type pavilion mated to a non-round crown. Half-moon facets, which connect the symmetric pavilion facets to the girdle, characterize such designs. See page 246 of Volume 2.
basal cleavage	A cleavage plane oriented parallel to the base of a crystal, as in topaz. See page 137 of Volume 2.
Beilby layer	A putative layer on the surface of materials being polished which results from molecular flow. Now discredited. See Chapter 8.11.1.
beryl	A beryllium aluminum silicate mineral family which includes the popular gemstones aquamarine, emerald, golden beryl, goshenite, heliodor, morganite, and bixbite. See Chapter 14.1.
bezel	An enclosing band of metal (as opposed to pins or claws), holding a gem in a mounting.
biaxial crystal	A crystal exhibiting two optical axes. Minerals which form in the orthorhombic, monoclinic, and triclinic crystal systems are biaxial. See Chapter 12.10. See also optical axis.
birefringence	The optical property of a material in which the refractive index depends on the polarization and direction of light passing through it. Birefringent materials split incoming rays, producing double refraction. Zircon and calcite are well-known birefringent gemstones. See Chapter 12.4.
Blender	A community supported freeware software package enabling three-dimensional scene creation and rendering. See Chapter 15.5.

BOG   Better Optimizer for GemRay. A free computer program to optimize the pavilion and crown facet angles of a gemstone. See Chapters 15.3.2 and 18.5.

bonded lap   A type of metal cutting lap with a relatively thin layer of diamond abrasive electroplated to its surface. See Chapter 3.2.3. See also sintered lap.

bort   A fine, graded diamond powder used for polishing. Also sometimes spelled boart. See Chapter 4.12.2.

boule   A drop-shaped crystal of synthetic gemstone produced by the flame fusion or Czochralski pulling process. See Chapter 6.6.2.

break facets   The pavilion or crown facets immediately bordering the girdle. The intersection of the break facets with the girdle facets usually forms the girdle line. Also known as girdle, cross, skill, skew, or halves facets.

brightness   The fraction of environmental light returned to the viewer from a gemstone. This fraction depends on the type of material, the gem cut, and the lighting environment. Many gemstone designs quote the ISO brightness. See page 196 of Volume 2.

brilliance   A general term describing a gemstone's appearance and encompassing brightness and scintillation.

brilliant (gem cut)   A gem having a pavilion characterized by symmetric break and main facets that emphasize sparkle. The standard round brilliant is the canonical brilliant cut. See Chapter 1.3.

briolette (gem cut)   An elongated, tear-shaped faceted gemstone, often drilled to hang as a pendant or bead. Similar to a pendeloque, but usually covered with regular triangular or quadrilateral facets and lacking a girdle.

brittle wear   An impact and fracture process in which abrasive particles grind away the surface. See Chapter 8.11.2.

bulk diffusion   see diffusion

C

C (facet diagram)   In a faceting diagram, C denotes the height of the crown of a gemstone above the girdle. See Chapter 10.8.1. See also L, P, T, U, W.

c-axis   One of the crystallographic axes of a mineral. The c-axis usually extends along the length of the crystal, and in pleochroic materials, will exhibit a different colour. Some tourmalines extinguish light traveling along the c-axis and are hence termed "closed c-axis" gems. See Chapter 12.10 for more.

cabochon   A polished, dome-shaped gem (i.e. not faceted). Often used with translucent and opaque minerals. See Chapter 1.2.

calipers   A metal, plastic, or composite tool for precise size measurement. Available with analog or digital readout. See Chapter 4.17.

CAM   Acronym for the Center-point Angle Method of establishing the gem outline. See Chapter 17.3.

CAM pre-form | A partially faceted gem whose outline has been created using the CAM technique. See Chapter 17.3.

Canada balsam | Along with cedarwood oil, Canada balsam is the traditional optical agent for filling fractures in emerald and other gemstones. It is a turpentine based on the resin of the balsam fir tree. See Chapter 13.2. See also optical agent.

carat | One fifth of a gram. Not to be confused with the measure of the purity of gold, which can be spelled carat or karat (see page 9).

cat's-eye | The optical effect, seen in tiger's eye and other gemstones, arising from light scattering from randomly oriented fibrous inclusions. Formally known as chatoyancy. See Chapter 12.7.3.

cedarwood oil | A traditional optical agent for filling fractures in emerald. Usually distilled from juniper and cypress trees, not cedar. See Chapter 13.2. See also Canada balsam and optical agent.

cerium oxide | Popular metal oxide polishing agent. See Chapter 4.12.1.

ceramic lap | An extremely hard type of polishing lap used with diamond bort. Ceramic laps produces the flattest facets and the sharpest meet points, but they can be a challenge to use. See Chapters 3.3.1 and 8.14.4.

charge | (verb) To load a lap with abrasive or polishing agent. (noun) The act of doing so, or the current load of abrasive, as in "the current charge of diamond is wearing out." See Chapters 3.2.2 and 8.14.

chatoyancy | see cat's-eye

cheater | A mechanism for adjusting the rotation of the quill slightly in a clockwise or counterclockwise direction. These adjustments are usually smaller than one setting of the index wheel. Hence, the cheater is also known as the index splitter. See Chapter 2.2.1.

chemical polishing | The finest yet least well understood polishing process. Chemical polishing produces the final, perfect surface finish through a combination of mechanical and chemical action. See Chapter 8.11.

chemical vapour deposition (CVD) | A method for synthesizing gemstones by condensing material directly from a vapour to the solid state. Currently used only with diamond. CVD produces relatively small but high quality diamonds. See Chapter 6.6.2.

CHIA | An mnemonic acronym to remember items to check before cutting a facet. Stands for "Cheater, Height, Index, Angle." See Chapter 8.9.2.

chromophore | Mineralogical name for the atoms that produce the colour in gemstones. These are usually trace impurity atoms, such as chromium which makes ruby red. See Chapter 12.3.2.

chrysoberyl | A beryllium aluminum oxide gem material. Although usually yellow or golden-green, the rare and highly prized alexandrite type exhibits a green to purple-red colour change. See Chapter 14.1.

CLAM   Acronym for the Corner Locator Angle Method of establishing the gem outline. See Chapter 17.5.

clarity   A measure of how well a gemstone transmits light. Clarity can be reduced by internal flaws. See Chapter 6.4.1.

cleavage, cleavage plane   Cleavage is the parting or splitting of a gemstone, or its tendency to do so. Cleavage planes are directions along a crystal in which the lattice is weaker, leading to such splitting. See Chapter 12.11.1.

collet   A metal collar or flange to hold a dop stick in the quill of a faceting machine. Collets achieve superior centering compared to other clamping methods.

colour   The property of a gemstone leading to our perception of the spectral composition of light emerging from it. Also referred to as hue. See Chapter 12.3.

colour center   A small zone in a crystal which absorbs a certain range of wavelengths of light, leading to a change in overall colour. See Chapter 13.1.1.

colour change   The property of a gemstone to exhibit a different body colour under differing lighting conditions. In natural gems, colour change is highly prized and can add considerably to value. Vargas has suggested the term "photochroism" for this property. See Chapter 12.3.5.

colour zone   A band, spot, or region of different colour than the rest of the gem. Placing a colour zone in the culet can spread the effect throughout the stone. See page 234.

composite lap   A cutting or polishing lap fabricated from a non-metallic composite material, such as plastic or resin. Composite laps are growing in popularity. See Chapter 3.

compound (chemical)   A substance formed by the joining of two or more chemical elements in a fixed ratio. Essentially all gemstones with the exception of diamond are chemical compounds. See Chapter 12.2.

concave faceting   Collective name for a variety of techniques which seek to produce concave, not flat, facets on a gemstone. The facets are usually cylindrical, driven by the shape of the *mandrel* which cuts them. Also known as optically magnified faceting or OMF.

conchoidal   The fracture pattern of most common gemstone materials. The name derives from the Greek word for "mussel-like," due to the shell-like concentric ridges of the broken material. See Chapter 12.11.2.

conductivity (thermal, electric)   The property of a material to convey heat or electricity. For example, copper has excellent electrical conductivity.

cone pre-form   A method for roughing out the approximate shape of a gemstone using the quill in free-wheeling mode. See Chapter 8.3.2.

Corian   An acrylic polymer material normally used for counter tops but which has become popular as a lap. See page 78.

corundum | A precious gem material with chemical formula Al_2O_3. By definition, red corundum is called ruby. All other colours are called sapphire. Also used as an abrasive. See Chapter 14.1.

critical angle | The minimum angle of incidence of light leaving a medium of higher refractive index which will produce total internal reflection. The pavilion angles must generally be steeper (larger) than the critical angle, in order to prevent light leaking out of the bottom of the gem, a situation known as a fish-eye. See Chapters 10.3 and 11.7.

crown | The portion of a gemstone above the girdle line. See Chapter 1.2.

crown break facets | The facets on the crown of a gemstone immediately bordering the girdle. See Chapter 1.2.

cryptocrystalline | A mineral property in which the crystalline nature of the material only becomes apparent on small physical scales, usually by examination with a polarizing microscope. Opposite of macrocrystalline. Chalcedony and Jasper are cryptocrystalline forms of quartz.

crystal, crystalline | A solid composed of arrayed atoms or molecules that display long range order. Most common gem materials are crystalline. See Chapter 12.10.

crystal axis, crystallographic axis | A direction of symmetry within a crystal. Most common gemstone materials have three crystallographic axes (hexagonal and trigonal materials have four). Crystal axes also determine the optical behaviour of the material. See Chapter 12.10.

crystal habit | The macroscopic appearance of a crystal, as opposed to its microscopic crystal system. The crystal habit often reflects the underlying crystal system, but there are many exceptions. See Chapter 12.10.1

crystal lattice | see lattice

crystal system | One of the basic geometric configurations in which crystals form. They include isometric, tetragonal, orthorhombic, monoclinic, triclinic, trigonal, and hexagonal. Some references include amorphous as a crystal system, while others count the trigonal and hexagonal systems as a single group. There are therefore six, seven, or eight distinct crystal systems. See Chapter 12.10.

cubic crystal system | A crystal system exhibiting three, equal-length crystal axes meeting at 90°. Also known as isometric. See Chapter 12.10.2.

cubic zirconia | A synthetic gemstone originally used as a diamond simulant. Cubic zirconia is popular among faceters due to its many available colours and its high refractive index and dispersion. It is the cubic form of ZrO_2. Often called CZ. See Chapter 14.1.

culet | The apex or deepest point of the pavilion. See Chapter 1.2. See also keel.

culet facet | A facet truncating the culet and generally placed parallel to the table. Older cut diamonds often had culet facets. Culet facet can also refer to the conventional facets meeting at the culet. See Figures 7-15 and 16-20.

curmudgeon   An ill-tempered, frequently older person full of stubborn ideas or opinions. Also known as a faceter. And proud of it.

cushion
(gem cut)   A gem design characterized by a geometric form (triangle, square, etc.) with rounded corners. This can prevent trapping of light and simplify mounting. See Figure 16-3.

cyanoacrylate
glue   A strong, fast-acting adhesive used in gem dopping. Very useful for heat sensitive gems. See Chapters 4.1.2 and 7.2.3.

Czochralski
pulling   A method for synthesizing gemstones using a seed crystal lowered into molten material and then withdrawn slowly. See Chapter 6.6.2.

D

density   A measure of the amount of matter confined in a given volume, usually expressed as grams per cubic centimeter. The density can be a distinguishing physical property of gemstone materials. See Chapter 12.8. See also specific gravity.

depth of cut
indicator   A mechanism for signaling that a certain cutting depth has been reached on a faceting machine. See Chapter 20.7.

diamond   The hardest gemstone material, consisting of pure elemental carbon. See Chapter 14.2 and page 81 of Volume 2.

diamond
compound   see bort

dichroism   see pleochroism

dichroscope   An instrument for visualizing the different colours of a pleochroic mineral. Most dichroscopes rely on polarization and hence are frequently called polariscopes. See Chapter 20.3.

diffraction   The breaking up of the colours of incoming light due to regular spaced structures within a mineral. The colours of opal arise due to diffraction. See Chapter 12.7.4.

diffusion   A method for artificially introducing colour into a gemstone through the slow absorption of colouring agent into the crystal. The surface diffusion process colours only the outer periphery of the gem, but the bulk or lattice diffusion technique goes much deeper and hence it is much harder to detect. See Chapter 13.1.1.

digital angle
encoder   see encoder

dispersion   The separation of incoming light into a spectrum, due to variation in the refractive index of the medium with wavelength. Strong dispersion is a desirable property in gemstones, as it leads to fire. See Chapter 12.6.

dop or dop
stick   A small straight rod, usually of metal, to which a gemstone is attached for faceting. The dop is inserted into the quill on the faceting machine. See Chapter 4.4.

dopping The procedure of attaching a piece of gem rough to a dop stick with wax or glue. See Chapter 7.

dop transfer The process of transferring a half-complete gemstone from one dop stick to another, in order to work on the other half. Conventionally, faceters cut and polish the pavilion first, execute a dop transfer, and then cut and polish the crown. See Chapters 5.6 and 7.3.2.

dop wax The traditional dopping adhesive. Dop wax is a mixture of wax, shellac, and filler material, and it is available with a variety of melting temperatures. See Chapters 4.1.1 and 7.2.1.

double refraction see birefringence

doublet An assembled gemstone consisting of two different materials bonded together at the girdle. See page 219. See also triplet.

dressing stick A tool for re-sharpening bonded and sintered cutting laps by scrubbing away cutting residue and metal, thereby exposing more diamond. See Chapter 4.9.1.

drip tank A reservoir and delivery system for water on a faceting machine. A steady flow of water cools and lubricates the lap and helps to remove swarf. See Chapter 2.2.1.

ductile grinding An abrasive process which occurs with grit sizes of a few microns and smaller. In ductile grinding, the abrasive particles push the surface material to the side, like a plough. This can leave residual internal stress. See Chapter 8.11.2.

E

ECED Acronym for the Equal Center to Edge Distance method of establishing the gem outline. See Chapter 17.2.

element (chemical) Any one of the simplest chemical substances that cannot be broken down further by chemical reactions. Oxygen, silicon, and aluminum are the three most common elements in the Earth's crust. Unsurprisingly, they are also common in gemstones. See Chapter 12.2.

emerald (gem cut) A traditional rectangular gem design with cut-off corners and long, parallel facets. The emerald cut emphasizes colour over sparkle. See Chapter 1.3 and Figure 16-31.

encoder, angle An electromechanical device for accurately (and precisely) measuring the cutting angle on a faceting machine. See Chapter 20.8.

epoxy resin A two-component commercial resin-based adhesive used for dopping. See Chapters 4.1.2 and 7.2.2.

euhedral (crystal habit) Having sharp, recognizable crystal faces.

extender fluid An oil or other fluid used to dilute and disperse diamond bort on a polishing lap. See Chapter 8.14.3.

F

facet	Any one of the many, small, flat surfaces on a cut gemstone. See Chapter 1.2.
faceted girdle	A gemstone girdle that has cut and polished facets, as opposed to a ground girdle. See Chapter 8.18.
faceter	A person who facets gems. Also occasionally the colloquial short form of faceting machine.
faceting	The act (and hobby!) of faceting gemstones.
faceting head	A sub-assembly of a faceting machine that usually includes the quill, index wheel, cheater, and cutting angle readout mechanism. See Chapter 2.2.1.
faceting machine	A machine for faceting gemstones, consisting of the faceting head, a mast or platform, a drive assembly, and a drip tank. See Chapter 2.2.
fancy (gem cut)	In the diamond world, any gem cut that is not a standard round brilliant is defined as a fancy cut. For coloured stones, a fancy cut generally refers to a non-conventional shape or combination of pavilion and crown.
feather	A layer of internal inclusions, usually small bubbles, resembling a feather or veil. See Chapter 12.12. Also see inclusion.
filling (treatment)	A method for concealing inclusions by filling the flaw with an optical agent, including natural and synthetic oils, glass, and resin. See Chapter 13.2.
findings	Metal parts used in jewelry construction and repair. This can include prongs for gem setting, bails, posts, etc. See page 126.
fire	The visual manifestation of dispersion in a gemstone, in the form of flashes of coloured light. See Chapter 12.6.
fisheye	A situation in which the cutting angles of a gemstone permit light to enter the crown and exit the pavilion. This light is lost to the viewer, resulting in a duller, less interesting scintillation pattern. The name refers to the appearance of less-than-fresh seafood at the market. See Chapter 10.3.
flame fusion	The earliest method of gemstone synthesis, in which powdered material falls through a hot flame and fuses in the form of a boule. See Chapter 6.6.2.
flaw	see inclusion
float, floating	The action of placing a facet that has no target meet points, and hence can be cut to arbitrary depth. For example, the GeM101 design of Chapter 5 has a floating table.
fluorescence	The property of a mineral to emit visible light when exposed to ultraviolet radiation. Fluorescence can be characteristic of a particular gem species or geographic origin, and it can be very effective in identifying fake gems. See Chapter 12.7.6.
flux process	A method for synthesizing gemstones in which the raw material is dissolved and then re-crystallized within a non-aqueous flux such as lead fluoride, lithium niobate, or boron oxide. See Chapter 6.6.2.

foiling A gem treatment in which a thin layer of metal or dielectric material is applied to the surface of the stone. This can produce dramatic colours as in Mystic Topaz or make up for poor optical performance, as in the case of traditional foil-back gemstones. See page 152 of Volume 2.

fracture The surface appearance of a mineral after it has been broken under stress. This can help in identification, although the vast majority of common gemstones exhibit conchoidal fracture. See Chapter 12.11.2.

Fraunhofer lines The dark absorption lines seen in the spectrum of the Sun. The BG and CF pairs of Fraunhofer lines define the wavelength ranges of two common measures of dispersion. See Chapter 12.6.1.

free-form (gem cut) A gem whose outline displays no regular symmetry. Free-form gems often follow the outline of the raw gem rough. See Figure 16-4.

free-wheel pre-form see cone pre-form

Fresnel loss The process by which a fraction of incident light is reflected on entering a gemstone. Fresnel loss produces much of the effect of luster. See Chapters 11.8 and 12.7.2.

G

garnet Any of a group of related silicate minerals, including pyrope, almandine, spessartine, uvarovite, grossular, and andradite garnet, as well as their mixtures. See Chapter 14.1.

gem, gemstone A precious stone of any kind, especially when cut and polished for ornament…but see Chapter 1.1.

gem rough Gemstone material in its raw, uncut form. See Chapter 6.

GemCAD A Computer Aided Design (CAD) program for producing gemstone designs. The original MS-DOS version has been supplanted by GemCADWin, which runs under Windows. Available at www.gemcad.com. See Chapter 15.3.1.

GemRay An MS-DOS ray tracing program (recently upgraded to Windows) that generates a visual representation of a cut gemstone and provides information about the brightness properties of the design under various lighting conditions. Available at www.gemcad.com. See Chapter 15.3.1.

GGG Gadolinium Gallium Garnet, a synthetic garnet gem material originally developed for opto-electronic applications. See Chapter 6.6.

girasol Adularescence in quartz. See Chapter 12.7.4.

girdle The midline or equator of a gemstone, between the crown and the pavilion. Amateurs usually produce faceted girdles, both as an indication of workmanship and to provide a reference between the pavilion and crown facets. See Chapters 1.2 and 8.18.

glass Amorphous silicon dioxide used as an inexpensive and colourful gem material. See Chapter 14.1.

gram or   A unit of weight equal to 1/1000th of a kilogram or about 1/29th of an ounce.
gramme   A carat is one fifth of a gram. See page 9.

grit   A general term for abrasive, as in "diamond grit." Grit also refers to the mesh size of the abrasive, as in "1200 grit diamond." See Chapter 3.2.1.

H

half-moon   see barion
facet

handpiece   A handheld faceting head which holds the dop stick at the correct angle and index setting in a platform-type faceting machine. See Chapter 2.2.2.

hard stop   see angle stop

hardness   A measure of how difficult it is to scratch a mineral. Not to be confused with toughness, which measures a material's resistance to breaking and chipping. See Chapter 12.9. See also Mohs hardness scale.

head, facet-   see faceting head
ing

heat   The property of a mineral which reacts to sudden change in temperature. In
sensitivity   the worst instances, this reaction can result in fracturing of the stone. Faceters should cold-dop heat sensitive materials.

heat   Any of a variety of methods for improving the colour or clarity of a gemstone
treatment   through elevated temperatures, often in the presence of an oxidizing or reducing atmosphere. See Chapter 13.

hexagonal   A crystal system characterized by three, coplanar, equal-length crystal axes
crystal system   meeting at 120°, and a fourth axis perpendicular to their shared plane. Closely related to the trigonal crystal system. See Chapter 12.10.2.

high-grading   The act of screening a lot of gem rough and removing the best stones prior to sale as a lot. If not openly declared, high-grading represents unethical business practice. See Chapter 6.5.

hydrothermal   A gemstone synthesis method in which the raw gem material is dissolved in
process   water at high temperature and pressure. Local cooling and introduction of a seed causes crystal growth. See Chapter 6.6.2.

I

idiochromatic   An idiochromatic mineral has intrinsic body colour arising from its native
mineral   chemistry. Peridot is an idiochromatic mineral. See page 85 of Volume 2. See also allochromatic.

immersion   A liquid with refractive index similar to that of the gem rough under study.
fluid   Immersing the rough in the liquid fills in surface defects and reduces distracting reflections, thereby revealing internal flaws. See Chapter 4.5.

inclusion   Any internal flaw which reduces the clarity of a gemstone. See Chapter 12.12. Also see feather and needle.

index gear see index wheel

index lock A mechanical device for fixing the index wheel setting. See Chapter 2.2.1.

index of refraction (usually represented by the symbol n) A measure of the speed of light in a given optical medium. Changes in n when traveling from one medium (i.e. air) to another (i.e. diamond) produce refraction, the heart and soul of gemstone optics. A larger index of refraction corresponds to a lower speed of light and hence a greater refractive power. See Chapters 11.3.1 and 12.5. Also called refractive index or RI.

index splitter see cheater

index wheel A usually interchangeable device for restricting the rotation angles of the quill and dop stick to specific fractions of a full circle. The most common index wheels divide a full rotation into 96, 32, 120 or 77 steps. The choice of index wheel determines the range of possible symmetry of the resulting gemstone. See Chapters 2.2.1 and 10.7.

index wheel transposition The act of transforming a particular gem design from one index wheel to another. See Chapter 10.7.

infrared The region of the electromagnetic spectrum with wavelengths longer than that of visible light. See Chapter 11.2.1. See also ultraviolet.

iridescence The visual effect of colour splitting due to the interaction of light with regularly spaced structures within a mineral. Precious opal displays iridescence. Closely related to adularescence and labradorescence. See Chapter 12.7.4.

irradiation (treatment) Any of a group of methods to improve or change the appearance of a gemstone by subjecting it to radiation. See Chapter 13.

ISO brightness see brightness

isometric crystal system see cubic crystal system

isotropic Having the same material properties (in particular the index of refraction) in all directions. Minerals forming in the isometric crystal system are isotropic, as are amorphous materials. Minerals with differing properties in different directions are termed anisotropic. See Chapter 12.4.

J

jamb peg A traditional faceting machine consisting of a hand-held dop stick placed in various holes to achieve the desired cutting angle. See Chapter 2.2.

jardin Term used in the trade to describe internal inclusions in emerald. See Chapter 12.12.1.

K

karat   A measure of the purity of gold, ranging up to 24-karat for pure gold. Also spelled carat. See page 9.

keel   The bottom ridge line of some gemstone designs that do not have a culet. The keel resembles the eponymous structure in a boat. See Chapter 1.2.

kerf   The groove or slot created by a cutting implement. In faceting, kerf refers to the width of wasted material produced by a trim saw. See page 128 and page 294.

key system (dops)   A system of grooves, holes, or flats which allow repeatable rotational alignment of a dop stick in a faceting machine or transfer fixture. See Chapter 4.4.1.

L

L (facet diagram)   In a faceting diagram, L denotes the length of the gemstone. L is usually the longest dimension in the girdle plane. See Chapter 10.8.1. See also C, P, T, U, and W.

labradorescence   Iridescent colour splitting in labradorite and spectrolite. The splitting occurs due to the interaction of light with thin layers of inter-grown twinning crystals. Closely related to iridescence and adularescence. See Chapter 12.7.4.

lap   A circular, usually metal or composite disk used for gemstone cutting and polishing. See Chapter 3.

lapidary   A general term referring to gems and precious stones or the art of working them.

laser drilling (treatment)   A high-tech method of reducing the visibility of inclusions by boring a hole to the site with a laser and then deploying bleaching agents or filler. Currently used only with diamond. See Chapter 13.2.

lattice   The regularly spaced arrangement of atoms and molecules in a crystal. See Chapter 12.10.

lattice diffusion   see diffusion

law of reflection   The law describing how light reflects from a surface. The law of reflection states that the angle of reflection measured from the surface perpendicular is equal to the angle of incidence measured from the same perpendicular. See Chapter 10.3.

law of refraction   see Snell's law

Linde A, Linde B   Commercial name for alumina polishing compound. Linde A consists of 0.3 micron aluminum oxide particles, while Linde B is approximately 5-10 times finer. See Chapter 4.12.1.

loupe A magnifier which either attaches to the user's eyeglasses or is held directly by the muscles surrounding the eyeball. See Chapter 4.7.

Lucite lap A plastic polishing lap usually used with metal oxides. See page 77.

luster The appearance of a gem in light reflected from its surface. Both the refractive index and the surface conditions of the stone influence the luster. See Chapter 12.7.2. See also surface reflection.

LuxRender A community supported freeware software package for photorealistic rendering of three-dimensional scenes. LuxRender is a so-called unbiased renderer and hence can reproduce the optical effects inside gemstones. Works with Blender. See Chapter 15.5.

M

macrocrystalline Exhibiting crystals large enough to see without magnification. See also cryptocrystalline.

magnetism The property of a material to be attracted to a magnet. The magnetic properties of a gemstone can be used for identification. See Chapter 12.13.5.

main facets Usually the largest and most important facets on the crown or pavilion. In a standard round brilliant, the pavilion main facets extend from the girdle to the culet, while the crown main facets extend from the girdle to the table. See Chapter 1.2.

marquise cut A type of elongated gemstone design characterized by pointed ends and round sides. Also called a navette, French for "little boat," since the shape resembles the hull of a sailboat. See Figures 16.3 and 17.1.

mast A vertical shaft to which the faceting head is clamped in a mast-type faceting machine. See Chapter 2.2.1.

mast faceting machine A type of faceting machine employing a mast to hold the faceting head. See Chapter 2.2.1.

master lap A thick, usually metal lap used as support for thinner, more flexible laps. Typically, you should use a master lap with laps thinner than ¼ inch (6 mm). Master laps can also serve as a reference for faceting machine alignment. See Chapter 3.

meet point A point in a gem design formed by the intersection of at least three facets and which acts as a target for the placement of subsequent facets. See Chapters 1.2 and 8.7. Sometimes written as a single word: meetpoint.

meet point faceting A method of cutting a gem design using meet points. Meet point designs usually produce more accurate results, since the facets are located using defined angles and facet intersections, rather than the faceter's judgment sitting at the machine. See Chapter 8.7.

mesh size A measure of the size of abrasive grains. See Chapter 3.2.1. See also grit.

metamict
The term applied to minerals that have had significant internal crystal alteration due to radiation. "Low" zircon is the best-known metamict gemstone. See page 160 of Volume 2.

methylene chloride
An aggressive solvent used on epoxy resin bonds. Methylene chloride is highly toxic and has been banned in some jurisdictions. See Chapter 4.3.

micron
One millionth of a meter, or one one-thousandth of a millimeter (or approximately 0.00004 inches). Visible light has a wavelength of approximately half a micron. Also called a micrometer.

mineral
A naturally occurring solid material with specific chemistry, regular crystal structure, and properties. See Chapter 1.1.1.

mineraloid
A mineraloid differs from a mineral in not having regular crystal structure. Amber and opal are mineraloids. See Chapter 1.1.1.

mixed cut
Formally, a mixed cut is the combination of a brilliant-type crown and a step-cut pavilion. The term has evolved to mean any combination of crown and pavilion based on different designs. See page 249 of Volume 2.

Mohs hardness scale
The traditional scale for measuring the hardness, or scratch resistance, of minerals. The Mohs scale ranges between 1 for talc and 10 for diamond, although it is by no means linear. See Chapter 12.9. See also toughness.

molecule
The smallest particle of a chemical compound, consisting of two or more atoms held together by chemical bonds. See Chapter 12.2.

monoclinic crystal system
A crystal system characterized by three crystal axes of different length, two of which meet at 90° while the third is inclined. See Chapter 12.10.2.

multi-colour (gem)
A gemstone which exhibits different body colour at different locations. For example, ametrine is multi-colour quartz. See Chapter 12.3.8.

N

needle
A long, needle-like inclusion in a gemstone. Usually the crystallized form of an impurity material. For example, rutile or tourmaline needles often appear in quartz. See page 208 and Chapter 12.12. See also inclusion.

NuBond lap
Commercial name for a permanently charged composite cutting and pre-polish lap from Raytech Industries. See Chapter 3.2.3.

O

oiling (treatment)
The practice of using oil or other optical agent to conceal internal fractures and flaws. Oiling is common practice in the emerald trade. See Chapter 13.2.

Old European Cut
A traditional gem design resembling a standard round brilliant, but with a culet facet parallel to the table at the base of the pavilion. See Figure 7-15 and page 241 of Volume 2.

Old Mine Cut
A traditional square cushion gem cut that is the modern evolution of the classical Triple-Cut Brilliant or Peruzzi design. See page 241 of Volume 2.

OMNI	A method for establishing the outline of a gemstone. OMNI is particularly appropriate for barion-type designs. See Chapter 17.4.
opal	An amorphous mineraloid that frequently displays iridescent colour. Much opal is opaque or translucent and hence is cut en cabochon. The transparent jelly, fire, cherry, and hyalite varieties are suitable for faceting. See Chapter 14.1.
opalescence	Adularescence in opal. See Chapter 12.7.4.
open transfer	A method for executing a dop transfer without a transfer jig. See page 256.
optical agent (treatment)	A transparent liquid or solid used to conceal internal fractures and flaws. Common optical agents include cedarwood oil, Canada balsam, Opticon, glass, and resin. See Chapter 13.2.
optical axis	The direction along an anisotropic crystal for which light displays only single refraction. Uniaxial minerals (tetragonal, hexagonal and trigonal crystal systems) will have one optical axis, usually parallel to the c-axis direction of the crystal. Biaxial minerals (orthorhombic, monoclinic, and triclinic crystal systems) will have two optical axes. See Chapter 12.10. See also biaxial, uniaxial.
optically magnified faceting	See concave faceting
Opticon	A commercial optical agent used to conceal internal fractures and flaws. See Chapter 13.2. See also optical agent.
orange peel	A polishing problem characterized by a mottled "orange peel" appearance, patchy glazed regions, and pitting. Common with harder gemstones, such as corundum, and frequently associated with NuBond 1200 or 3000 grit metal bonded laps. See page 341.
orientation	The act or rotating a piece of gemstone rough for optimal cutting properties. Many factors, including rough shape, pleochroism, inclusions, and colour zones will drive the choice of orientation. See Chapters 6.7 and 10.8.2.
orthorhombic crystal system	A crystal system characterized by three crystal axes of different lengths meeting at 90°. See Chapter 12.10.2.
oval (gem cut)	General term for an elongated round gem design. See Figure 16-3.
over-cut facet	A facet that has been cut too far, and is hence deeper than it should be. See also under-cut facet.
oxide	Familiar term for the metal oxide polishing compounds. See Chapter 4.12.1.

P

P (facet diagram)	In a faceting diagram, P denotes the depth of the pavilion measured from the girdle line to the culet or keel. See Chapter 10.8.1 See also C, L, T, U, W.

pavilion	The underbelly of a gem responsible for internally reflecting light rays and sending them back through the crown. See Chapter 1.2.
pavilion break facets	The facets on the pavilion of a gemstone immediately bordering the girdle. See Chapter 1.2.
pear cut	A teardrop or pear-shaped gemstone design. See Figure 16-3.
pendeloque (gem cut)	An elongated, pear-shaped gem cut suitable for pendants and earrings. Similar to a briolette.
peridot	A green magnesium iron silicate gemstone. See Chapter 14.1.
photochroism	Alternate term for colour-change. See Chapter 12.3.5. Promulgated by Vargas but not widely adopted.
piezoelectricity	The property of certain minerals to generate an electric voltage in response to applied mechanical stress. Piezoelectric crystals can also work the other way, changing their physical dimensions in response to an applied voltage. Quartz and tourmaline are piezoelectric gemstones. See Chapter 12.13.3. See also pyroelectricity, triboelectricity.
pinfire	Conventionally, the closely-spaced pinpoints or specks of colour in opal. In a faceted gemstone, pinfire refers to tiny flashes of colour produced by facet placement and the intrinsic dispersion of the material. See Chapter 16.5.5.
platen	A machined plate, usually of metal, which forms the mechanical interface between the spindle and the lap. See Chapter 2.2.1.
platform faceting machine	A type of faceting machine employing a handpiece-type faceting head and a support platform. See Chapter 2.2.2.
pleochroism	The property of a mineral to display different body colour when viewed along different crystal directions. A pleochroic mineral exhibiting two distinct colours is called dichroic (e.g. tourmaline), while one that displays three colours is termed trichroic (e.g. iolite). See Chapter 12.4.
point	One one-hundredth of a carat or 0.002 g. For example, a 25 point diamond weighs ¼ carat. See page 9.
point cut	The first and simplest of diamond gem designs achieved by smoothing the faces and removing flaws from the natural octahedral form. See page 240 of Volume 2.
polariscope	see dichroscope
polarized, polarization	Polarized light is light whose constituent photons have a non-random orientation of the oscillation of their electric field. This leads to polarization. Polarization effects are very important in some gemstones. For example, birefringent gemstones have a different index of refraction for light waves of differing polarization. See Chapters 11.2.2 and 12.4.
polish	(verb) The act of generating the final, smooth surface finish on a gemstone. (noun) The surface finish so produced.

polymorph   Polymorphs are different forms of the same, chemically identical, mineral. For example, polymorphism in silica (SiO_2) forms α-Quartz and β-Quartz (see page 135 of Volume 2), and cristobalite, the material that puts the colour in opal (see page 84 of Volume 2). See also allotrope.

Portuguese cut   A round brilliant-type gemstone design composed of many stacked layers of kite-shaped facets. See Figure 8-18.

pre-form   (Verb or Noun, sometimes appearing as a single word: preform) The act or result of cutting the approximate form of a gemstone, usually with a very coarse lap or grinding wheel (see Chapter 8.3). Pre-forming can also refer to the more accurate cutting methods which generate the correct gem outline. Such techniques include ECED, CAM, OMNI, and CLAM (see Chapter 17).

pre-former   A mechanical device which assists in pre-forming. See Chapter 4.11.2.

pre-polish   The intermediate state between cutting and polishing, usually executed with a 1200 Nubond lap or with 3000 or finer diamond grit. Proper pre-polish helps eliminate subsurface damage, thereby alleviating many polishing difficulties. See Chapter 8.13.

precision   A measure of how repeatable a certain result is. See page 392 of Volume 2. Also see accuracy.

Princess cut   A square or rectangular gemstone design featuring fans of facets radiating from each corner. The princess cut is the second most popular diamond design after the standard round brilliant. See Chapter 18.1.

protractor   A mechanical device for measuring the cutting angle on a faceting machine. See Chapter 2.2.

pyroelectricity   The property of certain minerals, such as tourmaline, to generate an electric voltage when exposed to heat. See Chapter 12.13.3. See also piezoelectricity and triboelectricity.

Q

quartz   A very common gemstone with chemical formula SiO_2. The quartz family includes amethyst, citrine, rock crystal, ametrine, rose quartz, prasiolite, oro-verde, and smoky quartz. See Chapter 14.1.

quill   The (usually) cylindrical shaft which holds the dop stick to the trunnion of a mast or platform-type faceting machine. See Chapter 2.2.

R

radiant cut   Invented by Henry Grossbard in 1977, the radiant cut brings some of the scintillation of a brilliant type design to rectangular and square gems. Originally designed for diamond, since adapted to coloured gemstones.

radiation treatment   see irradiation

radioactivity   The spontaneous emission of radiation due to the breakdown of unstable nuclei in a material. Radioactivity can also refer to the gamma rays, alpha particles, neutrons, electrons, etc. emitted in this way. See Chapter 12.13.4.

reflection   The process by which a light wave is thrown back from a surface such as a mirror. In gemstones, reflection can take the form of surface reflections (or Fresnel loss) or total internal reflection. See Chapters 11.7 and 11.8.

refraction   The bending of light due to variations in the speed of light in a medium. See Chapter 11.4.

refractive index or RI   see index of refraction

Refractol   A commercial immersion fluid for revealing internal flaws in gem rough. Refractol has a refractive index of 1.567, and is thus most suitable for lower index materials such as quartz and beryl. See Chapter 4.5.

refractometer   An instrument for measuring the refractive index of a sample. Compact, hand-held refractometers can be used with cut gemstones. See Chapter 12.5.3.

reversibility (of light)   The property of light waves that their paths can be traced in either direction. See Chapter 11.6.

rough   Gem rough refers to raw, minimally processed gemstone material. See Chapter 6.

rose cut   An early gemstone design consisting of a domed crown and no pavilion. See Figure 16-18. A double rose cut has both the crown and pavilion cut this way.

ruby   see corundum

rutilated quartz   Quartz crystals containing needle-like inclusions of rutile, or titanium dioxide. See Chapter 12.12.1.

S

sapphire   see corundum

schiller   see aventurescence

scintillation   The dynamic visual impact of a gemstone produced by the flashing of facets under changing lighting conditions. Also referred to as sparkle. See Chapter 16.5.3.

scissor cut   A gem design feature X-shaped intersecting facets for added sparkle and visual interest. See the Tabula Rosa design in Chapter 19.2.3.

scoring, scored lap   The process of gouging grooves into a metal polishing lap with the goal of improving retention of polishing compound, providing an escape path for cutting residue, and reducing heat buildup due to metal-to-gem contact. Opinions differ on the effectiveness of scored laps. See page 328.

shellac, shellac-alcohol mixture
: Shellac is the processed resin extracted from lac bugs. In addition to serving as the most important wood finish of the last millennium, shellac is the primary constituent of dop wax. When mixed with alcohol, shellac assists adhesion during dopping. See page 87 and Chapter 4.3.1. Also see dop wax.

shock sensitivity
: The property of a mineral in reaction to mechanical impact. Some gemstones, such as fluorite and opal, can be very shock sensitive and should be cut only with a fine-grit lap. Shock sensitivity is the opposite of toughness. See page 128 of Volume 2.

silicate mineral
: Minerals containing silicate groups of atoms. These silicate groups contain different ratios of silicon and oxygen. For example, peridot is a magnesium iron silicate with chemical formula $(Mg,Fe)_2SiO_4$. The silicate minerals constitute approximately 90% of the Earth's crust. See Chapter 12.2.

simulant
: A simulant material attempts to imitate the optical and, to a lesser extent, the physical properties of a gemstone, but simulants are not chemically identical to the material they imitate. For example, cubic zirconia is a diamond simulant. See Chapter 6.6. See also synthetic.

single cut
: An early, 8-sided diamond cut created by grinding the corners off a table cut.

single refraction
: The property of a mineral which displays only a single index of refraction, independent of direction or polarization. Minerals forming in the cubic crystal system, as well as amorphous materials, display single refraction. They are also isotropic. See Chapter 12.4. See also double refraction.

sintered lap
: A premium cutting lap with a thick layer of diamond matrix. Sintered laps provide steady cutting performance over an extremely long lifetime, and the surface can be renewed repeatedly with a dressing stick. See Chapter 3.2.3. See also bonded lap.

skull melting
: A gem synthesis process for materials with very high melting temperature, such as cubic zirconia. See Chapter 6.6.2.

slurry
: A fluid suspension of small particles in a liquid. For example, cerium oxide forms a slurry when mixed with water. See Chapter 8.14.2.

Snell's Law
: The law governing the refraction of light at the interface between two media. See Chapter 11.4.

soft stop
: see angle stop

soudé emerald
: A doublet or triplet gem imitating a real emerald. See page 219.

sparkle
: see scintillation

specific gravity
: see density

spectrometer, spectroscope
: An instrument for splitting incoming light and analyzing the relative brightness of its component wavelengths. Different materials will produce characteristic absorption features that can be used in identification. See page 86

of Volume 2. Spectrometers can also be used to measure the dispersion of a gemstone material. See Chapter 12.6.1.

spectrum The range of colours made visible by a spectrometer. See Chapter 11.2.1.

spindle The shaft connecting the drive mechanism of a faceting machine with the platen. See Chapter 2.2.1. Although usually used interchangeably with the term arbor, the arbor contains the spindle as well as precision ball bearings.

spinel A hard magnesium aluminum oxide gemstone. See Chapter 14.1.

splash pan A rigid or flexible tub encompassing the spindle, platen, and lap. The splash pan contains the spray produced by cutting and directs it down a drain. See Chapter 2.2.1.

splitting (facets) The act of cutting two facets at the location of an original, single facet, in order to add visual interest and scintillation. See page 229 of Volume 2.

standard round brilliant or SRB The Standard Round Brilliant is the most popular gem design in the world. In its most common form, the SRB has 57 facets: 24 on the pavilion, 16 on the girdle, and 33 on the crown, including the table. There are many variations, however. See Chapters 1.3 and 16.2.

star facets Small accent facets, usually adjacent to the table facet. See Figure 1-4.

star-stone see asteria

step cut Generic term for a gem design featuring multiple parallel facets. When cut in rectangular form with truncated corners, the step cut becomes the classic emerald design. See Chapter 18.2.6 for an example of a step cut crown. Also known as a trap cut from the Dutch word for stairs.

streak The streak property of a mineral refers to the colour it leaves when ground against a very hard surface. The streak can help in identification. See Chapter 12.11.3.

striae, striation Linear or curving features left in a synthesized gemstone due to internal stress. Striae are particularly diagnostic of flame fusion materials. See Chapter 6.6.1.

subsurface damage Microscopic cracks and fractures that propagate downward from the surface of a gem during rough grinding. Subsurface damage at the cutting stage is the leading cause of polishing "problems." See page 157 and page 302.

surface diffusion see diffusion

surface reflection Literally (partial) reflection off the surface as light enters a gemstone. See Fresnel loss and Chapter 11.8.

swarf Familiar term for the residue of stone, abrasive, and lubricant produced by cutting or polishing.

symmetry A measure of how much and in what ways a gem looks the same when you reflect it across a line or rotate it around its axis. See Chapter 10.7.

synthetic	Synthetic gems are artificial stones that are chemically identical to the material they are trying to imitate. For example, synthetic ruby, like the original, is Al_2O_3. See Chapter 6.6.

T

T (facet diagram)	In a faceting diagram, T denotes the width of the table facet. It is the long dimension of the table, while the symbol U indicates the short dimension. See Chapter 10.8.1. See also C, L, P, U, and W.
table cut	A very early and simple gemstone design produced by truncating one of the points of a native octahedral diamond crystal, thereby creating a table. See page 240 of Volume 2.
table facet	The uppermost and usually largest facet of a gemstone. The table is almost always parallel to the girdle. The alternative to a table is the apex crown. See Chapter 1.2 and page 21 of Volume 2.
tablet cut	A faceted gemstone with effectively two crowns and two tables. Usually cut square or rectangular. Tablet cuts produce thin gems that are well suited to darker materials in an earring or pendant setting. Tabula Rosa from Chapter 19.2.3 is a tablet cut.
tabling adapter	A mechanical device which permits cutting and polishing the table at a cutting angle considerably lower than 90° (usually 45°). See Chapter 4.15.
tangent ratio	Literally the ratio of the trigonometric tangents of two angles. Used in tangent ratio scaling. See Chapters 10.5 and 10.6.
tangent ratio scaling	A method for stretching or shrinking the pavilion or crown of a gemstone without altering its plan (or top) view. Tangent ratio scaling can be used to adjust the height of a gem to accommodate internal flaws, cutting errors, change of material, etc. See Chapters 10.5 and 10.6.
temporary center point (TCP)	An intersection point created by a number of facets and then later cut away. The TCP is most commonly associated with CAM or similar facets used to establish the outline of the gemstone. See page 158 and Chapter 17.3.
tenebrescence	The property of some gemstones whose colour fades in daylight but which can be restored by returning the gem to darkness for a period of time. Tenebrescent zircon displays this property. Also known as reverse photochromism. See Chapter 12.3.7.
test tier (of facets)	A tier of facets cut immediately after dop transfer to determine the correct cheater setting for proper rotational alignment. See Chapter 7.7.
tetragonal crystal system	A crystal system characterized by three crystal axes meeting at 90°. Two of the axes are of equal length, while the third is shorter or longer. See Chapter 12.10.2.
tier (of facets)	A group of facets with the same angle and center distance, but with differing and often symmetrically placed index settings. Tiers of facets are almost always cut as a group. For example, the pavilion mains of a standard round brilliant form a tier of facets.

TIR   See total internal reflection

topper   A thin cutting or polishing lap that is placed on another lap for support. See Chapter 3.2.3.

total internal reflection   Perfect reflection within an optical medium when the angle of incidence exceeds the critical angle. Often abbreviated to TIR. With properly selected cutting angles, the pavilion will exploit TIR to send light entering the crown of a gemstone back out to the viewer. See Chapter 11.7.

toughness   A measure of how difficult it is to break or chip a mineral via impact. Not to be confused with hardness, which measures a material's resistance to scratching. See Chapter 12.9.

tourmaline   A group of chemically complex silicate gemstones. See Chapter 14.1.

transfer cheat   The process of determining the correct cheater setting after dop transfer. Also the result of this process, as in "the transfer cheat is ¾ of a turn clockwise." See Chapters 5.7.1 and 7.6.

transfer jig   A mechanical device for assisting in accurate dop transfer. See Chapter 4.16.

translucent   The property of a material to transmit light but not images. In other words, photons can pass through the material, but due to scattering and other effects, they do not follow straight paths. Wax paper is translucent. The opposite of translucent is opaque.

transparent   The property of a material to transmit light without significant absorption and scattering and thus form images. Window glass is transparent. Faceted gemstones require transparency for proper performance. See Chapter 12.7.1.

transpose   see index wheel transposition

trap cut   see step cut

triboelectricity   The property of some materials to acquire an electric charge when rubbed against another material. Amber is the classic example of a triboelectric gemstone. See Chapter 12.13.3.

triboluminescence   The property of some materials to emit light when rubbed or mechanically stressed. Quartz has this property, as do Wint-O-Green Lifesavers. See page 148 of Volume 2.

trichroism   see pleochroism

triclinic crystal system   A crystal system characterized by three crystal axes of unequal length and which meet at non-right angles. See Chapter 12.10.2.

trigonal crystal system   A crystal system closely related to the hexagonal crystal system in having three, coplanar, equal-length crystal axes meeting at 120°, and a fourth axis perpendicular to their shared plane. Trigonal crystals have three-fold symmetry, while hexagonal crystals exhibit six-fold symmetry. See Chapter 12.10.2.

trigonometry   The mathematical discipline dealing with the relationships between the lengths of the sides of a triangle and its angles. Trigonometry encompasses the familiar sine, cosine, and tangent functions. See Chapter 10.2.

trim saw   A compact saw featuring a thin diamond-coated blade for precise lapidary work. See page 128.

triplet   An assembled gemstone consisting of three different materials bonded together along planes parallel to the girdle. See page 219. See also doublet.

trunnion   A mechanical device which allows the quill of a mast-type faceting machine to swing up and down through a range of angles. The trunnion binds the quill and dop stick to the mast and usually contains the index wheel and cheater mechanisms. See Chapter 2.2.1.

twinning, twinning plane   The phenomenon in which two or more crystals have grown together. The twinning plane separates these crystals. This phenomenon is relatively common in quartz and spinel. In a gemstone, the twinning plane can produce distracting reflections and be a point of mechanical weakness. See Chapter 12.12.

U

U (facet diagram)   In a faceting diagram, U denotes the short dimension of the table facet (the symbol T indicates the long dimension of the table). See Chapter 10.8.1. See also C, L, P, T and W.

Ultralap   Commercial variety of thin, flexible cutting and polishing laps from Moyco Precision Abrasives Inc. The cerium oxide Ultralap is the standard beginner's polishing lap. See Chapters 3.2.3, 3.3.2, 8.14.1, and page 170.

ultraviolet (UV)   The region of the electromagnetic spectrum with wavelengths shorter than that of visible light. See Chapter 11.2.1. See also infrared.

under-cut facet   A facet that has not been cut deep enough. See also over-cut facet.

uniaxial crystal   A crystal exhibiting one optical axis. Minerals which form in the tetragonal, hexagonal and trigonal crystal systems are uniaxial (see Chapter 12.10). See also optical axis.

V

veil   A thin layer of inclusions resembling a veil. See also feather, inclusion.

vernier   A secondary scale with finer gradations to assist in the accurate measurement of distance or angle. Calipers and mechanical cutting angle protractors frequently use vernier scales. See page 122 and Chapter 4.11.6.

volume factor   The ratio of the volume of a gemstone to the cube of its width. Usually written as Vol./W^3. See Chapter 10.8.1.

W

W (facet diagram)   In a faceting diagram, W is the width of the gemstone, usually the shortest dimension in the girdle plane. See Chapter 10.8.1 See also C, L, P, T, and U.

wavelength   The distance from one peak to the next in a light wave. The wavelength of visible light is approximately half a micron. See Chapter 11.2.

window, windowing   The condition in which incorrect cutting angles allow light to pass directly through the crown and pavilion of a gemstone, producing a window effect. See Chapter 10.3. See also fish-eye.

Y

YAG   Yttrium Aluminum Garnet, a synthetic garnet gem material originally developed for lasers and semiconductors. See Chapter 6.6.

yield   A measure of the final to initial weight of a gemstone. Experienced faceters usually achieve yields in the range of 25 to 40 percent. See Chapter 10.8.3.

Z

zircon   A zirconium silicate gemstone with high refractive index and dispersion. See Chapter 14.1.

I

Index

Note: This is a merged index from both volumes of Amateur Gemstone Faceting. Look for the volume number before each page entry. For example, I:69-73 refers to Volume 1, whereas II:148 is in Volume 2.

Image Credits

Unless stated otherwise below, all images in this book are the original work of the author.

CHAPTER 2

Figure 2-6 (left) Image of Ultra Tec splash pan courtesy of David Thompson.

Figure 2-9 (left) Image of Fac-Ette GemMaster courtesy of Roger Dery (spectralgems.net).

Figure 2-9 (right) Image of the Tradition Française courtesy of P. M. Lamouret of l'Atelier des Lapidaires. M. Lamouret notes that although the "Tradition Française" is in every way a modern faceting machine, potential users should receive some training before embarking on their first gemstone.

Figure 2-13 (left) Image of Poly-Metric Scintillator courtesy of Zane Hoffman, Poly-Metric Instruments. More information at www.polymetricinc.com

Figure 2-13 (right) Photograph of Graves Mark IV by Tom Herbst with the able assistance of Billy Bob Riley and the Old Pueblo Lapidary Club. This is the machine on which I cut my very first gem.

Figure 2–14 Images of hand faceting machine courtesy Walt Heitland.

Figure 2-19 Image of Patriot faceting machine courtesy of Charles Musitano, Jersey Instruments. More information at www.jerseyinstruments.com

Figure 2-20 Image of Ultra Tec V5 faceting machine courtesy of Joe Rubin of Ultra Tec. More information at ultratec-facet.com

Figure 2-21 Courtesy Popular Science magazine.

Figure 2-22 Image courtesy of Popular Mechanics. Originally published in the February 1971 issue.

CHAPTER 3

Figure 3-1 Image of the Palomar 200 inch telescope courtesy of Scott Kardel, Palomar Observatory.

CHAPTER 4

Figure 4-14 Image of Norbide dressing sticks courtesy of Wolfgang Klich, American Rotary Tools Co., www.artcotools.com

Fig 4-29 Image of trim saw courtesy of David Thompson.

CHAPTER 6

Figure 6-17 (left) Synthetic ruby image by Aram Dulyan on wikipedia.org. Image released into the public domain.

CHAPTER 7

Figure 7-4 (left) GUIU dop image courtesy of Joe Rubin of Ultra Tec. More information at ultratec-facet.com

CHAPTER 8

Figure 8-1 Photograph of Michelangelo's David courtesy of Rico Heil.

Figure 8-20 (left) Portrait of Isaac Newton by Godfrey Kneller (1689). This image is from wikipedia.org and is in the public domain.

Figure 8-20 (right) Portrait of Robert Hooke by Rita Greer (2004). Released under CopyLeft license (http://artlibre.org/licence/lal/en). This is a cropped version of the original work, which is visible at http://en.wikipedia.org/wiki/File:13_Portrait_of_Robert_Hooke.JPG.

Figure 8-22 Image of Sir George Beilby courtesy of the Society of Chemical Industry, www.soci.org

About the Author

Tom Herbst is an amateur faceter and all-round rock enthusiast. Born in eastern Ontario, Canada, he received his formal education in Montreal, Quebec, Waterloo, Ontario, and Ithaca, New York. A research astrophysicist in his "day" job, Tom specializes in the design, construction, and scientific exploitation of novel astronomical instrumentation.

Although he began collecting pretty rocks as a kid, it was not until his mid-thirties that Tom realized that creating gemstones is within everyone's grasp. A few faceting lessons and a homebuilt machine later, he was deep into the hobby and has never looked back.

Tom currently lives and works near Heidelberg Germany, along with his wife Inge, and their two teenage sons, Matthew and Timothy.

You can contact the author at tom@facetingbook.com

The author working on the proofs of Amateur Gemstone Faceting while on family vacation in 2013 (right).